JOHN DEWEY

THE MIDDLE WORKS, 1899–1924

Volume 1: 1899–1901

Edited by Jo Ann Boydston
With an Introduction by Joe R. Burnett

Carbondale and Edwardsville
SOUTHERN ILLINOIS UNIVERSITY PRESS
London and Amsterdam
FEFFER & SIMONS, INC.

CENTER FOR EDITIONS OF
AMERICAN AUTHORS
AN APPROVED TEXT
MODERN LANGUAGE
ASSOCIATION OF AMERICA
®

Editorial expenses for this edition have been met in part by grants from the National Endowment for the Humanities. Publishing expenses have been met in part by grants from the John Dewey Foundation and from Mr. Corliss Lamont.

Library of Congress Cataloging in Publication Data

Dewey, John, 1859–1952.
    The middle works, 1899–1924.

    Bibliography: p.
    Includes index.
    CONTENTS: v. 1: 1899–1901
    1. Dewey, John, 1859–1952. 2. Education—Philosophy.
LB875.D34   1976   370.1′092′4   76–7231
ISBN 0–8093–0753–7 (v. 1)

The Middle Works, 1899–1924

Advisory Board

CONTENTS

INTRODUCTION

By Joe R. Burnett

This first volume of The Middle Works series includes Dewey's publications in the years 1899–1901, roughly the middle years of his 1894–1904 stay at the University of Chicago. As he was throughout his professional life, Dewey was incredibly busy during these three years: he was actively involved in social and educational reform movements in Chicago and the State of Illinois; he was seeing his early efforts in establishing the University Laboratory School rewarded with increased support and with national attention; his work in psychology had brought him the presidency of the American Psychological Association; and he and his colleagues at the University of Chicago were developing conceptions of inquiry and psychology that were to revolutionize American philosophy. This last activity, most clearly foreshadowed by Dewey's 1900 article "Some Stages of Logical Thought," led William James to remark three years later about the work in philosophy and psychology at Chicago: The University

. . . has during the past six months given birth to the fruit of its ten years of gestation under John Dewey. The result is wonderful —a *real school* and *real Thought*. Important thought, too! Did you ever hear of such a city or such a university? Here we have thought, but no school. At Yale a school, but no thought. Chicago has both.[1]

What James was so lavishly celebrating in 1903 was the publication (dedicated to James) of *Studies in Logical Theory*,[2] the precursor of such important works by Dewey as *How We*

---

1. Letters to Ms. Henry Whitman, in *Letters of William James*, ed. Henry James (Boston: Atlantic Monthly Press, 1920) 2:201–2. Also see James's letter to John Jay Chapman, 2:257 and 310.
2. John Dewey, with the Co-operation of Members and Fellows of the Department of Philosophy, *Studies in Logical Theory*, The Decennial Publications, second series, vol. 11 (Chicago: University of Chicago Press, 1903).

Think,[3] *Logic: The Theory of Inquiry*,[4] and *Knowing and the Known*.[5] Although *The School and Society*[6] is the most widely known of Dewey's writings of this period, his contemporaneous studies in logical theory were more characteristic of his lifelong preoccupations.

Dewey's publications during his middle years, 1899–1924, are not sharply set off in either content or tone from those of the early years, 1882–1898,[7] but, although the *Early Works* themes are continued in the *Middle Works*, certain of those themes are significantly consolidated and advanced and others gradually are treated as only tangential. Among those consolidated and advanced are Dewey's works in both logic and social philosophy, discussed more fully below. Among the themes which received less and less attention are those concerned with idealistic philosophy and physiological psychology.

In the present volume, only the review of the first volume of Josiah Royce's two-volume series *The World and the Individual*[8] deals directly with the idealistic—mainly Hegelian—tradition, and only the two essays on mental development (pp. 175, 192) are heavily weighted with data drawn from physiology. In each area, Dewey shows himself eminently competent in the contemporary subject-matter and style of analysis, but quantitative comparison of this material with that in the *Early Works* shows these domains were becoming minor concerns. They are topics he mentions, both herein and later, with considerable expertise, but he

3. *How We Think* (Boston: D. C. Heath and Co., 1910; rev. ed., 1933).
4. *Logic: The Theory of Inquiry* (New York: Henry Holt and Co., 1938).
5. John Dewey and Arthur F. Bentley, *Knowing and the Known* (Boston: Beacon Press, 1949).
6. *The School and Society* (Chicago: University of Chicago Press, 1899). [*The Middle Works of John Dewey, 1899–1924*, ed. Jo Ann Boydston (Carbondale: Southern Illinois University Press, 1975) 1:2–109.]
7. *The Early Works of John Dewey, 1882–1898*, ed. Jo Ann Boydston, 5 vols. (Carbondale: Southern Illinois University Press, 1967–72).
8. Review of *The World and the Individual*, by Josiah Royce, *Philosophical Review* 9 (1900): 311–24, and ibid. 11 (1902): 392–407. [*Middle Works*, 1:241–56 and 2:120–37.] The second part of this review, published in 1902, appears in *Middle Works* 2, but in the present discussion is considered as a unit with the first part.

mentions them mainly to make points about other matters more central to his developing thought.

Whereas physiological psychology in time disappears almost completely from Dewey's attention, idealistic philosophy—though diminished in overall emphasis—remains at once a love and a considered danger: a love in the extent to which Hegel's variety and richness of insight, second only to Plato's, appealed to him,[9] and a considered danger in that the idealism of his chief contemporaries was an obstacle to dealing with the immediate and urgent problems of men. After a studied analysis of Royce's two volumes—a review written in the best in-house tradition of Hegelian scholarship—Dewey concludes with something approaching a "confession of faith" regarding idealism:

Either our experiences, yea, even the experiences of "us men" have ultimate meaning and worth, and the "Absolute" is only the most adequate possible construing of this meaning; or else, having it not, they are not available to give content to the Absolute. But a difference of form or type between our consciousness and the Absolute, simply once for all makes metaphysical method impossible.[10]

This early confession of faith was in time to be intellectually underpinned in four of Dewey's finest later works: *Experience and Nature*,[11] *A Common Faith*,[12] *Art as Experience*,[13] and *The Quest for Certainty*,[14] where we find the rationale, based upon reason and experience, for the faith. The problems of men, "us men," become the basis for a naturalistic philosophy.

Although his interest in physiological psychology was waning during these years, Dewey's interest in general psy-

9. "From Absolutism to Experimentalism," in *Contemporary American Philosophy*, ed. George P. Adams and William P. Montague (New York: Macmillan Co., 1930) 2:13–27. Cf. Jane M. Dewey, ed. (but which is partly autobiographical by John Dewey), in *The Philosophy of John Dewey*, 2d ed. (New York: Tudor Publishing Co., 1951), pp. 32–33.
10. Review of *The World and the Individual, Middle Works*, 2:137.
11. *Experience and Nature* (Chicago: Open Court Publishing Co., 1925).
12. *A Common Faith* (New Haven: Yale University Press, 1934).
13. *Art as Experience* (New York: Minton, Balch and Co., 1934).
14. *The Quest for Certainty* (New York: Minton, Balch and Co., 1929).

chology—gradually concentrated on social psychology—continued unabated, later to culminate in the publication of *Human Nature and Conduct*.[15] The 1899–1901 period provides insights into the way his views on general psychology were developing: within the decade 1890–1900 he has come full circle. Earlier, heavily absorbed in studies in psychology, he had argued in 1886 that the completed method of thought of philosophy was to be found in psychology; psychology is, in fact, the "completed method of philosophy."[16] In "Psychology and Philosophic Method," (pp. 113–30), and "Psychology and Social Practice," (pp. 131–50), Dewey begins to make significant qualifications. Here we find him arguing that psychology is, in an important sense, a political science, and, further, that psychology should play a role in "the necessary transition of science into philosophy; a passage that carries the verified and solid body of the one into the large and free form of the other" (p. 129). Thus the role of psychology has for Dewey within this ten year period undergone a complete transition: from philosophy's master to philosophy's servant to only one of the social science servants of philosophy (p. 150).

Dewey's negativism toward the psychology of his day can be attributed in part to his own changing interests; but part of it must also be attributed to the character of most of the contemporary psychology. Just as he rejected Roycean idealism because it subsumed human experience under that of an Absolute, so he accused the psychologists of subsuming human experience under categories of particular states of consciousness. Such states of consciousness, he argued, have no existence before the psychologists create them as abstractions from the "connected whole of experience."

Dewey does not "name names" of those psychologists whose theories and methodologies he attacks, but it seems clear that he had in mind members of the Leipzig school of Wilhelm Wundt, and particularly students of Wundt's who

15. *Human Nature and Conduct* (New York: Henry Holt and Co., 1922).
16. "Psychology as Philosophic Method," *Mind* 11 (1886): 165. [*Early Works*, 1:157.] Also see Lewis Hahn's "Introduction: From Intuitionalism to Absolutism," in *Early Works*, vol. 1, especially pp. 22 ff.

came to practice in America—such as G. Stanley Hall, James McKeen Cattell, Edward Bradford Titchener—and especially their less critical followers. What was in vogue with many psychologists was the desire to develop a science of the psyche, *sui generis*. As Dewey interpreted their mission, with good evidence, the way in which thought *functioned* was so sharply distinguished from the *nature* of the psyche or mind that the mind's functioning was ignored. This was a familiar problem for Dewey: he had faced the same problem, only slightly varied, in dealing with the reflex-arc concept a few years earlier,[17] a study which Edna Heidbreder says represented for Dewey "a hunting-down of the old enemy in a new and unlikely and apparently safe hiding place."[18] Dewey did not make the same mistake of over-simplification, which would have been choosing functionalism in psychology as *the* approach: he thought that the view of the structuralists was legitimate when balanced, and that functionalism was dangerous if not informed by structuralism and its demands (pp. 116–17).

During the 1899–1901 period Dewey does refer favorably to William James and Hugo Münsterberg as sources of inspiration in the development of his own perspectives; however, in neither case does he give an analytic treatment of the specific way in which they contributed to his thought. What he had to say later suggests that James perhaps was third only to Plato and Hegel in suggestive influence from philosophers.[19] He lauds Münsterberg in his 1899 address as President of the American Philosophical Association, but within less than a decade he saw Münsterberg as an enemy of practical pedagogy *and* philosophic theory. What Dewey had liked in the early work of Münsterberg, just after James had brought Münsterberg to Harvard, was the emphasis upon

---

17. "The Reflex Arc Concept in Psychology," *Psychological Review* 3 (1896): 357–70. [*Early Works*, 5:96–109.] For an unusually succinct, fine summary of Dewey's argument in this essay, see Lewis Hahn's "Dewey's Philosophy and Philosophic Method," in *Guide to the Works of John Dewey*, ed. Jo Ann Boydston (Carbondale: Southern Illinois University Press, 1970), esp. pp. 27–28.
18. Edna Heidbreder, *Seven Psychologies* (New York: D. Appleton-Century Co., 1933), p. 213.
19. Cf. "From Absolutism to Experimentalism," p. 21.

the factors of volition and interest. Dewey, too, thought these
factors very important in the determination of how young
children should be educated; but Dewey was still working
(and would continue to work for the rest of his life) on a
concept of developmental logic-psychology. Münsterberg, to
Dewey's way of thinking, had made a classic mistake in philosophy, after a good beginning, in his theorizing about how
young children learn. Dewey was ready to agree that "will"
and "interest" were tremendously important in learning, especially in young children, but he was sharp in his criticism
of Münsterberg when the latter came to argue that in every
case will took precedence over other causal elements in experience. Münsterberg's voluntarism, he felt, faced the same
problems as every type of

thoroughgoing monism. When any one phase or factor of the experienced world is generalized to the point of being treated as
Ultimate, as the "Real" which explains all else, that ultimate loses
all distinguishing or differential character, and hence becomes
useless for explaining anything.[20]

Dewey's disagreement with prevailing approaches to the
study of psychology led him to diffuse his own continuing
interest throughout his other studies, notably logical theory.
For example, although "Some Stages of Logical Thought"
(pp. 151–74) touches only covertly on educational psychology, it anticipates rather fully the stages of thought so significantly related to education in How We Think. This article
is to my knowledge the first extensive, albeit schematic, attempt by Dewey to formulate the pattern of inquiry.[21] The
interest and importance of this essay stem from several
points: it is, first, a very concise theory of inquiry; second,
it is a theory of "developmental logic" as much as a theory
of developmental psychology; third, it is almost a "cultural
epoch" or "recapitulation" theory of thought. As a theory of

20. Review of The Eternal Values, by Hugo Münsterberg, Philo-
    sophical Review 19 (1910): 188.
21. However, one should note Dewey's earlier (1887), systematic
    discussion of "processes" and "stages" of knowledge in Psychol-
    ogy. This discussion is primarily a physiological/psychological
    one: the notion of systematic processes and stages of inquiry is,
    at best, barely implicit. [Cf. Early Works, vol. 2, pt. 1: "Knowl-
    edge."]

inquiry, a theory of "the complete act of thought"—an expression Dewey used in the first edition of *How We Think* but not in the second—it was built upon and refined in *How We Think, Logic: The Theory of Inquiry*, and *Knowing and the Known*.

But here the stages are correlated with stages in the history of philosophy, leading the reader to infer that a contemporary act of thought somehow recapitulates the best approaches to thinking as they developed historically, and that early philosophers ignored or at least did not utilize the later stages. It is interesting to note that this particular article was published at a time when Dewey had been working with educators who seemed at times absolutely obsessed with the cultural epoch or recapitulation theory.[22] Even though at the

22. The theory borrowed from the already rather vague biological notion that "ontogeny recapitulates phylogeny"; that is, the human individual develops through stages which have marked similarities to the stages of creatures in evolutionary development. Thus, the human zygote develops in such a fashion that it appears to be first merely cellular, then fish, then reptilian, then low primate, etc., until birth as high primate, Cro-Magnon, one of us. Baldly stated, the cultural epoch, recapitulation, theory maintained that the life of thought in the child followed the developmental process of thought in (particularly) western culture. The young child thinks like a savage first, then like an epic hero in Greco-Roman times, then like feudal nobility, then like a scientist. So, the curriculum follows accordingly: give the child myths and fables in early education, Homer and Virgil slightly later, tales of knights and kings still later, and then Newton and Darwin to bring him into the age of science. As it figured in the educational thought of some followers of G. Stanley Hall (one of Dewey's mentors at Johns Hopkins) and others, the curriculum would draw from the materials of prehistory for the infant, from patriarchal periods for childhood, from tribal history for adolescence, from the feudal stage for late adolescence, and from monarchial and age-of-science history for adulthood! (Cf. Merle Curti, *The Social Ideas of American Educators* [New York: Charles Scribner's Sons, 1935], on Hall.)

This particular view was carried (as anything so simple deserved to be) to the heights of absurdity by several educators given inspiration by philosophers. Cf., in particular, R. W. Pringle, *Adolescence and High School Problems* (Boston: D. C. Heath, 1922).

Dewey's most studied responses to the subject of cultural epoch theory are to be found in "Interpretation of the Culture-Epoch Theory," *Early Works*, 5:247; "Interpretation of Savage Mind," *Middle Works*, 2:39–66; particularly "Culture Epoch Theory," in *A Cyclopedia of Education*, ed. Paul Monroe (New York: Macmillan Co., 1911) 2:240–42; and *Democracy and Education* (New York: Macmillan Co., 1916), pp. 84–89. Also see Chapter 6 (and notes thereto) of Melvin C. Baker's *Foundations*

time he took the theory seriously, it dropped almost completely from his later work. But in 1900 he certainly seemed
to be trying a variant of the theory on "for size."

I wish to show how a variety of modes of thinking, easily
recognizable in the progress of both the race and the individual,
may be identified and arranged as successive species of the relationship which doubting bears to assurance. . . . The presumption is that the function of questioning is one which has continually grown in intensity and range, that doubt is continually
chased back, and, being cornered, fights more desperately, and
thus clears the ground more thoroughly. Its successive stations or
arrests constitute stages of thinking (p. 151).

Without mentioning him by name in "Some Stages of
Logical Thought," Dewey does implicitly recognize the work
of Charles Sanders Peirce by his prominent use of the concept of "doubt." Indeed, Dewey here defines thought as a
"doubt-inquiry function," (p. 172), and makes clear, as did
Peirce, that doubt is not a matter of subjective perspective
but of an unsettled objective situation.

Dewey's interest in logical theory, so apparent in his
work during this period, found continuing and full expression throughout the years that followed, but as the contents
of the present volume show, his published writings in 1899–
1901 were chiefly in education. His work in that field had already caused the University of Chicago's Laboratory School,
under his administration, to be widely recognized by the major educators of the day. But it was not only the work at the
Laboratory School that gave Dewey the chance for great im-
pact. This was the period in which secondary education got
its first great impetus in America, and resources—teachers,
administrators, and state-school legal relations and structures
—for educating thousands upon thousands of additional students simply were not present. American educational and
political leaders looked abroad for models that would help
them make rational an educational system which, even

---

of John Dewey's Educational Theory (New York: King's Crown
Press, Columbia University, 1955). Arthur Wirth's uniformly
fine work, John Dewey as Educator: His Design for Work in Education (1894–1904) (New York: John Wiley and Sons, 1966),
has a brief but very perceptive account in Chapter 8 regarding
Dewey's approach to the cultural epoch theory.

more than Topsy, had "just growed." The model they chose was European, and particularly (through the work of Horace Mann and Henry Barnard) the Germanic model.[23]

It perhaps is not surprising that the educational theory dominant in Europe at the time should have been brought back to serve as an intellectual defense for the organizational structure being sought and not-very-selectively adapted. Not only is it not surprising that it should be brought back, it is not surprising that it was accepted in large part. European (Germanic and French, mainly) academic training of the "best" American scholars was already a way of American academic life. American philosophers and psychologists were being asked to accept for instrumentation the very ideas in which they had been inculcated.

The streams of European thought that flowed into America were many, and they cannot be dealt with adequately here, but they must be mentioned. There was Christian idealism, whose educational influence was championed by the Moravian theologian and educator, John Amos Comenius—who wrote in the 1600s and whose educational prescriptions had a major influence on English education. There was an ambiguous heritage stemming from English empiricism and the educational prescriptions that John Locke "uncomfortably" associated with it—seeming not to realize that his empiricism was philosophy and his theory of education was political, practical, and pretty much disassociated from his philosophy. There was romantic voluntarism, stemming from Rousseau into the work of the Swiss educator, Johann Heinrich Pestalozzi, whose theories of education received considerable support by both European and American educators interested in the education of the very young. There was the influence of German objective idealism—originating with Hegel, Fichte, and Goethe—and apparently heav-

---

23. For a good account of Dewey's response to educators of his day, see Melvin C. Baker, *Foundations of John Dewey's Educational Theory*, Chapter 6. Also see Darnell Rucker, *The Chicago Pragmatists* (Minneapolis: University of Minnesota Press, 1969). Merle Curti's *Social Ideas of American Educators* remains as one of the finest volumes which places Dewey's educational thought and career in the context of American educational developments at the turn of the century.

ily influencing such important educational theorists as Jo-
hann Friedrich Herbart (also a philosopher of note) and
Friedrich Wilhelm Froebel in Europe, and William Torrey
Harris and G. Stanley Hall in America.[24]

Now it was the latter influence—the Germanic—which
came to predominate in the United States, just as it was the
influence most closely associated with the state supervised
system of education in Europe that also came to predominate in the United States. Most of the schoolmen in America
were philosophically untutored, yet they were trying to utilize the philosophies associated with the state structures being adopted. Dewey, with his competence in European philosophy and demonstrated interest in American education,
quickly found himself called upon to exposit, criticize, and
help apply the "foreign" philosophies.

Beyond his work at the Laboratory School, and his expertise in the philosophies that were competing for acceptance, Dewey had already begun developing an original social
and educational philosophy that took account of the unique
aspects of American industrialization, technology, and urbanization. He was knowledgeable about and even sympathetic to European theorizing, but had already begun to tailor
a social and educational philosophy which, by being based
upon scientific method à la Darwin, the American experience, and American concepts of democracy, was guaranteed
to appeal to many American educators.

In his writings on education included in this volume,
Dewey addresses educational problems from two perspectives, the first of which—how to coordinate aspects of logical
inquiry with physiological/psychological maturation—has already been touched upon. The second perspective, not separate except by a distinction of reason, is provided by his
pervasive consideration of the need for a rich, dynamic, and
viable social order.

The School and Society best illustrates this perspective.

24. Cf. Reginald D. Archambault, ed., *John Dewey: Lectures in the
    Philosophy of Education, 1899.* (New York: Random House,
    1966), pp. xv–xx. Archambault's work presents a "clean" edit-
    ing of lectures which Dewey gave at the University of Chicago
    in 1899, and Archambault has an admirable introduction for the
    volume and the period.

It would be easy to interpret this volume, as it usually has been interpreted, as concerned only with schools and the socialization process. But the fact is that by 1900 Dewey was moving away from a direct concern with practical pedagogy. He never conceived the Laboratory School at the University of Chicago as a model for broad-scale emulation: it was to be, as plainly and simply as possible, a *laboratory* school. It was not to be, as Arthur Wirth notes, "a normal school for the training of teachers, nor a model school offering specific answers for the immediate problems of the public schools."[25]

The School and Society is the early anticipation of such major later works as *Democracy and Education*,[26] *Reconstruction in Philosophy*,[27] *The Problems of Men*,[28] and *A Common Faith*. Constant neither in theme nor tone, the volume in its final, full form was, as the Textual Commentary points out, a work "put-together" for a reader who reads as he runs by one who wrote as he ran. The main theme of the book is, nevertheless, ringingly clear: industrialization, urbanization, science, and technology have created a revolution never "in all history so rapid, so extensive, so complete" (p. 6)—a revolution the schools cannot ignore.

After the period of years covered by the works in this volume, the practice of education came to assume less importance in the total bulk of Dewey's writing. By 1900 Dewey was becoming a philosopher of culture. Within four years he stopped discussing matters of practical pedagogy at any

25. Wirth, *Dewey as Educator*, p. 73. Cf. William W. Brickman's "Introduction" to *Schools of Tomorrow* (New York: E. P. Dutton and Co., 1962). Citing the "Preface," by Dewey, Brickman comments:

> In his preface, Dewey states, "We have tried to show what actually happens when schools start out to put into practice, each in its own way, some of the theories that have been pointed to since Plato . . ." and "how the applications arise from their theories and the direction that education in this country seems to be taking at the present time." This is exactly what the book does. It does not pretend to offer "a complete theory of education" or an analysis of educational systems or viewpoints, and it is not intended as a textbook for future teachers in service (p. xxiii).

26. *Democracy and Education* (New York: Macmillan Co., 1916).
27. *Reconstruction in Philosophy* (New York: Henry Holt and Co., 1920).
28. *The Problems of Men* (New York: The Philosophical Library, 1946).

length. Even *Democracy and Education*, which he claimed
as his major philosophical work for many years,[29] is a work
of social, political, and educational philosophy rather than
of practical pedagogy, for here are some of his earliest, clear-
est, and most theoretical statements about democracy as a
way of life.

During these pivotal years, the systems of American
public elementary and secondary schools were growing tremendously, educating many thousands more students than
in the two previous decades and helping turn America into
at least a "salad bowl" if not a "melting pot." Dewey had
considerable acquaintance with schools in the common sec-
tor, but his important function in this period was to call attention to the challenge of the future rather than to offer
careful, critical observations of actual conditions. He was,
for example, curiously uncritical of higher education during
this period: the main problems lay in the schools that were
preparing children for higher education and he was more
concerned about a philosophy for articulating elementary,
secondary, and higher education than with analyzing our
college and university system. As he wrote years later:

> While I cannot write an account of intellectual development
> without giving it the semblance of a continuity that it does not in
> fact own, there are . . . points that seem to stand out. One is the
> importance that the practice and theory of education have had for
> me: especially the education of the young, for I have never been
> able to feel much optimism regarding the possibilities of "higher"
> education when it is built upon warped and weak foundations.[30]

It was the "warped and weak foundations" that Dewey
and his followers tried hardest to shore up. Dewey's own
approach was through advocating techniques for restoring/
developing a sense of community in an era during which industrialization, science, technology, and urbanization were
destroying community as known in a mainly agrarian,
communal-neighborhood, extended-family America.

Dewey's response during the Chicago years can be interpreted as a simplistic one, which consisted mainly of seeking to restore/develop community by having children engage

29. "From Absolutism to Experimentalism," p. 23.
30. "From Absolutism to Experimentalism," p. 22.

in occupations that were central to the life of their families and friends. This interpretation is plausible because Dewey was working intensively with children during the Chicago years. It also is plausible because he was actively engaged in reform politics and adult education for those outside the mainstream of political, economic, and social power in Chicago. In a word, it is possible to interpret Dewey as nostalgic for older ways much as, I think, Morton and Lucia White interpret him in their provocative volume, *The Intellectual Versus the City*.[31] Dewey's conceptions of occupations, of child psychology, of elementary and secondary schooling, of the roles of such curriculum items as manual training, history, and geography—all touched upon here in *The School and Society*, the items from the *Elementary School Record*, and *The Educational Situation*—certainly do make it seem that Dewey longed for the kind of person-to-person relationship characteristic of an older social order. So he did, in the education of children, but it must not be forgotten that there was a profoundly radical strain in Dewey's developing political thought which was first to emerge most noticeably in *The Public and Its Problems* in 1927. But, as early as 1888, in *The Ethics of Democracy*,[32] he was arguing that industrial and political relations demanded that there be a "democracy of wealth" rather than economic aristocracy. He skirted the issue of whether this entailed socialism or communism: the issue he confronted then and later was the systemic changes which were required in order to raise social life to the ethical ideal embodied in the concept of democracy.

So, it is easy to read the Dewey publications of this period and conclude that he thought to make the social order in America more democratic merely by finding formal techniques to provide primary-group relationships which had budded informally and personally in pre-industrial, prescientific America. From this point of view, it also is easy to say that Dewey wanted to change society primarily by changing individuals—by helping them to become more communicative, more cooperative, and more analytical in

31. Morton White and Lucia White, *The Intellectual Versus the City* (New York: New American Library, 1962), chap. 10.
32. *The Ethics of Democracy, Early Works*, 1:227.

thought, morals, and skills. He did want this, but the fact should not be overlooked that, during the Chicago years, he had not renounced the conviction that major, systemic changes in society were also necessary. Dewey agrees with neither of the old contentions that, on the one hand, society cannot be changed except that individuals are first changed and, on the other hand, that individuals cannot be changed until societies are changed; rather, he argues both conjointly.

About the private man of the years 1899–1901, little can be said: the time span is too brief, and Dewey was singularly reticent in speaking publicly about the University of Chicago administration and about his hopes and ambitions apparently frustrated by that administration. Unlike Thorstein Veblen, who published a critical, theoretical account of American higher education so obviously generalized from his experiences at the University of Chicago,[33] Dewey never spelled out the difficulties that led him to resign abruptly, with no job or contract elsewhere. Not even after he accepted, in 1904, the position at Columbia that he held until the end of his professional career did he write publicly about the last difficult years at Chicago.[34]

As for the public man, these years along with the previous five at the University of Chicago represent a period when Dewey made significant advances in what has been called his search for "unity of thought and action."[35] Although Dewey himself, writing in his seventy-first year, disclaimed any great continuity and systematic unity in his thought, he nonetheless pointed to four "special points" in his intellectual development. All four of these figured prominently in the Chicago years. "The importance that the practice and theory of education have had" found expression in day-by-day

33. See Thorstein Veblen's 1916 "Preface" to *The Higher Learning in America* (Stanford: Academic Reprints, 1954).
34. See the following, for instance. George Dykhuizen, with "Introduction" by Harold Taylor, *The Life and Mind of John Dewey*, ed. Jo Ann Boydston (Carbondale: Southern Illinois University Press, 1973), chaps. 5, 6, and 7. Robert McCaul, in *John Dewey: Master Educator*, ed. William W. Brickman and Stanley Lehrer (New York: Society for the Advancement of Education, 1961), chaps. 4, 5, 6.
35. William Robert McKenzie, "Introduction: Toward Unity of Thought and Action," in *Early Works*, 5:xiii–xx.

experiences at the Laboratory School as well as in the numerous writings on education; he took the first steps in "the construction of a logic . . . which would apply without abrupt breach of continuity" to both "science" and "morals"; "the influence of William James" chiefly the "objective strain" of the *Psychology* with its "roots in a return to the earlier biological conception of the *psyche*, . . . worked its way more and more into all [his] ideas." And, finally, "the objective biological approach of the Jamesian psychology led straight to the perception of the importance of distinctive social categories, especially communication and participation."[36]

10 December 1974

36. "From Absolutism to Experimentalism," pp. 22, 23, 24, and 25.

The School and Society

Publisher's Note*

The first three chapters of this book were delivered as lectures before an audience of parents and others interested in the University Elementary School, in the month of April of the year 1899. Mr. Dewey revised them in part from a stenographic report, and unimportant changes and the slight adaptations necessary for the press have been made in his absence. The lectures retain therefore the unstudied character as well as the power of the spoken word. As they imply more or less familiarity with the work of the Elementary School, Mr. Dewey's supplementary statement of this has been added.

* To 1899 printing.

Author's Note*

A second printing affords a grateful opportunity for recalling that this little book is a sign of the cooperating thoughts and sympathies of many persons. Its indebtedness to Mrs. Emmons Blaine is partly indicated in the dedication. From my friends Mr. and Mrs. George Herbert Mead came that interest, unflagging attention to detail, and artistic taste which, in my absence, remade colloquial remarks until they were fit to print, and then saw the results through the press with the present attractive result—a mode of authorship made easy, which I recommend to others fortunate enough to possess such friends.

It would be an extended paragraph which should list all the friends whose timely and persisting generosity has made possible the school which inspired and defined the ideas of

* February 1900 printing.

these pages. These friends, I am sure, would be the first to recognize the peculiar appropriateness of especial mention of the names of Mrs. Charles R. Crane and Mrs. William R. Linn.

And the school itself in its educational work is a joint undertaking. Many have engaged in shaping it. The clear and experienced intelligence of my wife is wrought everywhere into its texture. The wisdom, tact, and devotion of its instructors have brought about a transformation of its original amorphous plans into articulate form and substance with life and movement of their own. Whatever the issue of the ideas presented in this book, the satisfaction coming from the cooperation of the diverse thoughts and deeds of many persons in undertaking to enlarge the life of the child will abide.

January 5, 1900.

Author's Note to Second Edition

The present edition includes some slight verbal revisions of the three lectures constituting the first portion of the book. The latter portion is included for the first time, containing material borrowed, with some changes, from the author's contributions to the *Elementary School Record*, long out of print.

The writer may perhaps be permitted a word to express his satisfaction that the educational point of view presented in this book is not so novel as it was fifteen years ago; and his desire to believe that the educational experiment of which the book is an outgrowth has not been without influence in the change.

July, 1915.

1. THE SCHOOL AND SOCIAL PROGRESS

We are apt to look at the school from an individualistic standpoint, as something between teacher and pupil, or between teacher and parent. That which interests us most is naturally the progress made by the individual child of our acquaintance, his normal physical development, his advance in ability to read, write, and figure, his growth in the knowledge of geography and history, improvement in manners, habits of promptness, order, and industry—it is from such standards as these that we judge the work of the school. And rightly so. Yet the range of the outlook needs to be enlarged. What the best and wisest parent wants for his own child, that must the community want for all of its children. Any other ideal for our schools is narrow and unlovely; acted upon, it destroys our democracy. All that society has accomplished for itself is put, through the agency of the school, at the disposal of its future members. All its better thoughts of itself it hopes to realize through the new possibilities thus opened to its future self. Here individualism and socialism are at one. Only by being true to the full growth of all the individuals who make it up, can society by any chance be true to itself. And in the self-direction thus given, nothing counts as much as the school, for, as Horace Mann said, "Where any thing is growing, one former is worth a thousand re-formers."

Whenever we have in mind the discussion of a new movement in education, it is especially necessary to take the broader, or social, view. Otherwise, changes in the school institution and tradition will be looked at as the arbitrary inventions of particular teachers; at the worst transitory fads, and at the best merely improvements in certain details—and this is the plane upon which it is too customary to consider school changes. It is as rational to conceive of the locomotive or the telegraph as personal devices. The modification going

on in the method and curriculum of education is as much a
product of the changed social situation, and as much an effort to meet the needs of the new society that is forming, as
are changes in modes of industry and commerce.

It is to this, then, that I especially ask your attention:
the effort to conceive what roughly may be termed the "New
Education" in the light of larger changes in society. Can we
connect this "New Education" with the general march of
events? If we can, it will lose its isolated character; it will
cease to be an affair which proceeds only from the over-
ingenious minds of pedagogues dealing with particular
pupils. It will appear as part and parcel of the whole social
evolution, and, in its more general features at least, as inevitable. Let us then ask after the main aspects of the social
movement; and afterwards turn to the school to find what
witness it gives of effort to put itself in line. And since it is
quite impossible to cover the whole ground, I shall for the
most part confine myself to one typical thing in the modern
school movement—that which passes under the name of
manual training—hoping if the relation of that to changed
social conditions appears, we shall be ready to concede the
point as well regarding other educational innovations.

I make no apology for not dwelling at length upon the
social changes in question. Those I shall mention are writ so
large that he who runs may read. The change that comes first
to mind, the one that overshadows and even controls all
others, is the industrial one—the application of science resulting in the great inventions that have utilized the forces of
nature on a vast and inexpensive scale: the growth of a
world-wide market as the object of production, of vast manufacturing centres to supply this market, of cheap and rapid
means of communication and distribution between all its
parts. Even as to its feebler beginnings, this change is not
much more than a century old; in many of its most important
aspects it falls within the short span of those now living. One
can hardly believe there has been a revolution in all history
so rapid, so extensive, so complete. Through it the face of the
earth is making over, even as to its physical forms; political
boundaries are wiped out and moved about, as if they were
indeed only lines on a paper map; population is hurriedly

gathered into cities from the ends of the earth; habits of living are altered with startling abruptness and thoroughness; the search for the truths of nature is infinitely stimulated and facilitated, and their application to life made not only practicable, but commercially necessary. Even our moral and religious ideas and interests, the most conservative because the deepest-lying things in our nature, are profoundly affected. That this revolution should not affect education in some other than a formal and superficial fashion is inconceivable.

Back of the factory system lies the household and neighborhood system. Those of us who are here today need go back only one, two, or at most three generations, to find a time when the household was practically the centre in which were carried on, or about which were clustered, all the typical forms of industrial occupation. The clothing worn was for the most part made in the house; the members of the household were usually familiar also with the shearing of the sheep, the carding and spinning of the wool, and the plying of the loom. Instead of pressing a button and flooding the house with electric light, the whole process of getting illumination was followed in its toilsome length, from the killing of the animal and the trying of fat to the making of wicks and dipping of candles. The supply of flour, of lumber, of foods, of building materials, of household furniture, even of metal ware, of nails, hinges, hammers, etc., was produced in the immediate neighborhood, in shops which were constantly open to inspection and often centres of neighborhood congregation. The entire industrial process stood revealed, from the production on the farm of the raw materials till the finished article was actually put to use. Not only this, but practically every member of the household had his own share in the work. The children, as they gained in strength and capacity, were gradually initiated into the mysteries of the several processes. It was a matter of immediate and personal concern, even to the point of actual participation.

We cannot overlook the factors of discipline and of character-building involved in this kind of life: training in habits of order and of industry, and in the idea of responsibility, of obligation to do something, to produce something,

in the world. There was always something which really
needed to be done, and a real necessity that each member of
the household should do his own part faithfully and in cooperation with others. Personalities which became effective
in action were bred and tested in the medium of action.
Again, we cannot overlook the importance for educational
purposes of the close and intimate acquaintance got with
nature at first hand, with real things and materials, with the
actual processes of their manipulation, and the knowledge of
their social necessities and uses. In all this there was continual training of observation, of ingenuity, constructive
imagination, of logical thought, and of the sense of reality
acquired through first-hand contact with actualities. The educative forces of the domestic spinning and weaving, of the
saw-mill, the grist-mill, the cooper shop, and the blacksmith
forge, were continuously operative.

No number of object-lessons, got up *as* object-lessons
for the sake of giving information, can afford even the
shadow of a substitute for acquaintance with the plants and
animals of the farm and garden acquired through actual
living among them and caring for them. No training of sense-
organs in school, introduced for the sake of training, can begin to compete with the alertness and fullness of sense-life
that comes through daily intimacy and interest in familiar
occupations. Verbal memory can be trained in committing
tasks, a certain discipline of the reasoning powers can be
acquired through lessons in science and mathematics; but,
after all, this is somewhat remote and shadowy compared
with the training of attention and of judgment that is acquired in having to do things with a real motive behind and
a real outcome ahead. At present, concentration of industry
and division of labor have practically eliminated household
and neighborhood occupations—at least for educational purposes. But it is useless to bemoan the departure of the good
old days of children's modesty, reverence, and implicit
obedience, if we expect merely by bemoaning and by exhortation to bring them back. It is radical conditions which
have changed, and only an equally radical change in education suffices. We must recognize our compensations—the increase in toleration, in breadth of social judgment, the larger

acquaintance with human nature, the sharpened alertness in reading signs of character and interpreting social situations, greater accuracy of adaptation to differing personalities, contact with greater commercial activities. These considerations mean much to the city-bred child of today. Yet there is a real problem: how shall we retain these advantages, and yet introduce into the school something representing the other side of life—occupations which exact personal responsibilities and which train the child in relation to the physical realities of life?

When we turn to the school, we find that one of the most striking tendencies at present is toward the introduction of so-called manual training, shop-work, and the household arts—sewing and cooking.

This has not been done "on purpose," with a full consciousness that the school must now supply that factor of training formerly taken care of in the home, but rather by instinct, by experimenting and finding that such work takes a vital hold of pupils and gives them something which was not to be got in any other way. Consciousness of its real import is still so weak that the work is often done in a half-hearted, confused, and unrelated way. The reasons assigned to justify it are painfully inadequate or sometimes even positively wrong.

If we were to cross-examine even those who are most favorably disposed to the introduction of this work into our school system, we should, I imagine, generally find the main reasons to be that such work engages the full spontaneous interest and attention of the children. It keeps them alert and active, instead of passive and receptive; it makes them more useful, more capable, and hence more inclined to be helpful at home; it prepares them to some extent for the practical duties of later life—the girls to be more efficient house managers, if not actually cooks and seamstresses; the boys (were our educational system only adequately rounded out into trade schools) for their future vocations. I do not underestimate the worth of these reasons. Of those indicated by the changed attitude of the children I shall indeed have something to say in my next talk, when speaking directly of the relationship of the school to the child. But the point of view

is, upon the whole, unnecessarily narrow. We must conceive
of work in wood and metal, of weaving, sewing, and cooking,
as methods of living and learning, not as distinct studies.

We must conceive of them in their social significance, as
types of the processes by which society keeps itself going, as
agencies for bringing home to the child some of the primal
necessities of community life, and as ways in which these
needs have been met by the growing insight and ingenuity of
man; in short, as instrumentalities through which the school
itself shall be made a genuine form of active community life,
instead of a place set apart in which to learn lessons.

A society is a number of people held together because
they are working along common lines, in a common spirit,
and with reference to common aims. The common needs and
aims demand a growing interchange of thought and growing
unity of sympathetic feeling. The radical reason that the
present school cannot organize itself as a natural social unit
is because just this element of common and productive
activity is absent. Upon the playground, in game and sport,
social organization takes place spontaneously and inevitably.
There is something to do, some activity to be carried on, requiring natural divisions of labor, selection of leaders and
followers, mutual cooperation and emulation. In the schoolroom the motive and the cement of social organization are
alike wanting. Upon the ethical side, the tragic weakness of
the present school is that it endeavors to prepare future members of the social order in a medium in which the conditions
of the social spirit are eminently wanting.

The difference that appears when occupations are made
the articulating centres of school life is not easy to describe
in words; it is a difference in motive, of spirit and atmosphere. As one enters a busy kitchen in which a group of
children are actively engaged in the preparation of food, the
psychological difference, the change from more or less passive and inert recipiency and restraint to one of buoyant outgoing energy, is so obvious as fairly to strike one in the face.
Indeed, to those whose image of the school is rigidly set the
change is sure to give a shock. But the change in the social
attitude is equally marked. The mere absorbing of facts and
truths is so exclusively individual an affair that it tends very

naturally to pass into selfishness. There is no obvious social motive for the acquirement of mere learning, there is no clear social gain in success thereat. Indeed, almost the only measure for success is a competitive one, in the bad sense of that term—a comparison of results in the recitation or in the examination to see which child has succeeded in getting ahead of others in storing up, in accumulating, the maximum of information. So thoroughly is this the prevailing atmosphere that for one child to help another in his task has become a school crime. Where the school work consists in simply learning lessons, mutual assistance, instead of being the most natural form of cooperation and association, becomes a clandestine effort to relieve one's neighbor of his proper duties. Where active work is going on, all this is changed. Helping others, instead of being a form of charity which impoverishes the recipient, is simply an aid in setting free the powers and furthering the impulse of the one helped. A spirit of free communication, of interchange of ideas, suggestions, results, both successes and failures of previous experiences, becomes the dominating note of the recitation. So far as emulation enters in, it is in the comparison of individuals, not with regard to the quantity of information personally absorbed, but with reference to the quality of work done—the genuine community standard of value. In an informal but all the more pervasive way, the school life organizes itself on a social basis.

Within this organization is found the principle of school discipline or order. Of course, order is simply a thing which is relative to an end. If you have the end in view of forty or fifty children learning certain set lessons, to be recited to a teacher, your discipline must be devoted to securing that result. But if the end in view is the development of a spirit of social cooperation and community life, discipline must grow out of and be relative to such an aim. There is little of one sort of order where things are in process of construction; there is a certain disorder in any busy workshop; there is not silence; persons are not engaged in maintaining certain fixed physical postures; their arms are not folded; they are not holding their books thus and so. They are doing a variety of things, and there is the confusion, the bustle, that results from activity. But out of the occupation, out of doing things that are to produce results, and out of doing these in a social and cooperative way, there is born a discipline of its own kind and type. Our whole conception of school discipline changes when we get this point of view. In critical moments we all realize that the only discipline that stands by us, the only training that becomes intuition, is that got through life itself. That we learn from experience, and from books or the sayings of others *only* as they are related to experience, are not mere phrases. But the school has been so set apart, so isolated from the ordinary conditions and motives of life, that the place where children are sent for discipline is the one place in the world where it is most difficult to get experience — the mother of all discipline worth the name. It is only when a narrow and fixed image of traditional school discipline dominates that one is in any danger of overlooking that deeper and infinitely wider discipline that comes from having a part to do in constructive work, in contributing to a result which, social in spirit, is none the less obvious and tangible in form — and hence in a form with reference to which responsibility may be exacted and accurate judgment passed.

The great thing to keep in mind, then, regarding the introduction into the school of various forms of active occupation, is that through them the entire spirit of the school is renewed. It has a chance to affiliate itself with life, to become the child's habitat, where he learns through directed living, instead of being only a place to learn lessons having an abstract and remote reference to some possible living to be done in the future. It gets a chance to be a miniature community, an embryonic society. This is the fundamental fact, and from this arise continuous and orderly streams of instruction. Under the industrial *régime* described, the child, after all, shared in the work, not for the sake of the sharing, but for the sake of the product. The educational results secured were real, yet incidental and dependent. But in the school the typical occupations followed are freed from all economic stress. The aim is not the economic value of the products, but the development of social power and insight. It is this liberation from narrow utilities, this openness to the possibilities of the human spirit that makes these practical activities in the school allies of art and centres of science and history.

The unity of all the sciences is found in geography. The significance of geography is that it presents the earth as the enduring home of the occupations of man. The world without its relationship to human activity is less than a world. Human industry and achievement, apart from their roots in the earth, are not even a sentiment, hardly a name. The earth is the final source of all man's food. It is his continual shelter and protection, the raw material of all his activities, and the home to whose humanizing and idealizing all his achievement returns. It is the great field, the great mine, the great source of the energies of heat, light, and electricity; the great scene of ocean, stream, mountain, and plain, of which all our agriculture and mining and lumbering, all our manufacturing and distributing agencies, are but the partial elements and factors. It is through occupations determined by this environment that mankind has made its historical and political progress. It is through these occupations that the intellectual and emotional interpretation of nature has been developed. It is through what we do in and with the world that we read its meaning and measure its value.

In educational terms, this means that these occupations in the school shall not be mere practical devices or modes of routine employment, the gaining of better technical skill as cooks, seamstresses, or carpenters, but active centres of scientific insight into natural materials and processes, points of departure whence children shall be led out into a realization of the historic development of man. The actual significance of this can be told better through one illustration taken from actual school work than by general discourse.

There is nothing which strikes more oddly upon the average intelligent visitor than to see boys as well as girls of ten, twelve, and thirteen years of age engaged in sewing and weaving. If we look at this from the standpoint of preparation of the boys for sewing on buttons and making patches, we get a narrow and utilitarian conception—a basis that hardly justifies giving prominence to this sort of work in the school. But if we look at it from another side, we find that this work gives the point of departure from which the child can trace and follow the progress of mankind in history, getting an insight also into the materials used and the mechanical principles involved. In connection with these occupations, the historic development of man is recapitulated. For example, the children are first given the raw material— the flax, the cotton plant, the wool as it comes from the back of the sheep (if we could take them to the place where the sheep are sheared, so much the better). Then a study is made of these materials from the standpoint of their adaptation to the uses to which they may be put. For instance, a comparison of the cotton fibre with wool fibre is made. I did not know until the children told me, that the reason for the late development of the cotton industry as compared with the woolen is that the cotton fibre is so very difficult to free by hand from the seeds. The children in one group worked thirty minutes freeing cotton fibres from the boll and seeds, and succeeded in getting out less than one ounce. They could easily believe that one person could gin only one pound a day by hand, and could understand why their ancestors wore woolen instead of cotton clothing. Among other things discovered as affecting their relative utilities was the shortness of the cotton fibre as compared with that of wool, the former averaging, say, one-third of an inch in length, while the latter run to three inches in length; also that the fibres of cotton are smooth and do not cling together, while the wool has a certain roughness which makes the fibres stick, thus assisting the spinning. The children worked this out for themselves with the actual material, aided by questions and suggestions from the teacher.

They then followed the processes necessary for working the fibres up into cloth. They re-invented the first frame for carding the wool—a couple of boards with sharp pins in them for scratching it out. They re-devised the simplest process for spinning the wool—a pierced stone or some other weight through which the wool is passed, and which as it is twirled draws out the fibre; next the top, which was spun on the floor, while the children kept the wool in their hands until it was gradually drawn out and wound upon it. Then the children are introduced to the invention next in historic order, working it out experimentally, thus seeing its necessity, and tracing its effects, not only upon that particular industry, but upon modes of social life—in this way passing in review the entire process up to the present complete loom, and all that goes with the application of science in the use of our present available powers. I need not speak of the science involved in this—the study of the fibres, of geographical features, the conditions under which raw materials are grown, the great centres of manufacture and distribution, the physics involved in the machinery of production; nor, again, of the historical side—the influence which these inventions have had upon humanity. You can concentrate the history of all mankind into the evolution of the flax, cotton, and wool fibres into clothing. I do not mean that this is the only, or the best, centre. But it is true that certain very real and important avenues to the consideration of the history of the race are thus opened—that the mind is introduced to much more fundamental and controlling influences than appear in the political and chronological records that usually pass for history.

Now, what is true of this one instance of fibres used in fabrics (and, of course, I have only spoken of one or two elementary phases of that) is true in its measure of every material used in every occupation, and of the processes employed. The occupation supplies the child with a genuine motive; it gives him experience at first hand; it brings him into contact with realities. It does all this, but in addition it is liberalized throughout by translation into its historic and social values and scientific equivalencies. With the growth of the child's mind in power and knowledge it ceases to be a pleasant occupation merely, and becomes more and more a medium, an instrument, an organ of understanding—and is thereby transformed.

This, in turn, has its bearing upon the teaching of science. Under present conditions, all activity, to be successful, has to be directed somewhere and somehow by the scientific expert—it is a case of applied science. This connection should determine its place in education. It is not only that the occupations, the so-called manual or industrial work in the school, give the opportunity for the introduction of science which illuminates them, which makes them material, freighted with meaning, instead of being mere devices of hand and eye; but that the scientific insight thus gained becomes an indispensable instrument of free and active participation in modern social life. Plato somewhere speaks of the slave as one who in his actions does not express his own ideas, but those of some other man. It is our social problem now, even more urgent than in the time of Plato, that method, purpose, understanding, shall exist in the consciousness of the one who does the work, that his activity shall have meaning to himself.

When occupations in the school are conceived in this broad and generous way, I can only stand lost in wonder at the objections so often heard, that such occupations are out of place in the school because they are materialistic, utilitarian, or even menial in their tendency. It sometimes seems to me that those who make these objections must live in quite another world. The world in which most of us live is a world in which everyone has a calling and occupation, something to do. Some are managers and others are subordinates. But the great thing for one as for the other is that each shall have had the education which enables him to see within his daily work all there is in it of large and human significance. How many of the employed are today mere appendages to the machines which they operate! This may be due in part to the machine itself, or the *régime* which lays so much stress upon the products of the machine; but it is certainly due in large part to the fact that the worker has had no opportunity to develop his imagination and his sympathetic insight as to the social and scientific values found in his work. At present, the impulses which lie at the basis of the industrial system are either practically neglected or positively distorted during the school period. Until the instincts of construction and production are systematically laid hold of in the years of childhood and youth, until they are trained in social directions, enriched by historical interpretation, controlled and illuminated by scientific methods, we certainly are in no position even to locate the source of our economic evils, much less to deal with them effectively.

If we go back a few centuries, we find a practical monopoly of learning. The term *possession* of learning is, indeed, a happy one. Learning was a class matter. This was a necessary result of social conditions. There were not in existence any means by which the multitude could possibly have access to intellectual resources. These were stored up and hidden away in manuscripts. Of these there were at best only a few, and it required long and toilsome preparation to be able to do anything with them. A high-priesthood of learning, which guarded the treasury of truth and which doled it out to the masses under severe restrictions, was the inevitable expression of these conditions. But, as a direct result of the industrial revolution of which we have been speaking, this has been changed. Printing was invented; it was made commercial. Books, magazines, papers were multiplied and cheapened. As a result of the locomotive and telegraph, frequent, rapid, and cheap intercommunication by mails and electricity was called into being. Travel has been rendered easy; freedom of movement, with its accompanying exchange of ideas, indefinitely facilitated. The result has been an intellectual revolution. Learning has been put into circulation. While there still is, and probably always will be, a particular class having the special business of inquiry in hand, a distinctively learned class is henceforth out of the question. It is an anachronism. Knowledge is no longer an immobile solid; it has been liquefied. It is actively moving in all the currents of society itself.

It is easy to see that this revolution, as regards the materials of knowledge, carries with it a marked change in the attitude of the individual. Stimuli of an intellectual sort pour in upon us in all kinds of ways. The merely intellectual life, the life of scholarship and of learning, thus gets a very altered value. Academic and scholastic, instead of being titles of honor, are becoming terms of reproach.

But all this means a necessary change in the attitude of the school, one of which we are as yet far from realizing the full force. Our school methods, and to a very considerable extent our curriculum, are inherited from the period when learning and command of certain symbols, affording as they did the only access to learning, were all-important. The ideals of this period are still largely in control, even where the outward methods and studies have been changed. We sometimes hear the introduction of manual training, art and science into the elementary, and even the secondary schools, deprecated on the ground that they tend toward the production of specialists—that they detract from our present scheme of generous, liberal culture. The point of this objection would be ludicrous if it were not often so effective as to make it tragic. It is our present education which is highly specialized, one-sided and narrow. It is an education dominated almost entirely by the mediæval conception of learning. It is something which appeals for the most part simply to the intellectual aspect of our natures, our desire to learn, to accumulate information, and to get control of the symbols of learning; not to our impulses and tendencies to make, to do, to create, to produce, whether in the form of utility or of art. The very fact that manual training, art and science are objected to as technical, as tending toward mere specialism, is of itself as good testimony as could be offered to the specialized aim which controls current education. Unless education had been virtually identified with the exclusively intellectual pursuits, with learning as such, all these materials and methods would be welcome, would be greeted with the utmost hospitality.

While training for the profession of learning is regarded as the type of culture, or a liberal education, the training of a mechanic, a musician, a lawyer, a doctor, a farmer, a merchant, or a railroad manager is regarded as purely technical and professional. The result is that which we see about us everywhere—the division into "cultured" people and "workers," the separation of theory and practice. Hardly one per cent of the entire school population ever attains to what we call higher education; only five per cent to the grade of our high school; while much more than half leave on or before the completion of the fifth year of the elementary grade. The simple facts of the case are that in the great majority of human beings the distinctively intellectual interest is not dominant. They have the so-called practical impulse and disposition. In many of those in whom by nature intellectual interest is strong, social conditions prevent its adequate realization. Consequently by far the larger number of pupils leave school as soon as they have acquired the rudiments of learning, as soon as they have enough of the symbols of reading, writing, and calculating to be of practical use to them in getting a living. While our educational leaders are talking of culture, the development of personality, etc., as the end and aim of education, the great majority of those who pass under the tuition of the school regard it only as a narrowly practical tool with which to get bread and butter enough to eke out a restricted life. If we were to conceive our educational end and aim in a less exclusive way, if we were to introduce into educational processes the activities which appeal to those whose dominant interest is to do and to make, we should find the hold of the school upon its members to be more vital, more prolonged, containing more of culture.

But why should I make this labored presentation? The obvious fact is that our social life has undergone a thorough and radical change. If our education is to have any meaning for life, it must pass through an equally complete transformation. This transformation is not something to appear suddenly, to be executed in a day by conscious purpose. It is already in progress. Those modifications of our school system which often appear (even to those most actively concerned with them, to say nothing of their spectators) to be mere changes of detail, mere improvement within the school mechanism, are in reality signs and evidences of evolution. The introduction of active occupations, of nature study, of elementary science, of art, of history; the relegation of the merely symbolic and formal to a secondary position; the change in the moral school atmosphere, in the relation of pupils and teachers—of discipline; the introduction of more active, expressive, and self-directing factors—all these are not mere accidents, they are necessities of the larger social evolution. It remains but to organize all these factors, to appreciate them in their fullness of meaning, and to put the ideas and ideals involved into complete, uncompromising possession of our school system. To do this means to make each one of our schools an embryonic community life, active with types of occupations that reflect the life of the larger society, and permeated throughout with the spirit of art, history, and science. When the school introduces and trains each child of society into membership within such a little community, saturating him with the spirit of service, and providing him with the instruments of effective self-direction, we shall have the deepest and best guarantee of a larger society which is worthy, lovely, and harmonious.

2. THE SCHOOL AND THE LIFE OF THE CHILD

Last week I tried to put before you the relationship between the school and the larger life of the community, and the necessity for certain changes in the methods and materials of school work, that it might be better adapted to present social needs.

Today I wish to look at the matter from the other side, and consider the relationship of the school to the life and development of the children in the school. As it is difficult to connect general principles with such thoroughly concrete things as little children, I have taken the liberty of introducing a great deal of illustrative matter from the work of the University Elementary School, that in some measure you may appreciate the way in which the ideas presented work themselves out in actual practice.

Some few years ago I was looking about the school supply stores in the city, trying to find desks and chairs which seemed thoroughly suitable from all points of view—artistic, hygienic, and educational—to the needs of the children. We had a great deal of difficulty in finding what we needed, and finally one dealer, more intelligent than the rest, made this remark: "I am afraid we have not what you want. You want something at which the children may work; these are all for listening." That tells the story of the traditional education. Just as the biologist can take a bone or two and reconstruct the whole animal, so, if we put before the mind's eye the ordinary schoolroom, with its rows of ugly desks placed in geometrical order, crowded together so that there shall be as little moving room as possible, desks almost all of the same size, with just space enough to hold books, pencils and paper, and add a table, some chairs, the bare walls, and possibly a few pictures, we can reconstruct the only educational activity that can possibly go on in such a place. It is all made "for listening"—because simply studying lessons out of a book is only another kind of listening; it marks the dependency of one mind upon another. The attitude of listening means, comparatively speaking, passivity, absorption; that there are certain ready-made materials which are there, which have been prepared by the school superintendent, the board, the teacher, and of which the child is to take in as much as possible in the least possible time.

There is very little place in the traditional schoolroom for the child to work. The workshop, the laboratory, the materials, the tools with which the child may construct, create, and actively inquire, and even the requisite space, have been for the most part lacking. The things that have to do with these processes have not even a definitely recognized place in education. They are what the educational authorities who write editorials in the daily papers generally term "fads" and "frills." A lady told me yesterday that she had been visiting different schools trying to find one where activity on the part of the children preceded the giving of information on the part of the teacher, or where the children had some motive for demanding the information. She visited, she said, twenty-four different schools before she found her first instance. I may add that that was not in this city.

Another thing that is suggested by these schoolrooms, with their set desks, is that everything is arranged for handling as large numbers of children as possible, for dealing with children *en masse*, as an aggregate of units; involving, again, that they be treated passively. The moment children act they individualize themselves; they cease to be a mass, and become the intensely distinctive beings that we are acquainted with out of school, in the home, the family, on the playground, and in the neighborhood.

On the same basis is explicable the uniformity of method and curriculum. If everything is on a "listening" basis, you can have uniformity of material and method. The ear, and the book which reflects the ear, constitute the medium which is alike for all. There is next to no opportunity for adjustment to varying capacities and demands. There is a certain amount—a fixed quantity—of ready-made results and accomplishments to be acquired by all children alike in a given time. It is in response to this demand that the curricu-

lum has been developed from the elementary school up through the college. There is just so much desirable knowledge, and there are just so many needed technical accomplishments in the world. Then comes the mathematical problem of dividing this by the six, twelve, or sixteen years of school life. Now give the children every year just the proportionate fraction of the total, and by the time they have finished they will have mastered the whole. By covering so much ground during this hour or day or week or year, everything comes out with perfect evenness at the end—provided the children have not forgotten what they have previously learned. The outcome of all this is Matthew Arnold's report of the statement, proudly made to him by an educational authority in France, that so many thousands of children were studying at a given hour, say eleven o'clock, just such a lesson in geography; and in one of our own western cities this proud boast used to be repeated to successive visitors by its superintendent.

I may have exaggerated somewhat in order to make plain the typical points of the old education: its passivity of attitude, its mechanical massing of children, its uniformity of curriculum and method. It may be summed up by stating that the centre of gravity is outside the child. It is in the teacher, the text-book, anywhere and everywhere you please except in the immediate instincts and activities of the child himself. On that basis there is not much to be said about the *life* of the child. A good deal might be said about the studying of the child, but the school is not the place where the child *lives*. Now the change which is coming into our education is the shifting of the centre of gravity. It is a change, a revolution, not unlike that introduced by Copernicus when the astronomical centre shifted from the earth to the sun. In this case the child becomes the sun about which the appliances of education revolve; he is the centre about which they are organized.

If we take an example from an ideal home, where the parent is intelligent enough to recognize what is best for the child, and is able to supply what is needed, we find the child learning through the social converse and constitution of the family. There are certain points of interest and value to him in the conversation carried on: statements are made, inquiries arise, topics are discussed, and the child continually learns. He states his experiences, his misconceptions are corrected. Again the child participates in the household occupations, and thereby gets habits of industry, order, and regard for the rights and ideas of others, and the fundamental habit of subordinating his activities to the general interest of the household. Participation in these household tasks becomes an opportunity for gaining knowledge. The ideal home would naturally have a workshop where the child could work out his constructive instincts. It would have a miniature laboratory in which his inquiries could be directed. The life of the child would extend out of doors to the garden, surrounding fields, and forests. He would have his excursions, his walks and talks, in which the larger world out of doors would open to him.

Now, if we organize and generalize all of this, we have the ideal school. There is no mystery about it, no wonderful discovery of pedagogy or educational theory. It is simply a question of doing systematically and in a large, intelligent, and competent way what for various reasons can be done in most households only in a comparatively meagre and haphazard manner. In the first place, the ideal home has to be enlarged. The child must be brought into contact with more grown people and with more children in order that there may be the freest and richest social life. Moreover, the occupations and relationships of the home environment are not specially selected for the growth of the child; the main object is something else, and what the child can get out of them is incidental. Hence the need of a school. In this school the life of the child becomes the all-controlling aim. All the media necessary to further the growth of the child centre there. Learning?—certainly, but living primarily, and learning through and in relation to this living. When we take the life of the child centred and organized in this way, we do not find that he is first of all a listening being; quite the contrary.

The statement so frequently made that education means "drawing out" is excellent, if we mean simply to contrast it with the process of pouring in. But, after all, it is difficult to connect the idea of drawing out with the ordinary doings of the child of three, four, seven, or eight years of age. He is already running over, spilling over, with activities of all kinds. He is not a purely latent being whom the adult has to approach with great caution and skill in order gradually to draw out some hidden germ of activity. The child is already intensely active, and the question of education is the question of taking hold of his activities, of giving them direction. Through direction, through organized use, they tend toward valuable results, instead of scattering or being left to merely impulsive expression.

If we keep this before us, the difficulty I find uppermost in the minds of many people regarding what is termed the new education is not so much solved as dissolved; it disappears. A question often asked is: If you begin with the child's ideas, impulses and interests, all so crude, so random and scattering, so little refined or spiritualized, how is he going to get the necessary discipline, culture, and information? If there were no way open to us except to excite and indulge these impulses of the child, the question might well be asked. We should either have to ignore and repress the activities, or else to humor them. But if we have organization of equipment and of materials, there is another path open to us. We can direct the child's activities, giving them exercise along certain lines, and can thus lead up to the goal which logically stands at the end of the paths followed.

"If wishes were horses, beggars would ride." Since they are not, since really to satisfy an impulse or interest means to work it out, and working it out involves running up against obstacles, becoming acquainted with materials, exercising ingenuity, patience, persistence, alertness, it of necessity involves discipline—ordering of power—and supplies knowledge. Take the example of the little child who wants to make a box. If he stops short with the imagination or wish, he certainly will not get discipline. But when he attempts to realize his impulse, it is a question of making his idea definite, making it into a plan, of taking the right kind of wood, measuring the parts needed, giving them the necessary proportions, etc. There is involved the preparation of materials, the sawing, planing, the sand-papering, making all the edges and corners to fit. Knowledge of tools and processes is inevitable. If the child realizes his instinct and makes the box, there is plenty of opportunity to gain discipline and perseverance, to exercise effort in overcoming obstacles, and to attain as well a great deal of information.

So undoubtedly the little child who thinks he would like to cook has little idea of what it means or costs, or what it requires. It is simply a desire to "mess around," perhaps to imitate the activities of older people. And it is doubtless possible to let ourselves down to that level and simply humor that interest. But here, too, if the impulse is exercised, utilized, it runs up against the actual world of hard conditions, to which it must accommodate itself; and there again come in the factors of discipline and knowledge. One of the children became impatient recently, at having to work things out by a long method of experimentation, and said: "Why do we bother with this? Let's follow a recipe in a cook-book." The teacher asked the children where the recipe came from, and the conversation showed that if they simply followed this they would not understand the reasons for what they were doing. They were then quite willing to go on with the experimental work. To follow that work will, indeed, give an illustration of just the point in question. Their occupation happened that day to be the cooking of eggs, as making a transition from the cooking of vegetables to that of meats. In order to get a basis of comparison they first summarized the constituent food elements in the vegetables and made a preliminary comparison with those found in meat. Thus they found that the woody fibre or cellulose in vegetables corresponded to the connective tissue in meat, giving the element of form and structure. They found that starch and starchy products were characteristic of the vegetables, that mineral salts were found in both alike, and that there was fat in both—a small quantity in vegetable food and a large amount in animal. They were prepared then to take up the study of albumen as the characteristic feature of animal food, corresponding to starch in the vegetables, and were ready to consider the conditions requisite for the proper treatment of albumen—the eggs serving as the material of experiment.

They experimented first by taking water at various tem-

CHILD'S DRAWING OF A CAVE AND TREES

peratures, finding out when it was scalding, simmering, and boiling hot, and ascertained the effect of the various degrees of temperature on the white of the egg. That worked out, they were prepared, not simply to cook eggs, but to understand the principle involved in the cooking of eggs. I do not wish to lose sight of the universal in the particular incident. For the child simply to desire to cook an egg, and accordingly drop it in water for three minutes, and take it out when he is told, is not educative. But for the child to realize his own impulse by recognizing the facts, materials and conditions involved, and then to regulate his impulse through that recognition, is educative. This is the difference, upon which I wish to insist, between exciting or indulging an interest and realizing it through its direction.

Another instinct of the child is the use of pencil and paper. All children like to express themselves through the medium of form and color. If you simply indulge this interest by letting the child go on indefinitely, there is no growth that is more than accidental. But let the child first

CHILD'S DRAWING OF A FOREST

express his impulse, and then through criticism, question, and suggestion bring him to consciousness of what he has done, and what he needs to do, and the result is quite different. Here, for example, is the work of a seven-year-old child. It is not average work, it is the best work done among the little children, but it illustrates the particular principle of which I have been speaking. They had been talking about the primitive conditions of social life when people lived in caves. The child's idea of that found expression in this way: the cave is neatly set up on the hill side in an impossible way. You see the conventional tree of childhood—a vertical line with horizontal branches on each side. If the child had been allowed to go on repeating this sort of thing day by day, he would be indulging his instinct rather than exercising it. But the child was now asked to look closely at trees, to compare those seen with the one drawn, to examine more closely and consciously into the conditions of his work. Then he drew trees from observation.

Finally he drew again from combined observation,

memory, and imagination. He made again a free illustration, expressing his own imaginative thought, but controlled by detailed study of actual trees. The result was a scene representing a bit of forest; so far as it goes, it seems to me to have as much poetic feeling as the work of an adult, while at the same time its trees are, in their proportions, possible ones, not mere symbols.

If we roughly classify the impulses which are available in the school, we may group them under four heads. There is the social instinct of the children as shown in conversation, personal intercourse, and communication. We all know how self-centred the little child is at the age of four or five. If any new subject is brought up, if he says anything at all, it is: "I have seen that"; or, "My papa or mamma told me about that." His horizon is not large; an experience must come immediately home to him, if he is to be sufficiently interested to relate it to others and seek theirs in return. And yet the egoistic and limited interest of little children is in this manner capable of infinite expansion. The language instinct is the simplest form of the social expression of the child. Hence it is a great, perhaps the greatest of all educational resources.

Then there is the instinct of making—the constructive impulse. The child's impulse to do finds expression first in play, in movement, gesture, and make-believe, becomes more definite, and seeks outlet in shaping materials into tangible forms and permanent embodiment. The child has not much instinct for abstract inquiry. The instinct of investigation seems to grow out of the combination of the constructive impulse with the conversational. There is no distinction between experimental science for little children and the work done in the carpenter shop. Such work as they can do in physics or chemistry is not for the purpose of making technical generalizations or even arriving at abstract truths. Children simply like to do things, and watch to see what will happen. But this can be taken advantage of, can be directed into ways where it gives results of value, as well as be allowed to go on at random.

And so the expressive impulse of the children, the art instinct, grows also out of the communicating and construc-

tive instincts. It is their refinement and full manifestation.
Make the construction adequate, make it full, free, and
flexible, give it a social motive, something to tell, and you
have a work of art. Take one illustration of this in connection with the textile work—sewing and weaving. The
children made a primitive loom in the shop; here the constructive instinct was appealed to. Then they wished to do
something with this loom, to make something. It was the
type of the Indian loom, and they were shown blankets
woven by the Indians. Each child made a design kindred in
idea to those of the Navajo blankets, and the one which
seemed best adapted to the work in hand was selected. The
technical resources were limited, but the coloring and form
were worked out by the children. Examination shows that it
took patience, thoroughness, and perseverance to do the
work. It involved not merely discipline and information of
both a historical sort and the elements of technical design,
but also something of the spirit of art in adequately conveying an idea.

One more instance of the connection of the art side
with the constructive side: The children had been studying
primitive spinning and carding, when one of them, twelve
years of age, made a picture of one of the older children
spinning. Here is another piece of work which is not quite
average; it is better than the average. It is an illustration of
two hands and the drawing out of the wool to get it ready
for spinning. This was done by a child eleven years of age.
But, upon the whole, with the younger children especially,
the art impulse is connected mainly with the social instinct—
the desire to tell, to represent.

Now, keeping in mind these fourfold interests—the
interest in conversation or communication; in inquiry, or
finding out things; in making things, or construction; and
in artistic expression—we may say they are the natural resources, the uninvested capital, upon the exercise of which
depends the active growth of the child. I wish to give one
or two illustrations, the first from the work of children
seven years of age. It illustrates in a way the dominant
desire of the children to talk, particularly about folks and
of things in relation to folks. If you observe little children,

CHILD'S DRAWING OF HANDS SPINNING

you will find they are interested in the world of things mainly in its connection with people, as a background and medium of human concerns. Many anthropologists have told us there are certain identities in the child interests with those of primitive life. There is a sort of natural recurrence of the child mind to the typical activities of primitive peoples; witness the hut which the boy likes to build in the yard, playing hunt, with bows, arrows, spears, and so on. Again the question comes: What are we to do with this interest—are we to ignore it, or just excite and draw it out? Or shall we get hold of it and direct it to something ahead, something better? Some of the work that has been planned for our seven-year-old children has the latter end in view— to utilize this interest so that it shall become a means of seeing the progress of the human race. The children begin by imagining present conditions taken away until they are in contact with nature at first hand. That takes them back to a hunting people, to a people living in caves or trees and getting a precarious subsistence by hunting and fishing. They imagine as far as possible the various natural physical conditions adapted to that sort of life; say, a hilly, woody slope, near mountains and a river where fish would be abundant. Then they go on in imagination through the hunting to the semi-agricultural stage, and through the nomadic to the settled agricultural stage. The point I wish to make is that there is abundant opportunity thus given for actual study, for inquiry which results in gaining information. So, while the instinct primarily appeals to the social side, the interest of the child in people and their doings is carried on into the larger world of reality. For example, the children had some idea of primitive weapons, of the stone arrow-head, etc. That provided occasion for the testing of materials as regards their friability, their shape, texture, etc., resulting in a lesson in mineralogy, as they examined the different stones to find which was best suited to the purpose. The discussion of the iron age supplied a demand for the construction of a smelting oven made out of clay, and of considerable size. As the children did not get their drafts right at first, the mouth of the furnace not being in proper relation to the vent as to size and position, instruction in the principles of combustion, the nature of drafts and of fuel, was required. Yet the instruction was not given ready-made; it was first needed, and then arrived at experimentally. Then the children took some material, such as copper, and went through a series of experiments, fusing it, working it into objects; and the same experiments were made with lead and other metals. This work has been also a continuous course in geography, since the children have had to imagine and work out the various physical conditions necessary to the different forms of social life implied. What would be the physical conditions appropriate to pastoral life? to the beginning of agriculture? to fishing? What would be the natural method of exchange between these peoples? Having worked out such points in conversation, they have afterward represented them in maps and sand-molding. Thus they have gained ideas of the various forms of the configuration of the earth, and at the same time have seen them in their relation to human activity, so that they are not simply external facts, but are fused and welded with social conceptions regarding the life and progress of humanity.

CHILD'S DRAWING OF A GIRL SPINNING

The result, to my mind, justifies completely the conviction that children, in a year of such work (of five hours a week altogether), get infinitely more acquaintance with facts of science, geography, and anthropology than they get where information is the professed end and object, where they are simply set to learning facts in fixed lessons. As to discipline, they get more training of attention, more power of interpretation, of drawing inferences, of acute observation and continuous reflection, than if they were put to working out arbitrary problems simply for the sake of discipline.

I should like at this point to refer to the recitation. We all know what it has been—a place where the child shows off to the teacher and the other children the amount of information he has succeeded in assimilating from the text-book. From this other standpoint, the recitation becomes pre-eminently a social meeting place; it is to the school what the spontaneous conversation is at home, excepting that it is more organized, following definite lines. The recitation becomes the social clearing-house, where experiences and ideas are exchanged and subjected to criticism, where mis-conceptions are corrected, and new lines of thought and inquiry are set up.

This change of the recitation from an examination of knowledge already acquired to the free play of the children's communicative instinct, affects and modifies all the language work of the school. Under the old *régime* it was unques-tionably a most serious problem to give the children a full and free use of language. The reason was obvious. The natural motive for language was seldom offered. In the pedagogical text-books language is defined as the medium of expressing thought. It becomes that, more or less, to adults with trained minds, but it hardly needs to be said that lan-guage is primarily a social thing, a means by which we give our experiences to others and get theirs again in return. When it is taken away from its natural purpose, it is no wonder that it becomes a complex and difficult problem to teach language. Think of the absurdity of having to teach language as a thing by itself. If there is anything the child will do before he goes to school, it is to talk of the things that interest him. But when there are no vital interests appealed to in the school, when language is used simply for the repetition of lessons, it is not surprising that one of the chief difficulties of school work has come to be instruction in the mother-tongue. Since the language taught is unnatural, not growing out of the real desire to communicate vital impressions and convictions, the freedom of children in its use gradually disappears, until finally the high-school teacher has to invent all kinds of devices to assist in getting any spontaneous and full use of speech. Moreover, when the language instinct is appealed to in a social way, there is a continual contact with reality. The result is that the child always has something in his mind to talk about, he has something to say; he has a thought to express, and a thought is not a thought unless it is one's own. On the traditional method, the child must say something that he has merely learned. There is all the difference in the world between having something to say and having to say something. The child who has a variety of materials and facts wants to talk about them, and his language becomes more refined and full, because it is controlled and informed by realities. Reading and writing, as well as the oral use of language, may be taught on this basis. It can be done in a *related* way, as the outgrowth of the child's social desire to recount his experiences and get in return the experiences of others, directed always through contact with the facts and forces which determine the truth communicated.

I shall not have time to speak of the work of the older children, where the original crude instincts of construction and communication have been developed into something like scientifically directed inquiry, but I will give an illustration of the use of language following upon this experimental work. The work was on the basis of a simple experiment of the commonest sort, gradually leading the children out into geological and geographical study. The sentences that I am going to read seem to me poetic as well as "scientific." "A long time ago when the earth was new, when it was lava, there was no water on the earth, and there was steam all round the earth up in the air, as there were many gases in the air. One of them was carbon dioxide. The steam became clouds, because the earth began to cool off, and after a while it began to rain, and the water came down and dissolved the carbon dioxide from the air." There is a good deal more science in that than probably would be apparent at the outset. It represents some three months of work on the part of the child. The children kept daily and weekly records, but this is part of the summing up of the quarter's work. I call this language poetic, because the child has a clear image and has a personal feeling for the realities imaged. I extract sentences from two other records to illustrate further the vivid use of language when there is a vivid experience back of it. "When the earth was cold enough to condense, the water, with the help of carbon dioxide, *pulled* the calcium out of the rocks into a large body of water where the little animals could get it." The other reads as follows: "When the earth cooled, calcium was in the rocks. Then the carbon dioxide and water united and formed a solution, and, as it ran, it *tore* out the calcium and carried it on to the sea, where there were little animals who took it out of solution." The use of such words as "pulled" and "tore" in connection with the process of chemical combination evidences a personal realization which compels its own appropriate expression.

If I had not taken so much time in my other illustrations, I should like to show how, beginning with very simple material things, the children are led on to larger fields of investigation, and to the intellectual discipline that is the accompaniment of such research. I will simply mention the experiment in which the work began. It consisted in making precipitated chalk, used for polishing metals. The children, with simple apparatus—a tumbler, lime water, and a glass tube—precipitated the calcium carbonate out of the water; and from this beginning went on to a study of the processes by which rocks of various sorts, igneous, sedimentary, etc., had been formed on the surface of the earth and the places they occupy; then to points in the geography of the United States, Hawaii, and Puerto Rico; to the effects of these various bodies of rock, in their various configurations, upon the human occupations; so that this geological record finally rounded itself out into the life of man at the present time. The children saw and felt the connection between these geologic processes taking place ages and ages ago, and the physical conditions determining the industrial occupations of today.

Of all the possibilities involved in the subject, "The School and the Life of the Child," I have selected but one, because I have found that that one gives people more difficulty, is more of a stumbling-block, than any other. One may be ready to admit that it would be most desirable for the school to be a place in which the child should really live, and get a life-experience in which he should delight and find meaning for its own sake. But then we hear this inquiry: How, upon this basis, shall the child get the needed information; how shall he undergo the required discipline? Yes, it has come to this, that with many, if not most, people the

normal processes of life appear to be incompatible with
getting information and discipline. So I have tried to indicate,
in a highly general and inadequate way (for only the
school itself, in its daily operation, could give a detailed and
worthy representation), how the problem works itself out—
how it is possible to lay hold upon the rudimentary instincts
of human nature, and, by supplying a proper medium, so to
control their expression as not only to facilitate and enrich
the growth of the individual child, but also to supply the
same results, and far more, of technical information and
discipline that have been the ideals of education in the past.

But although I have selected this especial way of approach (as a concession to the question almost universally
raised), I am not willing to leave the matter in this more
or less negative and explanatory condition. Life is the great
thing after all; the life of the child at its time and in its
measure, no less than the life of the adult. Strange would it
be, indeed, if intelligent and serious attention to what the
child *now* needs and is capable of in the way of a rich,
valuable, and expanded life should somehow conflict with
the needs and possibilities of later, adult life. "Let us live
with our children" certainly means, first of all, that our children shall live—not that they shall be hampered and stunted
by being forced into all kinds of conditions, the most remote
consideration of which is relevancy to the present life of
the child. If we seek the kingdom of heaven, educationally,
all other things shall be added unto us—which, being interpreted, is that if we identify ourselves with the real instincts
and needs of childhood, and ask only after its fullest assertion and growth, the discipline and information and culture
of adult life shall all come in their due season.

Speaking of culture reminds me that in a way I have
been speaking only of the outside of the child's activity—
only of the outward expression of his impulses toward saying,
making, finding out, and creating. The real child, it hardly
need be said, lives in the world of imaginative values and
ideas which find only imperfect outward embodiment. We
hear much nowadays about the cultivation of the child's
"imagination." Then we undo much of our own talk and
work by a belief that the imagination is some special part of

the child that finds its satisfaction in some one particular
direction—generally speaking, that of the unreal and make-
believe, of the myth and made-up story. Why are we so hard
of heart and so slow to believe? The imagination is the
medium in which the child lives. To him there is everywhere
and in everything that occupies his mind and activity at all
a surplusage of value and significance. The question of the
relation of the school to the child's life is at bottom simply
this: Shall we ignore this native setting and tendency, dealing not with the living child at all, but with the dead image
we have erected, or shall we give it play and satisfaction? If
we once believe in life and in the life of the child, then will
all the occupations and uses spoken of, then will all history
and science, become instruments of appeal and materials of
culture to his imagination, and through that to the richness
and the orderliness of his life. Where we now see only the
outward doing and the outward product, there, behind all
visible results, is the re-adjustment of mental attitude, the
enlarged and sympathetic vision, the sense of growing
power, and the willing ability to identify both insight and
capacity with the interests of the world and man. Unless
culture be a superficial polish, a veneering of mahogany
over common wood, it surely is this—the growth of the
imagination in flexibility, in scope, and in sympathy, till the
life which the individual lives is informed with the life of
nature and of society. When nature and society can live in
the schoolroom, when the forms and tools of learning are
subordinated to the substance of experience, then shall
there be an opportunity for this identification, and culture
shall be the democratic password.

3. WASTE IN EDUCATION

The subject announced for today was "Waste in Education." I should like first to state briefly its relation to the two preceding lectures. The first dealt with the school in its social aspects, and the necessary re-adjustments that have to be made to render it effective in present social conditions. The second dealt with the school in relation to the growth of individual children. Now the third deals with the school as itself an institution, in relation both to society and to its own members—the children. It deals with the question of organization, because all waste is the result of the lack of it, the motive lying behind organization being promotion of economy and efficiency. This question is not one of the waste of money or the waste of things. These matters count; but the primary waste is that of human life, the life of the children while they are at school, and afterward because of inadequate and perverted preparation.

So, when we speak of organization, we are not to think simply of the externals; of that which goes by the name "school system"—the school board, the superintendent, and the building, the engaging and promotion of teachers, etc. These things enter in, but the fundamental organization is that of the school itself as a community of individuals, in its relations to other forms of social life. All waste is due to isolation. Organization is nothing but getting things into connection with one another, so that they work easily, flexibly, and fully. Therefore in speaking of this question of waste in education, I desire to call your attention to the isolation of the various parts of the school system, to the lack of unity in the aims of education, to the lack of coherence in its studies and methods.

I have made a chart (I) which, while I speak of the isolations of the school system itself, may perhaps appeal to the eye and save a little time in verbal explanations. A paradoxical friend of mine says there is nothing so obscure as an illustration, and it is quite possible that my attempt to illustrate my point will simply prove the truth of his statement.

The blocks represent the various elements in the school system, and are intended to indicate roughly the length of time given to each division, and also the overlapping, both in time and in subjects studied, of the individual parts of the system. With each block is given the historical conditions in which it arose and its ruling ideal.

The school system, upon the whole, has grown from the top down. During the Middle Ages it was essentially a cluster of professional schools—especially law and theology. Our present university comes down to us from the Middle Ages. I will not say that at present it is a mediæval institution, but it had its roots in the Middle Ages, and it has not outlived all mediæval traditions regarding learning.

The kindergarten, rising with the present century, was a union of the nursery and of the philosophy of Schelling; a wedding of the plays and games which the mother carried on with her children, to Schelling's highly romantic and symbolic philosophy. The elements that came from the actual study of child life—the continuation of the nursery— have remained a life-bringing force in all education; the Schellingesque factors made an obstruction between it and the rest of the school system, brought about isolations.

The line drawn over the top indicates that there is a certain interaction between the kindergarten and the primary school; for, so far as the primary school remained in spirit foreign to the natural interests of child life, it was isolated from the kindergarten, so that it is a problem, at present, to introduce kindergarten methods into the primary school; the problem of the so-called connecting class. The difficulty is that the two are not one from the start. To get a connection the teacher has had to climb over the wall instead of entering in at the gate.

On the side of aims, the ideal of the kindergarten was the moral development of the children, rather than instruction or discipline; an ideal sometimes emphasized to the point of sentimentality. The primary school grew practically

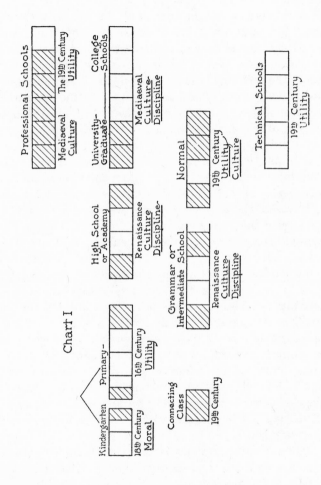

Chart I

out of the popular movement of the sixteenth century, when along with the invention of printing and the growth of commerce, it became a business necessity to know how to read, write, and figure. The aim was distinctly a practical one; it was utility; getting command of these tools, the symbols of learning, not for the sake of learning, but because they gave access to careers in life otherwise closed.

The division next to the primary school is the grammar school. The term is not much used in the West, but is common in the eastern states. It goes back to the time of the revival of learning—a little earlier perhaps than the conditions out of which the primary school originated, and, even when contemporaneous, having a different ideal. It had to do with the study of language in the higher sense; because, at the time of the Renaissance, Latin and Greek connected people with the culture of the past, with the Roman and Greek world. The classic languages were the only means of escape from the limitations of the Middle Ages. Thus there sprang up the prototype of the grammar school, more liberal than the university (so largely professional in character), for the purpose of putting into the hands of the people the key to the old learning, that men might see a world with a larger horizon. The object was primarily culture, secondarily discipline. It represented much more than the present grammar school. It was the liberal element in the college, which, extending downward, grew into the academy and the high school. Thus the secondary school is still in part just a lower college (having an even higher curriculum than the college of a few centuries ago) or a preparatory department to a college, and in part a rounding up of the utilities of the elementary school.

There appear then two products of the nineteenth century, the technical and normal schools. The schools of technology, engineering, etc., are, of course, mainly the development of nineteenth-century business conditions, as the primary school was the development of business conditions of the sixteenth century. The normal school arose because of the necessity for training teachers, with the idea partly of professional drill, and partly that of culture.

Without going more into detail, we have some eight

different parts of the school system as represented on the chart, all of which arose historically at different times, having different ideals in view, and consequently different methods. I do not wish to suggest that all of the isolation, all of the separation, that has existed in the past between the different parts of the school system still persists. One must, however, recognize that they have never yet been welded into one complete whole. The great problem in education on the administrative side is how to unite these different parts.

Consider the training schools for teachers—the normal schools. These occupy at present a somewhat anomalous position, intermediate between the high school and the college, requiring the high-school preparation, and covering a certain amount of college work. They are isolated from the higher subject-matter of scholarship, since, upon the whole, their object has been to train persons *how* to teach, rather than *what* to teach; while, if we go to the college, we find the other half of this isolation—learning *what* to teach, with almost a contempt for methods of teaching. The college is shut off from contact with children and youth. Its members, to a great extent, away from home and forgetting their own childhood, become eventually teachers with a large amount of subject-matter at command, and little knowledge of how this is related to the minds of those to whom it is to be taught. In this division between what to teach and how to teach, each side suffers from the separation.

It is interesting to follow out the interrelation between primary, grammar, and high schools. The elementary school has crowded up and taken many subjects previously studied in the old New England grammar school. The high school has pushed its subjects down. Latin and algebra have been put in the upper grades, so that the seventh and eighth grades are, after all, about all that is left of the old grammar school. They are a sort of amorphous composite, being partly a place where children go on learning what they already have learned (to read, write, and figure), and partly a place of preparation for the high school. The name in some parts of New England for these upper grades was "Intermediate School." The term was a happy one; the work was simply intermediate between something that had been and something that was going to be, having no special meaning on its own account.

Just as the parts are separated, so do the ideals differ —moral development, practical utility, general culture, discipline, and professional training. These aims are each especially represented in some distinct part of the system of education; and with the growing interaction of the parts, each is supposed to afford a certain amount of culture, discipline, and utility. But the lack of fundamental unity is witnessed in the fact that one study is still considered good for discipline, and another for culture; some parts of arithmetic, for example, for discipline and others for use; literature for culture; grammar for discipline; geography partly for utility, partly for culture; and so on. The unity of education is dissipated, and the studies become centrifugal; so much of this study to secure this end, so much of that to secure another, until the whole becomes a sheer compromise and patchwork between contending aims and disparate studies. The great problem in education on the administrative side is to secure the unity of the whole, in the place of a sequence of more or less unrelated and overlapping parts and thus to reduce the waste arising from friction, reduplication and transitions that are not properly bridged.

In this second symbolic diagram (II) I wish to suggest that really the only way to unite the parts of the system is to unite each to life. We can get only an artificial unity so long as we confine our gaze to the school system itself. We must look at it as part of the larger whole of social life. This block (A) in the centre represents the school system as a whole. (1) At one side we have the home, and the two arrows represent the free interplay of influences, materials, and ideas between the home life and that of the school. (2) Below we have the relation to the natural environment, the great field of geography in the widest sense. The school building has about it a natural environment. It ought to be in a garden, and the children from the garden would be led on to surrounding fields, and then into the wider country, with all its facts and forces. (3) Above is represented business life, and the necessity for free play between the school

Chart Ⅱ

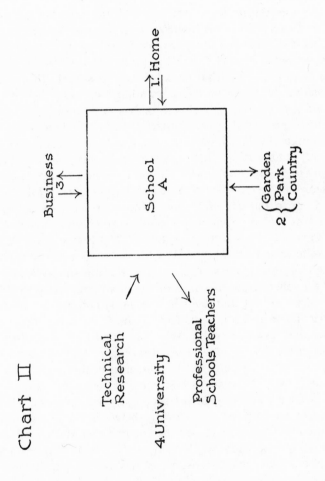

Business
3

School
A

1. Home

Garden
Park
Country
2

Technical
Research

4. University

Professional
Schools Teachers

and the needs and forces of industry. (4) On the other side is the university proper, with its various phases, its laboratories, its resources in the way of libraries, museums, and professional schools.

From the standpoint of the child, the great waste in the school comes from his inability to utilize the experiences he gets outside the school in any complete and free way within the school itself; while, on the other hand, he is unable to apply in daily life what he is learning at school. That is the isolation of the school—its isolation from life. When the child gets into the schoolroom he has to put out of his mind a large part of the ideas, interests, and activities that predominate in his home and neighborhood. So the school, being unable to utilize this everyday experience, sets painfully to work, on another tack and by a variety of means, to arouse in the child an interest in school studies. While I was visiting in the city of Moline a few years ago, the superintendent told me that they found many children every year who were surprised to learn that the Mississippi River in the text-book had anything to do with the stream of water flowing past their homes. The geography being simply a matter of the schoolroom, it is more or less of an awakening to many children to find that the whole thing is nothing but a more formal and definite statement of the facts which they see, feel, and touch every day. When we think that we all live on the earth, that we live in an atmosphere, that our lives are touched at every point by the influences of the soil, flora, and fauna, by considerations of light and heat, and then think of what the school study of geography has been, we have a typical idea of the gap existing between the everyday experiences of the child, and the isolated material supplied in such large measure in the school. This is but an instance, and one upon which most of us may reflect long before we take the present artificiality of the school as other than a matter of course or necessity.

Though there should be organic connection between the school and business life, it is not meant that the school is to prepare the child for any particular business, but that there should be a natural connection of the everyday life of the child with the business environment about him, and that it is the affair of the school to clarify and liberalize this connection, to bring it to consciousness, not by introducing special studies, like commercial geography and arithmetic, but by keeping alive the ordinary bonds of relation. The subject of compound-business-partnership is probably not in many of the arithmetics nowadays, though it was there not a generation ago, for the makers of text-books said that if they left out anything they could not sell their books. This compound-business-partnership originated as far back as the sixteenth century. The joint-stock company had not been invented, and as large commerce with the Indies and Americas grew up, it was necessary to have an accumulation of capital with which to handle it. One man said, "I will put in this amount of money for six months," and another, "So much for two years," and so on. Thus by joining together they got money enough to float their commercial enterprises. Naturally, then, "compound partnership" was taught in the schools. The joint-stock company was invented; compound partnership disappeared, but the problems relating to it stayed in the arithmetics for two hundred years. They were kept after they had ceased to have practical utility, for the sake of mental discipline—they were "such hard problems, you know." A great deal of what is now in the arithmetics under the head of percentage is of the same nature. Children of twelve and thirteen years of age go through gain and loss calculations, and various forms of bank discount so complicated that the bankers long ago dispensed with them. And when it is pointed out that business is not done this way, we hear again of "mental discipline." And yet there are plenty of real connections between the experience of children and business conditions which need to be utilized and illuminated. The child should study his commercial arithmetic and geography, not as isolated things by themselves, but in their reference to his social environment. The youth needs to become acquainted with the bank as a factor in modern life, with what it does, and how it does it; and then relevant arithmetical processes would have some meaning—quite in contradistinction to the time-absorbing and mind-killing examples in percentage, partial payments, etc., found in all our arithmetics.

The connection with the university, as indicated in this chart, I need not dwell upon. I simply wish to indicate that there ought to be a free interaction between all the parts of the school system. There is much of utter triviality of subject-matter in elementary and secondary education. When we investigate it, we find that it is full of facts taught that are not facts, which have to be unlearned later on. Now, this happens because the "lower" parts of our system are not in vital connection with the "higher." The university or college, in its idea, is a place of research, where investigation is going on, a place of libraries and museums, where the best resources of the past are gathered, maintained and organized. It is, however, as true in the school as in the university that the spirit of inquiry can be got only through and with the attitude of inquiry. The pupil must learn what has meaning, what enlarges his horizon, instead of mere trivialities. He must become acquainted with truths, instead of things that were regarded as such fifty years ago, or that are taken as interesting by the misunderstanding of a partially educated teacher. It is difficult to see how these ends can be reached except as the most advanced part of the educational system is in complete interaction with the most rudimentary.

The next chart (III) is an enlargement of the second. The school building has swelled out, so to speak, the surrounding environment remaining the same, the home, the garden and country, the relation to business life and the university. The object is to show what the school must become to get out of its isolation and secure the organic connection with social life of which we have been speaking. It is not our architect's plan for the school building that we hope to have; but it is a diagrammatic representation of the idea which we want embodied in the school building. On the lower side you see the dining room and the kitchen, at the top the wood and metal shops, and the textile room for sewing and weaving. The centre represents the manner in which all come together in the library, that is to say, in a collection of the intellectual resources of all kinds that throw light upon the practical work, that give it meaning and liberal value. If the four corners represent practice, the interior represents the theory of the practical activities. In other words, the object of

Chart III

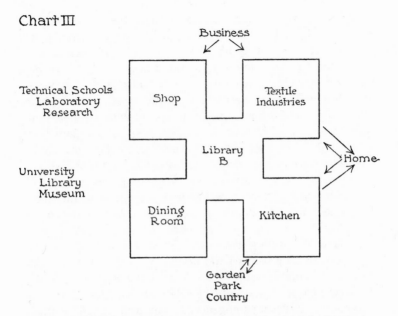

these forms of practice in the school is not found chiefly in themselves, or in the technical skill of cooks, seamstresses, carpenters and masons, but in their connection, on the social side, with the life without; while on the individual side they respond to the child's need of action, of expression, of desire to do something, to be constructive and creative, instead of simply passive and conforming. Their great significance is that they keep the balance between the social and individual sides—the chart symbolizing particularly the connection with the social. Here on one side is the home. How naturally the lines of connection play back and forth between the home and the kitchen and the textile room of the school! The child can carry over what he learns in the home and utilize it in the school; and the things learned in the school he applies at home. These are the two great things in breaking down isolation, in getting connection—to have the child come to school with all the experience he has got outside the school, and to leave it with something to be immediately used in his everyday life. The child comes to the traditional school with a healthy body and a more or less unwilling mind, though, in fact, he does not bring both his body and mind with him;

he has to leave his mind behind, because there is no way to use it in the school. If he had a purely abstract mind, he could bring it to school with him, but his is a concrete one, interested in concrete things, and unless these things get over into school life, he cannot take his mind with him. What we want is to have the child come to school with a whole mind and a whole body, and leave school with a fuller mind and an even healthier body. And speaking of the body suggests that, while there is no gymnasium in these diagrams, the active life carried on in its four corners brings with it constant physical exercise, while our gymnasium proper will deal with the particular weaknesses of children and their correction, and will attempt more consciously to build up the thoroughly sound body as the abode of the sound mind.

That the dining room and kitchen connect with the country and its processes and products it is hardly necessary to say. Cooking may be so taught that it has no connection with country life, and with the sciences that find their unity in geography. Perhaps it generally has been taught without these connections being really made. But all the materials that come into the kitchen have their origin in the country; they come from the soil, are nurtured through the influences of light and water, and represent a great variety of local environments. Through this connection, extending from the garden into the larger world, the child has his most natural introduction to the study of the sciences. Where did these things grow? What was necessary to their growth? What their relation to the soil? What the effect of different climatic conditions? and so on. We all know what the old-fashioned botany was: partly collecting flowers that were pretty, pressing and mounting them; partly pulling these flowers to pieces and giving technical names to the different parts, finding all the different leaves, naming all their different shapes and forms. It was a study of plants without any reference to the soil, to the country, or to growth. In contrast, a real study of plants takes them in their natural environment and in their uses as well, not simply as food, but in all their adaptations to the social life of man. Cooking becomes as well a most natural introduction to the study of chemistry, giving the child here also something which he can at once bring to bear upon his daily experience. I once heard a very intelligent woman say that she could not understand how science could be taught to little children, because she did not see how they could understand atoms and molecules. In other words, since she did not see how highly abstract facts could be presented to the child independently of daily experience, she could not understand how science could be taught at all. Before we smile at this remark, we need to ask ourselves if she is alone in her assumption, or whether it simply formulates the principle of almost all our school practice.

The same relations with the outside world are found in the carpentry and the textile shops. They connect with the country, as the source of their materials, with physics, as the science of applying energy, with commerce and distribution, with art in the development of architecture and decoration. They have also an intimate connection with the university on the side of its technological and engineering schools; with the laboratory, and its scientific methods and results.

To go back to the square which is marked the library (Chart III, B): if you imagine rooms half in the four corners and half in the library, you will get the idea of the recitation room. That is the place where the children bring the experiences, the problems, the questions, the particular facts which they have found, and discuss them so that new light may be thrown upon them, particularly new light from the experience of others, the accumulated wisdom of the world— symbolized in the library. Here is the organic relation of theory and practice; the child not simply doing things, but getting also the *idea* of what he does; getting from the start some intellectual conception that enters into his practice and enriches it; while every idea finds, directly or indirectly, some application in experience, and has some effect upon life. This, I need hardly say, fixes the position of the "book" or reading in education. Harmful as a substitute for experience, it is all-important in interpreting and expanding experience.

The other chart (IV) illustrates precisely the same idea. It gives the symbolic upper story of this ideal school. In the upper corners are the laboratories; in the lower corners are the studios for art work, both the graphic and auditory arts.

Chart IV

Laboratories
Research

University

Library
Museum

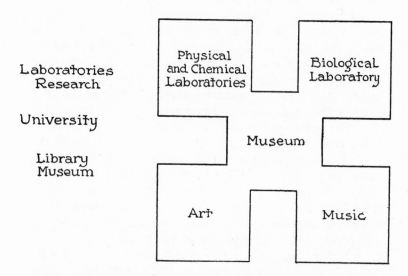

The questions, the chemical and physical problems, arising in the kitchen and shop, are taken to the laboratories to be worked out. For instance, this past week one of the older groups of children doing practical work in weaving which involved the use of the spinning wheel, worked out the diagrams of the direction of forces concerned in treadle and wheel, and the ratio of velocities between wheel and spindle. In the same manner, the plants with which the child has to do in cooking, afford the basis for a concrete interest in botany, and may be taken and studied by themselves. In a certain school in Boston science work for months was centred in the growth of the cotton plant, and yet something new was brought in every day. We hope to do similar work with all the types of plants that furnish materials for sewing and weaving. These examples will suggest, I hope, the relation which the laboratories bear to the rest of the school.

The drawing and music, or the graphic and auditory arts, represent the culmination, the idealization, the highest point of refinement of all the work carried on. I think everybody who has not a purely literary view of the subject recognizes that genuine art grows out of the work of the artisan. The art of the Renaissance was great, because it grew out of the manual arts of life. It did not spring up in a separate atmosphere, however ideal, but carried on to their spiritual meaning processes found in homely and everyday forms of life. The school should observe this relationship. The merely artisan side is narrow, but the mere art, taken by itself, and grafted on from without, tends to become forced, empty, sentimental. I do not mean, of course, that all art work must be correlated in detail to the other work of the school, but simply that a spirit of union gives vitality to the art, and depth and richness to the other work. All art involves physical organs—the eye and hand, the ear and voice; and yet it is something more than the mere technical skill required by the organs of expression. It involves an idea, a thought, a spiritual rendering of things; and yet it is other than any number of ideas by themselves. It is a living union of thought and the instrument of expression. This union is symbolized by saying that in the ideal school the art work might be considered to be that of the shops, passed through the alembic of library and museum into action again.

Take the textile room as an illustration of such a synthesis. I am talking about a future school, the one we hope, some time, to have. The basal fact in that room is that it is a workshop, doing actual things in sewing, spinning, and weaving. The children come into immediate connection with the materials, with various fabrics of silk, cotton, linen and wool. Information at once appears in connection with these materials; their origin, history, their adaptation to particular uses, and the machines of various kinds by which the raw materials are utilized. Discipline arises in dealing with the problems involved, both theoretical and practical. Whence does the culture arise? Partly from seeing all these things reflected through the medium of their scientific and historic conditions and associations, whereby the child learns to appreciate them as technical achievements, as thoughts precipitated in action; and partly because of the introduction of the art idea into the room itself. In the ideal school there would be something of this sort: first, a complete industrial museum, giving samples of materials in various stages of manufacture, and the implements, from the simplest to the most complex, used in dealing with them; then a collection of photographs and pictures illustrating the landscapes and the scenes from which the materials come, their native homes, and their places of manufacture. Such a collection would be a vivid and continual lesson in the synthesis of art, science, and industry. There would be, also, samples of the more perfect forms of textile work, as Italian, French, Japanese, and Oriental. There would be objects illustrating motives of design and decoration which have entered into production. Literature would contribute its part in its idealized representation of the world-industries, as the Penelope in the *Odyssey*—a classic in literature because the character is an adequate embodiment of a certain industrial phase of social life. So, from Homer down to the present time, there is a continuous procession of related facts which have been translated into terms of art. Music lends its share, from the Scotch song at the wheel to the spinning song of Marguerite, or of Wagner's Senta. The shop becomes a pictured museum, appealing to the eye. It would have not only materials,— beautiful woods and designs,—but would give a synopsis of the historical evolution of architecture in its drawings and pictures.

Thus I have attempted to indicate how the school may be connected with life so that the experience gained by the child in a familiar, commonplace way is carried over and made use of there, and what the child learns in the school is carried back and applied in everyday life, making the school an organic whole, instead of a composite of isolated parts. The isolation of studies as well as of parts of the school system disappears. Experience has its geographical aspect, its artistic and its literary, its scientific and its historical sides. All studies arise from aspects of the one earth and the one life lived upon it. We do not have a series of stratified earths, one of which is mathematical, another physical, another historical, and so on. We should not be able to live very long in any one taken by itself. We live in a world where all sides are bound together. All studies grow out of relations in the one great common world. When the child lives in varied but concrete and active relationship to this common world, his studies are naturally unified. It will no longer be a problem to correlate studies. The teacher will not have to resort to all sorts of devices to weave a little arithmetic into the history lesson, and the like. Relate the school to life, and all studies are of necessity correlated.

Moreover, if the school is related as a whole to life as a whole, its various aims and ideals—culture, discipline, information, utility—cease to be variants, for one of which we must select one study and for another another. The growth of the child in the direction of social capacity and service, his larger and more vital union with life, becomes the unifying aim; and discipline, culture and information fall into place as phases of this growth.

I wish to say one word more about the relationship of our particular school to the University. The problem is to unify, to organize, education, to bring all its various factors together, through putting it as a whole into organic union with everyday life. That which lies back of the pedagogical school of the University is the necessity of working out something to serve as a model for such unification, extending from work beginning with the four-year-old child up through the graduate work of the University. Already we have much help from the University in scientific work planned, sometimes even in detail, by heads of the departments. The graduate student comes to us with his researches and methods, suggesting ideas and problems. The library and museum are at hand. We want to bring all things educational together; to break down the barriers that divide the education of the little child from the instruction of the maturing youth; to identify the lower and the higher education, so that it shall be demonstrated to the eye that there is no lower and higher, but simply education.

Speaking more especially with reference to the pedagogical side of the work: I suppose the oldest university chair of pedagogy in our country is about twenty years old—that of the University of Michigan, founded in the latter seventies. But there are only one or two that have tried to make a connection between theory and practice. They teach for the most part by theory, by lectures, by reference to books, rather than through the actual work of teaching itself. At Columbia, through the Teachers College, there is an extensive and close connection between the University and the training of teachers. Something has been done in one or two other places along the same line. We want an even more intimate union here, so that the University shall put all its resources at the disposition of the elementary school, contributing to the evolution of valuable subject-matter and right method, while the school in turn will be a laboratory in which the student of education sees theories and ideas demonstrated, tested, criticized, enforced, and the evolution of new truths. We want the school in its relation to the University to be a working model of a unified education.

A word as to the relation of the school to educational interests generally. I heard once that the adoption of a certain method in use in our school was objected to by a teacher on this ground: "You know that it is an experimental school. They do not work under the same conditions that we are subject to." Now, the purpose of performing an experiment is that other people need not experiment; at least need not experiment so much, may have something definite and positive to go by. An experiment demands particularly favorable conditions in order that results may be reached both freely and securely. It has to work unhampered, with all the needed resources at command. Laboratories lie back of all the great business enterprises of today, back of every great factory, every railway and steamship system. Yet the laboratory is not a business enterprise; it does not aim to secure for itself the conditions of business life, nor does the commercial undertaking repeat the laboratory. There is a difference between working out and testing a new truth, or a new method, and applying it on a wide scale, making it available for the mass of men, making it commercial. But the first thing is to discover the truth, to afford all necessary facilities, for this is the most practical thing in the world in the long run. We do not expect to have other schools literally imitate what we do. A working model is not something to be copied; it is to afford a demonstration of the feasibility of the principle, and of the methods which make it feasible. So (to come back to our own point) we want here to work out the problem of the unity, the organization of the school system in itself, and to do this by relating it so intimately to life as to demonstrate the possibility and necessity of such organization for all education.

4. THREE YEARS OF THE UNIVERSITY ELEMENTARY SCHOOL[1]

The school was started the first week in January, three years ago. I shall try this afternoon to give a brief statement of the ideas and problems that were in mind when the experiment was started, and a sketch of the development of the work since that time. We began in a small house in Fifty-seventh Street, with fifteen children. We found ourselves the next year with twenty-five children in Kimbark Avenue, and then moved in January to Rosalie Court, the larger quarters enabling us to take forty children. The next year the numbers increased to sixty, the school remaining at Rosalie Court. This year we have had ninety-five on the roll at one time, and are located at 5412 Ellis Avenue, where we hope to stay till we have a building and grounds of our own.

The children during the first year of the school were between the ages of six and nine. Now their ages range between four and thirteen—the members of the oldest group being in their thirteenth year. This is the first year that we have children under six, and this has been made possible through the liberality of friends in Honolulu, H. I., who are building up there a memorial kindergarten along the same lines.

The expenses of the school during the first year, of two terms only, were between $1,300 and $1,400. The expenses this year will be about $12,000. Of this amount $5,500 will come from tuitions; $5,000 has been given by friends interested in the school, and there remains about $1,500 yet to be raised for the conduct of the school. This is an indication of the increase of expenses. The average expense per pupil is about the same since the start, i.e., $120 per child per school year. Relatively speaking, this year the expenses of the school took something of a jump, through the expense of moving to a new building, and the repairs and changes there

1. Stenographic report of a talk by John Dewey at a meeting of the Parents' Association of the University Elementary School, February, 1899; somewhat revised.

necessary. An increase in the staff of teachers has also enlarged the work as well as the debits of the school. Next year
(1899–1900) we hope to have about 120 children, and apparently the expenses will be about $2,500 more than this.
Of this amount $2,000 will be met by the increase in tuition
from the pupils. The cost of a child to the school, $120 a
year, is precisely the tuition charged by the University for
students and is double the average tuition charged by the
school. But it is not expected that the University tuition will
come anywhere near meeting the expense involved there.
One reason for not increasing the tuition here, even if it
were advisable for other reasons, is that it is well to
emphasize, from an educational point of view, that elementary as well as advanced education requires endowment.
There is every reason why money should be spent freely for
the organization and maintenance of foundation work in
education as well as for the later stages.

The elementary school has had from the outset two
sides: one, the obvious one of instruction of the children who
have been entrusted to it; the other, relationship to the
University, since the school is under the charge, and forms a
part of the pedagogical work of the University.

When the school was started, there were certain ideas in
mind—perhaps it would be better to say questions and problems; certain points which it seemed worth while to test. If
you will permit one personal word, I should like to say that it
is sometimes thought that the school started out with a
number of ready-made principles and ideas which were to
be put into practice at once. It has been popularly assumed
that I am the author of these ready-made ideas and principles which were to go into execution. I take this opportunity
to say that the educational conduct of the school, as well as
its administration, the selection of subject-matter, and the
working out of the course of study, as well as actual instruction of children, have been almost entirely in the hands
of the teachers of the school; and that there has been a
gradual development of the educational principles and
methods involved, not a fixed equipment. The teachers
started with question marks, rather than with fixed rules,
and if any answers have been reached, it is the teachers in

the school who have supplied them. We started upon the whole with four such questions, or problems:

1. What can be done, and how can it be done, to bring the school into closer relation with the home and neighborhood life—instead of having the school a place where the child comes solely to learn certain lessons? What can be done to break down the barriers which have unfortunately come to separate the school life from the rest of the everyday life of the child? This does not mean, as it is sometimes, perhaps, interpreted to mean, that the child should simply take up in the school things already experienced at home and study them, but that, so far as possible, the child shall have the same attitude and point of view in the school as in the home; that he shall find the same interest in going to school, and in there doing things worth doing for their own sake, that he finds in the plays and occupations which busy him in his home and neighborhood life. It means, again, that the motives which keep the child at work and growing at home shall be used in the school, so that he shall not have to acquire another set of principles of actions belonging only to the school—separate from those of the home. It is a question of the unity of the child's experience, of its actuating motives and aims, not of amusing or even interesting the child.

2. What can be done in the way of introducing subject-matter in history and science and art, that shall have a positive value and real significance in the child's own life; that shall represent, even to the youngest children, something worthy of attainment in skill or knowledge; as much so to the little pupil as are the studies of the high-school or college student to him? You know what the traditional curriculum of the first few years is, even though many modifications have been made. Some statistics have been collected showing that 75 or 80 per cent of the first three years of a child in school are spent upon the form—not the substance—of learning, the mastering of the symbols of reading, writing, and arithmetic. There is not much positive nutriment in this. Its purpose is important—is necessary—but it does not represent the same kind of increase in a child's intellectual and moral experience that is represented by positive truth of

history and nature, or by added insight into reality and beauty. One thing, then, we wanted to find out is how much can be given a child that is really worth his while to get, in knowledge of the world about him, of the forces in the world, of historical and social growth, and in capacity to express himself in a variety of artistic forms. From the strictly educational side this has been the chief problem of the school. It is along this line that we hope to make our chief contribution to education in general; we hope, that is, to work out and publish a positive body of subject-matter which may be generally available.

3. How can instruction in these formal, symbolic branches—the mastering of the ability to read, write, and use figures intelligently—be carried on with everyday experience and occupation as their background and in definite relations to other studies of more inherent content, and be carried on in such a way that the child shall feel their necessity through their connection with subjects which appeal to him on their own account? If this can be accomplished, he will have a vital motive for getting the technical capacity. It is not meant, as has been sometimes jocosely stated, that the child learn to bake and sew at school, and to read, write, and figure at home. It is intended that these formal subjects shall not be presented in such large doses at first as to be the exclusive objects of attention, and that the child shall be led by that which he is doing to feel the need for acquiring skill in the use of symbols and the immediate power they give. In any school, if the child realizes the motive for the use and application of number and language he has taken the longest step toward securing the power; and he can realize the motive only as he has some particular—not some general and remote—use for the symbols.

4. Individual attention. This is secured by small groupings—eight or ten in a class—and a large number of teachers supervising systematically the intellectual needs and attainments and physical well-being and growth of the child. To secure this we have now 135 hours of instructors' time per week, that is, the time of nine teachers for three hours per day, or one teacher per group. It requires but a few words to make this statement about attention to individual powers

and needs, and yet the whole of the school's aims and methods, moral, physical, intellectual, are bound up in it.

I think these four points present a fair statement of what we have set out to discover. The school is often called an experimental school, and in one sense that is the proper name. I do not like to use it too much, for fear parents will think we are experimenting upon the children, and that they naturally object to. But it is an experimental school—at least I hope so—with reference to education and educational problems. We have attempted to find out by trying, by doing—not alone by discussion and theorizing—*whether* these problems may be worked out, and *how* they may be worked out.

Next a few words about the means that have been used in the school in order to test these four questions, and to supply their answers, and first as to the place given to hand-work of different kinds in the school. There are three main lines regularly pursued: (*a*) the shop-work with wood and tools, (*b*) cooking work, and (*c*) work with textiles—sewing and weaving. Of course, there is other hand-work in connection with science, as science is largely of an experimental nature. It is a fact that may not have come to your attention that a large part of the best and most advanced scientific work involves a great deal of manual skill, the training of the hand and eye. It is impossible for one to be a first-class worker in science without this training in manipulation, and in handling apparatus and materials. In connection with the history work, especially with the younger children, hand-work is brought in in the way of making implements, weapons, tools, etc. Of course, the art work is another side— drawing, painting, and modelling. Logically, perhaps, the gymnasium work does not come in here, but as a means of developing moral and intellectual control through the medium of the body it certainly does. The children have one-half hour per day of this form of physical exercise. Along this line we have found that hand-work, in large variety and amount, is the most easy and natural method of keeping up the same attitude of the child in and out of the school. The child gets the largest part of his acquisitions through his bodily activities, until he learns to work systematically with the intellect. That is the purpose of this work in the school, to direct these activities, to systematize and organize them, so that they shall not be as haphazard and as wandering as they are outside of school. The problem of making these forms of practical activity work continuously and definitely together, leading from one factor of skill to another, from one intellectual difficulty to another, has been one of the most difficult, and at the same time one in which we have been most successful. The various kinds of work, carpentry, cooking, sewing, and weaving, are selected as involving different kinds of skill, and demanding different types of intellectual attitude on the part of the child, and because they represent some of the most important activities of the everyday outside world: the question of living under shelter, of daily food and clothing, of the home, of personal movement and exchange of goods. He gets also the training of sense-organs, of touch, of sight, and the ability to coordinate eye and hand. He gets healthy exercise; for the child demands a much larger amount of physical activity than the formal program of the ordinary school permits. There is also a continual appeal to memory, to judgment, in adapting ends to means, a training in habits of order, industry, and neatness in the care of the tools and utensils, and in doing things in a systematic, instead of a haphazard, way. Then, again, these practical occupations make a background, especially in the earlier groups, for the later studies. The children get a good deal of chemistry in connection with cooking, of number work and geometrical principles in carpentry, and a good deal of geography in connection with their theoretical work in weaving and sewing. History also comes in with the origin and growth of various inventions, and their effects upon social life and political organization.

Perhaps more attention, upon the whole, has been given to our second point, that of positive subject-matter, than to any other thing. On the history side the curriculum is now fairly well worked out. The younger children begin with the home and occupations of the home. In the sixth year the intention is that the children should study occupations outside the home, the larger social industries—farming, mining, lumber, etc.—that they may see the complex and various social industries on which life depends, while incidentally they investigate the use of the various materials—woods, metals, and the processes applied—thus getting a beginning of scientific study. The next year is given to the historical development of industry and invention—starting with man as a savage and carrying him through the typical phases of his progress upward, until the iron age is reached and man begins to enter upon a civilized career. The object of the study of primitive life is not to keep the child interested in lower and relatively savage stages, but to show him the steps of progress and development, especially along the line of invention, by which man was led into civilization. There is a certain nearness, after all, in the child to primitive forms of life. They are much more simple than existing institutions. By throwing the emphasis upon the progress of man, and upon the way advance has been made, we hope to avoid the objections that hold against paying too much attention to the crudities and distracting excitements of savage life.

The next two or three years, *i.e.*, the fourth and fifth grades, and perhaps the sixth, will be devoted to American history. It is then that history, properly speaking, begins, as the study of primitive life can hardly be so called.

Then comes Greek history and Roman, in the regular chronological order, each year having its own work planned with reference to what has come before and after.

The science work was more difficult to arrange and systematize, because there was so little to follow—so little that has been already done in an organized way. We are now at work upon a program,[2] and I shall not speak in detail about it. The first two or three years cultivate the children's powers of observation, lead them to sympathetic interest in the habits of plants and animals, and to look at things with reference to their uses. Then the centre of the work becomes geographical—the study of the earth, as the most central thing. From this almost all the work grows out, and to it the work goes back. Another standpoint in the science work is that of the application of natural forces to the service of man through machines. Last year a good deal of work was done in electricity (and will be repeated this year), based on

2. This year's program is published in the *Elementary School Record*.

the telegraph and telephone—taking up the things that can easily be grasped.

In mechanics they have studied locks and clocks with reference to the adaptation of the various parts of the machinery. All this work makes a most excellent basis for more formal physics later on. Cooking gives opportunity for getting a great many ideas of heat and water, and of their effects. The scientific work taken up in the school differs mainly from that of other schools in having the experimental part— physics and chemistry—emphasized, and is not confined simply to nature study—the study of plants and animals. Not that the latter is less valuable, but that we find it possible to introduce the physical aspects from the first.

If I do not spend a large amount of time in speaking of the music and art work, it is not because they are not considered valuable and important—certainly as much so as any other work done in the school, not only in the development of the child's moral and æsthetic nature, but also from a strictly intellectual point of view. I know of no work in the school that better develops the power of attention, the habit of observation and of consecutiveness, of seeing parts in relation to a whole.

I shall now say a few words about the administrative side of the school. At the outset we mixed up the children of different ages and attainments as much as possible, believing there were mental advantages in the give-and-take thus secured, as well as the moral advantages in having the older assume certain responsibilities in the care of the younger. As the school grew, it became necessary to abandon the method, and to group the children with reference to their common capacities. These groupings, however, are based, not on ability to read and write, but upon similarity of mental attitude and interest, and upon general intellectual capacity and mental alertness. There are ways in which we are still trying to carry out the idea of mixing up the children, that we may not build the rigid stepladder system of the "graded" school. One step in this direction is having the children move about and come in contact with different teachers. While there are difficulties and evils connected with this, I think one of the most useful things in the school is that children come into intimate relation with a number of different personalities. The children also meet in general assemblies—for singing, and for the report of the whole school work as read by members of the different groups. The older children are also given a half hour a week in which to join some of the younger groups, and, if possible, as in hand-work, enter into the work of the younger children. In various ways we are attempting to keep a family spirit throughout the school, and not the feeling of isolated classes and grades.

The organization of the teaching force has gradually become departmental, as the needs of the work have indicated its chief branches. So we now have recognized divisions of Science, History, Domestic or Household Arts, Manual Training in the limited sense (wood and metals), Music, Art (that is, drawing, water colors, clay-modelling, etc.), and Gymnasium. As the work goes on into the secondary period, the languages and mathematics will also of necessity assume a more differentiated and distinct position. As it is sometimes said that correlated or thoroughly harmonized work cannot be secured upon this basis, I am happy to say that our experience shows positively that there are no intrinsic difficulties. Through common devotion to the best development of the child, through common loyalty to the main aims and methods of the school, our teachers have demonstrated that in education, as in business, the best organization is secured through proper regard for natural divisions of labor, interest, and training. The child secures the advantage in discipline and knowledge of contact with experts in each line, while the individual teachers serve the common thought in diverse ways, thus multiplying and reinforcing it.

Upon the moral side, that of so-called discipline and order, where the work of the University Elementary School has perhaps suffered most from misunderstanding and misrepresentation, I shall say only that our ideal has been, and continues to be, that of the best form of family life, rather than that of a rigid graded school. In the latter, the large number of children under the care of a single teacher, and the very limited number of modes of activity open to the pupils, have made necessary certain fixed and somewhat external forms of "keeping order." It would be very stupid to copy these, under the changed conditions of our school, its small groups permitting and requiring the most intimate personal acquaintance of child and teacher, and its great variety of forms of work, with their differing adaptations to the needs of different children. If we have permitted to our children more than the usual amount of freedom, it has not been in order to relax or decrease real discipline, but because under our particular conditions larger and less artificial responsibilities could thus be required of the children, and their entire development of body and spirit be more harmonious and complete. And I am confident that the parents who have entrusted their children to us for any length of time will agree in saying that, while the children like, or love, to come to school, yet work, and not amusement, has been the spirit and teaching of the school; and that this freedom has been granted under such conditions of intelligent and sympathetic oversight as to be a means of upbuilding and strengthening character.

At the end of three years, then, we are not afraid to say that some of our original questions have secured affirmative answers. The increase of our children from fifteen to almost one hundred, along with a practical doubling of fees, has shown that parents are ready for a form of education that makes individual growth its sole controlling aim. The presence of an organized corps of instructors demonstrates that thoroughly educated teachers are ready to bring to elementary education the same resources of training, knowledge, and skill that have long been at the command of higher education. The everyday work of the school shows that children can live in school as out of it, and yet grow daily in wisdom, kindness, and the spirit of obedience—that learning may, even with little children, lay hold upon the substance of truth that nourishes the spirit, and yet the forms of knowledge be observed and cultivated; and that growth may be genuine and thorough, and yet a delight.

5. THE PSYCHOLOGY OF ELEMENTARY EDUCATION

Naturally, most of the public is interested in what goes on day by day in a school in direct relation to the children there. This is true of parents who send their boys and girls for the sake of the personal results they wish to secure, not for the sake of contributing to educational theory. In the main, it is true of visitors to a school who recognize, in varying degrees, what is actually done with the children before their eyes, but who rarely have either the interest or the time to consider the work in relation to underlying problems. A school cannot lose sight of this aspect of its work, since only by attending to it can the school retain the confidence of its patrons and the presence of its pupils.

Nevertheless a school conducted by a department of a university must have another aspect. From the university standpoint, the most important part of its work is the scientific—the contribution it makes to the progress of educational thinking. The aim of educating a certain number of children would hardly justify a university in departing from the tradition which limits it to those who have completed their secondary instruction. Only the scientific aim, the conduct of a laboratory, comparable to other scientific laboratories, can furnish a reason for the maintenance by a university of an elementary school. Such a school is a laboratory of applied psychology. That is, it has a place for the study of mind as manifested and developed in the child, and for the search after materials and agencies that seem most likely to fulfill and further the conditions of normal growth.

It is not a normal school or a department for the training of teachers. It is not a model school. It is not intended to demonstrate any one special idea or doctrine. Its task is the problem of viewing the education of the child in the light of the principles of mental activity and processes of growth made known by modern psychology. The problem by its nature is an infinite one. All that any school can do is to make contributions here and there, and to stand for the necessity of considering education, both theoretically and practically, in this light. This being the end, the school conditions must, of course, agree. To endeavor to study the process and laws of growth under such artificial conditions as prevent many of the chief facts of child life from showing themselves is an obvious absurdity.

In its practical aspect, this laboratory problem takes the form of the construction of a course of study which harmonizes with the natural history of the growth of the child in capacity and experience. The question is the selection of the kind, variety, and due proportion of subjects, answering most definitely to the dominant needs and powers of a given period of growth, and of those modes of presentation that will cause the selected material to enter vitally into growth. We cannot admit too fully or too freely the limits of our knowledge and the depths of our ignorance in these matters. No one has a complete hold scientifically upon the chief psychological facts of any one year of child life. It would be sheer presumption to claim that just the material best fitted to promote this growth has as yet been discovered. The assumption of an educational laboratory is rather that enough is known of the conditions and modes of growth to make intelligent inquiry possible; and that it is only by acting upon what is already known that more can be found out. The chief point is such experimentation as will add to our reasonable convictions. The demand is to secure arrangements that will permit and encourage freedom of investigation; that will give some assurance that important facts will not be forced out of sight; conditions that will enable the educational practice indicated by the inquiry to be sincerely acted upon, without the distortion and suppression arising from undue dependence upon tradition and preconceived notions. It is in this sense that the school would be an experimental station in education.

What, then, are the chief working hypotheses that have been adopted from psychology? What educational counterparts have been hit upon as in some degree in line with the adopted psychology?

The discussion of these questions may be approached by

pointing out a contrast between contemporary psychology and the psychology of former days. The contrast is a triple one. Earlier psychology regarded mind as a purely individual affair in direct and naked contact with an external world. The only question asked was of the ways in which the world and the mind acted upon each other. The entire process recognized would have been in theory exactly the same if there were one mind living alone in the universe. At present the tendency is to conceive individual mind as a function of social life—as not capable of operating or developing by itself, but as requiring continual stimulus from social agencies, and finding its nutrition in social supplies. The idea of heredity has made familiar the notion that the equipment of the individual, mental as well as physical, is an inheritance from the race: a capital inherited by the individual from the past and held in trust by him for the future. The idea of evolution has made familiar the notion that mind cannot be regarded as an individual, monopolistic possession, but represents the outworkings of the endeavor and thought of humanity; that it is developed in an environment which is social as well as physical, and that social needs and aims have been most potent in shaping it—and the chief difference between savagery and civilization is not in the naked nature which each faces, but the social heredity and social medium.

Studies of childhood have made it equally apparent that this socially acquired inheritance operates in the individual only under present social stimuli. Nature must indeed furnish its physical stimuli of light, sound, heat, etc., but the significance attaching to these, the interpretation made of them, depends upon the ways in which the society in which the child lives acts and reacts in reference to them. The bare physical stimulus of light is not the entire reality; the interpretation given to it through social activities and thinking confers upon it its wealth of meaning. It is through imitation, suggestion, direct instruction, and even more indirect unconscious tuition, that the child learns to estimate and treat the bare physical stimuli. It is through the social agencies that he recapitulates in a few short years the progress which it has taken the race slow centuries to work out.

Educational practice has exhibited an unconscious

adaptation to and harmony with the prevailing psychology; both grew out of the same soil. Just as mind was supposed to get its filling by direct contact with the world, so all the needs of instruction were thought to be met by bringing the child mind into direct relation with various bodies of external fact labelled geography, arithmetic, grammar, etc. That these classified sets of facts were simply selections from the social life of the past was overlooked; equally so that they had been generated out of social situations and represented the answers found for social needs. No social element was found in the subject-matter nor in the intrinsic appeal which it made to the child; it was located wholly outside in the teacher—in the encouragements, admonitions, urgings, and devices of the instructor in getting the child's mind to work upon a material which in itself was only accidentally lighted up by any social gleam. It was forgotten that the maximum appeal, and the full meaning in the life of the child, could be secured only when the studies were presented not as bare external studies, but from the standpoint of the relation they bear to the life of society. It was forgotten that to become integral parts of the child's conduct and character they must be assimilated not as mere items of information, but as organic parts of his present needs and aims—which in turn are social.

In the second place, the older psychology was a psychology of knowledge, of intellect. Emotion and endeavor occupied but an incidental and derivative place. Much was said about sensations—next to nothing about movements. There was discussion of ideas and of whether they originated in sensations or in some innate mental faculty; but the possibility of their origin in and from the needs of action was ignored. Their influence upon conduct, upon behavior, was regarded as an external attachment. Now we believe (to use the words of Mr. James) that the intellect, the sphere of sensations and ideas, is but a "middle department which we sometimes take to be final, failing to see, amid the monstrous diversity of the length and complication of the cogitations which may fill it, that it can have but one essential function—the function of defining the direction which our activity, immediate or remote, shall take."

Here also was a preëstablished harmony between educational practice and psychological theory. Knowledge in the schools was isolated and made an end in itself. Facts, laws, information have been the staple of the curriculum. The controversy in educational theory and practice was between those who relied more upon the sense-element in knowledge, upon contact with things, upon object-lessons, etc., and those who emphasized abstract ideas, generalizations, etc.—reason, so-called, but in reality other people's ideas as formulated in books. In neither case was there any attempt to connect either the sense-training or the logical operations with the problems and interests of the life of practice. Here again an educational transformation is indicated if we are to suppose that our psychological theories stand for any truths of life.

The third point of contrast lies in the modern conception of the mind as essentially a process—a process of growth, not a fixed thing. According to the older view mind was mind, and that was the whole story. Mind was the same throughout, because fitted out with the same assortment of faculties whether in child or adult. If any difference was made it was simply that some of these ready-made faculties—such as memory—came into play at an earlier time, while others, such as judging and inferring, made their appearance only after the child, through memorizing drills, had been reduced to complete dependence upon the thought of others. The only important difference that was recognized was one of quantity, of amount. The boy was a little man and his mind was a little mind—in everything but the size the same as that of the adult, having its own ready-furnished equipment of faculties of attention, memory, etc. Now we believe in the mind as a growing affair, and hence as essentially changing, presenting distinctive phases of capacity and interest at different periods. These are all one and the same in the sense of continuity of life, but all different in that each has its own distinctive claims and offices. "First the blade, then the ear, and then the full corn in the ear."

It is hardly possible to overstate the agreement of education and psychology at this point. The course of study was thoroughly, even if unconsciously, controlled by the assumption that since mind and its faculties are the same

throughout, the subject-matter of the adult, logically arranged facts and principles, is the natural "study" of the
child—simplified and made easier of course, since the wind
must be tempered to the shorn lamb. The outcome was the
traditional course of study in which again child and adult
minds are absolutely identified, except as regards the mere
matter of amount or quantity of power. The entire range of
the universe is first subdivided into sections called studies;
then each one of these studies is broken up into bits, and
some one bit assigned to a certain year of the course. No
order of development was recognized—it was enough that the
earlier parts were made easier than the later. To use the
pertinent illustration of Mr. W. S. Jackman in stating the
absurdity of this sort of curriculum: "It must seem to
geography teachers that Heaven smiled on them when it
ordained but four or five continents, because starting in far
enough along the course it was so easy, that it really seemed
to be natural, to give one continent to each grade, and then
come out right in the eight years."

If once more we are in earnest with the idea of mind
as growth, this growth carrying with it typical features distinctive of its various stages, it is clear that an educational
transformation is again indicated. It is clear that the selection and grading of material in the course of study must be
done with reference to proper nutrition of the dominant
directions of activity in a given period, not with reference to
chopped-up sections of a ready-made universe of knowledge.

It is, of course, comparatively easy to lay down general
propositions like the foregoing; easy to use them to criticize
existing school conditions; easy by means of them to urge the
necessity of something different. But art is long. The difficulty is in carrying such conceptions into effect—in seeing
just what materials and methods, in what proportion and
arrangement, are available and helpful at a given time. Here
again we must fall back upon the idea of the laboratory.
There is no answer in advance to such questions as these.
Tradition does not give it because tradition is founded upon
a radically different psychology. Mere reasoning cannot give
it because it is a question of fact. It is only by trying that
such things can be found out. To refuse to try, to stick blindly

to tradition, because the search for the truth involves experimentation in the region of the unknown, is to refuse the only step which can introduce rational conviction into education.

Hence the following statement simply reports various lines of inquiry started during the last five years, with some of the results more recently indicated. These results can, of course, make no claim to be other than tentative, excepting in so far as a more definite consciousness of what the problems are, clearing the way for more intelligent action in the future, is a definitive advance. It should also be stated that practically it has not as yet been possible, in many cases, to act adequately upon the best ideas obtained, because of administrative difficulties, due to lack of funds—difficulties centering in the lack of a proper building and appliances, and in inability to pay the amounts necessary to secure the complete time of teachers in some important lines. Indeed, with the growth of the school in numbers, and in the age and maturity of pupils, it is becoming a grave question how long it is fair to the experiment to carry it on without more adequate facilities.

In coming now to speak of the educational answers which have been sought for the psychological hypotheses, it is convenient to start from the matter of the stages of growth. The first stage (found in the child say of from four to eight years of age) is characterized by directness of social and personal interests, and by directness and promptness of relationship between impressions, ideas, and action. The demand for a motor outlet for expression is urgent and immediate. Hence the subject-matter for these years is selected from phases of life entering into the child's own social surroundings, and, as far as may be, capable of reproduction by him in something approaching social form—in play, games, occupations, or miniature industrial arts, stories, pictorial imagination, and conversation. At first the material is such as lies nearest the child himself, the family life and its neighborhood setting; it then goes on to something slightly more remote, social occupations (especially those having to do with the interdependence of city and country life), and then extends itself to the historical evolution of typical occupations and of the social forms connected with them. The material is not presented as lessons, as something to be learned, but rather as something to be taken up into the child's own experience, through his own activities, in weaving, cooking, shop-work, modelling, dramatic plays, conversation, discussion, story-telling, etc. These in turn are direct agencies. They are forms of motor or expressive activity. They are emphasized so as to dominate the school program, in order that the intimate connection between knowing and doing, so characteristic of this period of child life, may be maintained. The aim, then, is not for the child to go to school as a place apart, but rather in the school so to recapitulate typical phases of his experience outside of school, as to enlarge, enrich, and gradually formulate it.

In the second period, extending from eight or nine to eleven or twelve, the aim is to recognize and respond to the change which comes into the child from his growing sense of the possibility of more permanent and objective results, and of the necessity for the control of agencies for the skill necessary to reach these results. When the child recognizes distinct and enduring ends which stand out and demand attention on their own account, the previous vague and fluid unity of life is broken up. The mere play of activity no longer directly satisfies. It must be felt to accomplish something—to lead up to a definite and abiding outcome. Hence the recognition of rules of action—that is, of regular means appropriate to reaching permanent results—and of the value of mastering special processes so as to give skill in their use.

Hence, on the educational side, the problem is, as regards the subject-matter, to differentiate the vague unity of experience into characteristic typical phases, selecting such as clearly illustrate the importance to mankind of command over specific agencies and methods of thought and action in realizing its highest aims. The problem on the side of method is an analogous one: to bring the child to recognize the necessity of a similar development within himself— the need of securing for himself practical and intellectual control of such methods of work and inquiry as will enable him to realize results for himself.

On the more direct social side, American history (especially that of the period of colonization) is selected as furnishing a typical example of patience, courage, ingenuity, and continual judgment in adapting means to ends, even in the face of great hazard and obstacle; while the material itself is so definite, vivid, and human as to come directly within the range of the child's representative and constructive imagination and thus becomes, vicariously at least, a part of his own expanding consciousness. Since the aim is not "covering the ground," but knowledge of social processes used to secure social results, no attempt is made to go over the entire history, in chronological order, of America. Rather a series of types is taken up: Chicago and the northwestern Mississippi valley; Virginia, New York, and the Puritans and Pilgrims in New England. The aim is to present a variety of climatic and local conditions, to show the different sorts of obstacles and helps that people found, and a variety of historic traditions, and customs and purposes of different people.

The method involves presentation of a large amount of detail, of minutiæ of surroundings, tools, clothing, household utensils, foods, modes of living day by day, so that the child can reproduce the material as life, not as mere historic information. In this way, social processes and results become realities. Moreover, to the personal and dramatic identification of the child with the social life studied, characteristic of the earlier period, there now supervenes an *intellectual* identification—the child puts himself at the standpoint of the problems that have to be met and rediscovers, so far as may be, ways of meeting them.

The general standpoint—the adaptation of means to ends—controls also the work in science. For purposes of convenience, this may be regarded as now differentiated into two sides—the geographical and the experimental. Since, as just stated, the history work depends upon an appreciation of the natural environment as affording resources and presenting urgent problems, considerable attention is paid to the physiography, mountains, rivers, plains, and lines of natural travel and exchange, flora and fauna of each of the colonies. This is connected with field excursions in order that the child may be able to supply from observation, as far as possible, the data to be used by constructive imagination, in reproducing more remote environments.

The experimental side devotes itself to a study of

processes which yield typical results of value to men. The
activity of the child in the earlier period is directly productive, rather than investigative. His experiments are modes of
active doing—almost as much so as his play and games.
Later he tries to find out how various materials or agencies
are manipulated in order to give certain results. It is thus
clearly distinguished from experimentation in the scientific
sense—such as is appropriate to the secondary period—
where the aim is the discovery of facts and verification of
principles. Since the practical interest predominates, it is a
study of applied science rather than of pure science. For
instance, processes are selected found to have been of importance in colonial life—bleaching, dyeing, soap and can-
dle-making, manufacture of pewter dishes, making of cider
and vinegar, leading to some study of chemical agencies, of
oils, fats, elementary metallurgy. "Physics" is commenced
from the same applied standpoint. A study is made of the
use and transfer of energy in the spinning-wheel and looms;
everyday uses of mechanical principles are taken up—in
locks, scales, etc., going on later to electric appliances and
devices—bells, the telegraph, etc.

The relation of means to ends is emphasized also in
other lines of work. In art, attention is given to practical
questions of perspective, of proportion of spaces and masses,
balance, effect of color combinations and contrasts, etc. In
cooking, the principles of food-composition and of effects of
various agencies upon these elements are taken up, so that
the children may deduce, as far as possible, their own rules.
In sewing, methods of cutting, fitting (as applied to dolls'
clothing) come up, and later on the technical sequence of
stitches, etc.

It is clear that with the increasing differentiation of
lines of work and interest, leading to greater individuality
and independence in various studies, great care must be
taken to find the balance between, on one side, undue
separation and isolation, and on the other, a miscellaneous
and casual attention to a large number of topics, without
adequate emphasis and distinctiveness to any. The first
principle makes work mechanical and formal, divorces it
from the life-experience of the child, and from effective in-

fluence upon conduct. The second makes it scrappy and vague, and leaves the child without definite command of his own powers, or clear consciousness of purposes. It is perhaps only in the present year that the specific principle of the conscious relation of means to ends has emerged as the unifying principle of this period; and it is hoped that emphasis of this in all lines of work will have a decidedly cumulative and unifying effect upon the child's development.

Nothing has been said, as yet, of one of the most important agencies or means in extending and controlling experience—command of the social or conventional symbols—symbols of language, including those of quantity. The importance of these instrumentalities is so great that the traditional or three R's curriculum is based upon them—from 60 to 80 per cent of the time program of the first four or five years of elementary schools being devoted to them, the smaller figure representing selected rather than average schools.

These subjects are social in a double sense. They represent the tools which society has evolved in the past as the instruments of its intellectual pursuits. They represent the keys which will unlock to the child the wealth of social capital which lies beyond the possible range of his limited individual experience. While these two points of view must always give these arts a highly important place in education, they also make it necessary that certain conditions should be observed in their introduction and use. In a wholesale and direct application of the studies no account is taken of these conditions. The chief problem at present relating to the three R's is recognition of these conditions and the adaptation of work to them.

The conditions may be reduced to two: (1) The need that the child shall have in his own personal and vital experience a varied background of contact and acquaintance with realities, social and physical. This is necessary to prevent symbols from becoming a purely second-hand and conventional substitute for reality. (2) The need that the more ordinary, direct, and personal experience of the child shall furnish problems, motives, and interests that necessitate recourse to books for their solution, satisfaction, and pursuit.

Otherwise, the child approaches the book without intellectual hunger, without alertness, without a questioning attitude, and the result is the one so deplorably common: such abject dependence upon books as weakens and cripples vigor of thought and inquiry, combined with reading for mere random stimulation of fancy, emotional indulgence, and flight from the world of reality into a make-belief land.

The problem here is then (1) to furnish the child with a sufficiently large amount of personal activity, in occupations, expression, conversation, construction, and experimentation, so that his individuality, moral and intellectual, shall not be swamped by a disproportionate amount of the experience of others to which books introduce him; and (2) so to conduct this more direct experience as to make the child feel the need of resort to and command of the traditional social tools—furnish him with motives and make his recourse to them intelligent, an addition to his powers, instead of a servile dependency. When this problem shall be solved, work in language, literature, and number will not be a combination of mechanical drill, formal analysis and appeal, even if unconscious, to sensational interests; and there will not be the slightest reason to fear that books and all that relates to them will not take the important place to which they are entitled.

It is hardly necessary to say that the problem is not yet solved. The common complaint that children's progress in these traditional school studies is sacrificed to the newer subjects that have come into the curriculum is sufficient evidence that the exact balance is not yet struck. The experience thus far in the school, even if not demonstrative, indicates the following probable results: (1) the more direct modes of activity, constructive and occupation work, scientific observation, experimentation, etc., present plenty of opportunities and occasions for the necessary use of reading, writing (and spelling), and number work. These things may be introduced, then, not as isolated studies, but as organic outgrowths of the child's experience. The problem is, in a systematic and progressive way, to take advantage of these occasions. (2) The additional vitality and meaning which these studies thus secure make possible a very considerable reduction of the time ordinarily devoted to them. (3) The final use of the symbols, whether in reading, calculation, or composition, is more intelligent, less mechanical; more active, less passively receptive; more an increase of power, less a mere mode of enjoyment.

On the other hand, increasing experience seems to make clear the following points: (1) that it is possible, in the early years, to appeal, in teaching the recognition and use of symbols, to the child's power of production and creation; as much so in principle as in other lines of work seemingly much more direct, and that there is the advantage of a limited and definite result by which the child may measure his progress. (2) Failure sufficiently to take account of this fact results in an undue postponement of some phases of these lines of work, with the effect that the child, having progressed to a more advanced plane intellectually, feels what earlier might have been a form of power and creation to be an irksome task. (3) There is a demand for periodic concentration and alternation in the school program of the time devoted to these studies—and of all studies where mastery of technique or special method is advisable. That is to say, instead of carrying all subjects simultaneously and at an equal pace upon the program, at times one must be brought to the foreground and others relegated to the background, until the child is brought to the point of recognizing that he has a power or skill, which he can now go ahead and use independently.

The third period of elementary education is upon the borderland of secondary. It comes when the child has a sufficient acquaintance of a fairly direct sort with various forms of reality and modes of activity; and when he has sufficiently mastered the methods, the tools of thought, inquiry, and activity, appropriate to various phases of experience, to be able profitably to specialize upon distinctive studies and arts for technical and intellectual aims. While the school has a number of children who are in this period, the school has not, of course, been in existence long enough so that any typical inferences can be safely drawn. There certainly seems to be reason to hope, however, that with the consciousness of difficulties, needs, and resources gained in the experience of the last five years, children can be brought to and through this period without sacrifice of thoroughness, mental discipline, or command of technical tools of learning, and with a positive enlargement of life, and a wider, freer, and more open outlook upon it.

6. FROEBEL'S EDUCATIONAL PRINCIPLES

One of the traditions of the Elementary School of the University of Chicago is of a visitor who, in its early days, called to see the kindergarten. On being told that the school had not as yet established one, she asked if there were not singing, drawing, manual training, plays and dramatizations, and attention to the children's social relations. When her questions were answered in the affirmative, she remarked, both triumphantly and indignantly, that that was what she understood by a kindergarten, and that she did not know what was meant by saying that the school had no kindergarten. The remark was perhaps justified in spirit, if not in letter. At all events, it suggests that in a certain sense the school endeavors throughout its whole course—now including children between four and thirteen—to carry into effect certain principles which Froebel was perhaps the first consciously to set forth. Speaking still in general, these principles are:

1. That the primary business of school is to train children in cooperative and mutually helpful living; to foster in them the consciousness of mutual interdependence; and to help them practically in making the adjustments that will carry this spirit into overt deeds.

2. That the primary root of all educative activity is in the instinctive, impulsive attitudes and activities of the child, and not in the presentation and application of external material, whether through the ideas of others or through the senses; and that, accordingly, numberless spontaneous activities of children, plays, games, mimic efforts, even the apparently meaningless motions of infants—exhibitions previously ignored as trivial, futile, or even condemned as positively evil—are capable of educational use; nay, are the foundation stones of educational method.

3. That these individual tendencies and activities are

organized and directed through the uses made of them in
keeping up the cooperative living already spoken of; taking
advantage of them to reproduce on the child's plane the
typical doings and occupations of the larger, maturer society
into which he is finally to go forth; and that it is through
production and creative use that valuable knowledge is secured and clinched.

So far as these statements correctly represent Froebel's
educational philosophy, the school should be regarded as its
exponent. An attempt is making to act upon them with as
much faith and sincerity in their application to children of
twelve as to children of four. This attempt, however, to
assume what might be called the kindergarten attitude
throughout the whole school makes necessary certain modifications of the work done in what is more technically known
as the kindergarten period—that is, with the children between the ages of four and six. It is necessary only to state
reasons for believing that in spite of the apparently radical
character of some of them they are true to the spirit of
Froebel.

As Regards Play and Games

Play is not to be identified with anything which the
child externally does. It rather designates his mental attitude in its entirety and in its unity. It is the free play, the
interplay, of all the child's powers, thoughts, and physical
movements, in embodying, in a satisfying form, his own
images and interests. Negatively, it is freedom from economic pressure—the necessities of getting a living and sup-
porting others—and from the fixed responsibilities attaching
to the special callings of the adult. Positively, it means that
the supreme end of the child is fullness of growth—fullness
of realization of his budding powers, a realization which
continually carries him on from one plane to another.

This is a very general statement, and taken in its
generality is so vague as to be innocent of practical bearing.
Its significance in detail, in application, however, means the
possibility, and in many respects the necessity, of quite a

radical change of kindergarten procedure. To state it baldly, the fact that "play" denotes the psychological attitude of the child, not his outward performances, means complete emancipation from the necessity of following any given or prescribed system, or sequence of gifts, plays, or occupations. The judicious teacher will certainly look for suggestions to the activities mentioned by Froebel (in his *Mother Play* and elsewhere), and to those set forth in such minute detail by his disciples; but she will also remember that the principle of play requires her carefully to investigate and criticize these things, and decide whether they are really activities for her own children, or just things which may have been vital in the past to children living in different social conditions. So far as occupations, games, etc., simply perpetuate those of Froebel and his earlier disciples, it may fairly be said that in many respects the presumption is against them—the presumption is that in the worship of the external doings discussed by Froebel we have ceased to be loyal to his principle.

The teacher must be absolutely free to get suggestions from any and from every source, asking herself but these two questions: Will the proposed mode of play appeal to the child as his own? Is it something of which he has the instinctive roots in himself, and which will mature the capacities that are struggling for manifestation in him? And again: Will the proposed activity give that sort of expression to these impulses that will carry the child on to a higher plane of consciousness and action, instead of merely exciting him, and then leaving him just where he was before, plus a certain amount of nervous exhaustion and appetite for more excitation in the future?

There is every evidence that Froebel studied carefully—inductively we might now say—the children's plays of his own time, and the games which mothers played with their infants. He also took great pains—as in his *Mother Play*—to point out that certain principles of large import were involved. He had to bring his generation to consciousness of the fact that these things were not merely trivial and childish because done by children, but were essential factors in their growth. But I do not see the slightest evidence that

he supposed that just these plays, and only these plays, had
meaning, or that his philosophic explanation had any motive
beyond that just suggested. On the contrary, I believe that
he expected his followers to exhibit their following by continuing his own study of contemporary conditions and activities, rather than by literally adhering to the plays he had
collected. Moreover, it is hardly likely that Froebel himself
would contend that in his interpretation of these games he
did more than take advantage of the best psychological and
philosophical insight available to him at the time; and we
may suppose that he would have been the first to welcome
the growth of a better and more extensive psychology
(whether general, experimental, or as child-study), and
would avail himself of its results to reinterpret the activities,
to discuss them more critically, going from the new standpoint into the reasons that make them educationally valuable.

Symbolism

It must be remembered that much of Froebel's symbolism is the product of two peculiar conditions of his own
life and work. In the first place, on account of inadequate
knowledge at that time of the physiological and psychological
facts and principles of child growth, he was often forced to
resort to strained and artificial explanations of the value
attaching to the plays, etc. To the impartial observer it is
obvious that many of his statements are cumbrous and far-
fetched, giving abstract philosophical reasons for matters
that may now receive a simple, everyday formulation. In the
second place, the general political and social conditions of
Germany were such that it was impossible to conceive continuity between the free, cooperative social life of the kindergarten and that of the world outside. Accordingly, he could
not regard the "occupations" of the schoolroom as literal
reproductions of the ethical principles involved in community life—the latter were often too restricted and authoritative to serve as worthy models.

Accordingly he was compelled to think of them as symbolic of abstract ethical and philosophical principles. There certainly is change enough and progress enough in the social conditions of the United States of today, as compared with those of the Germany of his day, to justify making kindergarten activities more natural, more direct, and more real representations of current life than Froebel's disciples have done. Even as it is, the disparity of Froebel's philosophy with German political ideals has made the authorities in Germany suspicious of the kindergarten, and has been undoubtedly one force operating in transforming its social simplicity into an involved intellectual technique.

Imagination and Play

An excessive emphasis on symbolism is sure to influence the treatment of imagination. It is of course true that a little child lives in a world of imagination. In one sense, he can only "make believe." His activities represent or stand for the life that he sees going on around him. Because they are thus representative they may be termed symbolic, but it should be remembered that this make-believe or symbolism has reference to the activities suggested. Unless they are, to the child, as real and definite as the adult's activities are to him, the inevitable result is artificiality, nervous strain, and either physical and emotional excitement, or else deadening of powers.

There has been a curious, almost unaccountable, tendency in the kindergarten to assume that because the value of the activity lies in what it stands for to the child, therefore the materials used must be as artificial as possible, and that one must keep carefully away from real things and real acts on the part of the child. Thus one hears of gardening activities which are carried on by sprinkling grains of sand for seeds; the child sweeps and dusts a make-believe room with make-believe brooms and cloths; he sets a table using only paper cut in the flat (and even then cut with reference to geometric design, rather than to dishes), instead of toy tea things with which the child outside of the kindergarten plays. Dolls, toy locomotives, and trains of cars, etc., are tabooed as altogether too grossly real—and hence not cultivating the child's imagination.

All this is surely mere superstition. The imaginative play of the child's mind comes through the cluster of suggestions, reminiscences, and anticipations that gather about the things he uses. The more natural and straightforward these are, the more definite basis there is for calling up and holding together all the allied suggestions which make his imaginative play really representative. The simple cooking, dish-washing, dusting, etc., which children do are no more prosaic or utilitarian to them than would be, say, the game of the Five Knights. To the children these occupations are surcharged with a sense of the mysterious values that attach to whatever their elders are concerned with. The materials, then, must be as "real," as direct and straightforward, as opportunity permits.

But the principle does not end here—the reality symbolized must also lie within the capacities of the child's own appreciation. It is sometimes thought the use of the imagination is profitable in the degree it stands for very remote metaphysical and spiritual principles. In the great majority of such cases it is safe to say that the adult deceives himself. He is conscious of both the reality and the symbol, and hence of the relation between them. But since the truth or reality represented is far beyond the reach of the child, the supposed symbol is not a symbol to him at all. It is simply a positive thing on its own account. Practically about all he gets out of it is its own physical and sensational meaning, plus, very often, a glib facility in phrases and attitudes that he learns are expected of him by the teacher—without, however, any mental counterpart. We often teach insincerity, and instill sentimentalism, and foster sensationalism when we think we are teaching spiritual truths by means of symbols. The realities reproduced, therefore, by the child should be of as familiar, direct, and real a character as possible. It is largely for this reason that in the kindergarten of our school the work centres so much about the reproduction of home and neighborhood life. This brings us to the topic of

Subject-matter

The home life in its setting of house, furniture, utensils, etc., together with the occupations carried on in the home, offers, accordingly, material which is in a direct and real relationship to the child, and which he naturally tends to reproduce in imaginative form. It is also sufficiently full of ethical relations and suggestive of moral duties to afford plenty of food for the child on his moral side. The program is comparatively unambitious compared with that of many kindergartens, but it may be questioned whether there are not certain positive advantages in this limitation of the subject-matter. When much ground is covered (the work going over, say, industrial society, army, church, state, etc.), there is a tendency for the work to become over-symbolic. So much of this material lies beyond the experience and capacities of the child of four and five that practically all he gets out of it is the physical and emotional reflex—he does not get any real penetration into the material itself. Moreover, there is danger, in these ambitious programs, of an unfavorable reaction upon the child's own intellectual attitude. Having covered pretty much the whole universe in a purely make-believe fashion, he becomes blasé, loses his natural hunger for the simple things of direct experience, and approaches the material of the first grades of the primary school with a feeling that he has had all that already. The later years of a child's life have their own rights, and a superficial, merely emotional anticipation is likely to do the child serious injury.

Moreover, there is danger that a mental habit of jumping rapidly from one topic to another be induced. The little child has a good deal of patience and endurance of a certain type. It is true that he has a liking for novelty and variety; that he soon wearies of an activity that does not lead out into new fields and open up new paths for exploration. My plea, however, is not for monotony. There is sufficient variety in the activities, furnishings, and instrumentalities of the homes from which the children come to give continual diversity. It touches the civic and the industrial life at this and that point; these concerns can be brought in, when desirable, without going beyond the unity of the main topic. Thus there is an opportunity to foster that sense which is at the basis of attention, and of all intellectual growth, a sense of continuity.

This continuity is often interfered with by the very methods that aim at securing it. From the child's standpoint unity lies in the subject-matter—in the present case, in the fact that he is always dealing with one thing: home life. Emphasis is continually passing from one phase of this life to another; one occupation after another, one piece of furniture after another, one relation after another, etc., receive attention; but they all fall into building up one and the same mode of living, although bringing now this feature, now that, into prominence. The child is working all the time *within a unity*, giving different phases of its clearness and definiteness, and bringing them into coherent connection with each other. When there is a great diversity of subject-matter, continuity is apt to be sought simply on the formal side; that is, in schemes of sequence, "schools of work," a rigid program of development followed with every topic, a "thought for the day" from which the work is not supposed to stray. As a rule such sequence is purely intellectual, hence is grasped only by the teacher, quite passing over the head of the child. Hence the program for the year, term, month, week, etc., should be made out on the basis of estimating how much of the common subject-matter can be covered in that time, not on the basis of intellectual or ethical principles. This will give both definiteness and elasticity.

Method

The peculiar problem of the early grades is, of course, to get hold of the child's natural impulses and instincts, and to utilize them so that the child is carried on to a higher plane of perception and judgment, and equipped with more efficient habits; so that he has an enlarged and deepened consciousness, and increased control of powers of action. Wherever this result is not reached, play results in mere amusement and not in educative growth.

Upon the whole, constructive or "built up" work (with, of course, the proper alternation of story, song, and game which may be connected, so far as is desirable, with the ideas involved in the construction) seems better fitted than anything else to secure these two factors—initiation in the child's own impulse and termination upon a higher plane. It brings the child in contact with a great variety of material: wood, tin, leather, yarn, etc.; it supplies a motive for using these materials in real ways instead of going through exercises having no meaning except a remote symbolic one; it calls into play alertness of the senses and acuteness of observation; it demands clear-cut imagery of the ends to be accomplished, and requires ingenuity and invention in planning; it makes necessary concentrated attention and personal responsibility in execution, while the results are in such tangible form that the child may be led to judge his own work and improve his standards.

A word should be said regarding the psychology of imitation and suggestion in relation to kindergarten work. There is no doubt that the little child is highly imitative and open to suggestions; there is no doubt that his crude powers and immature consciousness need to be continually enriched and directed through these channels. But on this account it is imperative to discriminate between a use of imitation and suggestion which is so external as to be thoroughly non-psychological, and a use which is justified through its organic relation to the child's own activities. As a general principle no activity should be *originated* by imitation. The start must come from the child; the model or copy may then be supplied in order to assist the child in imaging more definitely what it is that he really wants—in bringing him to consciousness. Its value is not as model to copy in action, but as guide to clearness and adequacy of conception. Unless the child can get away from it to his own imagery when it comes to execution, he is rendered servile and dependent, not developed. Imitation comes in to reinforce and help out, not to initiate.

There is no ground for holding that the teacher should not suggest anything to the child until he has *consciously* expressed a want in that direction. A sympathetic teacher is quite likely to know more clearly than the child himself what his own instincts are and mean. But the suggestion must *fit in* with the dominant mode of growth in the child; it must serve simply as stimulus to bring forth more adequately what the child is already blindly striving to do. Only by watching the child and seeing the attitude that he assumes toward suggestions can we tell whether they are operating as factors in furthering the child's growth, or whether they are external, arbitrary impositions interfering with normal growth.

The same principle applies even more strongly to so-called dictation work. Nothing is more absurd than to suppose that there is no middle term between leaving a child to his own unguided fancies and likes or controlling his activities by a formal succession of dictated directions. As just intimated, it is the teacher's business to know what powers are striving for utterance at a given period in the child's development, and what sorts of activity will bring these to helpful expression, in order then to supply the requisite stimuli and needed materials. The suggestion, for instance, of a playhouse, the suggestion that comes from seeing objects that have already been made to furnish it, from seeing other children at work, is quite sufficient definitely to direct the activities of a normal child of five. Imitation and suggestion come in naturally and inevitably, but only as instruments to help him carry out his own wishes and ideas. They serve to make him realize, to bring to consciousness, what he already is striving for in a vague, confused, and therefore ineffective way. From the psychological standpoint it may safely be said that when a teacher has to rely upon a series of dictated directions, it is just because the child has no image of his own of what is to be done or why it is to be done. Instead, therefore, of gaining power of control by conforming to directions, he is really losing it—made dependent upon an external source.

In conclusion, it may be pointed out that such subject-matter and the method connect directly with the work of the six-year-old children (corresponding to the first grade of primary work). The play reproduction of the home life passes naturally on into a more extended and serious study of the larger social occupations upon which the home is dependent; while the continually increasing demands made upon the child's own ability to plan and execute carry him over into more controlled use of attention upon more distinctively intellectual topics. It must not be forgotten that the readjustment needed to secure continuity between "kindergarten" and "first-grade" work cannot be brought about wholly from the side of the latter. The school change must be as gradual and insensible as that in the growth of the child. This is impossible unless the subprimary work surrenders whatever isolates it, and hospitably welcomes whatever materials and resources will keep pace with the full development of the child's powers, and thus keep him always prepared, ready, for the next work he has to do.

By occupation is not meant any kind of "busy work" or exercises that may be given to a child in order to keep him out of mischief or idleness when seated at his desk. By occupation I mean a mode of activity on the part of the child which reproduces, or runs parallel to, some form of work carried on in social life. In the University Elementary School these occupations are represented by the shop-work with wood and tools; by cooking, sewing, and by the textile work.

The fundamental point in the psychology of an occupation is that it maintains a balance between the intellectual and the practical phases of experience. As an occupation it is active or motor; it finds expression through the physical organs—the eyes, hands, etc. But it also involves continual observation of materials, and continual planning and reflection, in order that the practical or executive side may be successfully carried on. Occupation as thus conceived must, therefore, be carefully distinguished from work which educates primarily for a trade. It differs because its end is in itself; in the growth that comes from the continual interplay of ideas and their embodiment in action, not in external utility.

It is possible to carry on this type of work in other than trade schools, so that the entire emphasis falls upon the manual or physical side. In such cases the work is reduced to a mere routine or custom, and its educational value is lost. This is the inevitable tendency wherever, in manual training for instance, the mastery of certain tools, or the production of certain objects, is made the primary end, and the child is not given, wherever possible, intellectual responsibility for selecting the materials and instruments that are most fit, and given an opportunity to think out his own model and plan of work, led to perceive his own errors, and find out how to correct them—that is, of course, within the range of his capacities. So far as the external result is held in view, rather than the mental and moral states and growth involved in the process of reaching the result, the work may be called manual, but cannot rightly be termed an occupation. Of course the tendency of all mere habit, routine, or custom is to result in what is unconscious and mechanical. That of occupation is to put the maximum of consciousness into whatever is done.

This enables us to interpret the stress laid (a) upon personal experimenting, planning, and re-inventing in connection with the textile work, and (b) its parallelism with lines of historical development. The first requires the child to be mentally quick and alert at every point in order that he may do the outward work properly. The second enriches and deepens the work performed by saturating it with values suggested from the social life which it recapitulates.

Occupations, so considered, furnish the ideal occasions for both sense-training and discipline in thought. The weakness of ordinary lessons in observation, calculated to train the senses, is that they have no outlet beyond themselves, and hence no necessary motive. Now, in the natural life of the individual and the race there is always a reason for sense-observation. There is always some need, coming from an end to be reached, that makes one look about to discover and discriminate whatever will assist him. Normal sensations operate as clues, as aids, as stimuli, in directing activity in what has to be done; they are not ends in themselves. Separated from real needs and motives, sense-training becomes a mere gymnastic and easily degenerates into acquiring what are hardly more than mere knacks or tricks in observation, or else mere excitement of the sense-organs.

The same principle applies in normal *thinking*. It also does not occur for its own sake, nor end in itself. It arises from the need of meeting some difficulty, in reflecting upon the best way of overcoming it, and thus leads to planning, to projecting mentally the result to be reached, and deciding upon the steps necessary and their serial order. This concrete logic of action long precedes the logic of pure speculation or abstract investigation, and through the mental habits that it forms is the best of preparations for the latter.

Another educational point upon which the psychology

of occupations throws helpful light is the place of interest in school work. One of the objections regularly brought against giving in school work any large or positive place to the child's interest is the impossibility on such a basis of proper selection. The child, it is said, has all kinds of interests, good, bad, and indifferent. It is necessary to decide between the interests that are really important and those that are trivial; between those that are helpful and those that are harmful; between those that are transitory or mark immediate excitement, and those which endure and are permanently influential. It would seem as if we had to go beyond interest to get any basis for using interest.

Now, there can be no doubt that occupation-work possesses a strong interest for the child. A glance into any school where such work is carried on will give sufficient evidence of this fact. Outside of the school, a large portion of the children's plays are simply more or less miniature and haphazard attempts at reproducing social occupations. There are certain reasons for believing that the type of interest which springs up along with these occupations is of a thoroughly healthy, permanent, and really educative sort; and that by giving a larger place to occupations we should secure an excellent, perhaps the very best, way of making an appeal to the child's spontaneous interest, and yet have, at the same time, some guarantee that we are not dealing with what is merely pleasure-giving, exciting, or transient.

In the first place, every interest grows out of some instinct or some habit that in turn is finally based upon an original instinct. It does not follow that all instincts are of equal value, or that we do not inherit many instincts which need transformation, rather than satisfaction, in order to be useful in life. But the instincts which find their conscious outlet and expression in occupation are bound to be of an exceedingly fundamental and permanent type. The activities of life are of necessity directed to bringing the materials and forces of nature under the control of our purposes; of making them tributary to ends of life. Men have had to work in order to live. In and through their work they have mastered nature, they have protected and enriched the conditions of their own life, they have been awakened to the sense of their own

powers—have been led to invent, to plan, and to rejoice in
the acquisition of skill. In a rough way, all occupations may
be classified as gathering about man's fundamental relations
to the world in which he lives through getting food to maintain life; securing clothing and shelter to protect and orna-
ment it, and thus, finally, to provide a permanent home in
which all the higher and more spiritual interests may centre.
It is hardly unreasonable to suppose that interests which
have such a history behind them must be of the worthy sort.

However, these interests as they develop in the child not
only recapitulate past important activities of the race, but
reproduce those of the child's present environment. He continually sees his elders engaged in such pursuits. He daily
has to do with things which are the results of just such
occupations. He comes in contact with facts that have no
meaning, except in reference to them. Take these things out
of the present social life and see how little would remain—
and this not only on the material side, but as regards intellectual, æsthetic, and moral activities, for these are largely
and necessarily bound up with occupations. The child's instinctive interests in this direction are, therefore, constantly
reinforced by what he sees, feels, and hears going on around
him. Suggestions along this line are continually coming to
him; motives are awakened; his energies are stirred to action.
Again, it is not unreasonable to suppose that interests which
are touched so constantly, and on so many sides, belong to
the worthy and enduring type.

In the third place, one of the objections made against
the principle of interest in education is that it tends to dis-
integration of mental economy by constantly stirring up the
child in this way or that, destroying continuity and thoroughness. But an occupation (such as the textile one) is of necessity a continuous thing. It lasts not only for days, but for
months and years. It represents, not a stirring of isolated
and superficial energies, but rather a steady, continuous organization of power along certain general lines. The same is
true, of course, of any other form of occupation, such as
shop-work with tools, or as cooking. The occupations articulate a vast variety of impulses, otherwise separate and
spasmodic, into a consistent skeleton with a firm backbone.

It may well be doubted whether, wholly apart from some such regular and progressive modes of action, extending as cores throughout the entire school, it would be permanently safe to give the principle of "interest" any large place in school work.

8. THE DEVELOPMENT OF ATTENTION

The subprimary or kindergarten department is under-taking the pedagogical problems growing out of an attempt to connect kindergarten work intimately with primary, and to readapt traditional materials and technique to meet present social conditions and our present physiological and psychological knowledge.

Little children have their observations and thoughts mainly directed towards people: what they do, how they behave, what they are occupied with, and what comes of it. Their interest is of a personal rather than of an objective or intellectual sort. Its intellectual counterpart is the story-form, not the task, consciously defined end, or problem— meaning by story-form something psychical, the holding together of a variety of persons, things, and incidents through a common idea that enlists feeling; not an outward relation or tale. Their minds seek wholes, varied through episode, enlivened with action and defined in salient features—there must be go, movement, the sense of use and operation—inspection of things separated from the idea by which they are carried. Analysis of isolated detail of form and structure neither appeals nor satisfies.

Material provided by existing social occupations is calculated to meet and feed this attitude. In previous years the children have been concerned with the occupations of the home, and the contact of homes with one another and with outside life. Now they may take up typical occupations of society at large—a step farther removed from the child's egoistic, self-absorbed interest, and yet dealing with something personal and something which touches him.

From the standpoint of educational theory, the following features may be noted:

    1. The study of natural objects, processes, and relations is placed in a human setting. During the year, a con-

siderably detailed observation of seeds and their growth, of
plants, woods, stones, animals, as to some phases of structure and habit, of geographical conditions of landscape, cli-
mate, arrangement of land and water, is undertaken. The
pedagogical problem is to direct the child's power of observation, to nurture his sympathetic interest in characteristic
traits of the world in which he lives, to afford interpreting
material for later more special studies, and yet to supply a
carrying medium for the variety of facts and ideas through
the dominant spontaneous emotions and thoughts of the
child. Hence their association with human life. Absolutely
no separation is made between the "social" side of the work,
its concern with people's activities and their mutual de-
pendencies, and the "science," regard for physical facts and
forces—because the conscious distinction between man and
nature is the result of later reflection and abstraction, and to
force it upon the child here is not only to fail to engage his
whole mental energy, but to confuse and distract him. The
environment is always that in which life is situated and
through which it is circumstanced; and to isolate it, to make
it with little children an object of observation and remark
by itself, is to treat human nature inconsiderately. At last,
the original open and free attitude of the mind to nature is
destroyed; nature has been reduced to a mass of meaningless details.

In its emphasis upon the "concrete" and "individual,"
modern pedagogical theory often loses sight of the fact that
the existence and presentation of an individual physical
thing—a stone, an orange, a cat—is no guarantee of *concreteness*—that this is a psychological affair, whatever appeals to the mind as a whole, as a self-sufficient centre of
interest and attention. The reaction from this external and
somewhat dead standpoint often assumes, however, that the
needed clothing with human significance can come only by
direct personification, and we have that continued symboli-
zation of a plant, cloud or rain which makes only pseudo-
science possible; which, instead of generating love for nature
itself, switches interest to certain sensational and emotional
accompaniments, and leaves it, at last, dissipated and burnt
out. And even the tendency to approach nature through the

medium of literature, the pine tree through the fable of the
discontented pine, etc., while recognizing the need of the
human association, fails to note that there is a more straightforward road from mind to the object—direct through connection with life itself; and that the poem and story, the
literary statement, have their place as reinforcements and
idealizations, not as foundation stones. What is wanted, in
other words, is not to fix up a connection of child mind and
nature, but to give free and effective play to the connection
already operating.

2. This suggests at once the practical questions that
are usually discussed under the name of "correlation," questions of such interaction of the various matters studied and
powers under acquisition as will avoid waste, and maintain
unity of mental growth. From the standpoint adopted the
problem is one of differentiation, rather than of correlation
as ordinarily understood. The unity of life, as it presents
itself to the child, binds together and carries along the
different occupations, the diversity of plants, animals, and
geographic conditions; drawing, modelling, games, constructive work, numerical calculations are ways of carrying certain features of it to mental and emotional satisfaction and
completeness. Not much attention is paid in this year to
reading and writing; but it is obvious that if this were regarded as desirable, the same principle would apply. It is
the community and continuity of the subject-matter that
organizes, that correlates; correlation is not through devices
of instruction which the teacher employs in tying together
things in themselves disconnected.

3. Two recognized demands of primary education are
often, at present, not unified, or are even opposed. The need
of the familiar, the already experienced, as a basis for moving upon the unknown and remote, is a commonplace. The
claims of the child's imagination as a factor is at least beginning to be recognized. The problem is to work these two
forces together, instead of separately. The child is too often
given drill upon familiar objects and ideas under the sanc-
tion of the first principle, while he is introduced with equal
directness to the weird, strange, and impossible to satisfy
the claims of the second. The result, it is hardly too much to

say, is a twofold failure. There is no special connection between the unreal, the myth, the fairy tale, and the play of mental imagery. Imagination is not a matter of an impossible subject-matter, but a constructive way of dealing with any subject-matter under the influence of a pervading idea. The point is not to dwell with wearisome iteration upon the familiar and under the guise of object-lessons to keep the senses directed at material which they have already made acquaintance with, but to enliven and illumine the ordinary, commonplace, and homely by using it to build up and appreciate situations previously unrealized and alien. And this also is culture of imagination. Some writers appear to have the impression that the child's imagination has outlet only in myth and fairy tale of ancient time and distant place, or in weaving egregious fabrications regarding sun, moon, and stars; and have even pleaded for a mythical investiture of all "science"—as a way of satisfying the dominating imagination of the child. But fortunately these things are exceptions, are intensifications, are relaxations of the average child; not his pursuits. The John and Jane that most of us know let their imaginations play about the current and familiar contacts and events of life—about father and mother and friend, about steamboats and locomotives, and sheep and cows, about the romance of farm and forest, of seashore and mountain. What is needed, in a word, is to afford occasion by which the child is moved to educe and exchange with others his store of experiences, his range of information, to make new observations correcting and extending them in order to keep his images moving, in order to find mental rest and satisfaction in definite and vivid realization of what is new and enlarging.

With the development of reflective attention come the need and the possibility of a change in the mode of the child's instruction. In the previous paragraphs we have been concerned with the direct, spontaneous attitude that marks the child till into his seventh year—his demand for new experiences, and his desire to complete his partial experiences by building up images and expressing them in play. This attitude is typical of what writers call spontaneous attention, or, as some say, non-voluntary attention.

The child is simply absorbed in what he is doing; the occupation in which he is engaged lays complete hold upon him. He gives himself without reserve. Hence, while there is much energy spent, there is no *conscious* effort; while the child is intent, to the point of engrossment, there is no *conscious* intention.

With the development of a sense of more remote ends, and of the need of directing acts so as to make them means for these ends (a matter discussed in *Middle Works of John Dewey*, 1:226–29), we have the transition to what is termed indirect, or, as some writers prefer to say, voluntary, attention. A result is imaged, and the child attends to what is before him or what he is immediately doing, because it helps to secure the result. Taken by itself, the object or the act might be indifferent or even repulsive. But because it is felt to belong to something desirable or valuable, it borrows the latter's attracting and holding power.

This is the transition to "voluntary" attention, but only the transition. The latter comes fully into being only when the child entertains results in the form of problems or questions, the solution of which he is to seek for himself. In the intervening stage (in the child from eight to, say, eleven or twelve), while the child directs a series of intervening activities on the basis of some end he wishes to reach, this end is something to be done or made, or some tangible result to be reached; the problem is a practical difficulty, rather than an intellectual question. But with growing power, the child can conceive of the end as something to be found out, discovered; and can control his acts and images so as to help in the inquiry and solution. This is reflective attention proper.

In history work there is change from the story and biography form, from discussion of questions that arise, to the formulation of questions. Points about which difference of opinion is possible, matters upon which experience, reflection, etc., can be brought to bear, are always coming up in history. But to use the discussion to develop this matter of doubt and difference into a definite problem, to bring the child to feel just what the difficulty is, and then throw him upon his own resources in looking up material bearing upon the point, and upon his judgment in bringing it to bear, or getting a solution, is a marked intellectual advance. So in the science there is a change from the practical attitude of making and using cameras to the consideration of the problems intellectually involved in this—to principles of light, angular measurements, etc., which give the theory or explanation of the practice.

In general, this growth is a natural process. But the proper recognition and use of it is perhaps the most serious problem in instruction upon the intellectual side. A person who has gained the power of reflective attention, the power to hold problems, questions, before the mind, *is* in so far, intellectually speaking, educated. He has mental discipline— power *of* the mind and *for* the mind. Without this the mind remains at the mercy of custom and external suggestions. Some of the difficulties may be barely indicated by referring to an error that almost dominates instruction of the usual type. Too often it is assumed that attention can be given directly to any subject-matter, if only the proper will or disposition be at hand, failure being regarded as a sign of unwillingness or indocility. Lessons in arithmetic, geography, and grammar are put before the child, and he is told to attend in order to learn. But excepting as there is some question, some doubt, present in the mind as a *basis* for this attention, *reflective* attention is impossible. If there is sufficient *intrinsic* interest in the material, there will be direct or spontaneous attention, which is excellent so far as it goes, but which merely of itself does not give power of thought or internal mental control. If there is not an inherent attracting power in the material, then (according to his temperament and training, and the precedents and expectations of the school) the teacher will either attempt to surround the material with foreign attractiveness, making a bid or offering a bribe for attention by "making the lesson interesting"; or else will resort to counterirritants (low marks, threats of nonpromotion, staying after school, personal disapprobation, expressed in a great variety of ways, naggings, continuous calling upon the child to "pay attention," etc.); or, probably, will use some of both means.

But (1) the attention thus gained is never more than partial, or divided; and (2) it always remains dependent upon something external—hence, when the attraction ceases or the pressure lets up, there is little or no gain in inner or intellectual control. And (3) such attention is always for the sake of "learning," *i.e., memorizing ready-made answers to possible questions to be put by another.* True, reflective attention, on the other hand, always involves judging, reasoning, deliberation; it means that the child has a *question of his own,* and is actively engaged in seeking and selecting relevant material with which to answer it, considering the bearings and relations of this material—the kind of solution it calls for. The problem is one's own; hence also the impetus, the stimulus to attention, is one's own; hence also the training secured is one's own—it is discipline, or gain in power of control; that is, a *habit* of considering problems.

It is hardly too much to say that in the traditional education so much stress has been laid upon the presentation to the child of ready-made material (books, object-lessons, teacher's talks, etc.), and the child has been so almost exclusively held to bare responsibility for reciting upon this ready-made material, that there has been only accidental occasion and motive for developing reflective attention. Next to no consideration has been paid to the fundamental necessity —leading the child to realize a problem as his own, so that he is self-induced to attend in order to find out its answer. So completely have the conditions for securing this self-putting of problems been neglected that the very idea of voluntary attention has been radically perverted. It is regarded as measured by unwilling effort—as activity called out by foreign and so repulsive material under conditions of strain, instead of as self-initiated effort. "Voluntary" is treated as meaning the reluctant and disagreeable instead of the free, the self-directed, through personal interest, insight, and power.

9. THE AIM OF HISTORY IN ELEMENTARY EDUCATION

If history be regarded as just the record of the past, it is hard to see any grounds for claiming that it should play any large rôle in the curriculum of elementary education. The past is the past, and the dead may be safely left to bury its dead. There are too many urgent demands in the present, too many calls over the threshold of the future, to permit the child to become deeply immersed in what is forever gone by. Not so when history is considered as an account of the forces and forms of social life. Social life we have always with us; the distinction of past and present is indifferent to it. Whether it was lived just here or just there is a matter of slight moment. It is life for all that; it shows the motives which draw men together and push them apart, and depicts what is desirable and what is hurtful. Whatever history may be for the scientific historian, for the educator it must be an indirect sociology—a study of society which lays bare its process of becoming and its modes of organization. Existing society is both too complex and too close to the child to be studied. He finds no clues into its labyrinth of detail, and can mount no eminence whence to get a perspective of arrangement.

If the aim of historical instruction is to enable the child to appreciate the values of social life, to see in imagination the forces which favor and let men's effective cooperation with one another, to understand the sorts of character that help on and that hold back, the essential thing in its presentation is to make it moving, dynamic. History must be presented not as an accumulation of results or effects, a mere statement of what happened, but as a forceful, acting thing. The motives—that is, the motors—must stand out. To study history is not to amass information, but to use information in constructing a vivid picture of how and why men did thus and so; achieved their successes and came to their failures.

When history is conceived as dynamic, as moving, its economic and industrial aspects are emphasized. These are but technical terms which express the problem with which humanity is unceasingly engaged; how to live, how to master and use nature so as to make it tributary to the enrichment of human life. The great advances in civilization have come through those manifestations of intelligence which have lifted man from his precarious subjection to nature, and revealed to him how he may make its forces cooperate with his own purposes. The social world in which the child now lives is so rich and full that it is not easy to see how much it cost, how much effort and thought lie back of it. Man has a tremendous equipment ready at hand. The child may be led to translate these ready-made resources into fluid terms; he may be led to see man face to face with nature, without inherited capital, without tools, without manufactured materials. And, step by step, he may follow the processes by which man recognized the needs of his situation, thought out the weapons and instruments that enable him to cope with them; and may learn how these new resources opened new horizons of growth and created new problems. The industrial history of man is not a materialistic or merely utilitarian affair. It is a matter of intelligence. Its record is the record of how man learned to think, to think to some effect, to transform the conditions of life so that life itself became a different thing. It is an ethical record as well; the account of the conditions which men have patiently wrought out to serve their ends.

The question of how human beings live, indeed, represents the dominant interest with which the child approaches historic material. It is this point of view which brings those who worked in the past close to the beings with whom he is daily associated, and confers upon him the gift of sympathetic penetration.

The child who is interested in the way in which men lived, the tools they had to do with, the new inventions they made, the transformations of life that arose from the power and leisure thus gained, is eager to repeat like processes in his own action, to remake utensils, to reproduce processes, to rehandle materials. Since he understands their problems and

their successes only by seeing what obstacles and what resources they had from nature, the child is interested in field
and forest, ocean and mountain, plant and animal. By building up a conception of the natural environment in which
lived the people he is studying, he gets his hold upon their
lives. This reproduction he cannot make excepting as he
gains acquaintance with the natural forces and forms with
which he is himself surrounded. The interest in history gives
a more human coloring, a wider significance, to his own
study of nature. His knowledge of nature lends point and
accuracy to his study of history. This is the natural "correlation" of history and science.

This same end, a deepening appreciation of social life,
decides the place of the biographic element in historical
instruction. That historical material appeals to the child most
completely and vividly when presented in individual form,
when summed up in the lives and deeds of some heroic
character, there can be no doubt. Yet it is possible to use
biographies so that they become a collection of mere stories,
interesting, possibly, to the point of sensationalism, but yet
bringing the child no nearer to comprehension of social life.
This happens when the individual who is the hero of the tale
is isolated from his social environment; when the child is not
brought to feel the social situations which evoked his acts and
the social progress to which his deeds contributed. If biography is presented as a dramatic summary of social needs
and achievements, if the child's imagination pictures the
social defects and problems that clamored for the man and
the ways in which the individual met the emergency, then
the biography is an organ of social study.

A consciousness of the social aim of history prevents
any tendency to swamp history in myth, fairy story, and
merely literary renderings. I cannot avoid the feeling that
much as the Herbartian school has done to enrich the elementary curriculum in the direction of history, it has often
inverted the true relationship existing between history and
literature. In a certain sense the *motif* of American colonial
history and of De Foe's *Robinson Crusoe* are the same. Both
represent man who has achieved civilization, who has attained a certain maturity of thought; who has developed

ideals and means of action, but is suddenly thrown back upon his own resources, having to cope with a raw and often hostile nature, and to regain success by sheer intelligence, energy, and persistence of character. But when *Robinson Crusoe* supplies the material for the curriculum of the third- or fourth-grade child, are we not putting the cart before the horse? Why not give the child the reality with its much larger sweep, its intenser forces, its more vivid and lasting value for life, using the *Robinson Crusoe* as an imaginative idealization in a particular case of the same sort of problems and activities? Again, whatever may be the worth of the study of savage life in general, and of the North American Indians in particular, why should that be approached circuitously through the medium of *Hiawatha*, instead of at first hand, employing indeed the poem to furnish the idealized and culminating touches to a series of conditions and struggles which the child has previously realized in more specific form? Either the life of the Indian presents some permanent questions and factors in social life, or it has next to no place in a scheme of instruction. If it has such a value, this should be made to stand out on its own account, instead of being lost in the very refinement and beauty of a purely literary presentation.

The same end, the understanding of character and social relations in their natural dependence, enables us, I think, to decide upon the importance to be attached to chronological order in historical instruction. Considerable stress has of late been laid upon the supposed necessity of following the development of civilization through the successive steps in which it actually took place—beginning with the valleys of the Euphrates and the Nile, and coming on down through Greece, Rome, etc. The point urged is that the present depends upon the past, and each phase of the past upon a prior past.

We are here introduced to a conflict between the logical and psychological interpretation of history. If the aim be an appreciation of what social life is and how it goes on, then, certainly, the child must deal with what is near in spirit, not with the remote. The difficulty with the Babylonian or Egyptian life is not so much its remoteness in time, as its remoteness from the present interests and aims of social life. It does not simplify enough and does not generalize enough; or, at least, it does not do so in the right way. It does it by omission of what is significant now, rather than by presenting these factors arranged on a lower scale. Its salient features are hard to get at and to understand, even by the specialist. It undoubtedly presents factors which contributed to later life, and which modified the course of events in the stream of time. But the child has not arrived at a point where he can appreciate abstract causes and specialized contributions. What he needs is a picture of typical relations, conditions, and activities. In this respect, there is much of pre-historic life which is much closer to him than the complicated and artificial life of Babylon or of Egypt. When a child is capable of appreciating institutions, he is capable of seeing what special institutional idea each historic nation stands for, and what factor it has contributed to the present complex of institutions. But this period arrives only when the child is beginning to be capable of abstracting causes in other realms as well; in other words, when he is approaching the time of secondary education.

In this general scheme three periods or phases are recognized: first comes the generalized and simplified history—history which is hardly history at all in the local or chronological sense, but which aims at giving the child insight into, and sympathy with, a variety of social activities. This period includes the work of the six-year-old children in studying typical occupations of people in the country and city at present; of the seven-year-old children in working out the evolution of inventions and their effects upon life, and of the eight-year-old children in dealing with the great movements of migration, exploration, and discovery which have brought the whole round world into human ken. The work of the first two years is evidently quite independent of any particular people or any particular person—that is, of historical data in the strict sense of the term. At the same time, plenty of scope is provided through dramatization for the introduction of the individual factor. The account of the great explorers and the discoverers serves to make the transition to what is local and specific, that which depends upon certain specified persons who lived at certain specified places and times.

This introduces us to the second period where local conditions and the definite activities of particular bodies of people become prominent—corresponding to the child's growth in power of dealing with limited and positive fact. Since Chicago, since the United States, are localities with which the child can, by the nature of the case, most effectively deal, the material of the next three years is derived directly and indirectly from this source. Here, again, the third year is a transitional year, taking up the connections of American life with European. By this time the child should be ready to deal not with social life in general, or even with the social life with which he is most familiar, but with certain thoroughly differentiated and, so to speak, peculiar types of social life; with the special significance of each and the particular contribution it has made to the whole world history. Accordingly, in the next period the chronological order is followed, beginning with the ancient world about the Mediterranean and coming down again through European history to the peculiar and differentiating factors of American history.

The program is not presented as the only one meeting the problem, but as a contribution, the outcome not of thought but of considerable experimenting and shifting of subjects from year to year, to the problem of giving material which takes vital hold upon the child and at the same time leads on, step by step, to more thorough and accurate knowledge of both the principles and facts of social life, and makes a preparation for later specialized historic studies.

Essays

"CONSCIOUSNESS" AND EXPERIENCE[1]
[Psychology and Philosophic Method]

Every science in its final standpoint and working aims is controlled by conditions lying outside itself—conditions that subsist in the practical life of the time. With no science is this as obviously true as with psychology. Taken without nicety of analysis, no one would deny that psychology is specially occupied with the individual; that it wishes to find out those things that proceed peculiarly from the individual, and the mode of their connection with him. Now, the way in which the individual is conceived, the value that is attributed to him, the things in his make-up that arouse interest, are not due at the outset to psychology. The scientific view regards these matters in a reflected, a borrowed, medium. They are revealed in the light of social life. An autocratic, an aristocratic, a democratic society propound such different estimates of the worth and place of individuality; they procure for the individual as an individual such different sorts of experience; they aim at arousing such different impulses and at organizing them according to such different purposes, that the psychology arising in each must show a different temper.

In this sense, psychology is a political science. While the professed psychologist, in his conscious procedure, may easily cut his subject-matter loose from these practical ties and references, yet the starting-point and goal of his course are none the less socially set. In this conviction I venture to

1. Delivered as a public address before the Philosophic Union of the University of California, with the title "Psychology and Philosophic Method," May, 1899, and published in the *University Chronicle* for August, 1899. Reprinted, with slight verbal changes, mostly excisions.

[First published in *University* (of California) *Chronicle* 2 (1899): 159–79, with the title "Psychology and Philosophic Method." Reprinted separately, Berkeley: The University Press, 1899, 23 pp., and in *The Influence of Darwin on Philosophy* (New York: Henry Holt and Co., 1910), pp. 242–70, with the title " 'Consciousness' and Experience."]

introduce to an audience that could hardly be expected to be interested in the technique of psychology, a technical subject, hoping that the human meaning may yet appear.

There is at present a strong, apparently a growing tendency to conceive of psychology as an account of the consciousness of the individual, considered as something in and by itself; consciousness, the assumption virtually runs, being of such an order that it may be analyzed, described, and explained in terms of just itself. The statement, as commonly made, is that psychology is an account of consciousness, *qua* consciousness; and the phrase is supposed to limit psychology to a certain definite sphere of fact that may receive adequate discussion for scientific purposes, without troubling itself with what lies outside. Now if this conception be true, there is no intimate, no important connection of psychology and philosophy at large. That philosophy, whose range is comprehensive, whose problems are catholic, should be held down by a discipline whose voice is as partial as its material is limited, is out of the range of intelligent discussion.

But there is another possibility. If the individual of whom psychology treats be, after all, a social individual, any absolute setting off and apart of a sphere of consciousness as, even for scientific purposes, self-sufficient, is condemned in advance. All such limitation, and all inquiries, descriptions, explanations that go with it, are only preliminary. "Consciousness" is but a symbol, an anatomy whose life is in natural and social operations. To know the symbol, the psychical letter, is important; but its necessity lies not within itself, but in the need of a language for reading the things signified. If this view be correct, we cannot be so sure that psychology is without large philosophic significance. Whatever meaning the individual has for the social life that he both incorporates and animates, that meaning has psychology for philosophy.

This problem is too important and too large to suffer attack in an evening's address. Yet I venture to consider a portion of it, hoping that such things as appear will be useful clues in entering wider territory. We may ask what is the effect upon psychology of considering its material as something so distinct as to be capable of treatment without in-

volving larger issues. In this inquiry we take as representative
some such account of the science as this: Psychology deals
with consciousness "as such" in its various modes and
processes. It aims at an isolation of each such as will permit
accurate description: at statement of its place in the serial
order such as will enable us to state the laws by which one
calls another into being, or as will give the natural history of
its origin, maturing, and dissolution. It is both analytic and
synthetic—analytic in that it resolves each state into its
constituent elements; synthetic in that it discovers the
processes by which these elements combine into complex
wholes and series. It leaves alone—it shuts out—questions
concerning the validity, the objective import of these modifications: of their value in conveying truth, in effecting goodness, in constituting beauty. For it is just with such questions
of worth, of validity, that philosophy has to do.

Some such view as this is held by the great majority of
working psychologists today. A variety of reasons have con-
spired to bring about general acceptance. Such a view seems
to enroll one in the ranks of the scientific men rather than
of the metaphysicians—and there are those who distrust the
metaphysicians. Others desire to take problems piecemeal
and in detail, avoiding that excursion into ultimates, into
that never-ending panorama of new questions and new possibilities that seems to be the fate of the philosopher. While
no temperate mind can do other than sympathize with this
view, it is hardly more than an expedient. For, as Mr. James
remarks, after disposing of the question of free-will by
relegating it to the domain of the metaphysician:—"Meta-
physics means only an unusually obstinate attempt to think
clearly and consistently"—and clearness and consistency are
not things to be put off beyond a certain point. When the
metaphysician chimes in with this new-found modesty of
the psychologist, so different from the disposition of Locke
and Hume and the Mills, salving his metaphysical conscience
with the remark—it hardly possesses the dignity of a conviction—that the partial sciences, just because they are
partial, are not expected to be coherent with themselves nor
with one another; when the metaphysician, I say, praises the
psychologist for sticking to his last, we are reminded that

another motive is also at work. There is a half-conscious
irony in this abnegation of psychology. It is not the first time
that science has assumed the work of Cinderella; and, since
Mr. Huxley has happily reminded her, she is not altogether
oblivious, in her modesty, of a possible future check to the
pride of her haughty sister, and of a certain coronation that
shall mark her coming to her own.

But, be the reasons as they may, there is little doubt of
the fact. Almost all our working psychologists admit, nay,
herald this limitation of their work. I am not presumptuous
enough to set myself against this array. I too proclaim myself of those who believe that psychology has to do (at a
certain point, that is) with "consciousness as such." But I do
not believe that the limitation is final. Quite the contrary: if
"consciousness" or "state of consciousness" be given intel-
ligible meaning, I believe that this conception is the open
gateway into the fair fields of philosophy. For, note you, the
phrase is an ambiguous one. It may mean one thing to the
metaphysician who proclaims: Here finally we have psychology recognizing her due metes and bounds, giving bonds
to trespass no more. It may mean quite another thing to the
psychologist in his work—whatever he may happen to say
about it. It may be that the psychologist deals with states of
consciousness as the significant, the analyzable and describable form, to which he reduces the things he is studying.
Not that they *are* that existence, but that they are its indications, its clues, in shape for handling by scientific methods.
So, for example, does the paleontologist work. Those curiously shaped and marked forms to which he is devoted are
not life, nor are they the literal termini of his endeavor; but
through them as signs and records he construes a life. And
again, the painter-artist might well say that he is concerned
only with colored paints as such. Yet none the less through
them as registers and indices, he reveals to us the mysteries
of sunny meadow, shady forest, and twilight wave. These are
the things-in-themselves of which the oils on his palette are
phenomena.

So the preoccupation of the psychologist with states of
consciousness may signify that they are the media, the concrete conditions to which he purposely reduces his material,

in order *through them*, as methodological helps, to get at and understand that which is anything but a state of consciousness. To him, however, who insists upon the fixed and final limitation of psychology, the state of consciousness is not the shape some fact takes from the exigency of investigation; it is literally the full fact itself. It is not an intervening term; it bounds the horizon. Here then the issue defines itself. I conceive that states of consciousness (and I hope you will take the phrase broadly enough to cover all the specific data of psychology) have no existence before the psychologist begins to work. He brings them into existence. What we are really after is the process of experience, the way in which it arises and behaves. We want to know its course, its history, its laws. We want to know its various typical forms; how each originates; how it is related to others; the part it plays in maintaining an inclusive, expanding, connected course of experience. Our problem as psychologists is to learn its *modus operandi*, its method.

The paleontologist is again summoned to our aid. In a given district he finds a great number and variety of footprints. From these he goes to work to construct the structure and the life habits of the animals that made them. The tracks exist undoubtedly; they are there; but yet he deals with them not as final existences but as signs, phenomena in the literal sense. Imagine the hearing that the critic would receive who should inform the paleontologist that he is transcending his field of scientific activity; that his concern is with footprints as such, aiming to describe each, to analyze it into its simplest forms, to compare the different kinds with one another so as to detect common elements, and finally, thereby, to discover the laws of their arrangement in space!

Yet the immediate data are footprints, and footprints only. The paleontologist does in a way do all these things that our imaginary critic is urging upon him. The difference is not that he arbitrarily lugs in other data; that he invents entities and faculties that are not there. The difference is in his standpoint. His interest is in the animals, and the data are treated in whatever way seems likely to serve this interest. So with the psychologist. He is continually and perforce occupied with minute and empirical investigation of special facts—states of consciousness, if you please. But these neither define nor exhaust his scientific problem. They are his footprints, his clues through which he places before himself the life-process he is studying—with the further difference that his footprints are not after all given to him, but are developed by his investigation.[2]

The supposition that these states are somehow existent by themselves and in this existence provide the psychologist with ready-made material is just the supreme case of the "psychological fallacy": the confusion of experience as it is to the one experiencing with what the psychologist makes out of it with his reflective analysis.

The psychologist begins with certain operations, acts, functions as his data. If these fall out of sight in the course of discussion, it is only because having been taken for granted, they remain to control the whole development of the inquiry, and to afford the sterling medium of redemption. Acts such as perceiving, remembering, intending, loving give the points of departure; they alone are concrete experiences. To understand these experiences, under what conditions they arise and what effects they produce, analysis into states of consciousness occurs. And the modes of consciousness that are figured remain unarranged and unimportant, save as they may be translated back into acts.

To remember is to do something, as much as to shoe a horse, or to cherish a keepsake. To propose, to observe, to be kindly affectioned, are terms of value, of practice, of operation; just as digestion, respiration, locomotion express functions, not observable "objects." But there is an object that may be described: lungs, stomach, leg-muscles, or whatever. Through the structure we present to ourselves the function;

2. This is a fact not without its bearings upon the question of the nature and value of introspection. The objection that introspection "alters" the reality and hence is untrustworthy, most writers dispose of by saying that, after all, it need not alter the reality so very much—not beyond repair—and that, moreover, memory assists in restoring the ruins. It would be simpler to admit the fact: that the purpose of introspection is precisely to effect the right sort of alteration. If introspection should give us the original experience again, we should just be living through the experience over again in direct fashion; as psychologists we should not be forwarded one bit. Reflection upon this obvious proposition may bring to light various other matters worthy of note.

it appears laid out before us, spread forth in detail—objectified in a word. The anatomist who devotes himself to this detail may, if he please (and he probably does please to concentrate his devotion) ignore the function: to discover what is there, to analyze, to measure, to describe, gives him outlet enough. But nevertheless it is the function that fixed the point of departure, that prescribed the problem and that set the limits, physical as well as intellectual, of subsequent investigation. Reference to function makes the details discovered other than a jumble of incoherent trivialities. One might as well devote himself to the minute description of a square yard of desert soil were it not for this translation. States of consciousness are the morphology of certain functions.[3] What is true of analysis, of description, is true equally of classification. Knowing, willing, feeling, name states of consciousness not in terms of themselves, but in terms of acts, attitudes, found in experience.[4]

Explanation, even of an "empirical sort," is as impossible as determination of a "state" and its classification, when we rigidly confine ourselves to modifications of consciousness as a self-existent. Sensations are always defined, classified, and explained by reference to conditions which, ac-

3. Thus to divorce "structure psychology" from "function psychology" is to leave us without possibility of scientific comprehension of function, while it deprives us of all standard of reference in selecting, observing, and explaining the structure.

4. The following answer may fairly be anticipated: "This is true of the operations cited, but only because complex processes have been selected. Such a term as 'knowing' does of course express a function involving a system of intricate references. But, for that very reason, we go back to the sensation, which is the genuine type of the 'state of consciousness' as such, pure and unadulterate and unsophisticated." The point is large for a footnote, but the following considerations are instructive: (1) The same psychologist will go on to inform us that sensations, as we experience them, are networks of reference—they are perceptual, and more or less conceptual even. From which it would appear that whatever else they are or are not, the sensations, for which self-enclosed existence is claimed, are *not* states of consciousness. And (2) we are told that these are reached by scientific abstraction in order to account for complex forms. From which it would appear that they are hypothecated as products of interpretation and for purposes of further interpretation. Only the delusion that the more complex forms are just aggregates (instead of being acts, like seeing, hoping, etc.) prevents recognition of the point in question—that the "state of consciousness" is an instrument of inquiry or methodological appliance.

cording to the theory, are extraneous—sense-organs and stimuli. The whole physiological side assumes a ludicrously anomalous aspect on this basis.[5] While experimentation is retained, and even made much of, it is at the cost of logical coherence. To experiment with reference to a bare state of consciousness is a performance of which one cannot imagine the nature, to say nothing of doing it; while to experiment with reference to acts and the conditions of their occurrence is a natural and straightforward undertaking. Such simple processes as association are concretely inexplicable when we assume states of consciousness as existences by themselves. As recent psychology testifies, we again have to resort to conditions that have no place nor calling on the basis of the theory—the principle of habit, of neural action, or else some connection in the object.[6]

We have only to note that there are two opposing schools in psychology to see in what an unscientific status is the subject. We have only to consider that these two schools are the result of assuming states of consciousness as existences *per se* to locate the source of the scientific scandal. No matter what the topic, whether memory or association or attention or effort, the same dualisms present themselves, the same necessity of choosing between two schools. One, lost in the distinctions that it has developed, denies the function because it can find objectively presented only states of consciousness. So it abrogates the function, regarding it as a mere aggregate of such states, or as a purely external and factitious relation between them. The other school, recognizing that this procedure explains away rather than explains, the values of experience, attempts to even up by declaring that certain functions are themselves immediately

5. On the other hand, if what we are trying to get at is just the course and procedure of experiencing, of course any consideration that helps distinguish and make comprehensible that process is thoroughly pertinent.

6. It may avoid misunderstanding if I anticipate here a subsequent remark: that my point is not in the least that "states of consciousness" require some "synthetic unity" or faculty of substantial mind to effect their association. Quite the contrary; for this theory also admits the "states of consciousness" as existences in themselves also. My contention is that the "state of consciousness" as such is always a methodological product, developed in the course and for the purposes of psychological analysis.

given data of consciousness, existing side by side with the "states," but indefinitely transcending them in worth, and apprehended by some higher organ. So against the elementary contents and external associations of the analytic school in psychology, we have the complicated machinery of the intellectualist school, with its pure self-consciousness as a source of ultimate truths, its hierarchy of intuitions, its ready-made faculties. To be sure, these "spiritual faculties" are now largely reduced to some one comprehensive form— Apperception, or Will, or Attention, or whatever the fashionable term may be. But the principle remains the same; the assumption of a function as a given existent, distinguishable in itself and acting upon other existences—as if the functions digestion and vision were regarded as separate from organic structures, somehow acting upon them from the outside so as to bring cooperation and harmony into them![7] This division into psychological schools is as reasonable as would be one of botanists into rootists and flowerists; of those proclaiming the root to be the rudimentary and essential structure, and those asserting that since the function of seed-bearing is the main thing, the flower is really the controlling "synthetic" principle. Both sensationalist and intellectualist suppose that psychology has some special sphere of "reality" or of experience marked off for it within which the data are just lying around, self-existent and ready-made, to be picked up and assorted as pebbles await the visitor on the beach. Both alike fail to recognize that the psychologist first has experience to deal with; the same experience that the zoölogist, geologist, chemist, mathematician, and historian deal with, and that what characterizes his specialty is not some data or existences which he may call uniquely his own; but the problem raised—the problem of the *course* of the acts that constitute experiencing.

Here psychology gets its revenge upon those who would rule it out of possession of important philosophical bearing. As a matter of fact, the larger part of the questions that are being discussed in current epistemology and what is termed

7. The "functions" are in truth ordinary everyday acts and attitudes: seeing, smelling, talking, listening, remembering, hoping, loving, fearing.

metaphysic of logic and ethic arise out of (and are hopelessly compromised by) this original assumption of "consciousness as such"—in other words, are provoked by the
exact reason that is given for denying to psychology any essential meaning for epistemology and metaphysic. Such is
the irony of the situation. The epistemologist's problem is,
indeed, usually put as the question of how the subject can so
far "transcend" itself as to get valid assurance of the objective world. The very phraseology in which the problem is
put reveals the thoroughness of the psychologist's revenge.
Just and only because experience has been reduced to "states
of consciousness" as independent existences, does the question of self-transcendence have any meaning. The entire
epistemological industry is one—shall I say it—of a Sisyphean
nature. *Mutatis mutandis*, the same holds of the metaphysic
of logic, ethic, and æsthetic. In each case, the basic problem
has come to be how a mere state of consciousness can be the
vehicle of a system of truth, of an objectively valid good, of
beauty which is other than agreeable feeling. We may, indeed, excuse the psychologist for not carrying on the special
inquiries that are the business of logical, ethical, and
æsthetical philosophy; but can we excuse ourselves for
forcing his results into such a shape as to make philosophic
problems so arbitrary that they are soluble only by arbitrarily
wrenching scientific facts?

Undoubtedly we are between two fires. In placing upon
psychology the responsibility of discovering the method of
experience, as a sequence of acts and passions, do we not
destroy just that limitation to concrete detail which now
constitutes it a science? Will not the psychologist be the first
to repudiate this attempt to mix him up in matters philosophical? We need only to keep in mind the specific facts involved in the term Course or Process of Experience to avoid
this danger. The immediate preoccupation of the psychologist is with very definite and empirical facts—questions
like the limits of audition, of the origin of pitch, of the
structure and conditions of the musical scale, etc. Just so the
immediate affair of the geologist is with particular rock-
structures, of the botanist with particular plants, and so on.
But through the collection, description, location, classification

of rocks the geologist is led to the splendid story of world-forming. The limited, fixed, and separate piece of work is dissolved away in the fluent and dynamic drama of the earth. So, the plant leads with inevitableness to the whole process of life and its evolution.

In form, the botanist still studies the genus, the species, the plant—hardly, indeed, that; rather the special parts, the structural elements, of the plant. In reality, he studies life itself; the structures are the indications, the signature through which he renders transparent the mystery of life growing in the changing world. It was doubtless necessary for the botanist to go through the Linnean period—the period of engagement with rigid detail and fixed classifications; of tearing apart and piecing together; of throwing all emphasis upon peculiarities of number, size, and appearance of matured structure; of regarding change, growth, and function as external, more or less interesting, attachments to form. Examination of this period is instructive; there is much in contemporary investigation and discussion that is almost unpleasantly reminiscent in its suggestiveness. The psychologist should profit by the intervening history of science. The conception of evolution is not so much an additional law as it is a face-about. The fixed structure, the separate form, the isolated element, is henceforth at best a mere stepping-stone to knowledge of process, and when not at its best, marks the end of comprehension, and betokens failure to grasp the problem.

With the change in standpoint from self-included existence to including process, from structural unit of composition to controlling unity of function, from changeless form to movement in growth, the whole scheme of values is transformed. Faculties are definite directions of development; elements are products that are starting-points for new processes; bare facts are indices of change; static conditions are modes of accomplished adjustment. Not that the concrete, empirical phenomenon loses in worth, much less that unverifiable "metaphysical" entities are impertinently introduced; but that our aim is the discovery of a process of actions in its adaptations to circumstance. If we apply this evolutionary logic in psychology, where shall we stop? Ques-

tions of limits of stimuli in a given sense, say hearing, are
in reality questions of temporary arrests, adjustments marking the favorable equilibrium of the whole organism; they
connect with the question of the use of sensation in general
and auditory sensations in particular for life-habits; of the
origin and use of localized and distinguished perception; and
this, in turn, involves within itself the whole question of
space and time recognition; the significance of the thing-and-
quality experience, and so on. And when we are told that the
question of the origin of space experience has nothing at all
to do with the question of the nature and significance of the
space experienced, the statement is simply evidence that the
one who makes it is still at the static standpoint; he believes
that things, that relations, have existence and significance
apart from the particular conditions under which they come
into experience, and apart from the special service rendered
in those particular conditions.

Of course, I am far from saying that every psychologist
must make the whole journey. Each individual may contract,
as he pleases, for any section or subsection he prefers; and
undoubtedly the well-being of the science is advanced by
such division of labor. But psychology goes over the whole
ground, from detecting every distinct act of experiencing, to
seeing what need calls out the special organ fitted to cope
with the situation, and discovering the machinery through
which it operates to keep a-going the course of action.

But, I shall be told, the wall that divides psychology
from philosophy cannot be so easily treated as non-existent.
Psychology is a matter of natural history, even though it may
be admitted that it is the natural history of the course of experience. But philosophy is a matter of values; of the criticism and justification of certain validities. One deals, it is
said, with genesis, with conditions of temporal origin and
transition; the other with analysis, with eternal constitution.
I shall have to repeat that just this rigid separation of genesis
and analysis seems to me a survival from a pre-evolutionary,
a pre-historic age. It indicates not so much an assured barrier
between philosophy and psychology as the distance dividing
philosophy from all science. For the lesson that mathema-
ticians first learned, that physics and chemistry pondered

over, in which the biological disciplines were finally tutored, is that sure and delicate analysis is possible only through the patient study of conditions of origin and development. The method of analysis in mathematics is the method of construction. The experimental method is the method of making, of following the history of production; the term "cause" that has (when taken as an existent entity) so hung on the heels of science as to impede its progress, has universal meaning when read as condition of appearance in a process. And, as already intimated, the conception of evolution is no more and no less the discovery of a general law of life than it is the generalization of all scientific method. Everywhere analysis that cannot proceed by examining the successive stages of its subject, from its beginning up to its culmination, that cannot control this examination by discovering the conditions under which successive stages appear, is only preliminary. It may further the invention of proper tools of inquiry, it may help define problems, it may serve to suggest valuable hypotheses. But as science it breathes an air already tainted. There is no way to sort out the results flowing from the subject-matter itself from those introduced by the assumptions and presumptions of our own reflection. Not so with natural history when it is worthy of its name. Here the analysis is the unfolding of the existence itself. Its distinctions are not pigeonholes of our convenience; they are stakes that mark the parting of the ways in the process itself. Its classifications are not a grasp at factors resisting further analysis; they are the patient tracings of the paths pursued. Nothing is more out of date than to suppose that interest in genesis is interest in reducing higher forms to cruder ones: it is interest in locating the exact and objective conditions under which a given fact appears, and in relation to which accordingly it has its meaning. Nothing is more naïve than to suppose that in pursuing "natural history" (term of scorn in which yet resides the dignity of the world-drama) we simply learn something of the temporal conditions under which a given value appears, while its own eternal essential quality remains as opaque as before. Nature knows no such divorce of quality and circumstance. Things come when they are wanted and as they are wanted; their quality is precisely the response they give to the conditions that call for them, while the furtherance they afford to the movement of their whole is their meaning. The severance of analysis and genesis, instead of serving as a ready-made test by which to try out the empirical, temporal events of psychology from the rational abiding constitution of philosophy, is a brand of philosophic dualism: the supposition that values are externally obtruded and statically set in irrelevant rubbish.

There are those who will admit that "states of consciousness" are but the cross-sections of flow of behavior, arrested for inspection, made in order that we may reconstruct experience in its life-history. Yet in the knowledge of the course and method of our experience, they will hold that we are far from the domain proper of philosophy. Experience, they say, is just the historic achievement of finite individuals; it tells the tale of approach to the treasures of truth, of partial victory, but larger defeat, in laying hold of the treasure. But, they say, reality is not the path to reality, and record of devious wanderings in the path is hardly a safe account of the goal. Psychology, in other words, may tell us something of how we mortals lay hold of the world of things and truths; of how we appropriate and assimilate its contents; and of how we react. It may trace the issues of such approaches and apprehensions upon the course of our own individual destinies. But it cannot wisely ignore nor sanely deny the distinction between these individual strivings and achievements and the "Reality" that subsists and supports its own structure outside these finite futilities. The processes by which we turn over The Reality into terms of our fragmentary unconcluded, inconclusive experiences are so extrinsic to the Reality itself as to have no revealing power with reference to it. There is the *ordo ad universum*, the subject of philosophy; there is the *ordo ad individuum*, the subject of psychology.

Some such assumption as this lies latent, I am convinced, in all forswearings of the kinship of psychology and philosophy. Two conceptions hang together. The opinion that psychology is an account only and finally of states of consciousness, and therefore can throw no light upon the objects with which philosophy deals, is twin to the doctrine that the whole conscious life of the individual is not organic to the world. The philosophic basis and scope of this doctrine lie beyond examination here. But even in passing one cannot avoid remarking that the doctrine is almost never consistently held; the doctrine logically carried out leads so directly to intellectual and moral scepticism that the theory usually prefers to work in the dark background as a disposition and temper of thought rather than to make a frank statement of itself. Even in the half-hearted expositions of the process of human experience as something merely annexed to the reality of the universe, we are brought face to face to the consideration with which we set out: the dependence of theories of the individual upon the position at a given time of the individual practical and social. The doctrine of the accidental, futile, transitory significance of the individual's experience as compared with eternal realities; the notion that at best the individual is simply realizing for and in himself what already has fixed completeness in itself is congruous only with a certain intellectual and political scheme and must modify itself as that shifts. When such rearrangement comes, our estimate of the nature and importance of psychology will mirror the change.

When man's command of the methods that control action was precarious and disturbed; when the tools that subject the world of things and forces to use and operation were rare and clumsy, it was unavoidable that the individual should submit his perception and purpose blankly to the blank reality beyond. Under such circumstances, external authority must reign; the belief that human experience in itself is approximate, not intrinsic, is inevitable. Under such circumstances, reference to the individual, to the subject, is a resort only for explaining error, illusion, and uncertainty. The necessity of external control and external redemption of experience reports itself in a low valuation of the self, and of all the factors and phases of experience that spring from the self. That the psychology of mediævalism should appear only as a portion of its theology of sin and salvation is as obvious as that the psychology of the Greeks should be a chapter of cosmology.

As against all this, the assertion is ventured that psychology, supplying us with knowledge of the behavior of experience, is a conception of democracy. Its postulate is that since experience fulfills itself in individuals, since it administers itself through their instrumentality, the account of the course and method of this achievement is a significant and indispensable affair.

Democracy is possible only because of a change in intellectual conditions. It implies tools for getting at truth in detail, and day by day, as we go along. Only such possession justifies the surrender of fixed, all-embracing principles to which, as universals, all particulars and individuals are subject for valuation and regulation. Without such possession, it is only the courage of the fool that would undertake the venture to which democracy has committed itself—the ordering of life in response to the needs of the moment in accordance with the ascertained truth of the moment. Modern life involves the deification of the here and the now; of the specific, the particular, the unique, that which happens once and has no measure of value save such as it brings with itself. Such deification is monstrous fetishism, unless the deity be there; unless the universal lives, moves, and has its being in experience as individualized.[8] This conviction of the value

8. This is perhaps a suitable moment to allude to the absence, in this discussion, of reference to what is sometimes termed rational psychology—the assumption of a separate, substantialized ego, soul, or whatever, existing side by side with particular experiences and "states of consciousness," acting upon them and acted upon by them. In ignoring this and confining myself to the "states of consciousness" theory and the "natural history" theory, I may appear not only to have unduly narrowed the concerns at issue, but to have weakened my own point, as this doctrine seems to offer a special vantage ground whence to defend the close relationship of psychology and philosophy. The "narrowing," if such it be, will have to pass—from limits of time and other matters. But the other point I cannot concede. The independently existing soul restricts and degrades individuality, making of it a separate thing outside of the full flow of things, alien to things experienced and consequently in either mechanical or miraculous relations to them. It is vitiated by just the quality already objected to—that psychology has a separate piece of reality apportioned to it, instead of occupying itself with the manifestation and operation of any and all existences in reference to concrete action. From this point of view, the "states of consciousness" attitude is a much more hopeful and fruitful one. It ignores certain considerations, to be sure; and when it turns its ignoring into denial, it leaves us with curious hieroglyphics. But after all, there is a key; these symbols can be read;

of the individualized finds its further expression in psychology, which undertakes to show how this individualization proceeds, and in what aspect it presents itself.

Of course, such a conception means something for philosophy as well as for psychology; possibly it involves for philosophy the larger measure of transformation. It involves surrender of any claim on the part of philosophy to be the sole source of some truths and the exclusive guardian of some values. It means that philosophy be a method; not an assurance company, nor a knight errant. It means an alignment with science. Philosophy may not be sacrificed to the partial and superficial clamor of that which sometimes officiously and pretentiously exhibits itself as Science. But there is a sense in which philosophy must go to school to the sciences; must have no data save such as it receives at their hands; and be hospitable to no method of inquiry or reflection not akin to those in daily use among the sciences. As long as it claims for itself special territory of fact, or peculiar modes of access to truth, so long must it occupy a dubious position. Yet this claim it has to make until psychology comes to its own. There is something in experience, something in things, which the physical and the biological sciences do not touch; something, moreover, which is not just more experiences or more existences; but without which their materials are inexperienced, unrealized. Such sciences deal only with what *might* be experienced; with the content of experience, provided and assumed there be experience. It is psychology which tells us how this possible experience loses its barely hypothetical character, and is stamped with categorical unquestioned experiencedness; how, in a word, it becomes here and now in some uniquely individualized life. Here is the necessary transition of science into philosophy; a passage that carries the verified and solid body of the one into the large and free form of the other.

---

they may be translated into terms of the course of experience. When thus translated, selfhood, individuality, is neither wiped out nor set up as a miraculous and foreign entity; it is seen as the unity of reference and function involved in all things when fully experienced—the pivot about which they turn.

[NOTE: I have let this paper stand much as written, though now conscious that much more is crowded into it than could properly be presented in one paper. The drift of the ten years from '99 to '09 has made, I venture to believe, for increased clearness in the main positions of the paper: The revival of a naturalistic realism, the denial of the existence of "consciousness," the development of functional and dynamic psychology (accompanied by aversion to interpretation of functions as faculties of a soul-substance)—all of these tendencies are sympathetic with the aim of the paper. There is another reason for letting it stand: the new functional and pragmatic empiricism proffered in this volume has been constantly objected to on the ground that its conceptions of knowledge and verification lead only to subjectivism and solipsism. The paper may indicate that the identification of experience with bare states of consciousness represents the standpoint of the critic, not of the empiricism criticized, and that it is for him, not for me, to fear the subjective implications of such a position. The paper also clearly raises the question as to how far the isolation of "consciousness" from nature and social life, which characterizes the procedure of many psychologists of today, is responsible for keeping alive quite unreal problems in philosophy.]

PSYCHOLOGY AND SOCIAL PRACTICE[1]

In coming before you I had hoped to deal with the problem of the relation of psychology to the social sciences—and through them to social practice, to life itself. Naturally, in anticipation, I had conceived a systematic exposition of fundamental principles covering the whole ground, and giving every factor its due rating and position. That discussion is not ready today. I am loath, however, completely to withdraw from the subject, especially as there happens to be a certain phase of it with which I have been more or less practically occupied within the last few years. I have in mind the relation of Psychology to Education. Since education is primarily a social affair, and since educational science is first of all a social science, we have here a section of the whole field. In some respects there may be an advantage in approaching the more comprehensive question through the medium of one of its special cases. The absence of elaborated and coherent view may be made up for by a background of experience, which shall check the projective power of reflective abstraction, and secure a translation of large words and ideas into specific images. This special territory, moreover, may be such as to afford both sign-posts and broad avenues to the larger sphere—the place of psychology among the social sciences. Because I anticipate such an outcome, and because I shall make a survey of the broad field from the special standpoint taken, I make no apology for presenting this discussion to an Association of Psychologists rather than to a gathering of educators.

1. Address of the President before the American Psychological Association, New Haven, 1899.

[First published in *Psychological Review* 7 (1900): 105–24 and in *Science*, n.s. 11 (1900): 321–33. Reprinted separately as University of Chicago Contributions to Education, no. 2 (Chicago: University of Chicago Press, 1901), 42 pp.]

In dealing with this particular question, it is impossible not to have in mind the brilliant and effective discourses recently published by my predecessor in this chair. I shall accordingly make free to refer to points, and at times to words, in his treatment of the matter. Yet, as perhaps I hardly need say, it is a problem of the most fundamental importance for both psychology and social theory that I wish to discuss, not any particular book or article. Indeed with much of what Dr. Münsterberg says about the uselessness and the danger for the teacher of miscellaneous scraps of child-study, of unorganized information regarding the nervous system, and of crude and uninterpreted results of laboratory experiment, I am in full agreement. It is doubtless necessary to protest against a hasty and violent bolting of psychological facts and principles which, of necessity, destroys their scientific form. It is necessary to point out the need of a preliminary working over of psychological material, adapting it to the needs of education. But these are minor points. The main point is whether the standpoint of psychological science, as a study of *mechanism*, is indifferent and opposed to the demands of education with its free interplay of personalities in their vital attitudes and aims.

I.

The school practice of today has a definite psychological basis. Teachers are already possessed by specific psychological assumptions which control their theory and their practice. The greatest obstacle to the introduction of certain educational reforms is precisely the permeating persistence of the underlying psychological creed. Traced back to its psychological ultimates, there are two controlling bases of existing methods of instruction. One is the assumption of a fundamental distinction between child psychology and the adult psychology where, in reality, identity reigns, viz.: in the region of the motives and conditions which make for mental power. The other is the assumption of likeness where marked difference is the feature most significant for educational purposes; I mean the specialization of aims and habits in the adult, compared with the absence of specialization in the child, and the connection of undifferentiated status with the full and free growth of the child.

The adult is primarily a person with a certain calling and position in life. These devolve upon him certain *specific* responsibilities which he has to meet, and call into play certain formed habits. The child is primarily one whose calling is *growth*. He is concerned with arriving at specific ends and purposes—instead of having a general framework already developed. He is engaged in *forming* habits rather than in definitely utilizing those already formed. Consequently he is absorbed in getting that all-around contact with persons and things, that range of acquaintance with the physical and ideal factors of life, which shall afford the background and material for the specialized aims and pursuits of later life. He is, or should be, busy in the formation of a flexible variety of habits whose sole immediate criterion is their relation to *full growth*, rather than in acquiring certain *skills* whose value is measured by their reference to specialized technical accomplishments. This is the radical psychological and biological distinction, I take it, between the child and the adult. It is because of this distinction that children are neither physiologically nor mentally describable as "little men and women."

The full recognition of this distinction means of course the selection and arrangement of all school materials and methods for the facilitation of full normal growth, trusting to the result in growth to provide the instrumentalities of later specialized adaptation. If education means the period of prolonged infancy, it means nothing less than this. But look at our school system and ask whether the 3 R's are taught, either as to subject-matter or as to method, with reference to growth, to its present demands and opportunities; or as technical acquisitions which are to be needed in the specialized life of the adult. Ask the same questions about geography, grammar and history. The gap between psychological theory and the existing school practice becomes painfully apparent. We readily realize the extent to which the present school system is dominated by carrying over into child life a standpoint and method which are significant in the psychology of the adult.

The narrow scope of the traditional elementary curriculum, the premature and excessive use of logical analytic methods, the assumption of ready-made faculties of observation, memory, attention, etc., which can be brought into play if only the child chooses to do so, the ideal of formal discipline—all these find a large measure of their explanation in neglect of just this psychological distinction between the child and the adult. The hold of these affairs upon the school is so fixed that it is impossible to shake it in any fundamental way, excepting by a thorough appreciation of the actual psychology of the case. This appreciation cannot be confined to the educational leaders and theorists. No individual instructor can be sincere and whole-hearted, to say nothing of intelligent, in carrying into effect the needed reforms, save as he genuinely understands the scientific basis and necessity of the change.

But in another direction there is the assumption of a fundamental difference: namely, as to the *conditions* which secure intellectual and moral progress and power.[2] No one seriously questions that, with an adult, power and control are obtained through realization of personal ends and problems, through personal selection of means and materials which are relevant, and through personal adaptation and application of what is thus selected, together with whatever of experimentation and of testing is involved in this effort. Practically every one of these three conditions of increase in power for the adult is denied for the child. For him problems and aims are determined by another mind. For him the material that is relevant and irrelevant is selected in advance by another mind. And, upon the whole, there is such an attempt to teach him a ready-made method for applying his material to the solution of his problems, or the reaching of his ends, that the factor of experimentation is reduced to the minimum. With the adult we unquestioningly assume that an attitude of personal inquiry, based upon the possession of a problem which interests and absorbs, is a necessary precondition of mental growth. With the child we assume that the precondition is rather the willing disposition which makes him ready to submit to any problem and mate-

2. I owe this point specifically (as well as others more generally) to my friend and colleague, Mrs. Ella Flagg Young.

rial presented from without. *Alertness* is our ideal in one case; *docility* in the other. With one, we assume that power of attention develops in dealing with problems which make a personal appeal, and through personal responsibility for determining what is relevant. With the other we provide next to no opportunities for the evolution of problems out of immediate experience, and allow next to no free mental play for selecting, assorting and adapting the experiences and ideas that make for their solution. How profound a revolution in the position and service of text-book and teacher, and in methods of instruction depending therefrom, would be effected by a sincere recognition of the psychological identity of child and adult in these respects can with difficulty be realized.

Here again it is not enough that the educational commanders should be aware of the correct educational psychology. The rank and file, just because they are persons dealing with persons, must have a sufficient grounding in the psychology of the matter to realize the necessity and the significance of what they are doing. Any reform instituted without such conviction on the part of those who have to carry it into effect would never be undertaken in good faith, nor in the spirit which its ideal inevitably demands; consequently it could lead only to disaster.

At this point, however, the issue defines itself somewhat more narrowly. It may be true, it is true, we are told, that some should take hold of psychological methods and conclusions, and organize them with reference to the assistance which they may give to the cause of education. But this is not the work of the teacher. It belongs to the general educational theorist—the middleman between the psychologist and the educational practitioner. He should put the matter into such shape that the teacher may take the net results in the form of advice and rules for action; but the teacher who comes in contact with the living personalities must not assume the psychological attitude. If he does, he reduces persons to objects, and thereby distorts, or rather destroys, the ethical relationship which is the vital nerve of instruction (Münsterberg, *Psychology and Life*, p. 122, and pp. 136–38).

That there is some legitimate division of labor between the general educational theorist and the actual instructor, there is of course no doubt. As a rule, it will not be the one actively employed in instruction who will be most conscious of the psychological basis and equivalents of the educational work, nor most occupied in finding the pedagogical rendering of psychological facts and principles. Of necessity, the stress of interest will be elsewhere. But we have already found reason for questioning the possibility of making the somewhat different direction of interest into a rigid dualism of a legislative class on one side and an obedient subject class on the other. Can the teacher ever receive "obligatory prescriptions"? Can he receive from another a statement of the means by which he is to reach his ends, and not become hopelessly servile in his attitude? Would not such a result be even worse than the existing mixture of empiricism and inspiration?—just because it would forever fossilize the empirical element and dispel the inspiration which now quickens routine. Can a passive, receptive attitude on the part of the instructor (suggesting the soldier awaiting orders from a commanding general) be avoided, unless the teacher, as a student of psychology, himself sees the reasons and import of the suggestions and rules that are proffered him?

I quote a passage that seems of significance: "Do we not lay a special linking science everywhere else between the theory and practical work? We have engineering between physics and the practical workingmen in the mills; we have a scientific medicine between the natural sciences and the physician" (p. 138). The sentences suggest, in an almost startling way, that the real essence of the problem is found in an *organic* connection between the two extreme terms— between the theorist and the practical worker—through the medium of the linking science. The decisive matter is the extent to which the ideas of the theorist actually project themselves, through the kind offices of the middleman, into the consciousness of the practitioner. It is the participation by the practical man in the theory, through the agency of the linking science, that determines at once the effectiveness of the work done, and the moral freedom and personal development of the one engaged in it. It is because the physician no longer follows rules, which, however rational in themselves, are yet arbitrary to him (because grounded in principles that he does not understand), that his work is becoming liberal, attaining the dignity of a profession, instead of remaining a mixture of *empiricism and quackery.* It is because, alas, engineering makes only a formal and not a real connection between physics and the practical workingmen in the mills that our industrial problem is an ethical problem of the most serious kind. The question of the amount of wages the laborer receives, of the purchasing value of this wage, of the hours and conditions of labor, are, after all, secondary. The problem primarily roots in the fact that the mediating science does not connect with his *consciousness,* but merely with his outward actions. He does not appreciate the significance and bearing of what he does; and he does not perform his work because of sharing in a larger scientific and social consciousness. If he did, he would be free. All other proper accompaniments of wage, and hours, healthful and inspiring conditions would be added unto him, because he would have entered into the ethical kingdom. Shall we seek analogy with the teacher's calling in the workingmen in the mill, or in the scientific physician?

It is quite likely that I shall be reminded that I am overlooking an essential difference. The physician, it will be said, is dealing with a body which either is in itself a pure object, a causal interplay of anatomical elements, or is something which lends itself naturally and without essential loss to treatment from this point of view; while the case is quite different in the material with which the teacher deals. Here is personality, which is destroyed when regarded as an object. But the gap is not so pronounced nor so serious as this objection implies. The physician after all is not dealing with a lifeless body; with a simple anatomical structure, or interplay of mechanical elements. Life-functions, active operations, are the reality which confronts him. We do not have to go back many centuries in the history of medicine to find a time when the physician attempted to deal with these functions directly and immediately. They were so overpoweringly present, they forced themselves upon him so obviously and so constantly that he had no resource save a mixture of magic and empiricism: magic, so far as he followed methods derived from uncritical analogy, or from purely general speculation on the universe and life; empiricism, so long as he just followed procedures which had been found helpful before in cases which somewhat resembled the present. We have only to trace the intervening history of medicine to appreciate that it is precisely the ability to state function in terms of structure, to reduce life in its active operations to terms of a causal mechanism, which has taken the medical calling out of this dependence upon a vibration between superstition and routine. Progress has come by taking what is really an activity *as if* it were only an object. It is the capacity to effect this transformation of life-activity which measures both the scientific character of the physician's procedure and his practical control, the certainty and efficacy of what he, as a living man, does in relation to some other living man.

It is an old story, however, that we must not content ourselves with analogies. We must find some specific reason in the principles of the teacher's own activities for believing that psychology—the ability to transform a living personality into an objective mechanism for the time being—is not merely an incidental help, but an organic necessity. Upon the whole, the best efforts of teachers at present are partly paralyzed, partly distorted, and partly rendered futile precisely from the fact that they are in such immediate contact with sheer, unanalyzed personality. The relation is such a purely ethical and personal one that the teacher cannot get enough outside the situation to handle it intelligently and effectively. He is in precisely the condition in which the physician was when he had no recourse save to deal with health as entity or force on one side, and disease as opposing agency or invading influence upon the other. The teacher reacts *en bloc*, in a gross wholesale way, to something which he takes in an equally undefined and total way in the child. It is the inability to regard, upon occasion, both himself and the child as just objects working upon each other in specific ways that compels him to resort to purely arbitrary measures, to fall back upon mere routine traditions of school teaching, or to fly to the latest fad of pedagogical theorists—the latest

panacea peddled out in school journals or teachers' institutes
—just as the old physician relied upon his magic formula.

I repeat, it is the fundamental weakness of our teaching
force today (putting aside teachers who are actually incom-
petent by reason either of wrong motives or inadequate
preparation), that they react in gross to the child's exhibitions in gross without analyzing them into their detailed and
constituent elements. If the child is angry, he is dealt with
simply as an angry being; anger is an entity, a force, not a
symptom. If a child is inattentive, this again is treated as a
mere case of refusal to use the faculty or function of attention, of sheer unwillingness to act. Teachers tell you that a
child is careless or inattentive in the same final way in
which they would tell you that a piece of paper is white. It
is just a fact, and that is all there is of it. Now it is only
through some recognition of attention as a mechanism, some
awareness of the interplay of sensations, images and motor
impulses which constitute it as an objective fact that the
teacher can deal effectively with attention as a function.
And, of course, the same is true of memory, quick and useful
observation, good judgment and all the other practical
powers the teacher is attempting to cultivate.

Consideration of the abstract concepts of mechanism
and personality is important. Too much preoccupation with
them in a general fashion, however, without translation into
relevant imagery of actual conditions is likely to give rise
to unreal difficulties. The ethical personality does not go to
school naked; it takes with it the body as the instrument
through which all influences reach it, and through control of
which its ideas are both elaborated and expressed. The
teacher does not deal with personality at large, but as expressed in intellectual and practical impulses and habits. The
ethical personality is not formed—it is forming. The teacher
must provide stimuli leading to the equipment of personality
with active habits and interests. When we consider the problem of forming habits and interests we find ourselves at
once confronted with matters of this sort: What stimuli
shall be presented to the sense-organs and how? What stable
complexes of associations shall be organized? What motor
impulses shall be evoked, and to what extent? How shall

they be induced in such a way as to bring favorable stimuli under greater control, and to lessen the danger of excitation from undesirable stimuli? In a word, the teacher is dealing with the psychical factors that are concerned with furtherance of certain habits, and the inhibition of others—habits intellectual, habits emotional, habits in overt action.

Moreover, all the instruments and materials with which the teacher deals must be considered as psychical stimuli. Such consideration involves of necessity a knowledge of their reciprocal reactions—of what goes by the name of *causal mechanism*. The introduction of certain changes into a network of associations, the reinforcement of certain sensorimotor connections, the weakening or displacing of others— this is the psychological rendering of the greater part of the teacher's actual business. It is not that one teacher employs mechanical considerations, and that the other does not, appealing to higher ends; it is that one does not know his mechanism, and consequently acts servilely, superstitiously and blindly, while the other, knowing what he is about, acts freely, clearly and effectively.[3]

The same thing is true on the side of materials of instruction—the school studies. No amount of exaltation of teleological personality (however true, and however necessary the emphasis) can disguise from us the fact that instruction is an affair of bringing a child into intimate relations with concrete objects, positive facts, definite ideas and specific symbols. The symbols are objective things in arithmetic, reading and writing. The ideas are truths of history and of science. The facts are derived from such specific disciplines as geography and language, botany and astronomy. To suppose that by some influence of pure personality upon pure personality, conjoined with a knowledge of rules formulated by an educational theorist, an effective interplay of this body of physical and ideal objects with the life of the child can be effective, is, I submit, nothing but an appeal to magic, plus dependence upon servile routine. Symbols in

3. That some teachers get their psychology by instinct more effectively than others by any amount of reflective study may be unreservedly stated. It is not a question of manufacturing teachers, but of reinforcing and enlightening those who have a right to teach.

reading and writing and number are, both in themselves and in the way in which they stand for ideas, elements in a mechanism which has to be rendered operative within the child. To bring about this influence in the most helpful and economical way, in the most fruitful and liberating way, is absolutely impossible save as the teacher has some power to transmute symbols and contents into their working psychical equivalents: and save as he also has the power to see what it is in the child, as a psychical mechanism, that affords maximum leverage.

Probably I shall now hear that at present the danger is not of dealing with acts and persons in a gross, arbitrary way, but (so far as what is called new education is concerned) in treating the children too much as mechanism, and consequently seeking for all kinds of stimuli to stir and attract—that, in a word, the tendency to reduce instruction to a merely agreeable thing, weakening the child's personality and indulging his mere love of excitement and pleasure, is precisely the result of taking the psycho-mechanical point of view. I welcome the objection for it serves to clear up the precise point. It is through a partial and defective psychology that the teacher, in his reaction from dead routine and arbitrary moral and intellectual discipline, has substituted an appeal to the satisfaction of momentary impulse. It is not because the teacher has a knowledge of the psycho-physical mechanism, but because he has a *partial* knowledge of it. He has come to consciousness of certain sensations, and certain impulses, and of the ways in which these may be stimulated and directed, but he is in ignorance of the larger mechanism (just as a mechanism), and of the causal relations which subsist between the unknown part and the elements upon which he is playing. What is needed to correct his errors is not to inform him that he gets only misleading from taking the psychical point of view, but to reveal to him the scope and intricate interactions of the mechanism as a whole. Then he will realize that while he is gaining apparent efficacy in some superficial part of the mechanism, he is disarranging, dislocating and disintegrating much more fundamental factors in it. In a word he is operating not as a psychologist, but as a poor psychologist, and the only cure for a partial psychology is a fuller one. He is gaining the momentary attention of the child through an appeal to pleasant color, or exciting tone, or agreeable association, but at the expense of isolating one cog and ratchet in the machinery, and making it operate independently of the rest. In theory, it is as possible to demonstrate this to a teacher, showing how the faulty method reacts unhappily into the personality, as it is to locate the points of wrong construction, and of ineffective transfer of energy in a physical apparatus.

This suggests the admission made by writers in many respects as far apart as Dr. Harris and Dr. Münsterberg—that scientific psychology is of use on the pathological side— where questions of "physical and mental health" are concerned. But is there anything with which the teacher has concern that is not included in the ideal of physical and mental health? Does health define to us anything less than the teacher's whole end and aim? Where does pathology leave off in the scale and series of vicious aims and defective means? I see no line between the more obvious methods and materials which result in nervous irritation and fatigue, in weakening the power of vision, in establishing spinal curvatures, and others which, in more remote and subtle, but equally real ways, leave the child with, say, a muscular system which is only partially at the service of his ideas, with blocked and inert brain paths between eye and ear, and with a partial and disconnected development of the cerebral paths of visual imagery. What error in instruction is there which could not, with proper psychological theory, be stated in just such terms as these? A wrong method of teaching reading, wrong I mean in the full educational and ethical sense, is also a case of pathological use of the psycho-physical mechanism. A method is ethically defective that, while giving the child a glibness in the mechanical facility of reading, leaves him at the mercy of suggestion and chance environment to decide whether he reads the "yellow journal," the trashy novel, or the literature which inspires and makes more valid his whole life. Is it any less certain that this failure on the ethical side is repeated in some lack of adequate growth and connection in the psychical and physiological factors involved? If a knowledge of psychology is important to the teacher in the grosser and more overt cases of mental pathology, is it not even more important in these hidden and indirect matters—just because they are less evident and more circuitous in their operation and manifestation?

The argument may be summarized by saying that there is controversy neither as to the ethical character of education, nor as to the abstraction which psychology performs in reducing personality to an object. The teacher is, indeed, a person occupied with other persons. He lives in a social sphere—he is a member and an organ of a social life. His aims are social aims, the development of individuals taking ever more responsible positions in a circle of social activities continually increasing in radius and in complexity. Whatever he as a teacher effectively does, he does as a person, and he does with and towards persons. His methods, like his aims, when actively in operation, are practical, are social, are ethical, are anything you please—save merely *psychical*. In comparison with this, the material and the data, the standpoint and the methods of psychology, are abstract. They transform specific acts and relations of individuals into a flow of processes in consciousness; and these processes can be adequately identified and related only through reference to a biological organism. I do not think there is danger of going too far in asserting the social and teleological nature of the work of the teacher; or in asserting the abstract and partial character of the mechanism into which the psychologist, as a psychologist, transmutes the play of vital values.

Does it follow from this that any attempt on the part of the teacher to perform this abstraction, to see the pupil as a mechanism, to define his own relations and that of the study taught in terms of causal influences acting upon this mechanism, is useless and harmful? On the face of it, I cannot understand the logic which says that because mechanism is mechanism, and because acts, aims, values are vital, therefore a statement in terms of one is alien to the comprehension and proper management of the other. Ends are not compromised when referred to the means necessary to realize them. Values do not cease to be values when they are minutely and accurately measured. Acts are not destroyed when their operative machinery is made manifest. The state-

ment of the disparity of mechanism and actual life, be it
never so true, solves no problem. It is no distinction that may
be used off-hand to decide the question of the relation of
psychology to any form of practice. It is a valuable and necessary distinction; but it is only preliminary. The purport of
our discussion has, indeed, led us strongly to suspect any
ideal which exists purely at large, out of relation to machinery of execution, and equally a machinery that operates in no
particular direction.

The proposition that a description and explanation of
stones, iron and mortar, as an absolutely necessary causal
nexus of mechanical conditions, makes the results of physical science unavailable for purposes of practical life, would
hardly receive attention today. Every sky-scraper, every railway bridge is a refutation, compared with which oceans of
talk are futile. One would not find it easy to stir up a problem
even if he went on to include, in this same mechanical system, the steam derricks that hoist the stones and iron, and
the muscles and nerves of architect, mason and steel worker.
The simple fact is still too obvious: the more thorough-going
and complete the mechanical and causal statement, the more
controlled, the more economical are the discovery and
realization of human aims. It is not in spite of, nor in neglect
of, but because of the mechanical statement that human
activity has been freed, and made effective in thousands of
new practical directions, upon a scale and with a certainty
hitherto undreamed of. Our discussion tends to suggest that
we entertain a similar question regarding psychology only
because we have as yet made so little headway—just because
there is so little scientific control of our practice in these
directions; that at bottom our difficulty is local and circum-
stantial, not intrinsic and doctrinal. If our teachers were
trained as architects are trained; if our schools were actually
managed on a psychological basis as great factories are run
on the basis of chemical and physical science; if our psychology were sufficiently organized and coherent to give as
adequate a mechanical statement of human nature as
physics does of its material, we should never dream of discussing this question.

I cannot pass on from this phase of the discussion without at least incidental remark of the obverse side of the situation. The difficulties of psychological observation and interpretation are great enough in any case. We cannot afford to neglect any possible auxiliary. The great advantage of the psycho-physical laboratory is paid for by certain obvious defects. The completer control of conditions, with resulting greater accuracy of determination, demands an isolation, a ruling out of the usual media of thought and action, which leads to a certain remoteness, and easily to a certain artificiality. When the result of laboratory experiment informs us, for example, that repetition is the chief factor influencing recall, we must bear in mind that the result is obtained with nonsense material—*i.e.*, by excluding the conditions of ordinary memory. The result is pertinent if we state it thus: The more we exclude the usual environmental adaptations of memory the greater importance attaches to sheer repetition. It is dubious (and probably perverse) if we say: Repetition is the prime influence in memory.

Now this illustrates a general principle. Unless our laboratory results are to give us artificialities, mere scientific curiosities, they must be subjected to interpretation by gradual re-approximation to conditions of life. The results may be very accurate, very definitive in form; but the task of reviewing them so as to see their actual import is clearly one of great delicacy and liability to error. The laboratory, in a word, affords no final refuge that enables us to avoid the ordinary scientific difficulties of forming hypotheses, interpreting results, etc. In some sense (from the very accuracy and limitations of its results) it adds to our responsibilities in this direction. Now the school, for psychological purposes, stands in many respects midway between the extreme simplifications of the laboratory and the confused complexities of ordinary life. Its conditions are those of life at large; they are social and practical. But it approaches the laboratory in so far as the ends aimed at are reduced in number, are definite, and thus simplify the conditions; and their psychological phase is uppermost—the formation of habits of attention, observation, memory, etc.—while in ordinary life these are secondary and swallowed up.

If the biological and evolutionary attitude is right in

looking at mind as fundamentally an instrument of adaptation, there are certainly advantages in any mode of approach
which brings us near to its various adaptations while they
are still forming, and under conditions selected with special
reference to promoting these adaptations (or faculties). And
this is precisely the situation we should have in a properly
organized system of education. While the psychological
theory would guide and illuminate the practice, acting upon
the theory would immediately test it, and thus criticize it,
bringing about its revision and growth. In the large and open
sense of the words psychology becomes a working hypothesis,
instruction is the experimental test and demonstration of the
hypothesis; the result is both greater practical control and
continued growth in theory.

   II.

   I must remind myself that my purpose does not conclude with a statement of the auxiliary relation of psychology
to education; but that we are concerned with this as a type
case of a wider problem—the relation of psychology to social
practice in general. So far I have tried to show that it is not
in spite of its statement of personal aims and social relations
in terms of mechanism that psychology is useful, but because of this transformation and abstraction. Through reduction of ethical relations to presented objects we are
enabled to get outside of the existing situation; to see it
objectively, not merely in relation to our traditional habits,
vague aspirations and capricious desires. We are able to see
clearly the factors which shape it, and therefore to get an
idea of how it may be modified. The assumption of an identical relationship of physics and psychology to practical life
is justified. Our freedom of action comes through its statement in terms of necessity. By this translation our control is
enlarged, our powers are directed, our energy conserved, our
aims illuminated.
   The school is an especially favorable place in which to
study the availability of psychology for social practice, because in the school the formation of a certain type of social

personality, with a certain attitude and equipment of working powers, is the express aim. In idea, at least, no other purpose restricts or compromises the dominance of the single purpose. Such is not the case in business, politics, and the professions. All these have upon their surface, taken directly, other ends to serve. In many instances these other aims are of far greater immediate importance; the ethical result is subordinate or even incidental. Yet as it profiteth a man nothing to gain the whole world and lose his own self, so indirectly and ultimately all these other social institutions must be judged by the contribution which they make to the value of human life. Other ends may be immediately uppermost, but these ends must in turn be means; they must subserve the interests of conscious life or else stand condemned.

In other words, the moment we apply an ethical standard to the consideration of social institutions, that moment they stand on exactly the same level as does the school, viz.: as organs for the increase in depth and area of the realized values of life. In both cases the statement of the mechanism, through which the ethical ends are realized, is not only permissible, but absolutely required. It is not merely incidentally, as a grateful addition to its normal task, that psychology serves us. The essential nature of the standpoint which calls it into existence, and of the abstraction which it performs, is to put in our possession the method by which values are introduced and effected in life. The statement of personality as an object, of social relations as a mechanism of stimuli and inhibitions, is precisely the statement of ends in terms of the method of their realization.

It is remarkable that men are so blind to the futility of a morality which merely blazons ideals, erects standards, asserts laws without finding in them any organic provision for their own realization. For ideals are held up to follow; standards are given to work by; laws are provided to guide action. The sole and only reason for their conscious moral statement is, in a word, that they may influence and direct conduct. If they cannot do this, not merely by accident, but of their own intrinsic nature, they are worse than inert. They are impudent impostors and logical self-contradictions.

When men derive their moral ideals and laws from custom, they also realize them through custom; but when they are in any way divorced from habit and tradition, when they are consciously proclaimed, there must be some substitute for custom as an organ of execution. We must know the method of their operation and know it in detail. Otherwise the more earnestly we insist upon our categorical imperatives, and upon their supreme right of control, the more flagrantly helpless we are as to their actual domination. The fact that conscious, as distinct from customary, morality and psychology have had a historic parallel march, is just the concrete recognition of the necessary equivalence between ends consciously conceived, and interest in the means upon which the ends depend. We have the same reality stated twice over: once as value to be realized, and once as mechanism of realization. So long as custom reigns, as tradition prevails, so long as social values are determined by instinct and habit, there is no conscious question as to the method of their achievement, and hence no need of psychology. Social institutions work of their own inertia, they take the individual up into themselves and carry him along in their own sweep. The individual is dominated by the mass life of his group. Institutions and the customs attaching to them take care of society both as to its ideals and its methods. But when once the values come to consciousness, when once a Socrates insists upon the organic relation of a reflective life and morality, then the means, the machinery by which ethical ideals are projected and manifested, comes to consciousness also. Psychology must needs be born as soon as morality becomes reflective.

Moreover, psychology, as an account of the mechanism of workings of personality, is the only alternative to an arbitrary and class view of society, to an aristocratic view in the sense of restricting the realization of the full worth of life to a section of society. The growth of a psychology that, as applied to history and sociology, tries to state the interactions of groups of men in familiar psychical categories of stimulus and inhibition, is evidence that we are ceasing to take existing social forms as final and unquestioned. The application of psychology to social institutions is the only scientific way of dealing with their ethical values in their present unequal distribution, their haphazard execution and their thwarted development. It marks just the recognition of the principle of sufficient reason in the large matters of social life. It is the recognition that the existing order is determined neither by fate nor by chance, but is based on law and order, on a system of existing stimuli and modes of reaction, through knowledge of which we can modify the practical outcome. There is no logical alternative save either to recognize and search for the mechanism of the interplay of personalities that controls the existing distributions of values, *or* to accept as final a fixed hierarchy of persons in which the leaders assert, on no basis save their own supposed superior personality, certain ends and laws which the mass of men passively receive and imitate. The effort to apply psychology to social affairs means that the determination of ethical values lies not in any set or class, however superior, but in the workings of the social whole; that the explanation is found in the complex interactions and interrelations which constitute this whole. To save personality in all, we must serve all alike —state the achievements of all in terms of mechanism, that is, of the exercise of reciprocal influence. To affirm personality independent of mechanism is to restrict its full meaning to a few, and to make its expression in the few irregular and arbitrary.

The anomaly in our present social life is obvious enough. With tremendous increase in control of nature, in ability to utilize nature for the indefinite extension and multiplication of commodities for human use and satisfaction, we find the actual realization of ends, the enjoyment of values growing unassured and precarious. At times it seems as if we were caught in a contradiction; the more we multiply means, the less certain and general is the use we are able to make of them. No wonder a Carlyle or a Ruskin puts our whole industrial civilization under a ban, while a Tolstoi proclaims a return to the desert. But the only way to see the situation steadily, and to see it as a whole, is to keep in mind that the entire problem is one of the development of science, *and of its application to life*. Our control of nature with the accompanying output of material commodities is the necessary result of the growth of physical science—of our ability to state things as interconnected parts of a mechanism. Physical science has for the time being far outrun psychical. We have mastered the physical mechanism sufficiently to turn out possible goods; we have not gained a knowledge of the conditions through which possible values become actual in life, and so are still at the mercy of habit, of haphazard, and hence of force.

Psychology, after all, simply states the mechanism through which conscious value and meaning are introduced into human experience. As it makes its way, and is progressively applied to history and all the social sciences, we can anticipate no other outcome than increasing control in the ethical sphere—the nature and extent of which can be best judged by considering the revolution that has taken place in the control of physical nature through a knowledge of her order. Psychology will never provide ready-made materials and prescriptions for the ethical life, any more than physics dictates off-hand the steam-engine and the dynamo. But science, both physical and psychological, makes known the conditions upon which certain results depend, and therefore puts at the disposal of life a method for controlling them. Psychology will never tell us just what to do ethically, nor just how to do it. But it will afford us insight into the conditions which control the formation and execution of aims, and thus enable human effort to expend itself sanely, rationally and with assurance. We are not called upon to be either boasters or sentimentalists regarding the possibilities of our science. It is best, for the most part, that we should stick to our particular jobs of investigation and reflection as they come to us. But we certainly are entitled in this daily work to be sustained by the conviction that we are not working in indifference to or at cross-purposes with the practical strivings of our common humanity. The psychologist, in his most remote and technical occupation with mechanism, is contributing his bit to that ordered knowledge which alone enables mankind to secure a larger and to direct a more equal flow of values in life.

SOME STAGES OF LOGICAL THOUGHT

The man in the street, when asked what he thinks about a certain matter, often replies that he does not think at all; he knows. The suggestion is that thinking is a case of active uncertainty set over against conviction or unquestioning assurance. When he adds that he does not have to think, but knows, the further implication is that thinking, when needed, leads to knowledge; that its purpose or object is to secure stable equilibrium. It is the purpose of this paper to show some of the main stages through which thinking, understood in this way, actually passes in its attempt to reach its most effective working; that is, the maximum of reasonable certainty.

I wish to show how a variety of modes of thinking, easily recognizable in the progress of both the race and the individual, may be identified and arranged as successive species of the relationship which doubting bears to assurance; as various ratios, so to speak, which the vigor of doubting bears to mere acquiescence. The presumption is that the function of questioning is one which has continually grown in intensity and range, that doubt is continually chased back, and, being cornered, fights more desperately, and thus clears the ground more thoroughly. Its successive stations or arrests constitute stages of thinking. Or to change the metaphor, just in the degree that what has been accepted as fact—the object of assurance—loses stable equilibrium, the tension involved in the questioning attitude increases, until a readjustment gives a new and less easily shaken equilibrium.

The natural tendency of man is not to press home a doubt, but to cut inquiry as short as possible. The practical man's impatience with theory has become a proverb; it

[First published in *Philosophical Review* 9 (1900): 465–89. Revised and reprinted in *Essays in Experimental Logic* (Chicago: University of Chicago Press, 1916), pp. 183–219.]

expresses just the feeling that, since the thinking process is of use only in substituting certainty for doubt, any apparent prolongation of it is useless speculation, wasting time and diverting the mind from important issues. To follow the line of least resistance is to cut short the stay in the sphere of doubts and suggestions, and to make the speediest return into the world where one can act. The result, of course, is that difficulties are evaded or surmounted rather than really disposed of. Hence, in spite of the opposition of the would-be practical man, the needs of practice, of economy, and of efficiency have themselves compelled a continual deepening of doubt and widening of the area of investigation.

It is within this evolution that we have to find our stages of thinking. The initial stage is where the doubt is hardly endured but not entertained; it is no welcome guest but an intruder, to be got rid of as speedily as possible. Development of alternative and competitive suggestions, the forming of suppositions (of ideas), goes but a little way. The mind seizes upon the nearest or most convenient instrument of dismissing doubt and re-attaining security. At the other end is the definitive and conscious search for problems, and the development of elaborate and systematized methods of investigation—the industry and technique of science. Between these limits come processes which have started out upon the path of doubt and inquiry, and then halted by the way.

In the first stage of the journey, beliefs are treated as something fixed and static. To those who are using them they are simply another kind of fact. They are used to settle doubts, but the doubts are treated as arising quite outside the ideas themselves. Nothing is further from recognition than that ideas themselves are open to doubt, or need criticism and revision. Indeed, the one who uses static meanings is not even aware that they originated and have been elaborated for the sake of dealing with conflicts and problems. The ideas are just "there," and they may be used like any providential dispensation to help men out of the troubles into which they have fallen.

Words are generally held responsible for this fixation of the idea, for this substantiation of it into a kind of thing.

A long line of critics has made us familiar with the invincible habit "of supposing that wherever there is a name there is some reality corresponding to it"; of supposing that general and abstract words have their equivalent objects somewhere *in rerum natura*, as have also singular and proper names. We know with what simplicity of self-confidence the English empirical school has accounted for the ontological speculation of Plato. Words tend to fix intellectual contents, and give them a certain air of independence and individuality. That some truth is here expressed there can be no question. Indeed, the attitude of mind of which we are speaking is well illustrated in the person who goes to the dictionary in order to settle some problem in morals, politics, or science; who would end some discussion regarding a material point by learning what meaning is attached to terms by the dictionary as authority. The question is taken as lying outside of the sphere of science or intellectual inquiry, since the meaning of the word—the idea—is unquestionable and fixed.

But this petrifying influence of words is after all only a superficial explanation. There must be some meaning present or the word could not fix it; there must be something which accounts for the disposition to use names as a medium of fossilization. There is, in truth, a certain real fact—an existent reality—behind both the word and the meaning it stands for. This reality is social usage. The person who consults a dictionary *is* getting an established fact when he turns there for the definition of a term. He finds the sense in which the word is currently used. Social customs are no less real than physical events. It is not possible to dispose of this fact of common usage by reference to mere convention, or any other arbitrary device. A form of social usage is no more an express invention than any other social institution. It embodies the permanent attitude, the habit taken towards certain recurring difficulties or problems in experience. Ideas, or meanings fixed in terms, show the scheme of values which the community uses in appraising matters that need consideration and which are indeterminate or unassured. They are held up as standards for all its members to follow. Here is the solution of the paradox. The fixed or static idea is a fact expressing an established social attitude, a custom. It is not merely verbal, because it denotes a force which operates, as all customs do, in controlling particular cases. But since it marks a mode of interpretation, a scheme for assigning values, a way of dealing with doubtful cases, it falls within the sphere of ideas. Or, coming to the life of the individual, the fixed meaning represents, not a state of consciousness fixed by a name, but a recognition of a habitual way of belief: a habit of understanding.

We find an apt illustration of fixed ideas in the rules prevalent in primitive communities, rules which minutely determine all acts in which the community as a whole is felt to have an interest. These rules are facts because they express customs, and carry with them certain sanctions. Their meaning does not cease with judicial utterance. They are made valid at once in a practical way against anyone who departs from them. Yet as rules they are ideas, for they express general ways of defining doubtful matters in experience, and of re-establishing certainty. An individual may fail in acknowledgment of them and explicit reference is then necessary. For one who has lost himself in the notion that ideas are psychical and subjective, I know of no better way to appreciate the significance of an idea than to consider that a social rule of judgment is nothing but a certain way of viewing or interpreting facts; as such it is an idea.

The point that is of special interest to us here, however, is that these ideas are taken as fixed and unquestionable, and that the cases to which they are to apply are regarded as in themselves equally fixed. So far as concerns the attitude of those who employ this sort of ideas, the doubt is simply as to what idea should be in a particular case. Even the Athenian Greeks, for instance, long kept up the form of indicting and trying a tree or implement through which some individual had been killed. There was a rule—a fixed idea—for dealing with all who offended against the community by destroying one of its citizens. The fact that an inanimate object, a thing without intention or volition, offended was not a material circumstance. It made no difference in the case; that is, there was no doubt as to the nature of the fact. It was as fixed as was the rule.

With advance in the complexity of life, however, rules

accumulate, and discrimination—that is, a certain degree of inquiring and critical attitude—enters in. Inquiry takes effect, however, in seeking among a collection of fixed ideas just the one to be used, rather than in directing suspicion against any rule or idea as such, or in an attempt to discover or constitute a new one. It is hardly necessary to refer to the development of casuistry, or to the multiplication of distinctions within dogmas, or to the growth of ceremonial law in cumbrous detail, to indicate what the outcome of this logical stage is likely to be. The essential thing is that doubt and inquiry are directed neither at the nature of the intrinsic fact itself, nor at the value of the idea as such, but simply at the manner in which one is attached to the other. Thinking falls outside both fact and idea, and into the sphere of their external connection. It is still a fiction of judicial procedure that there is already in existence some custom or law under which every possible dispute—that is, every doubtful or unassured case—falls, and that the judge only declares which law is applicable in the particular case. This point of view has tremendously affected the theory of logic in its historic development.

One of the chief, perhaps the most important instrumentalities in developing and maintaining fixed ideas is the need of instruction and the way in which it is given. If ideas were called into play only when doubtful cases actually arise, they could not help retaining a certain amount of vitality and flexibility; but the community always instructs its new members as to its way of disposing of these cases before they present themselves. Ideas are proffered, in other words, separated from present doubt, and remote from application, in order to escape future difficulties and the need of any thinking. In primitive communities this is the main purport of instruction, and it remains such to a very considerable degree. There is a pre-judgment rather than judgment proper. When the community uses its resources to fix certain ideas in the mind—that is, certain ways of interpreting and regarding experience—ideas are necessarily formulated so as to assume a rigid and independent form. They are doubly removed from the sphere of doubt. The attitude is uncritical and dogmatic in the extreme—so much so that one might question whether it is to be properly designated as a stage of thinking.

In this form ideas become the chief instruments of social conservation. Judicial decision and penal correction are restricted and ineffective methods of maintaining social institutions unchanged, compared with instilling in advance uniform ideas—fixed modes of appraising all social questions and issues. These set ideas thus become the embodiment of the values which any group has realized and intends to perpetuate. The fixation supports them against dissipation through attrition of circumstance, and against destruction through hostile attack. It would be interesting to follow out the ways in which such values are put under the protection of the gods and of religious rites, or themselves erected into quasi-divinities—as among the Romans. This, however, would hardly add anything to the logic of the discussion, although it would indicate the importance attached to the fixation of ideas, and the thoroughgoing character of the means used to secure immobilization.

The conserving value of the dogmatic attitude, the point of view which takes ideas as fixed, is not to be ignored. When society has no methods of science for protecting and perpetuating its achieved values, there is practically no other resort than such crystallization. Moreover, with any possible scientific progress, some equivalent of the fixed idea must remain. The nearer we get to the needs of action the greater absoluteness must attach to ideas. The necessities of action do not await our convenience. Emergencies continually present themselves where the fixity required for successful activity cannot be attained through the medium of investigation. The alternative to vacillation, confusion, and futility of action is importation to ideas of a positive and secured character, not in strict logic belonging to them. It is this sort of determination that Hegel seems to have in mind in what he terms *Verstand*—the understanding. "Apart from *Verstand*," he says, "there is no fixity or accuracy in the region either of theory or practice"; and, again, "*Verstand* sticks to fixity of characters and their distinctions from one another; it treats every meaning as having a subsistence of its own." In technical terminology, also, this is what is meant by "positing" ideas—hardening meanings.

In recognizing, however, that fixation of intellectual content is a pre-condition of effective action, we must not overlook the modification that comes with the advance of thinking into more critical forms. At the outset, fixity is taken as the rightful possession of the ideas themselves; it belongs to them and is their "essence." As the scientific spirit develops, we see that it is we who lend fixity to the ideas, and that this loan is for a purpose to which the meaning of the ideas is accommodated. Fixity ceases to be a matter of intrinsic structure of ideas, and becomes an affair of security in using them. Hence the important thing is the *way* in which we fix the idea—the manner of the inquiry which results in definition. We *take* the idea as if it were fixed, in order to secure the necessary stability of action. The crisis past, the idea drops its borrowed investiture, and reappears as surmise.

When we substitute for ideas, as uniform rules by which to decide doubtful cases, that making over of ideas which is requisite to make them fit, the quality of thought alters. We may fairly say that we have come into another stage. The idea is now regarded as essentially subject to change, as a manufactured article needing to be made ready for use. To determine the conditions of this transition lies beyond my purpose, since I have in mind only a descriptive setting forth of the periods through which, as a matter of fact, thought has passed in the development of the inquiry function, without raising the problem of its "why" and "how." At this point we shall not do more than note that, as the scheduled stock of fixed ideas grows larger, their application to specific questions becomes more difficult, prolonged, and roundabout. There has to be a definite hunting for the specific idea which is appropriate; there has to be comparison of it with other ideas. This comes to involve a certain amount of mutual compromise and modification before selection is possible. The idea thus gets somewhat shaken. It has to be made over so that it may harmonize with other ideas possessing equal worth. Often the very accumulation of fixed ideas commands this reconstruction. The dead weight of the material becomes so great that it cannot sustain itself without a readjustment of the centre of gravity. Simplification and systematization are required, and these call for reflec-

tion. Critical cases come up in which the fiction of an idea
or rule already in existence cannot be maintained. It is impossible to conceal that old ideas have to be radically modified before the situation can be dealt with. The friction of
circumstance melts away their congealed fixity. Judgment
becomes legislative.

Seeking illustrations at large, we find this change typi-
fied in Hebrew history, in the growing importance of the
prophet over the judge, in the transition from a justification
of conduct through bringing particular cases into conformity
with existent laws, into that effected by personal right-
mindedness enabling the individual to see the law in each
case for himself. Profoundly as this changed conception of
the relation between law and particular case affected moral
life, it did not, among Semites, directly influence the logical
sphere. With the Greeks, however, we find a continuous and
marked departure from positive declaration of custom. We
have assemblies meeting to discuss and dispute, and finally,
upon the basis of the considerations thus brought to view, to
decide. The man of counsel is set side by side with the man
of deed. Odysseus was much experienced, not only because
he knew the customs and ways of old, but even more because from the richness of his experience he could make the
pregnant suggestion to meet the new crisis. It is hardly too
much to say that it was the emphasis put by the Greek mind
upon discussion—at first as preliminary to decision, and
afterwards to legislation—which generated logical theory.

Discussion is thus an apt name for this attitude of thought.
It is bringing various beliefs together; shaking one against
another and tearing down their rigidity. It is conversation of
thoughts; it is dialogue—the mother of dialectic in more than
the etymological sense. No process is more recurrent in history than the transfer of operations carried on between different persons into the arena of the individual's own consciousness. The discussion which at first took place by
bringing ideas from different persons into contact, by introducing them into the forum of competition, and by subjecting them to critical comparison and selective decision, finally
became a habit of the individual with himself. He became
a miniature social assemblage, in which pros and cons were

brought into play struggling for the mastery—for final conclusion. In some such way we conceive reflection to be born.

It is evident that discussion, the agitation of ideas, if
judged from the standpoint of the older fixed ideas, is a destructive process. Ideas are not only shaken together and
apart, they are so shaken in themselves that their whole
validity becomes doubtful. Mind, and not merely beliefs, becomes uncertain. The attempt to harmonize different ideas
means that in themselves they are discrepant. The search for
a conclusion means that accepted ideas are only points of
view, and hence personal affairs. Needless to say it was the
Sophists who emphasized and generalized this negative
aspect—this pre-supposition of loss of assurance, of incon-
sistency, of "subjectivity." They took it as applying not only
to this, that, and the other idea, but to ideas as ideas. Since
ideas are no longer fixed contents, they are just expressions
of an individual's way of thinking. Lacking inherent value,
they merely express the interests that induce the individual
to look this way rather than that. They are made by the individual's point of view, and hence will be unmade if he can
be led to change his point of view. Where all was fixity, now
all is instability: where all was certitude, nothing now exists
save opinion based on prejudice, interest, or arbitrary choice.

The modern point of view, while condemning sophistry,
yet often agrees with it in limiting the reflective attitude as
such to self-involution and self-conceit. From Bacon down,
the appeal is to observation, to attention to facts, to concern
with the external world. The sole genuine guarantee of truth
is taken to be appeal to facts, and thinking as such is something different. If reflection is not considered to be merely
variable matter, it is considered to be at least an endless
mulling over of things. It is the futile attempt to spin truth
out of inner consciousness. It is introspection, and theorizing,
and mere speculation.

Such wholesale depreciation ignores the value inherent
even in the most subjective reflection, for it takes the settled
estate which is proof that thought is not needed, or that it
has done its work, as if it supplied the standard for the occasions in which problems are hard upon us, and doubt is
rife. It takes the conditions which come about after and be-

cause we have thought to measure the conditions which call
out thinking. Whenever we really need to reflect, we cannot
appeal directly to the "fact," for the adequate reason that the
stimulus to thinking arises just because "facts" have slipped
away from us. The fallacy is neatly committed by Mill in his
discussion of Whewell's account of the need of mental conception or hypothesis in "colligating" facts. He insists that
the conception is "obtained" from the "facts" in which "it
exists," is "impressed upon us from without," and also that
it is the "darkness and confusion" of the facts that make us
want the conception in order to create "light and order."[1]

Reflection involves running over various ideas, sorting
them out, comparing one with another, trying to get one
which will unite in itself the strength of two, searching for
new points of view, developing new suggestions, guessing,
suggesting, selecting and rejecting. The greater the problem,
and the greater the shock of doubt and resultant confusion
and uncertainty, the more prolonged and more necessary is
the process of "mere thinking." It is a more obvious phase
of biology than of physics, of sociology than of chemistry; but
it persists in established sciences. If we take even a mathematical proposition, not *after* it has been demonstrated —
and is thus capable of statement in adequate logical form —
but while in process of discovery and proof, the operation of
this subjective phase is manifest, so much so, indeed, that
a distinguished modern mathematician has said that the
paths which the mathematical inquirer traverses in any new
field are more akin to those of the experimentalist, and
even to those of the poet and artist, than to those of the
Euclidean geometer.

What makes the essential difference between modern
research and the reflection of, say, the Greeks, is not the
absence of "mere thinking," but the presence of conditions
for testing its results; the elaborate system of checks and
balances found in the technique of modern experimentation.
The thinking process does not now go on endlessly in terms
of itself, but seeks outlet through reference to particular
experiences. It is tested by this reference; not, however, as

1. *Logic*, Bk. IV, ch. 2, § 2.

if a theory could be tested by directly comparing it with facts—an obvious impossibility—but through use in facilitating commerce with facts. It is tested as glasses are tested; things are looked at through the medium of specific meanings to see if thereby they assume a more orderly and clearer aspect, if they are less blurred and obscure.

The reaction of the Socratic school against the Sophistic may serve to illustrate the third stage of thinking. This movement was not interested in the *de facto* shaking of received ideas and a discrediting of all thinking. It was concerned rather with the virtual appeal to a common denominator involved in bringing different ideas into relation with one another. In their comparison and mutual modification it saw evidence of the operation of a standard permanent meaning passing judgment upon their conflict, and revealing a common principle and standard of reference. It dealt not with the shaking and dissolution, but with a comprehensive permanent Idea finally to emerge. Controversy and discussion among different individuals may result in extending doubt, manifesting the incoherency of accepted ideas, and so throwing an individual into an attitude of distrust. But it also involves an appeal to a single thought to be accepted by both parties, thus putting an end to the dispute. This appeal to a higher court, this possibility of attaining a total and abiding intellectual object, which should bring into relief the agreeing elements in contending thoughts, and banish the incompatible factors, animated the Socratic search for the concept, the elaboration of the Platonic hierarchy of Ideas in which the higher substantiate the lower, and the Aristotelian exposition of the systematized methods by which general truths may be employed to prove propositions otherwise doubtful. At least this historic development will serve to illustrate what is involved in the transition from the second to the third stage; the transformation of discussion into reasoning, of subjective reflection into method of proof.

Discussion, whether with ourselves or others, goes on by suggestion of clues, as the uppermost object of interest opens a way here or there. It is discursive and haphazard. This gives it the devious tendency indicated in Plato's remark that it needs to be tied to the post of reason. It needs, that is, to have the ground or basis of its various component statements brought to consciousness in such a way as to define the exact value of each. The Socratic contention is the need of compelling the common denominator, the common subject underlying the diversity of views, to exhibit itself. It alone gives a sure standard by which the claims of all assertions may be measured. Until this need is met, discussion is a self-deceiving play with unjudged, unexamined matters, which, confused and shifting, impose themselves upon us.

We are familiar enough with the theory that the Socratic universal, the Platonic idea, was generated by an ignorant transformation of psychological abstractions into self-existent entities. To insist upon this as the key to the Socratic logic is mere caricature. The objectivity of the universal stood for the sense of something decisive and controlling in all reflection, which otherwise is just manipulation of personal prejudices. This sense is as active in modern science as it was in the Platonic dialectic. What Socrates felt was the opinionated, conceited quality of the terms used in the moral and political discussion of his day, as that contrasted with the subject-matter, which, if rightly grasped, would put an end to mere views and argumentations.

By Aristotle's time the interest was not so much in the existence of standards of decision in cases of doubt and dispute as in the technique of their use. The judge was firmly seated on the bench. The parties in controversy recognized his jurisdiction, and their respective claims were submitted for adjudicature. The need was for rules of procedure by which the judge might, in an obvious and impartial way, bring the recognized universal or decisive law to bear upon particular matters. Hence the elaboration of those rules of evidence, those canons of demonstrative force, which are the backbone of the Aristotelian logic. There was a code by which to decide upon the admissibility and value of proffered testimony—the rules of the syllogism. The figures and terms of the syllogism provided a scheme for deciding upon the exact bearing of every statement propounded. The plan of arrangement of major and minor premises, of major, minor, and middle terms, furnished a manifesto of the exact procedure to be followed in determining the probative force of each element in reasoning. The judge knew what testimony to permit, when and how it should be introduced, how it could be impeached or have its competence lessened, and how the evidence was to be arranged so that a summary would also be an exhibit of its value in establishing a conclusion.

This means that there now is a distinctive type of thinking marked off from mere discussion and reflection. It may be called either reasoning or proof. It is reasoning when we think of the regularity of the method for getting at and employing the unquestioned grounds which give validity to other statements. It is proof as regards the degree of logical desert thereby measured out to such propositions. Proof is the acceptance or rejection justified through the reasoning. To quote from Mill: "To give credence to a proposition as a conclusion from something else is to reason in the most extensive sense of the term. We say of a fact or statement, it is proved, when we believe its truth by reason of some other fact or statement from which it is said to follow."[2] Reasoning is marshalling a series of terms and propositions until we can bind some doubtful fact firmly to an unquestioned, although remote, truth; it is the regular way in which a certain proposition is brought to bear on a precarious one, clothing the latter with something of the peremptory quality of the former. So far as we reach this result, and so far as we can exhibit each step in the nexus and be sure it has been rightly performed, we have proof.

But questions still face us. How about that truth upon which we fall back as guaranteeing the credibility of other statements—how about our major premise? Whence does it derive its guarantee? *Quis custodes custodiet*?

We may, of course, in turn subsume it under some further major premise, but an infinite regress is impossible, and on this track we are finally left hanging in the air. For *practical* purposes, the unquestioned principle may be taken as signifying mutual concession or agreement—it denotes

---

2. *Logic*, Bk. II, ch. 1, § 1. I have changed the order of the sentences quoted, and have omitted some phrases.

that as a matter of fact its truth is not called in question by the parties concerned. This does admirably for settling arguments and controversies. It is a good way of amicably arranging matters among those already friends and fellow citizens. But scientifically, the widespread acceptance of an idea seems to testify to custom rather than to truth; prejudice is strengthened in influence, but hardly in value, by the number who share it; conceit is none the less self-conceit because it turns the heads of many.

Great interest was indeed afterward taken in the range of persons who hold truths in common. The *quod semper ubique omnibus* became of great importance. This, however, was not, in theory at least, because common agreement was supposed to constitute the major premise, but because it afforded confirmatory evidence of its self-evident and universal character.

Hence the Aristotelian logic necessarily assumes certain first or fundamental truths unquestioned and unquestionable, self-evident and self-evidencing, neither established nor modified by thought, but standing firm in their own right. This assumption was not, as modern dealers in formal logic would sometimes have it, an external psychological or metaphysical attachment to the theory of reasoning, to be omitted at will from logic as such. It was an essential factor of knowledge that there should be necessary propositions directly apprehended by reason and particular ones directly apprehended by sense. Reasoning could then join them. Without the truths we have only the play of subjective, arbitrary, futile opinion. *Judgment* has not taken place, and assertion is without warrant. Hence the scheduling of first truths is an organic part of any reasoning which is occupied with securing demonstration, surety of assent, or valid conviction. To deny the necessary place of ultimate truths in the logical system of Aristotle and his followers is to make them players in a game of social convention. It is to overlook, to invert, the fact that they were sincerely concerned with the question of attaining the grounds and process of assurance. Hence they were obliged to assume primary intuitions, metaphysical, physical, moral, and mathematical axioms, in order to get the pegs of certainty to which to tie the bundles of otherwise contingent propositions.

It would be going too far to claim that the regard for the authority of the church, of the fathers, of the Scriptures, of ancient writers, of Aristotle himself, so characteristic of the Middle Ages, was the direct outcome of this pre-supposition of truths fixed and unquestionable in themselves. But the logical connection is sure. The supply of absolute premises that Aristotle was able to proffer was scant. In his own generation and situation this paucity made comparatively little difference; for to the mass of men the great bulk of values was still carried by custom, by religious belief, and social institution. It was only in the comparatively small sphere of persons who had come under the philosophic influence, that need for the logical mode of confirmation was felt. In the mediæval period, however, all important beliefs required to be concentrated by some fixed principle giving them stay and power, for they were contrary to obvious common sense and natural tradition. The situation was exactly such as to call into active use the Aristotelian scheme of thought. Authority supplemented the meagreness of the store of universals known by direct intuition, the Aristotelian plan of reasoning afforded the precise instrumentality through which the vague and chaotic details of life could be reduced to order by subjecting them to authoritative rules.

It is not enough, however, to account for the ultimate major premises, for the unconditioned grounds upon which credibility is assigned. We have also to report where the other side comes from: matters so uncertain in themselves as to require that they have their grounds supplied from outside. The answer in the Aristotelian scheme is an obvious one. It is the very nature of sense, of ordinary experience, to supply us with matters which in themselves are only contingent. There is a certain portion of the intellectual sphere, that derived from experience, which is infected throughout by its unworthy origin. It stands forever condemned to be merely empirical—particular, more or less accidental, inherently irrational. You cannot make gold from dross, and the best that can be done for and with material of this sort is to bring it under the protection of truth which has warrant and weight in itself.

We may now characterize this stage of thinking with reference to our original remark that different stages denote various degrees in the evolution of the doubt-inquiry function. As compared with the period of fixed ideas, doubt is awake, and inquiry is active, but in itself it is rigidly limited. On one side it is bounded by fixed ultimate truths, whose very nature is that they cannot be doubted, which are not products or functions in inquiry, but bases that investigation fortunately rests upon. In the other direction all "matters of fact," all "empirical truths" belong to a particular sphere or kind of existence, and one intrinsically open to suspicion. The region is condemned in a wholesale way. In itself it exhales doubt; it cannot be reformed; it is to be shunned, or, if this is not possible, to be escaped from by climbing up a ladder of intermediate terms until we lay hold on the universal. The very way in which doubt is objectified, taken all in a piece, marks its lack of vitality. It is arrested and cooped up in a particular place. As with any doubtful character, the less of its company the better. Uncertainty is not realized as a necessary instrument in compelling experienced matters to reveal their meaning and inherent order.

This limitation upon inquiry settles the interpretation to be given thought at this stage—it is of necessity merely connective, merely mediating. It goes between the first principles—themselves, as to their validity, outside the province of thought—and the particulars of sense—also, as to their status and worth, beyond the dominion of thought. Thinking is subsumption—just placing a particular proposition under its universal. It is inclusion, finding a place for some questioned matter within a region taken as more certain. It is use of general truths to afford support to things otherwise shaky—an application that improves their standing, while leaving their content unchanged. This means that thought has only a formal value. It is of service in exhibiting and arranging grounds upon which any particular proposition may be acquitted or condemned, upon which anything already current may be assented to, or upon which belief may reasonably be withheld.

The metaphor of the law court is apt. There is assumed some matter to be either proved or disproved. As matter, as content, it is furnished. It is not to be found out. In the law court it is not a question of discovering what a man specifically is, but simply of finding reasons for regarding him as guilty or innocent. There is no all-around play of thought directed to the institution of something as fact, but a question of whether grounds can be adduced justifying acceptance of some proposition already set forth. The significance of such an attitude comes into relief when we contrast it with what is done in the laboratory. In the laboratory there is no question of proving that things are just thus and so, or that we must accept or reject a given statement; there is simply an interest in finding out what sort of things we are dealing with. Any quality or change that presents itself may be an object of investigation, or may suggest a conclusion, for it is judged, not by reference to preëxistent truths, but by its suggestiveness, by what it may lead to. The mind is open to inquiry in any direction. Or we may illustrate by the difference between the auditor and an actuary in an insurance company. One simply passes and rejects, issues vouchers, compares and balances statements already made out. The other investigates any one of the items of expense or receipt; inquires how it comes to be what it is, what facts, as regards, say, length of life, condition of money market, activity of agents, are involved, and what further researches and activities are indicated.

The illustrations of the laboratory and the expert remind us of another attitude of thought in which investigation attacks matters hitherto reserved. The growth, for example, of freedom of thought during the Renaissance was a revelation of the intrinsic momentum of the thought-process itself. It was not a mere reaction from and against mediæval scholasticism. It was the continued operation of the machinery which the scholastics had set a-going. Doubt and inquiry were extended into the region of particulars, of matters of fact, with the view of reconstituting them through discovery of their own structure, no longer with the intention of leaving that unchanged while transforming their claim to credence by connecting them with some authoritative principles. Thought no longer found satisfaction in appraising them in a scale of values according to their nearness to, or remoteness from, fixed truths. Such work had been done to a nicety, and it was futile to repeat it. Thinking must find a new outlet. It was out of employment, and set to discover new lands. Galileo and Copernicus were travelers—as much so as the crusader, Marco Polo, and Columbus.

Hence the fourth stage—covering what is popularly known as inductive and empirical science. Thought takes the form of inference instead of proof. Proof, as we have already seen, is accepting or rejecting a given proposition on the ground of its connection or lack of connection with some other proposition conceded or established. But inference does not terminate in any given proposition; it is after precisely those not given. It wants more facts, different facts. Thinking in the mode of inference insists upon terminating in an intellectual advance, in a consciousness of truths hitherto escaping us. Our thinking must not now "pass" certain propositions after challenging them, must not admit them because they exhibit certain credentials, showing a right to be received into the upper circle of intellectual society. Thinking endeavors to compel things as they present themselves, to yield up something hitherto obscure or concealed. This advance and extension of knowledge through thinking seems to be well designated by the term "inference." It does not certify what is otherwise doubtful, but "goes from the known to the unknown." It aims at pushing out the frontiers of knowledge, not at marking those already attained with sign-posts. Its technique is not a scheme for assigning status to beliefs already possessed, but is a method for making friends with facts and ideas hitherto alien. Inference reaches out, fills in gaps. Its work is measured not by the patents of standing it issues, but by the material increments of knowledge it yields. *Inventio* is more important than *judicium*, discovery than "proof."

With the development of empirical research, uncertainty or contingency is no longer regarded as infecting in a wholesale way an entire region, discrediting it save as it can be brought under the protecting ægis of universal truths as major premises. Uncertainty is now a matter of detail. It is the question whether the particular fact is really what it has been taken to be. It involves contrast, not of a fact as a fixed particular over against some fixed universal, but of the existing mode of apprehension with another possible better apprehension.

From the standpoint of reasoning and proof, the intellectual field is absolutely measured out in advance. Certainty is located in one part, intellectual indeterminateness or uncertainty in another. But when thinking becomes research, when the doubt-inquiry function comes to its own, the problem is just: What is the fact?

Hence the extreme interest in details as such; in observing, collecting, and comparing particular causes, in analysis of structure down to its constituent elements, interest in atoms, cells, and in all matters of arrangement in space and time. The microscope, telescope, and spectroscope, the scalpel and microtome, the kymograph and the camera are not mere material appendages to thinking; they are as integral parts of investigative thought as were *Barbara, Celarent*, etc., of the logic of reasoning. Facts must be discovered, and to accomplish this, apparent "facts" must be resolved into their elements. Things must be readjusted in order to be held free from intrusion of impertinent circumstance and misleading suggestion. Instrumentalities of extending and rectifying research are, therefore, of themselves organs of thinking. The specialization of the sciences, the almost daily birth of a new science, is a logical necessity— not a mere historical episode. Every phase of experience must be investigated, and each characteristic aspect presents its own peculiar problems which demand, therefore, their own technique of investigation. The discovery of difficulties, the substitution of doubt for quiescent acceptance, are more important than the sanctioning of belief through proof. Hence the importance of noting apparent exceptions, negative instances, extreme cases, anomalies. The interest is in the discrepant because that stimulates inquiry, not in the fixed universal which would terminate it once for all. Hence the roaming over the earth and through the skies for new facts which may be incompatible with old theories, and which may suggest new points of view.

To illustrate these matters in detail would be to write the history of every modern science. The interest in multiplying phenomena, in increasing the area of facts, in developing new distinctions of quantity, structure, and form, is obviously characteristic of modern science. But we do not always heed its logical significance—that it makes thinking to consist in the extension and control of contact with new material so as to lead regularly to the development of new experience.

The elevation of the region of facts—the formerly condemned region of the inherently contingent and variable—to something that invites and rewards inquiry, defines the import, therefore, of the larger aspects of modern science. This spirit prides itself upon being positivistic—it deals with the observed and the observable. It will have naught to do with ideas that cannot verify themselves by showing themselves *in propria persona*. It is not enough to present credentials from more sovereign truths. These are hardly acceptable even as letters of introduction. Refutation of Newton's claim, that he did not make hypotheses, by pointing out that no one was busier in this direction than he, and that scientific power is generally in direct ratio to ability to imagine possibilities, is as easy as it is irrelevant. The hypotheses, the thoughts, that Newton employed were of and about fact; they were for the sake of exacting and extending what can be apprehended. Instead of being sacrosanct truths affording a redemption by grace to facts otherwise ambiguous, they were the articulating of ordinary facts. Hence the notion of law changes. It is no longer something governing things and events from on high; it is the statement of their own order.

Thus the exiling of occult forces and qualities is not so much a specific achievement as it is a demand of the changed attitude. When thinking consists in the detection and determination of observable detail, forces, forms, qualities at large, are thrown out of employment. They are not so much proved non-existent as rendered nugatory. Disuse breeds their degeneration. When the universal is but the order of the facts themselves, the mediating machinery disappears along with the essences. There is substituted for the hierarchical world, in which each degree in the scale has its righteousness imputed from above, a world homogeneous in structure and in the scheme of its parts; the same in heaven, earth, and the uttermost parts of the sea. The ladder of values from the sublunary world with its irregular, extravagant, imperfect motion up to the stellar universe, with its self-returning perfect order, corresponded to the middle terms of the older logic. The steps were graduated, ascending from the indeterminate, unassured matter of sense up to the eternal, unquestionable truths of rational perception. But when interest is occupied in finding out what anything and everything is, any fact is just as good as its fellow. The observable world is a democracy. The difference which makes a fact what it is, is not an exclusive distinction, but a matter of position and quantity, an affair of locality and aggregation, traits which place all facts upon the same level, since all other observable facts also possess them, and are, indeed, conjointly responsible for them. Laws are not edicts of a sovereign binding a world of subjects otherwise lawless; they are the agreements, the compacts of facts themselves, or, in the familiar language of Mill, the common attributes, the resemblances.

The emphasis of modern science upon control flows from the same source. Interest is in the new, in extension, in discovery. Inference is the advance into the unknown, the use of the established to win new worlds from the void. This requires and employs regulation—that is, method—in procedure. There cannot be a blind attack. A plan of campaign is needed. Hence the so-called practical applications of science, the Baconian "knowledge is power," the Comteian "science is prevision," are not extra-logical addenda or supererogatory benefits. They are intrinsic to the logical method itself, which is just the orderly way of approaching new experiences so as to grasp and hold them.

The attitude of research is necessarily towards the future. The application of science to the practical affairs of life, as in the stationary engine, or telephone, does not differ in principle from the determination of wave-lengths of light through the experimental control of the laboratory. Science lives only in arranging for new contacts, new insights. The school of Kant agrees with that of Mill in asserting that judgment must, in order to be judgment, be synthetic or instructive; it must extend, inform, and purvey. When we recognize that this service of judgment in effecting growth of experience is not accidental, but that judgment means exactly the devising and using of suitable instrumentalities for this end, we remark that the so-called practical uses of science are only the further and freer play of the intrinsic movement of discovery itself.

We began with the assumption that thought is to be interpreted as a doubt-inquiry function, conducted for the purpose of arriving at that mental equilibrium known as assurance or knowledge. We assumed that various stages of thinking could be marked out according to the amount of play which they give to doubt, and the consequent sincerity with which thinking is identified with free inquiry. Modern scientific procedure, as just set forth, seems to define the ideal or limit of this process. It is inquiry emancipated, universalized, whose sole aim and criterion is discovery, and hence it marks the terminus of our description. It is idle to conceal from ourselves, however, that scientific procedure, as a practical undertaking, has not as yet reflected itself into any coherent and generally accepted theory of thinking, into any accepted doctrine of logic which is comparable to the Aristotelian. Kant's conviction that logic is a "complete and settled" science, which with absolutely "certain boundaries has gained nothing and lost nothing since Aristotle," is startlingly contradicted by the existing state of discussion of logical doctrine. The simple fact of the case is that there are at least three rival theories on the ground, each claiming to furnish the sole proper interpretation of the actual procedure of thought.

The Aristotelian logic is far from having withdrawn its claim. It still offers its framework as that into which the merely "empirical" results of observation and experimental inquiry must be fitted if they are to be regarded as really "proved." Another school of logicians, starting professedly from modern psychology, discredits the whole traditional industry, and reverses the Aristotelian theory of validity; it holds that only particular facts are self-supporting, and that the authority allowed to general principles is derivative and second hand. A third school of philosophy claims, by analysis of science and experience, to justify the conclusion that the universe itself is a construction of thought, giving evidence throughout of the pervasive and constitutive action of reason, and holds, consequently, that our logical processes are simply the reading off or coming to consciousness of the inherently rational structure already possessed by the universe in virtue of the presence within it of this pervasive and constitutive action of thought. It thus denies both the claim of the traditional logic, that matters of experienced fact are mere particulars having their rationality in an external ground, and the claim of the empirical logic, that thought is just a gymnastic by which we vault from one presented fact to another remote in space and time.

Which of the three doctrines is to be regarded as the legitimate exponent of the procedure of thought manifested in modern science? While the Aristotelian logic is willing to waive a claim to be regarded as expounder of the actual procedure, it still insists upon its right to be regarded as the sole ultimate umpire of the validity, or *proved* character of the results reached. But the empirical and transcendental logics stand face to face as rivals, each asserting that it alone tells the story of what science does and how it does it.

With the consciousness of this conflict, my discussion in its present, or descriptive, phase must cease. Its close, however, suggests a further question. In so far as we adopt the conception that thinking is itself a doubt-inquiry process, must we not deny the claims of all of the three doctrines to be the articulate voicing of the methods of experimental science? Do they not all agree in setting up something fixed outside inquiry, supplying both its material and its limit? That the first principle and the empirical matters of fact of the Aristotelian logic fall outside the thinking process, and condemn the latter to a purely external and go-between agency, has been already sufficiently descanted upon. But it is also true that the fixed particulars, given facts, or sensations—whatever the empirical logician starts from—are material given ready-made to the thought-process, and externally limiting inquiry, instead of being distinctions arising within and because of search for truth. Nor, as regards this point, is the transcendental in any position to throw stones at the empirical logic. Thought "in itself" is so far from a process of inquiry that it is taken to be the eternal, fixed structure of the universe; *our* thinking, involving doubt and investigation, is due wholly to our "finite," imperfect character, which condemns us to the task of merely imitating and reinstating "thought" in itself, once and forever complete, ready-made, fixed.

The practical procedure and practical assumptions of modern experimental science, since they make thinking essentially and not merely accidentally a process of discovery, seem irreconcilable with both the empirical and transcendental interpretations. At all events, there is here sufficient discrepancy to give occasion for further search: Does not an account of thinking, basing itself on modern scientific procedure, demand a statement in which all the distinctions and terms of thought—judgment, concept, inference, subject, predicate and copula of judgment, etc., *ad infinitum*—shall be interpreted simply and entirely as distinctive functions or divisions of labor within the doubt-inquiry process?

PRINCIPLES OF MENTAL DEVELOPMENT AS ILLUSTRATED IN EARLY INFANCY

Initiators of new scientific movements balance the obligations of gratitude under which they put their successors, by imposing on them forms of thinking and of classification which the latter only too rigidly follow. The beginning of any new movement always involves compromise. It brings to light new facts and considerations which are ultimately bound greatly to modify, if not to revolutionize, current standards and methods of interpretation. But at the outset the new wine is forced into old bottles. The new material is stowed away in the old pigeon-holes and classified from the point of view of the very rubrics which the material is destined to do away with. This principle is obviously exhibited in the present condition of child psychology. Fixing its attention upon growth, upon continuity of function, its controlling principle is essentially unitary. It will surely be one of the most effective instruments in doing away with the arbitrary distinctions and isolations which have constituted the heads for organizing psychical material in the past. It must end by substituting the idea of gradual differentiation for the notion of separate mental faculties, it must end by substituting the conception of organic interdependence and cooperation for the notion of mechanical juxtaposition and external association.

But, due chiefly probably to the influence of the great pioneer, Preyer, the data of child psychology is still organized under the most arbitrary, and be it added, misleading captions. Preyer, for example, put certain facts under sensation, although in every case the material described involves motor reactions, as is obvious with eye and ear, while much of it involves intelligent discrimination and identification. He in-

[First published in *Transactions of the Illinois Society for Child-Study* 4 (1899): 65–83. Not previously reprinted.]

cludes under the same head of sense, the emotions, which, without doubt, are closely connected with organic sensation, but which with equal certainty are conditioned in many cases, if not all, by motor reactions, and the higher of which, even in his own illustrations, are obviously dependent upon ideas. Under will he isolates certain motor phenomena, although by his own classification many of them are simple responses to sense stimuli, while others are the outcome of ideas. What rational ground can be given for putting the movements of the eye under the head of sensation, while those of the hand belong to will? In the case of the eye there is a coordination of the muscles in response to the stimulus of light; in the case of the hand there is a coordination of muscles in response to stimuli of contact. Surely the chief point, both theoretically and practically, is the unity of the type of process involved. To relegate one fact to the sphere of sensation and another to the compartment of will is to part asunder what God has most assuredly joined together. The same arbitrary isolation is found in relegating deliberate movements entirely to the will, thus disguising their identity of type with simple sensori-motor coordinations. If anything were needed to complete the confusion it is the fact that scarcely anything is now left in Preyer's arrangement for the rubric of intelligence excepting the development of speech— as if speech were not in origin a distinctly motor phenomenon, and all through its earlier development closely conditioned upon the development of wants, desires, and emotional reactions in general.

Recent observers have followed Preyer with only too great literalness. One of the more recent, one of the very best, of the biographical accounts of infancy, introduces a variation in putting all movements under the head of physical development—including even those which aim at the realization of ideas and are executed with effort; while senses, emotion, and intellect are sub-headings under the rubric of psychical development, coordinate with this physical development. I do not mention these facts for the sake of bringing carping criticism against Preyer and his followers. We must ever be grateful to them for the amount of detailed information they have collected, and the thoroughness and accuracy with which they have done the work. But just because so much data has been gathered together, either in unclassified heaps or with a literal adherence to classificatory headings devised before the genetic point of view arose, it becomes at once necessary and possible to search for more intrinsic principles of psychical growth with reference to which to collate and interpret facts. This work is urgently demanded for both practical or pedagogical, and for scientific purposes. Practically many intelligent parents, especially mothers, are repelled from the work of infant observation simply because there appears to be only a jungle of disconnected facts, all on the same level, with no leading points of survey or standards of reference. Moreover, the individuality of the living child is completely concealed in this uncontrolled accumulation of facts with resulting disjointed arrangements. The real child who interests, who holds attention, who is the object of attention and of education, is a living unity. From the concrete and educational standpoint, the mass of particular detail is of worth only as it can be treated as symptoms or indices to the rediscovery of the living unit of development. One reason, probably the chief reason that the results of child-study up to this time have been so comparatively infertile in application to education, is precisely because the forest has been lost in the trees, and a series of classifications under unreal headings like senses, movements, ideas, emotions, have been substituted for the concrete individuality. If you take any one of the half dozen more careful biographies of individual children and succeed in getting more than a slight idea of the character and temperament of the particular child in question, you will be more fortunate than I have been. Such glimpses as one gets at all are through occasional anecdotes and descriptive adjectives incidentally thrown in.

If all this were necessary in the cause of accuracy and thoroughness of science, we should undoubtedly be compelled to put up with it. But just the opposite is the case. Gathering unrelated facts and throwing them together in this disjected and wholesale way marks precisely the scientific, as well as the practical, limitation of current infant psychology. What would be thought of a botanist or a zoölogist who in studying

the life history of a plant or of an animal arbitrarily segre-
gated each change as it showed itself and then afterwards
classified his material under such headings as roots, stems,
leaves, flowers; or under the titles of legs, arms, trunk, and
tail? In a word, through forcing the observed facts under
the captions of the old faculty-psychology, we miss precisely
the peculiar scientific value of the genetic method. The fact
of growth, of continuity, is completely obscured in detail,
even though there may be much talk about it at large.
Growth is reduced to mere chronological sequence—to the
simple statement that certain things happened earlier and
other things later. There is no insight into continuity of
function; no way of connecting earlier and later facts into
a living unity. In any biological study, or study using the
genetic method, while the persistent and minute study of
details is absolutely indispensable, the minutiæ of structure
and the exact succession of changes are of importance simply
as they throw light upon the growth of the life process itself.
It is the life principle which is the real object of study; and
to sort the observed facts into pigeon-holes, irrespective of
their relation to life history, is to have the name but not the
reality of the genetic method.

But enough, probably more than enough, of negative
criticism. This, indeed, has been indulged in simply to define
the problem: the question whether any continuous function
of a typical character can be detected and traced, in its growing differentiations and ramifications, amid all the diversity
of phenomena which the infant life exhibits. As a working
hypothesis, I state that the principle of coordination or of
sensori-motor action supplies us with just such a centralizing principle—a principle which can be employed equally on
the physiological and the psychological side. In popular
language, this unit is an *act*, whether of greater or less complexity. Seeing and hearing are acts just as much as are
reaching, grasping and locomotion. "Sensation" is simply one
element in the act. On the other hand, grasping, speaking,
and creeping are no more merely muscular or motor phenomena than are seeing and hearing; they equally have a
sensory element involved. From a genetic standpoint the eye
and the ear are organs of action, of adjustment to the en-

vironment; while reaching and handling are equally organs for securing certain sensations—certain qualities or values of experience. Their distinction is not found in classing one under the head of sensation, another under the head of movement, and another under the head of intellect. Their differentia is found simply in the particular kind of adjustment set up by each.

As to method, this standpoint, as a working hypothesis, has very marked advantages. In the first place, as already suggested, it brings the physiological and psychological development into line with each other. In the second place, it makes the psychology of an infancy really genetic, that is, it brings it into harmony with the biological standpoint. Biologically the infant is not an isolated object or entity in the universe in whom the having of sensations, impulses, and ideas is a luxury or a mere object for scientific contemplation. He is a being who lives in an environment and who has got to do something in that environment. Biologically the chief thing in growth is precisely the building up and exhibition of the coordinations that enable the necessary adjustments to be made. In the third place, the only thing that can possibly be observed in another is, as Mr. Warner has brought out with great force, movement (*Mental Faculty*). This point of view when developed fixes the attention of the observer upon just what it is that he is to observe, namely, movements. But it also points out what the important thing is with regard to movement, namely, that it is a reaction whose value lies in its efficiency in completing the circuit of some act, or, more technically, of some coordination, or adjustment. The one question that the observer has to keep in mind all the time is simply what mode of action is now building up. The observer is freed from the intricate and fixed classificatory distinctions of sensations, ideas, purposive volition, etc., and his problem is defined simply as the discovery and interpretation of the stimulus which operates in calling out the movement as response.

So much for our general point of view. I propose now to apply it to organize in outline (since the limits of time permit only that) the chief facts already brought out by the great multitude of observers in infant psychology. I shall

start from the act, coordination, or sensori-motor adjustment as the fundamental fact, and attempt to trace the
growth of the act through its typical stages in the first year
or so of infant life.

For convenience I shall group the facts of the first
year or so of infant life under three main heads; not, of
course, that there are any abrupt endings or beginnings, but
trusting to the sequel to show that they are marked off from
each other by a particular type of coordination which, in its
process of formation, centralizes the subordinate facts of
that period. John Fiske has pointed out that the period of
prolonged infancy or individual helplessness is a fact of tremendous social importance. It necessitates something approaching permanency in social groupings and necessitates
habits of care and foresight. But as is often pointed out, it is
a fact of equal psychological importance. The pre-human
animal comes into existence either with coordinations already effected, or with the machinery for a relatively speedy
establishment of them at hand. Prolonged infancy or helplessness means precisely that such coordinations, even the
chief ones, have to be worked out, have to be learned. What
is definite instinct in the animal is unregulated impulsive
tendency in the human young. The child comes into the
world with a tendency to see, hear, reach, grasp, strike,
"locomote," and so on, but with a ready-made ability to do
none of these things. It is this state of affairs, with the necessities that it imposes, which gives the clue to understanding
the first stage of infancy, a period lasting in the rough up to
seventy-five to one hundred days in different children. The
essential characteristic of this epoch is the concomitant
growth of relatively independent systems of coordination
centering in different organs.

Physiological research has shown that the child comes
into the world with only his spinal cord and lower parts of
the brain in functional activity. For all practical purposes
the new-born baby is like an animal deprived of his cerebral
hemispheres. It is virtually a reflex machine; and indeed
there are only a few of the reflexes which are definitely established and even these are easily lost. The three chief ones
are the act of taking food or nursing, and the clutching of

the fingers about any object inserted within them, and the utterance of cries to conditions of temperature, etc., which affect respiration. So far as direct use is concerned, this is practically the child's whole stock in trade. Moreover, physiological research has shown that when the sensory motor brain centres of touching, seeing, hearing, develop in the first month, there are no functional cross-paths of communication. This corresponds precisely with the results of actual observation of the infant activity. When the child who is born practically deaf and blind, begins to see, to feel, and to hear, each of these activities develops independently of the others; each is isolated. Seeing has no meaning with reference to possible experiences of touching or hearing. In seeing, the child is simply learning to follow and fixate light stimuli with the eyes and head; because of lack of cross-reference, meaning or intellectual content does not attach to the activities.

First, upon the whole in order of time, comes the formation of the eye coordination, that is to say, the ability to use the eyes effectively as motor organs in order to control the stimulus of light. This involves at least five or six minor coordinations within itself. In the majority of cases the two eyes do not even work together. Normal associated movements have to be learned. This occurs, as a rule, for the waking hours at least, well within the first month, though uncoordinated movements continue in sleep for about three months, showing that the habit is not so thoroughly formed as to operate when the immediate stimulus of light is absent. Then, early in the second month, comes the capacity to fixate or gaze at an object instead of staring blankly into space. Almost contemporaneous with this is the ability to follow moving light with the two eyes. Almost a month after this comes winking, which, trivial as it is outwardly, is exceedingly important psychically as marking the ability to control the movement of the eye with reference to changes in light and shade. In the third month more definite accommodations with reference to distance begin to show themselves in ability to respond to objects at a distance of some feet away.

Without attempting to follow the development of the

function of other organs in detail, attention may be briefly
called to the hand and arm activity. At first reactions here
take place also comparatively independently, that is, the
stimulus is found in immediate contact of some object with
the hand, not in the activity of some other organ. Clasping
and holding on are the first intimations of this coordination,
they indeed being practically reflexes. Its reflex character
is obvious not only in its early appearance and certainty,
but in the fact that the thumb is not used. The power to
use the thumb, which may be put roughly at the beginning
of the third month, is so important that it might almost be
said to be an index of the transition from the first period
to the second. It shows that the movements of the hand are
no longer excited by bare contact, but have some relevancy
to the object as determined by the eye. Reaching out, grasping, pulling in, are all of them signs that the development
has passed into the second period.

The nature of the considerations upon which the second
period is discriminated from the first will serve to illustrate
a general principle of mental development as well as to provide the thread upon which a variety of apparently disconnected facts are hung. To take the former consideration first:
the characteristic of the first period, as already stated, is the
simultaneous and relatively independent maturing of the
functions corresponding to such organs as eye, ear, and hand
—independence in both a psychical and physiological sense.
But as each one of these functions reaches something like
adequate operation and thus becomes a habit, it ceases to
operate in this isolated way. The stress of activity is now
transferred to the elaboration of larger or more comprehensive coordinations into which two or more of the established habits enter as subordinate and contributing factors.
That which had been an end in itself now becomes a means,
in cooperation with others, to reaching a larger end. As soon
as a function is formed it normally must become at once a
habit or instrument for further use and application. To attempt to maintain it at its isolated culmination means
deterioration, not perfection.

As soon as the eye "follows light" regularly and successfully it can control, by its fixations, accommodations, and

following movements of head and two eyes, the stimulus for reaching and clasping. On the other side, so far as the hand can reach and clasp by itself, it gives something for the eyes to do—it cuts out work for the latter to attend to. The hands work for the sake of bringing things where the eyes can inspect them more successfully, and the eyes look with reference to helping the hands in what they are doing. Here we have an explanation of the fact noted by most observers, though apparently without appreciation of its meaning: viz., the child's expression, in looking, changes at this date. He no longer just blankly stares, or mechanically follows; he seems to watch, to observe. His attitude is inquiring and attentive, and so naturally he appears more intelligent. The reinforcement of tendency of the child to put everything into his mouth at this period has an analogous interpretation. The control now attained of the eye activity taken with the stimulus of hunger, becomes an inducement to the arms to reach and to retract things grasped into the mouth—thus indicating an adjustment of at least three modes of coordination. It is important to note that the histological study of the development of the nervous systems shows that the connecting fibres of so-called centres begin to function at this time.

Other phenomena characteristic of this period are holding the head erect, locating sounds (as evidenced by turning the head), getting bodily equilibrium (in sitting up), and the beginnings of locomotion—creeping, hitching, or rolling. These are clearly all cases of the mutual stimulation and reinforcement of separate types of action. During the first period the activity of the organism is seen in the so-called "random" and "excess" activities—throwing the arms and kicking the legs. These gradually become more and more symmetrical and rhythmic. But this coordination also goes its own way relatively unaffected by what hand, eye, or ear is doing. The stress of activity simply passes from one to another. But in the second period these more massive activities are also stimulated by eye and hand. The child who sees something, or who just touches it, stretches up his head or attempts to lift his whole body. It is at this period that the child, as we say, reaches up his arms to be taken up, or

"lifts up his stomach" (as the nurse says), the moment the
hands of another touch him. We are not justified in supposing that there is conscious desire on the child's part; but
there is certainly the interaction of stimuli. No one, I think,
can watch closely the succession of an infant's attempts to
sit up without seeing that it is very largely conditioned upon
his efforts to reach, grasp, or see and hear better.

The holding of the head erect means the ability to control it effectively with reference to seeing and hearing, and
the further uses to which these powers may be put. It is not
a mere coincidence that capacity to hold it up, and capacity
to turn it surely and accurately in the direction of sounds
are gained about the same time. The attainment of ability to
balance the body, as seen in sitting up, is, however, the
typical form of the principle under consideration, for it
signifies capacity of reciprocal control of touch, sight, hand,
and ear, by one another. It is, literally, a balancing of various
tendencies to act through relation to one another. The interaction of the various functions with one another means that
the organism as a whole is coming into play. Its psychological
equivalent is the possibility of attention.

Hence on the intellectual side the dawning of this coordination, through reciprocal influence of habits previously
formed in isolation, is signalized by the facts which are
summed up in the common remark that the baby is now beginning to be "like folks." The infant is no longer merely objectively cunning in the sense that it is an interesting object
for observation, but is subjectively so in the endeavors it
puts forth and the responses that it makes. There is a dawning of intelligence hardly describable, but recognized by
every parent in changed look of the eye, and in the less
mechanical and more human character of the smile. The
life is distinctly less physical and sensuous. Socially there
is a sympathetic response to the attitudes assumed and
words uttered by others—which has induced many observers
to say that children of three and four months old have
recognized their parents or nurses. These facts are easy to
interpret in the light of the principle already stated. What
we really mean here by the physical and the sensuous is
precisely the directness of reaction to stimulus. When the

eye reacts to light as light, the ear adjusts to sound as sound, and the hand to contact simply as contact, there is no further significance involved. It is stretching the point to speak of intelligence. But when there is translation from the terms of one activity into another, when what is heard means something for what can be seen, and what is seen means something for reaching and handling, there is significance; one experience points to, is a sign of another. It is this cross-reference, this mutuality of excitation and direction, which constitutes the essence of intelligence wherever found.

At the age of about six months power is developed to use sense discriminations as the bases of motor reactions, and motor reactions as ways of controlling the direction of the sense-organs. As one of the signs that the child is ready for a transition, for progress along a new line, may be noted ability to judge reaching distance with the eye. Long after the child gains considerable skill and interest in seizing and retracting, he overestimates and underestimates distances; as is evidenced in underreaching and overreaching. If he does not literally reach for the moon, he might do this, so far as his capacity to judge one experience in terms of another is concerned. But when, about the age of six months, the child ceases to try to get hold of objects not within reaching distance, it shows that a coordination is so effected that he can cash the check drawn by the eye in the medium of contact values. The baby in whom these powers of cross-reference are fairly established is clearly ready for another epoch.

As might be expected, this next period, extending, roughly speaking, to the twelfth or fourteenth month, consists in using the habits now acquired so as to gain new experiences. Evidences of this are seen (1) in the continual experimentations in which the baby engages; (2) in the efforts at locomotion witnessed in creeping; (3) in the emotional and intellectual phenomena of recognition, expectation, and disappointment, and (4) in the crude beginnings of the understanding of language.

By experimental adjustments we mean that the infant uses the motor control which he has secured in order to gain experiences from some other sense. Of course not too much or too intentional purpose should be ascribed to these attempts; but such experiences as the baby crumpling the paper, hearing a noise, and then continuing to rattle and tear in order to hear more sounds, illustrates what is meant. At first, this is doubtless purely accidental. But there is a marked difference between what happens now and what occurred in a previous stage. Then the sound made passed unnoticed. Now it receives sufficient attention so that it serves to keep up the same sort of activity. In the early months of this epoch these experimentations are of course quite crude and immediate. They consist in shaking a rattle to make a noise; in handling, pressing everything touched in order to get experiences of contact, resistance, and muscular power; in carrying the hand over objects, following outlines, to get the feeling of roughness, smoothness, varying degrees of projection and relief of surface; of moving the hands before the eyes, pressing one with the other, etc.; and in general in whatever pounding, twisting movements the child can execute which result in some conscious increment of experience.

Later on, more definite coordinations of the movements and the resulting experiences are secured, so that intentional adjustments, having a certain definite and orderly character occur. Their nature may be illustrated by quoting some observations of increasing degrees of complexity. The first is the case of an infant in its ninth month, recorded by Mrs. Hall (*Child-Study Monthly*). "The child struck a cup with his spoon and liking the sound repeated it several times. He then struck a sauce plate. As this gave a clearer, more ringing sound, he at once noticed the difference. His eyes opened wider and he hit first one and then the other as many as twenty times." The first part of the experience—repeatedly striking the cup to get a sound—is of the direct or primitive type. Such experiences as these constitute the greater part of the child's waking life during these months. Repetition often continues until actual fatigue sets in. But in the latter part of the experience there is evidently distinct adaptation of movements to secure specific sorts of experience. Now take this case occurring in the eleventh month as reported by Preyer. "The child struck several times with a spoon upon a plate. It happened accidentally while he was doing it that he touched the plate with the hand that was free. The sound was dulled and the child noticed the difference. He now took the spoon in the other hand, struck with it on the plate, dulled the sound again, and so on." Here we have, conscious or purposive adjustment. Movements are obviously employed as a means to secure an end which has struck the child's fancy.

The following case, occurring in the tenth month and reported by Mrs. Hall, gives an even more complex adjustment. "The baby was lifted up to look through the window when his attention was attracted by the upper part of the lower window-sash which the child could scarcely reach with the finger tips of his right hand. He succeeded in getting a firm hold and in pulling himself high enough to obtain a hold with the left hand also. In this way he raised himself so that he could look over the sash. After a moment, forgetting that it was his own effort that held him up, he loosened his hold and dropped back to his former level. He repeated the previous effort until he had regained his position, when desiring to grasp the window-shade, he again released his hold and once more dropped back. A third time he raised himself; this time he retained his hold with one hand while he pulled at the shade with the other. When he became tired he changed his hands, not loosening his hold with one hand until he had firmly grasped the sash with the other." Here we have not only certain acts used as means to secure results, but we have search for new means, following upon failure of the old ones and also rhythmical variation in the means employed so as to avoid fatigue and prolong the experience.

In this reciprocal adaptation of movements of the various parts of the body to each other, we have also the clue to the interest which the child takes at this period, first in creeping, and then in attempting to stand—at first, of course, by taking hold of objects. Creeping, which upon the average, comes at about the eighth month, means that the act of seeing suggests to the child the act of handling and manipulating the object seen. The object being out of reach, this cannot accomplish itself directly. As long as the baby cannot judge distance accurately, he has no stimulus to locomotion.

After he can judge reaching distance fairly accurately with the eye, there is still no motive to movement of the whole body, unless the acts of seeing and handling are so persistently coordinated with each other that one suggests the other. Let this be accomplished and the child begins to tip, twitch and contort his whole body in the direction of the thing seen. The child loses his balance and tumbles over a number of times, but gradually gains greater ability to control the movements of the various parts of the body, so as to get towards what is seen, and wanted. Here, then, also we have experimental adjustment—the hitching or creeping comes in as intermediary between a present experience and securing a more remote one. As the child gets a free habit of creeping, he soon, of course, begins to move about just for the fun of doing so—of getting a variety of new experiences; but at first it will be found that the efforts to change the position of the body find their chief motive in the attempts to reach and handle something which appeals to the eye.

On the intellectual side, recognition, expectation and comparison are the exact counterparts of the facts just discussed. In the early months of this period, the child begins to recognize a small number of persons and things which are of recurring importance in his life: mother, nurse, father, bottle, signs of preparation of food, etc. Now, recognition means that an experience reached through one organ does not merely stimulate or set going some other act, but is so definitely coordinated with that other as to be regarded as a sign of it. There is the crude beginning of an image which extends the scope of experience beyond what is immediately present. The sight of the mother, nurse, or bottle suggests other experiences with which it is customarily associated. Expectation, or anticipation, is thus at first always connected with recognition. The child recognizes persons and things on the basis of suggestion of some further experience habitually associated with them and he anticipates on the basis of what he recognizes. Both recognition and anticipation involve a presented experience and an imaged experience which are related as factors in a larger experience.

Comparison comes in here with more conscious recognition of the relationship. The infant compares different means with reference to the different results they accomplish, and *vice versa.* Recall for example, the instances quoted of striking, first a cup and then a saucer in order to get two different sounds; or the striking of a plate when the hand touched it and when it did not in order to secure two different sorts of sounds. There is, of course, no comparison in the abstract sense—that is, in the sense of an intellectual operation entirely separated from any practical end; but none the less the consciousness of two alternative results to be got by two different acts, involves comparison. Or, again, comparison may be seen in the selection of acts to serve as means in order to accomplish a desired end. This is obvious in the instance quoted of the effort of the child to maintain a standing position and at the same time play with the window shade.

When an image, however dim and crude, is formed, so that there is recognition and expectation, emotions, as distinct from direct pleasures and pains, begin also. The child up to this time has felt comfort when experiencing the satisfaction of hunger and agreeable bath, etc., and discomfort under opposite circumstances. But in these cases the occasion for the pleasure or pain is immediately operating on the child. But when the baby first shows irritation or anger at the loss of some object it is playing with, disappointment at not getting something which was expected, we have a feeling occasioned through the intervention of an image. The baby, for instance, is playing with a bright ring which rolls out of reach or is taken away from it; he begins to cry. The first occurrence of such an event marks a distinct epoch of development. It shows that an experience persists as an image when it ceases as a direct affair, and through its existence in the form of an image is capable of influencing the baby's sense of satisfaction. Such experiences happening in the sixth or seventh month are soon followed by evidences of obvious disappointment, as when the baby, catching sight of its bottle, cries when he does not receive it. This would be impossible unless some image, however vague, of satisfaction had intervened and then been frustrated. The change in the character of the baby's smile from something mechanical to something seemingly intelligent points in the same direction. The child takes evident pleasure in the presence of others, and often from the ninth or tenth month cries when left alone—to all

appearances simply from a sense of being alone. So, too, the
infant shows evident fear in the presence of unfamiliar persons; surprise when he finds himself in new surroundings
and oftentimes great pleasure in the return of mother or
nurse after an absence of hours or in some cases of days or
even weeks. There also is a certain pleasure taken in accomplishment, in the successful realization of an end. Here
we are standing upon rather slippery ground; but there can
be no mistaking the sense of elation which the baby shows
toward the end of this period when he first manages to stand
alone, or, the beginnings of personally referred emotions in
the child who, upon doing something, endeavors to attract the
attention of others before repeating it, and who then continues or discontinues according to the amount of attention
received.

During this period there are the beginnings of a sense of
language. Only in rare cases, does the infant employ more
than a few words as signs of objects, but in most instances
there is some understanding, not only of different tones of
the voice, but of some specific sounds. This, of course, means
that coordinations of an even more indirect character than
those already specified are forming. At first the sound may be
hardly more than an associated gesture, as when the baby
learns to say "by-by" and wave its hand. But when he shows
signs of expectation or of contentment upon hearing the word
"bottle" or "outdoors," the image certainly has no very direct
connection with what he has immediately experienced. It
marks quite an intellectual gain when the baby begins to
anticipate going outdoors upon seeing its bonnet and cloak.
But these at least have some actual connection with the going
out; they are really parts of the whole activity. But the word
"outdoors" bears no such relation. It cannot be directly
significant of what is going to happen, but only through the
conscious intervention in the child's mind of some further
image. Here then the child is entering upon ability to form
indirect and remote coordinations of a type to which no limit
can be fixed.

It is hardly necessary to insist that apprehension of the
meaning of words is an experience of the same type as the
others just discussed. It is simply a striking case—perhaps
the most striking—of using an experience derived through

one set of organs to secure experiences through the medium of another set. In the first period of a child's life an agreeable sound will often quiet restlessness, causing a cessation of a variety of motions; but it does so simply by concentrating all energy in a given path of discharge. In the second period, the child makes certain sounds recognized by those about him, proceeding from hunger, pain, impatience, or importunity. So far as others are concerned, these sounds serve as signs, but they are not consciously used as such. But when the child modifies his action upon hearing certain sounds such as, "wait," "outdoors," etc., it is not the direct presentation quality which is operative; this functions simply to call up the image of another experience which then affects action. The understanding and crude beginnings of language thus mark the perfecting of the type of adjustment in which one sort of experience is used to secure and control another. In becoming indirect or symbolic it marks, however, the transition to a further period and carries us beyond the limits of the period under discussion.

I conclude by summarizing the various principles involved in the foregoing discussion:

1. It is necessary to discover some single continuous function undergoing development in order to bring scientific relevancy and order into the various facts of child psychology, and in order to give them practical or pedagogical usefulness.

2. The principle of an act as a coordination of sensory stimulus and motor response affords such a centralizing principle.

3. The law is that each coordination is at first worked out more or less blindly simply by reaction to some excitation.

4. That periods of such development alternate rhythmically with periods of use or application in which the given coordination becomes a part of a larger coordination by actively cooperating with others of its own general order.

5. Development is not even and equable in all directions simultaneously. There are shifting, dominant centres of coordination. While one coordination is building up, all other activities are secondary and contributory. The forming coordination locates the centre of interest and decides the stress of effort at any particular time.

MENTAL DEVELOPMENT

References on Mental Development

I. GENERAL REFERENCE BOOKS

Mental Development: Methods and Processes. Baldwin.
Social and Ethical Interpretations in Mental Development.
  Baldwin.
The Child: A Study in the Evolution of Man. Chamberlain.
Studies of Childhood. Sully.
Series of Childhood Studies. Preyer.

II. SOME TOPICAL REFERENCES

1. Physical Development
   "Growth of Children in Height and Weight." *American
     Journal of Psychology,* IX (1898). Burk.
   Growth of Brain. Donaldson.
   The Study of Children. Warner.
   The Nervous System of the Child. Warner.
   The Development of the Child. Oppenheim.
   The Physical Nature of the Child. Rowe.
2. Periods of Mental Development
   The Child, Ch. 4. Chamberlain.
   Psychologic Foundations of Education. Harris.
   Philosophy of Education, Chs. 4, 5, 6. Rosenkranz.
   "Harris's *Psychologic Foundations of Education.*" *Educa-
     tional Review,* XVI (1898) [*Early Works,* 5:372–85].
     Dewey.
   The First Yearbook of the Herbart Society, pp. 70–121. Van
     Liew.
   "Herbartian System of Pedagogics." *Educational Review,* I
     (1891). De Garmo.
   "Constructive Work in the Common Schools." *Educational
     Review,* XVII (1899). Jackman.
3. Play and Games of Children
   "Education by Plays and Games." *Pedagogical Seminary,*
     III (1894). Johnson.

[First published by University of Chicago, 1900, 21 pages. Mimeographed. Not previously reprinted.]

"The Relation of Play to Education." *University of Chicago Record*, I (1896). Mead.

The Child, Ch. 2. Chamberlain.

Psychologic Foundations of Education, Ch. 34. Harris.

Social and Ethical Interpretations, pp. 139 and 242. Baldwin.

"Froebel's Educational Principles." *Elementary School Record*, pp. 143–51 [*Middle Works*, 1:81–91]. Dewey.

Play of Animals. Groos.

Studies on Children's Games. Barnes.

Social and Ethical Interpretations, Ch. 4. Baldwin.

Pedagogics of the Kindergarten. Froebel, translated by Jarvis.

4. Children's Art

The Child, Ch. 6. Chamberlain.

"Study of Children's Drawings." *Pedagogical Seminary*, IV (1896). Lukens.

"Study on Children's Drawings." *Pedagogical Seminary*, II (1892). Barnes.

Studies of Childhood, Chs. 9 and 10. Sully.

Mental Development: Methods and Processes, Ch. 5. Baldwin.

Social and Ethical Interpretations, Ch. 4. Baldwin.

5. Language of Children

"Psychology of Infant Language." *Psychological Review*, I (1894) [*Early Works*, 4:66–69]. Dewey.

The Child, Ch. 5. Chamberlain.

"The Learning of Language." *Pedagogical Seminary*, III (1896). Lukens.

"A Child's Vocabulary." *Educational Review*, VII (1894). Salisbury.

"A Study in Language Teaching." *Pedagogical Seminary*, IV (1897). Street.

"Language of Childhood." *American Journal of Psychology*, VI (1893). Tracy. (Found also in concluding chapter in his book, *Psychology of Childhood*.)

Social and Ethical Interpretations, Ch. 4. Baldwin.

6. Adolescence

"Study of Adolescence." *Pedagogical Seminary*, I (1891). Burnham.

"The New Life: A Study of Regeneration." *American Journal of Psychology*, VI (1893). Daniels.

"Moral and Religious Training of Children and Adolescents." *Pedagogical Seminary*, I (1891). G. S. Hall.

"Psychology and Pedagogy of Adolescence." *Pedagogical Seminary*, V (1897). Lancaster.

"Some Adolescent Reminiscences." *Journal of Pedagogy*, XI (1898). O'Shea.

The educative period of life, covering the first twenty to twenty-five years, may be roughly subdivided into four stages: (1) Early infancy, lasting two or two and a half years; (2) Later infancy, extending to the sixth or seventh year; (3) Childhood to the thirteenth or fourteenth year; and (4) Youth. For the purpose of these lectures we may omit the first stage and pass at once to

The Second Stage—Or Play Period

The first thing to note in this period is the character of the child's activities in relation to things. By eight or nine months there are quite a variety of objects which the child recognizes and responds to. These are things which are quite closely concerned with his own immediate satisfaction. They are the persons closest to him, as father, mother, nurse; things which have to do with the preparation and taking of food; with going out of doors, etc. But at the age of a year and a half, the child has built up quite a little world of things which are relatively independent of his own purely personal pleasures and pains. He recognizes, not simply his own bonnet and cloak as evidences of preparation for going out of doors, but the hats of other people. He recognizes doors, door-knobs, drawers, brushes, handkerchiefs, canes, spoons, at least a few flowers; a certain number of play-things, balls, blocks, and perhaps a pet doll. Now each of these things suggests to the child the characteristic use or function to which it is ordinarily put, and to this he responds at once in action. Hats are to put on and take off; drawers are to be pulled out and pushed in, door-knobs to be turned, handkerchiefs to be put to the nose, flowers to be smelled of, and so on. The child's waking activity is largely taken up with the continuous repetition of just such acts as these whenever the object presents itself. One can sometimes count such acts repeated twenty or thirty times without the slightest flagging of interest. These acts, moreover, are done quite ir-respective of any ulterior personal satisfaction. While at times, of course, the baby will push at the door as a sign that he wishes to go out, he is equally likely to be pushing it to and fro simply for the satisfaction of the act itself. There might almost be said to be an equation here. Things are to the child the acts which they suggest to him: the hat is something to be put on; the drawer is something to pull out, etc. But on the other hand, his activities are taken up with, absorbed in, things.

The comparison of this coordination with those reached in the earlier stages of infancy, will serve to sum up the progress made. Supposing we take a bright, polished door-knob. At first this is nothing but a light stimulus to the child. It is not even a thing, much less that definite object called the door-knob. The response is found simply in the movement of the eye in following or fixating the light. At the next stage the bright light stimulates reaching and grasping. The light is a stimulus to handling and thus is something hard, smooth and resisting as well as bright. Here the thing as an object of consciousness may be said to begin. But after all, this thing is hardly more than a cross-reference of the child's own activities of seeing and handling. It is hardly "objective." If, for purposes of illustration, we may suppose that the child comes to recognize the door-knob as something through whose use he can get away from the place where he is to a more desired spot, we have an illustration of the third stage. Here the thing is a means to some personal end. It is hardly yet an objective door-knob. It is rather an interesting instrument in securing some more interesting result. But at the epoch just discussed, when the child turns it simply for the sake of turning it, simply that he may effect the opening and shutting of the door, without any ulterior purpose, it is in principle just as much of an object to him as it is to any adult. Practically he has defined it; although he is still, of course, far from the capacity to give an intellectual formulation of his practical definition.

Such facts as we have been discussing are the natural transition to the play period. When the child's response is not to a single, sensory stimulus, but to an entire object; and when the response does not consist in getting a single isolated quality like hardness, through touch or sound, through the ear, but consists in putting the object to its appropriate use, direct stimulus has given way to indirect, or suggestion, and the response has ceased to be mere reaction and has become relevant—really a response. To the child at this period, the world of objects is a world of suggestions and of suggestions to be acted upon. The change from direct citation to indirect, or suggestion, marks an increase, not only in rationality of action, but of freedom. The child is no more enslaved to his sensations or to his sensations in respect to securing the satisfaction of his own appetites; but he rather utilizes sensations as ordered cues or signals for activity. Henceforth what we call the sensation is not, in all fairly familiar objects at least, an adequate stimulus to action. It calls forth a response not by itself, but in its relation to some larger organized movement, but that light taken as a sign or indication of that particular thing called a door-knob.

It is this growing freedom in activity which places it on the borderland of play. The child who repeatedly puts a hat on his father's head and takes it off again, is to all intents and purposes playing. He is performing an activity for the sake of satisfaction intrinsically involved therein. The doing, as affording an outlet for an idea or suggestion, suffices; and this, as we shall see, is the essential characteristic of play. It is simply the comparative poverty of the idea or suggestion, and the comparative simplicity of the response which marks it off from play as it later shows itself.

When the object calls out a complete response, not through its own habitual use but through an element of likeness to some other object; when, that is, suggestion has become roundabout and circuitous, then play proper may be said to begin. The child sees a watch chain hanging in a curved form, calls it a hammock and begins to swing it. He sees a string or strap and begins to shake it, calling out "gee gee," or "whoa whoa." He sees a stick and gets astride of it to ride it as a horse. He pushes a block and says "choo choo." Seeing a door it occurs to him to knock on it, to go in, say "how do you do," and repeat the operation several times. Mr. Sully tells of a baby who on seeing the round disc of a piano hammer, called it a "little owl"; and on seeing a compass needle vibrating called it a "bird." So far the latter instances are hardly more than such instances of projection as we found everywhere in language. But if the child had gone on, if he had continued to react as if the thing were a little owl or a bird it certainly would have been a full-fledged play. Other instances quoted by Mr. Sully, as when the child said of a dog panting after a run, "dat bow-wow like puff-puff" (locomotive), if not play itself, certainly shows the mental condition involved in all play.

Comparing such instances as these with those previously cited we find this difference. In the former cases the object as present (what we call technically a perception) serves to arouse the response. In the present case what is actually present operates only through the medium of intervening as-sociations—technically as part of an image. It is not likely that the child really confuses the pendant watch chain with a real hammock, and for that reason proceeds to swing it as if it were a hammock; it is rather that the particular object present ceases to interest or satisfy as an independent whole. It is reduced to a partial factor in a larger experience which has more meaning and thus serves as a suggestion to a richer and freer response. The point in question comes out clearly in the case of a little child, who upon seeing the head or leg broken off from a doll does not react to it for what it is in itself as directly presented, but proceeds to pet it, put it to bed, etc., just as it would with a whole doll. Here we have the whole essence of the childish imagination. It is the capacity to see in something which is physically and also mentally (as far as direct perception is concerned) a separate whole as if it were simply a part of a wider experience, and to respond to it on the basis of the unperceived factors which are imaginatively supplied.

We here come upon a principle which we shall see later on is of decided importance in the explanation of imagina-tion. It does not originate, as is often said, in picking out and piecing together parts of a number of disconnected ex-periences, but rather in the expansion of a given experience through suggestion, into a larger and richer whole. It con-sists in the capacity to see a whole in a part or to treat what is a whole in direct perception as if it were simply a part of a larger whole.

From the second or second and a half year, while the child continues of course to enlarge his world of directly per-

ceived objects, through performing the responses which are
appropriate to them, still the characteristic feature of his
conduct is precisely his responses to images—his reduction
of the actual object, ball, block, doll, chair, etc., to a
subsidiary factor in initiating or carrying on an experiment
of much wider scope, many of the elements of which are not
directly present at all: playing cars, building a house, feeding, petting and caring for a baby, and so on. Of this period,
throughout its whole scope, the following principles:

1. Image and play are not two independent affairs, but
factors in one and the same total experience. They are related
as stimulus and response; as were sensation and movement
on a lower plane of development. It is the very nature of the
image to find for itself an outlet in action—to express or
realize itself. There is no dam, physiologically, between the
excitation of energy in the brain which corresponds to the
image and the contraction of the muscles which corresponds
to the movement. The energy aroused must overflow and the
outgoing or motor nerves are the natural paths of discharge.
Thus the movement serves to maintain and build up the
image. An image which is not acted upon, or rather in this
period acted out, is fleeting; it dies. The image lives only in
its own motor expression. Hence the seemingly superabun-
dant display of physical energy in the child of this period.
His capacity to run about and do something all day till the
adult wearies simply in contemplation of it, to say nothing of
the propensity to engage continually in mischief, is not only
a help to physical growth, but is indispensable to full free
mental development.

2. It is accordingly the play period which protects the
child from undue specialization; which secures the time and
the opportunity for making a great number of experiments
and forming a great number of mental connections and interactions, which at the time were useless but which afterward
are of utmost importance in efficiency of practical life, to
say nothing of richness and depth of personal development.
As the animals in their play rehearse the typical activities of
their life species (as the kitten with the spool goes through
all the movements involved in catching a mouse) so the little
child in his play, in a much freer and profounder way, lives

in advance the typical experiences of the race, and yet does it wholly in terms of his own interest and capacities. It is almost impossible to estimate the extent of territory which the child explores on this play basis; the number of discoveries which he makes; the number of tentative adjustments which he sets up, that are capable, later on, with comparatively slight effort, of being transformed into habits that are of the utmost practical service. The child who has his play period reduced in extent and quality is cheated of his birthright. The tendency of this reduction comes from a variety of sources. Occasionally children at a very early age are set to work or to beg and thus have their powers confined through application to one very limited end. But more often the deprivation ensues because the economic position of the parents makes it impossible to secure the conditions for anything like full expression. Public nurseries, playgrounds, and kindergartens, are virtually an attempt on the part of society to compensate for the limitations thus put upon the child. But in more favored surroundings the child is often relatively stunted because adults are not willing to take the time and effort required; or have not the intelligence necessary to supply proper conditions—or even, in extreme cases to regard the play tendencies of the child as upon the whole exhibitions of a depraved desire to do as much mischief as possible.

3. There is in play no conscious distinction between process and product; between what is being done and what it is intended to accomplish. Play must be its own excuse, its own motive and justification. It is this which distinguishes it from work or labor, where the acts performed are not self-explanatory, but are aimed at a more remote end. It is this which gives the point of connection between play and artistic production, and has led some to regard play and the art impulse as identical in their origin. It is this which makes play the synonym of freedom and spontaneity. It is activity which interests just as activity, as the putting forth of energy in the realization of an image. The child's only want is to do what he is doing to the full. If it is to build a house, it is to build as high a one as possible; if it is playing soldier, to have as much parade and display as possible; if hunting Indians,

to have the maximum of sanguinary destruction; if playing school, to mimic to the extent of caricature the features which have particularly struck the child's attention.

The fact that in the play the interest is wholly inside the activity itself, comes out in a very clear and interesting way in the drawings which are characteristic of the fourth to sixth years of child life. There is complete disregard of actual size, proportion, and of actual structure of objects. Walls of houses are transparent so as to reveal the bed or chairs or table or people within; or if the outside of the house is drawn the window of the child's own room may be the only detail put in or may fill the whole side of the house. Birds will be larger than trees if the bird happens to represent the predominant interest. Drawings made about Christmas time have been seen in which the stocking was so much larger than the house that it had to be drawn at one side. In other words, the child conceives and executes that which represents objects, not as they are in themselves, or in their relations to each other, but as they are in relation to his own dominant interests. He conceives things not as part of an external world, but as elements in a sort of drama. His standard for judging size, proportion, material composition and structure is his own activity of interest.

While in one sense play is antithetical to work—namely as regards the fact that it is not controlled by any remote consideration—there is another sense in which it is not. The adult is generally conscious that he is playing. He feels the element of make-believe about it, of lack of full reality. To him it is amusement, recreation. All this is because, to the adult, it stands in contrast to what are considered the real affairs of life—the practical matters that have to do with family, profession, etc.; but play can have no such coloring to the child's mind just because for him there is no contrast. Play to the child is as serious as work to the adult—not serious of course in the sense of destroying spontaneity or encroaching upon freedom, but serious in the sense of ab- sorbing his full attention, of being for him at the time the only reality in existence.

It is a mistake therefore to suppose that play is equiva- lent to amusing the child or that it is opposed to serious and even strenuous endeavor. The child often works (in the sense of putting forth his utmost energies) when playing. Moreover many things which to the adult have become work or drudgery because of their associations with routine and with external ends, are to the child full of the delight and fascination of play; as, for example, washing dishes, setting a table, etc. Particularly, perhaps, in the educational use of play there is a tendency to overlook this fullness of absorption and activity on the part of the child and to exaggerate the element of make-believe.

The same line of statement applies to interpretation of the childish imagination. It is not to be identified with the mere fantastic or unreal. There is no psychological justification for identifying the scope and vividness of imagination simply with interest in fairy tales and myths or with the capacity to make impossible combinations. Primarily and normally the imagination is a power of realization, not of fanciful playing with unreals. Its defining-character is that it uses the actually seen or experienced thing as a basis about which are centred and gathered a large number of suggestions and appropriations. Of course as the child's experience is limited and his criteria for judging relations are very crude, much of this associated material will be irrelevant and inappropriate. But it is not these traits which make it imagination. There is not the slightest reason for supposing that imagination is cultivated and strengthened in proportion to the disparity between the actual, present material and the imaginative interpretation of it—as when a child uses cubical blocks for boats or balloons. If the child spontaneously does this no harm is likely to result; but when such interpretations are suggested to him by others, it actually interferes with the development of imagination. In such cases it is impossible to get a full and vivid realization of the scene. The child is likely to get habits of confused, incomplete, and half realized imagery—habits which are the greatest obstacle to educational growth on the intellectual side. It is equally a mistake to regard myth, fairy tale, and animistic interpretation of nature as peculiarly appropriate food for the imagery of the child. These undoubtedly have a certain place, varying very much with the temperament, bringing up, and surroundings of the child; but a place which in most cases is quite subordinate. Most children undoubtedly project to some extent weird and mythlike fancies about sun, moon, stars, clouds, and lightning; but fortunately in the normal child these are transitory and relatively insignificant in comparison with interest in dogs, and cats, horses and railroad trains, other real children and the actual occupations and doings of those with whom the child feels ties of interest. There are of course great differences due in the main to social environment. Some children with hard, limited, and sordid surroundings may need the shock of considerable contrast in order to stir and set free the forming of imagery. But children who receive the stimulation of a fairly complex and varied home life need to have their images brought out and cleared up through orderly and adequate expression rather than to have them simply excited by the application of an undue proportion of merely fanciful material. The child whose imagery is constantly excited beyond the possibility of objectification in active play or other expression, not only accumulates a great mass of unrelated and disintegrated images which have no relation to life; but has an appetite formed for continued excitation. Moreover, when the images do not find a natural outlet in action they are likely to react simply into the feelings and emotions so that the latter become strained or even morbid and sentimental. While, therefore, our knowledge of the psychology of the child leads us to attach the greatest importance to the value in growth of this image-play period, this knowledge points with equal positiveness to the need of utilizing the imagery instead of merely exciting it. The arousing of the image is in no sense an end in itself; it has as its function the enlarging and freedom of activity through its own motor expression. This expression in turn clarifies and corrects the imagery. It makes it more definite and brings to light the incongruities, impossibilities, and unrealities involved. The expression should operate continually as a selecting and discriminating factor. It should tend to weed out the fancies which do not lead anywhere and put a premium on those images which bring the child not only into fuller, but into more definite relation to the world of people and things in which he is to live.

In calling the entire period from—say two years and a half to seven years old—the play period, it is not meant of course to ignore or cover up the very great differences which characterize different stages within it. Unfortunately not all parts of this period have as yet been studied with sufficient fullness so that it is possible to trace fully and accurately the whole course of its development. We shall content ourselves with a brief comparison of its earlier and later parts. At first the formation of the image and the subsequent play reaction is dependent upon the presentation of some object which is quite directly associated with the image suggested which presents to the child's eye some marked sign of agreement. Such are the instances already cited (pp. 196–97). The play response consists, moreover, in simply doing the one or two things most directly suggested—shaking the string as if it were reins, saying "whoa, whoa," etc. But the image soon grows in scope and is less and less dependent upon stimulation through some object. The child gets chairs to stand for horses. He adds a carriage with a number of seats for different people. He drives to a particular spot, etc. This, as compared with the original shaking of the lines, shows the necessity the child is mentally under, of building up and enlarging his image through supplying relevant associations. The third year of the child's life is marked by this urgent impulse to expand an image. There are many evidences of this. It is at this time usually that the child becomes the incarnate question point. He demands to know the name of this, that, and the other thing—things with which he has not the slightest actual concern. He continually asks "why" and "what for." Observation, however, reveals that he is not after reasons in any scientific sense. He simply feels that the experience he has got hold of is fragmentary and partial and must be extended. This leads to questions which to the adult are very foolish, as well as to those which have the germ of rationality. When the child asks what is under a stone and is told the ground and then wants to know what is under the ground and so on indefinitely, we have a fair sample of this hunger in the child's mind, for enlargement of imagery. Just such serial questions as these, where the child asks about each answer the same thing that he had originally started upon, are characteristic of the child at this time. If he were really interested in the reason or explanation instead of thus travelling on indefinitely, he would recur to the fact which prompted the original inquiry and see how the two things fitted together. So far, however, as the child's questions are after origin or antecedents on the one side, and concern use on the other, he is putting bits of experience into such coherent relations with what precedes and comes after, as to supply the material for objective connections or real explanations later on.

Other instances of this desire on the part of the child for fullness and variety of imagery are seen in the growth of memory at this time. The tendency to recall previous experiences, to tell what happened in a particular place before, means of course a growing discontent with the experience as it actually presents itself and an attempt to fill out its meaning by referring it to its associations. The minute and careful observation which often characterizes children during this year, is to be explained on the same basis. When a new story or picture book interests the child, he will often dwell on it with loving persistence down to the minutest element involved. In his stories, moreover, he is likely to exact the insertion of every detail. Everyone who has told stories to children of this age is aware of the jealous insistence upon exactness of repetition and the introduction of all possible syntactically, particularly the use of prepositions and various connectives, evidences this same desire for totality of mental imagery. So too, at this period, there is often a habit of balancing statements over against each other, of using contrast and antithesis. For example, Mr. Sully tells a story which in itself is highly illustrative of this period. When a child is told "that's a little watch" he adds "that's not a big watch"; or another child, "that's E's cup, not mamma's cup." Many a fond parent has been shocked at this time by an apparently inexplicable and depraved tendency to tell lies. Often the most outrageous stories are concocted and insisted upon in spite of moral lectures or actual punishment. In cases not so extreme the child shows great ingenuity in inventing plausible excuses and modes of explaining away a situation which apparently tells seriously against the child. While at times there is undoubtedly actual inventiveness displayed, the manipulation of imagery to secure some desired result oftentimes in these cases is hardly more than spontaneous overflow of imagery. The following anecdote, while probably occurring at a later age, illustrates the point. A little girl, seeing a snake in the woods, met her brothers and told them she had seen a "sauger." They denied it was a sauger and said: "It did not have a red ring around its neck, did it?" The person in telling the story said: "My heated imagination saw just such a serpent as soon as their words were spoken and I declared it had a ring about its neck." In response to further suggestions she went on to say that it had scars and a little bell on its neck. The chief mental characteristic of this period being, as we have seen, the tendency for every image to find realization for itself, there is no well-defined objective standard for reality. Hence the easy transitions from exact truthfulness to various degrees of prevarication.

During the fourth year the demand for filling out each image by itself internally and of adding on associations in space and time externally, having satiated itself somewhat, there is a tendency to compare and combine various sorts of images into more complex wholes. The child is now not merely a hearer of stories, but begins to make them up and tell them on his own account. Language becomes discourse; that is, each individual sentence, being now relatively complete in itself, a succession of such questions bearing upon a common topic, is uttered. The child's questions are now aimed, not so much at carrying the image further, as towards really connecting it with other experiences. There enters a need of genuine explanation and interpretation. Discriminations which depend upon careful comparisons also become much more accurate as for example the correct naming of hues and shades of color. The dawning interest in the relations of experiences shows itself in the increasing attempts to employ distinctions of time, number, and order of growth—even though these attempts do not usually meet with success. In the sixth year the image has become much more topical in character; that is, it includes a considerable variety of experiences within its grasp in such a way as to form them into a related whole. The child is capable of playing with an increasingly greater number of persons, being able to adopt rapidly their suggestions without that friction with his own ideas which shows itself earlier, and also to subordinate easily his own immediate activity so as to fit it in to the larger play. The plays, moreover, are now largely mimic reproductions or dramatizations of quite complex social activities. The child plays store, or mother and children, or school, or imitates some other unit of social life.

The sixth year, as a rule, is essentially a period of transition. The child shows a greater interest in making things or making some specific outward result, as compared with the simply immediate doing. As the image gets complex, the child even in his plays begins to do things which have no immediate justification but which are necessary simply as links, simply as intermediate steps leading up to a more remote culmination. Such acts have an indicative or symbolic value. Their meaning is more or less a borrowed or transferred one; it consists in pointing on to some more critical and interesting event which lies beyond.

An interesting division now shows itself in the child's experience. On one hand he begins to get some ability to control his action on the basis of a result or product, instead of simply following the interest of immediate expression. This means that there is some capacity of setting up a specific end as an aim to be achieved and of manipulating the present with reference to this future result. In watching a number of children of this age playing a game like "Hide and Hoop" it will be found quite easy to mark them off into two groups. One will be able to regulate its activities by reference to the end to be reached—namely the touching of a goal before someone else does. They will select hiding places with care; will watch for good opportunities and then show some skill of adjustment in reaching the goal. The other group, except as somewhat carefully instructed, will be carried away by the momentary impetus of the activity itself. The children run to and fro and are amply satisfied with the pleasure had in the direct exercise of powers. There is little ability to concentrate attention on the end to be reached and to take all the intermediate steps with reference to that. The former group is evidently emerging into a different type of attitude and interest.

The child thus becomes capable of something like work on a small scale. He will put forth effort to do things which have no direct interest, because they are appreciated as necessary means in securing the result which is interesting. Such things, accordingly, are no longer looked at merely on their own account. They have become reduced to parts or elements in a somewhat extensive whole whose termination is in the future and thus they are viewed and estimated on the basis of the part they play or place they occupy in this larger whole. There is now a standard for judgment. One of the best opportunities for judging the child's progress in the matter will be found in his drawings. We have already stated that in the earlier period the sole standard is found in the region of the child's own dominant interest. During this time the child draws better from memory than from the object. He is simply expressing his own feeling and wish. Consequently the thing, if an attempt is made to hold his attention to it as furnishing a standard or model, interferes. But there comes a time when the child's expression, while its motive is still dramatic and illustrative, needs to be controlled by reference to real things. The inaccuracies, exaggerations and distortions can be felt and corrected through the medium of direct observation of objects. The result, in other words, as something which has a meaning of its own, a value no longer swallowed up in the immediate process of expression, is not sufficiently independent and external to exercise a controlling influence.

There is an interesting background to this period of the child's development. At the same time that he becomes conscious of more remote results and is willing to devote himself to things otherwise indifferent or unpleasant because they contribute to this result, he also shows aversion to doing things which previously had satisfied him. Any little acts of care and service which had previously been done simply as play, simply for the sake of doing them or the satisfaction of getting social approval, are now looked at and judged with reference to their actual purpose. The child does not identify this purpose with himself. He feels it rather as his mother's or his older brother's purpose. It is something foreign to him, outside his own aims; consequently he shows an aversion to everything connected with it. With the consciousness of definite ends which he can accomplish through his own activities, he begins to have a will of his own in a much more general sense than heretofore. He becomes less tractible, less responsive to direct suggestions from others. For the time being he seems to lose in sociability and amiability of disposition. He becomes more of a consciously independent individual. This is the natural outgrowth of his mental attitude, of his ability to conceive ends and to work with reference to them. It marks a critical occasion, however, in the child's moral development. With favorable surroundings, with insight, sympathy and tact on the part of others, there is opportunity to lead the child to identify these ends and purposes of his own with those of the persons about him; to lead him to appreciate that the current activities and aims of others are not so foreign to his own as they seem, but are really bound up with an adequate understanding of his own interests. In this way a broader and more intelligent morality substitutes itself for the child's previous plastic responsiveness to the suggestions of others. If on the other hand, the child at this period is continually thrown back on himself through experiencing simply opposition and rebuffs as regards his normal consciousness of having ends of his own, or if on the other hand he is simply humored and given undirected freedom in working out his ends without being led to see the need of interpreting them with reference to the purposes of others, the child substitutes a more conscious reflective selfishness for his previous naïve preoccupation with the dominant interests of the moment.

At the same time that the child begins to feel the need of accomplishing certain fairly definite external results, his imagery is more complex and all-including than at any previous time. Consequently there is an almost ludicrous disparity between his actual achievements and his ambitions and beliefs in his own powers. In idea there is nothing too great or difficult for the child, there is nothing which he cannot do and which he is not just going to do. He is about to be a great general or picture painter or carpenter or whatever else has momentarily caught his fancy. He plans in his images great things to make,—steamboats, railroads, theatres, etc.—plans which he is generally too wise to confide to unsympathetic adult ears. Just because of this disparity between profession and practice, between desire and achievement, here also is a critical moment in intellectual development. As the child becomes conscious of this gap he may practically solve the dilemma by surrendering the play of his imagery. He may give up his spontaneity, lose his originality and become satisfied with the narrow limits of his actual possibilities. He thus settles down into the relative routine of a humdrum existence. It is the commonest kind of remark that children who have been full of originality, ingenuity and characteristic flavor of individuality up to the time of six and seven only too often settle down into very commonplace beings, for the most part just like everybody else. In other cases the gap between imaginative tendency and practical accomplishment becomes hardened and fixed. The two things stand in no sort of relation to each other. The outward doing of the child is controlled by the external necessities of the case, by the commands of superiors, by the tasks that are imposed, etc., while the child's imagery runs riot internally on its own account. The outward doing is not inspired and illuminated by the play of individual imagery, nor is the image controlled in its development through reference to the conditions of its own realization. A state of divided attention supervenes and the child lives more or less in two separate worlds. While this is not so common as settling down into a humdrum commonplace existence, yet even the most ordinary child is likely to lead something of this double life, while to those of a naturally more vivid, fertile, and extensive imagination it becomes the dominating condition.

Without conscious appreciation of the psychological reasons for it, the critical character of this period has been practically realized. This is the period selected by common consent as the beginning of the school career, of consciously directed instruction. When the child can begin to conceive ends, to be interested in their realization and to control and direct his immediate overflow of energy on the basis of these ends, he is ripe for instruction. It becomes necessary to see to it in a somewhat systematic way that the ends which he conceives are those which are intrinsically important and valuable. It is necessary to gradually weed out those activities which do not lead anywhere, which carry with them no promise of achievement, of fulfillment in directions that count permanently. It becomes necessary to bring the child to consciousness of the larger ends and purposes which make society what it is, which keep alive civilization,—and to give him such consciousness of their significance as will cause him to adopt them as the regulating motives of his own life experience. As he appreciates these ends it is necessary that his own powers should be disciplined (*i.e.*, trained or directed) into effective means of execution. His natural and spontaneous imagery must be enlarged and controlled through taking in a knowledge of the world, natural and social, in which he lives. His motor powers must be developed into orderly habits and execution with reference to typical modes of social production and intercommunication—reading, writing, simple forms of hand work or manual training, etc.

Moreover, the need and opportunity of instruction are reinforced by the divergent tendencies already spoken of: the growth of independent individuality or will in relation to social conditions; and the diversity between the power to imagine and capacity to execute.

The Third Stage—Childhood

The period from seven years to twelve or thirteen years of age is physically one of slow development. As regards both height and weight boys and girls show much less marked increase during this time than during either the preceding period or the first years of the following. The curve representing the ratio of growth falls off decidedly at this time. While the full significance of this fact cannot be told, there can hardly be any doubt that the comparative cessation of outward growth means that energy is now being consumed in the building up of connections and adjustments which refine and complicate the powers already attained. Observation shows us that it is a period of intense motor activity. Children are continually taken up when left to themselves with various forms of overt physical action. They are restless and uneasy with their activities tending to discharge in a great variety of more or less uncontrolled ways. In the earlier period in the normal child the outward activity is upon the whole at the disposal of the image which possesses the child's mind. While activity is unstable, shifting and jumping from one thing to another, this for the most part is just because the child's ideas are so mobile and fluctuating. But now the child's physical activity appears as it were to get ahead of his intellectual development. The motor discharge for its own sake, more or less apart from an image to be carried out, gets a certain independence. The problem is now to find the ideas and purposes which will utilize this available energy and work it in the proper direction.

This change of emphasis in the child is seen in the growing transformation of plays into games. While no hard and fast line can be drawn between the two yet there is a marked psychological distinction. In playing the child's imagery runs on in more or less spontaneous fashion, one idea suggesting another, the outward activity following its lead. Upon the whole, it is plastic and subordinate. In a game there are certain specific acts which have to be performed and performed in a certain order. The movement of one child has to be adapted to the movements of another and there is a certain sequence which has to be observed. This comes out very clearly in even such simple games as tag, one old cat, hide and hoop, etc. Before this time, if there has been any such organization on the side of the outward activity it has been for the most part because the children were playing with a grown person who kept track of developments and made the proper suggestions at the proper time. Now children play with each other and the maintenance of a certain order following rules is the essence of a game. The play of imagery therefore has certain limits within which it must work. In certain games, as playing Indians, or soldiers, etc., a quite complex variety of image content may be introduced within these limits, but in other games of a more formal and set character constituting quite a large portion of the child's stock in trade, the simple adjustments, the ordering of acts and the reaching of an end either rhythmically or competitively, are the all-controlling points.

This indicates that, as already stated, the child can now entertain, somewhat definitely and constantly, the thought of an end to be reached. But it also indicates a new possibility of motor control for its own sake. The little child has not sufficient command of muscular coordination to shoot marbles, spin a top or skip a rope. Hence there can be no thought of finding satisfaction in the adjustment of a number of such acts into a game. With the capacity to control the execution of such movements, the child gets a start in a new direction of development. While for a time the reaching of the end securing some positive result, some actual accomplishment, predominates in the child's interest and attention, yet incidentally the simultaneous and serial adjustment of the means to each other has all the time to be looked out for. This phase of adjustment, this manipulation of means, as we may term it, gradually assumes greater prominence in the child's experience until it means quite as much to him as does the particular result reached. In his games for example the winning of a particular game comes to mean less as compared with skill as a player. The idea of command over the necessary adjustments (which is of course the psychological definition of skill) stands out somewhat on its own account. With the average child this shifting of interest is quite likely to show itself about the age of eight and a half or nine years. Games become more competitive because competition affords a measure of personal skill. A liking develops for puzzles— that is, for games in which the particular end is of no account, all the interest being simply in the manipulation of means to overcome difficulties. Children of normal development soon begin to desire more or less consciously an occasional piece of hard work in order to reinforce this consciousness of power and skill. They also exhibit a distrustfulness, a diffidence, a lack of self-confidence which they had not shown before. The crudity of result does not appeal to the younger child because it does not present itself as evidence of lack of power on his own part. Now he gets to a certain extent the reflex value of what he does—he sees that his work reflects upon him. As he thus measures his work he also measures himself in relation to his work and so feelings of superiority, of vanity and boasting alternate with self-depreciation and unwillingness to do things where an unsuccessful result is anticipated. The child's previous spontaneous tendency to carry every interesting image unreflectively into execution is now checked by a somewhat frequent "I can't."

This sense of the dependence of results upon an intervening mode of execution, upon the possession or attainment of skill, thus marks a new possibility in intellectual growth. Now is the time for the appeal to secure interest in methods or ways of doing things. Interest in skill, the tendency of the child to measure himself in particular lines according to the amount of skill which he possesses, can be transformed through segregation from its somewhat unduly personal and egotistic character into an objective interest in the ordering of the means which are requisite to secure certain types of results. This we may call an interest in technique. To read, to write, to draw, to play on a musical instrument successfully, means a certain command of technique—that is, of control over the ordering or adjustment of intervening steps. There is a certain mode or method of adjustment which remains fairly permanent in all the diversity of particular acts performed. The chief educational problem at this time is thus to carry the child over from interest in particular activities and results to interest in the general scheme, mode of arrangement, or technical skill that remains fairly uniform in all these various acts. Not merely are these particular capacities and abilities requisite for future development, but even more important still, a sense of power and a sense of limitations of power, is an indispensable condition for future healthy growth.

The normal course of development in this respect is greatly obscured from the fact that, upon the whole, this factor of skill or technique is prematurely forced upon the child. Instead of gradually awakening the child to a sense of his need of skill and the consciousness of the relation which the technical adjustments of reading, writing, ciphering, etc., bear to results which possess an intrinsic importance and value to the child, methods of school instruction have generally in the past taken the child of six years of age and set him to acquiring at once command of these arts. They are not only given to the child prematurely as regards his motor and intellectual development, but they are also given him out of their natural psychological relationship. Hence they do not appeal to the child as modes of action which he needs in order to secure results that appeal to him, but simply as isolated things. Because their end is not clearly appreciated, their value as means is not perceived. This interference with the natural process of psychological development greatly obscures and perverts the value of the results obtained by studying children at this period. It is very difficult to tell how much is due to the natural course of development and how much is due to the artificial conditions under which the child has been working and the habits that have resulted from these.

It is noteworthy that it is at about this age (namely from eight and a half to nine) that the finer muscular adjustments seem to come into play. It is a recognized principle of muscular development that growth is from coordination of the central or trunk muscles to the remote and peripheral – from the fundamental to the accessory. The central nerve connections which are necessary for the performance of the minuter acts of adjustment, involving the movements of hands or fingers do not seem to mature until about this age. But control of these adjustments is necessary for technical skill in writing, drawing, manual work, playing of the piano, etc. Hence the child up to this time is engaged in getting experience in framework, in outline, in its larger, coarser forms, and in the general relations which acts bear to each other. There is no adequate basis for interest in details or for interest in strictly accurate and refined ordering of acts in relation to one another. The observations which have been made, for instance, upon children's drawings, show that up to this time they are mostly diagrams even when purporting to reproduce objects. The child draws an apple, not the particular apple with its distinctive details, that is before his eyes (See Earl Barnes's *Studies in Education*). With ability to use hands and fingers in doing smaller things and in doing larger things more exactly, comes of necessity interest in observing the facts of form and structure and relationship which will make possible increased accuracy in accomplishing a result. Hence it is what we should naturally expect when we find that up to about this time children have defined objects mainly in terms of use and action—of how they behave and what good they are, while now they begin to define more by reference to the actual make-up of the thing itself, or by including the idea defined in a larger idea of which it is now regarded as a subordinate factor.

It is probable that if this interest in skill is duly utilized at the proper time and in its proper connections—it is followed by a period in which the child puts the power thus gained to use; in which he expands and enlarges his experience by employing his new command over means. In general, indeed, periods of concentration, of comparative reflection, seem to alternate with periods of expansion or of general out-going. It is not possible, however, to speak definitely regarding this particular period, partly because it has not as yet been sufficiently studied and partly because of the fact already noted, that the interpretation of results is made very difficult by not knowing how much is due to psychological development and how much is due to more or less artificial conditions of environment.

The Fourth Stage—Adolescence

The general period of adolescence may be conveniently subdivided into two periods: the first that of pubescence from—say thirteen to eighteen; the second that of adolescence proper, which according to Clouston, lasts till about twenty-four. The later portion is essentially a time of fixing the framework of the permanent habits and relationships of life. It is then that the person feels a calling to some profession and takes at least the preliminary steps for introduction into it. It is then that the general working theory of life-controlling ideas about conduct, religion, etc., is likely to be formed. It marks, in other words, the epoch of securing the final adjustment on the part of the individual of himself to the fundamental features of life. It marks the transition of the dependence of the individual, material and intellectual, upon others, to securing an independent psychical personality which shows itself in thinking and acting. The disturbances of this period are essentially connected with the sense of personality. They are emotional exaltations of self-consciousness and whatever is connected with it on one side (mania) or depressions of personality and its concerns (melancholia) on the other.

The essential characteristic of the pubescent period is of course that at this time we have through the sex factor the establishment of the larger relations of the individual to the race and to society. It is thus a period of tremendous enlargement of the sphere of interests, of the range of ideas and of stimuli of action. It is equally a period of personal readjustments in view of the larger scene thus opened up. We have had occasion to notice before that any marked change in the sphere and direction of activity throws the individual as it were, back upon himself, causing him to measure himself, to take stock of his own powers and ideas in reference to the new possibilities of action. This is preeminently true of the adolescent period. Having come to consciousness of the most fundamental relations and far-reaching influences of life, the youth has an entirely new point of view from which to consider himself. He feels and sees himself with reference to the expanding world about him. This new source of interests manifests itself in a new self-consciousness with both its healthy and its morbid manifestations. It shows itself in a modification of previously formed habits and acquired experiences in order to render them relevant to the needs of the new situation. It shows itself in the emotional disturbances and agitation which always accompany any break in the accustomed course of events and the making over of habitual powers to adapt them to novel circumstances. From every point of view—mental and moral as well as physical—we have a period of intense and expansive growth. What differentiates it from other periods of rapid growth is the fact that it is so essentially an epoch of reconstruction, of making over.

Intellectually this expansion takes place in the new interest in principles and generalizations and in the growth of power in discovering and formulating these larger, more universal relationships. Since socially and emotionally the youth feels himself a part of a larger world and is interested in the place which he occupies in this world and in the meaning which it has for him, his ideas try to keep pace with this personal readjustment. He tends to go beyond the limitations of his own particular experiences, to escape from the bonds of his own individual limitations and to discover and lose himself in the world of humanity, of the world which the race has formed for itself. In history, in literature, in science, the tendency at this time is to see larger wholes, to try to gather together facts otherwise scattered and to mass them as parts in the comprehensive whole. But this larger vision is possible only through the medium of generalized principles. It is a generalization which picks up a multitude of diverse and isolated facts and welds them into such coherent relations with each other that an underlying, inclusive totality can be felt or seen.

The younger child experiences things as unities or wholes; but of course the unities which he is capable of grasping are comparatively narrow and superficial. More than this however, it is personal interest, an interest of an almost egoistic character that alone is capable of conferring unity. The affair must either touch the child closely, or be capable of easy translation into his own concerns. Moreover, the relations which maintain the unity will be strictly those of action; it is the course, the march of events which binds details together. The whole must be of the nature of a story, an episode; must be dramatic. Later on, when the child is capable of appreciating the value of skill, he appreciates method or the arrangement of elements, the mutual adaptation of particular means in order to reach most effectively a given end. Here of course is something more nearly approaching intellectual generalization, but after all, the main interest is practical. The method, the scheme of relationship, does not hold the mind on its own account, but only with reference to the practical applications, the achievements, the results, that it makes possible.

With adolescence, however, dawns the sense of the larger world in which the individual is only one factor. The centre of gravity in interest shifts from the individual to the race—or if it remains in the individual it is in the individual as a member of the race. A relationship, a generalization, now means something on its own account; it is necessary in clearing up and realizing the sense of this larger objective world. It is the tie which holds and binds the individual into his participation in this world. It may even be said that the sense of unity is no longer the sense of an act or a dramatic whole, or of securing a result, a technical whole, but is a sense of organization. The relation,—the general principle, is whatever assists in securing the needed sense of organization.

At the same time the attitude toward details changes also. In one sense the individual up to this time has very little interest in details. Interest is too self-centred and too practical to permit of this. The details that go to make up a story, that present the picture of an act in vivid dramatic form, are of course of great interest. But, to the child, they are not details; they are simply vital parts of the story; they are the play of imagery making up the whole scene. Later on, the child is interested in a desired end. But even this is quite different from an interest in observation or accumulation of particulars on their own account. But when the mind is capable of reaching and grasping a new principle, details have a new meaning—they present themselves as cases, instances, samples or illustrations of the general law. The greater the number of different details observed and collected, the more vivid and precise is the hold on the principle. Indeed, the only way in which the generalization can be got hold of is by tracing out its operation in considerable variety and diversity of facts: in seeing that underneath all the apparent dissimilarity there is a common principle of work. The interest in general principles and in details do not therefore crowd each other out. On the contrary, they go together and, if properly appealed to, utilize each other. What might be called the morphological interest, the interest in the analysis of forms, details of structure, etc., first has independent vitality when these details are appreciated in the place which they occupy in a larger whole, as outward exhibitions or signs of the operation of these functions which are requisite to proper organization.

This growth of intellectual interest may be traced with reference to a plant, an animal or a mineral. The child at first is interested in the qualities and properties that appeal

immediately to him; in traits that are pretty or striking—
something, in a word that gives a direct outlet to the activity of his senses. He is interested in handling the stone,
feeling of it, pounding with it, scratching with it, etc.; in
picking the flower, smelling of it, etc. He is interested also
in the uses to which the things can be put, the various
products and articles of human utility that may be derived
from stone, plant or animal—particularly if these are presented in their points of contact with his own life. He is interested also in doing something with these objects,—in
planting the seed, watering and otherwise tending to his
plants; in feeding and taking care of his pet animal; in
trying to build something with the stones, etc. Interest in
details of form and structure and in principles or laws of life
or materials is strictly subordinated to these types of interest
of which we have just spoken.

Later on, when he feels the relationship between process
and result, when he sees that a given experience represents
an end which can be reached only through following a certain order, arranging and manipulating things in certain
ways, attitude towards objects changes somewhat. Appreciating the importance of rules—that is, of given sequences
—in his own conduct, he can be led to appreciate the
significance of similar order in other things. The way in
which a plant grows, an animal lives, in which the stone has
been formed and brought to its present condition; these
things interest him now, not merely as stories, but as his-
tories,—that is, as an ordered progress of events. The sense of
order, of method, in the growth of the plant, in the things
which the plant has to do, getting food materials from the
soil and air, breathing, circulating its nutritive materials,
etc., is the form which the general principle takes at this
time. The interest in details is made more precise and definite
through observation of the organs which are of use in keeping up these processes, in finding the particular parts of the
plant or animal which do the particular things in question.
In fine, at this point, the general means a rule of order in
change, the detail or particular means the special means or
instrument which must operate in order to accomplish effectively a certain thing.

With adolescence the process of life and growth becomes

of interest, becomes a mental whole of itself quite apart from its subordination to reaching any particular end. It is no longer the growth of this or that plant, a plant which is individually familiar to the child, of this or that pet animal but the fact of growth itself, which becomes of absorbing interest. Because the growth is thus a mental unit in itself, it has of course its own laws and principles. Only as these laws, these generalizations, are discovered, can the mind have any clear image of what the process of growth really is. Details, particulars, gain a corresponding value; they are no longer unessential or distracting; they are no longer of importance only when they can be shown to perform some definite result. They have meaning because they exhibit the complete workings of the general principle. They are the detail,—that is, the actual embodiment and evidence of the principle.

This may be summed up by saying that truth now appeals as an intrinsic and independent end of its own, and that accordingly there is an interest in investigation and discovery because of the relation which these are felt to bear to the ascertainment of genuine and valid truths. Investigations have shown that before the age of pubescence there is comparatively little spontaneous critical sense; there is very little natural tendency to doubt and to carry on investigations for the sake of settling doubts. The child takes things on their own evidence as they come to him; he takes them on authority. It is enough if the various elements will fit together so as to give him a constant mental picture. Now there is likely to arise a demand for evidence, for proof; a feeling that inquiry is a process which has truth for its goal and standard, and that, therefore, it cannot be conducted promiscuously and haphazard; that there are certain ties which the presumed law or apparent fact must submit to; certain conditions which it must fulfill before it can be accepted as valid.

In emphasizing the new intellectual point of view which arises at this time, it is important of course not to overlook the underlying continuity of development. There is something which stands for unity, for totality and organization, at every stage. There is the counterpart in each period of the factor of generalization or relationship in the whole, and of particulars or details. If the characteristic interest and attitude of each point of view is adequately lived up to and utilized, we may expect a comparative and easily graded transition from one period to another,—a transition so natural as to be practically insensible. It seems probable that at present there is a tendency to exaggerate certain of its extreme and almost sordid features as compared with the average course of events in the average child, and partly because the shock of transition is greater than it need be, through the partial and artificial development of the previous period.

GROUP IV. HISTORICAL DEVELOPMENT
OF INVENTIONS AND OCCUPATIONS

Average age of children between seven and seven and a half years. Fourteen children in group divided into two sub-groups. The group is under the charge of Miss Katherine B. Camp, and details of work are planned and carried out by her.

General Principles

As what has been said* regarding imagination and experienced fact, regarding correlation, and regarding the relation of the social or human, and science or physical aspects of the work, applies equally well here, it remains only to note the traits which differentiate the work.

The work is taken up historically, with its factors drawn out longitudinally, so to speak, instead of as they are co-existent in current life. There are two reasons for this:

1. It permits and requires greater definiteness, corresponding to the gain of mental concentration made in the year—greater abstractness, if the word is used in the sense of an ₍intentional simplification of existing experience, through elimination of certain elements and emphasis of others, conducted to bring out a special idea. For instance, farming, as studied in the previous year, simply shows what certain people do; what things they come in contact with, how they use them, and how the farmer serves other people. The agricultural stage, taken in historic perspective, while reviewing much of this material, throws emphasis upon the peculiar needs in man's life which call forth this occupation, and the way in which it reacts upon the make-up of society. In one case, the matter is taken up as a situation to be

* Pp. 97–100, this volume.
[First published in the *Elementary School Record*, no. 1 (1900): 21–23. Not previously reprinted.]

FORMS OF CLAY BOWLS

realized; in the other as something whose typical motive and effects are to be discovered and traced. The historical statement is used, then, as a method of *analysis* of existing social life, not as affording information about something past and gone—although it is found that the children take in much of the material got together by anthropologists.

2. The historic approach also requires attention to the sequence and order of progress in its larger and more obvious features; it brings into play ideas of causality, and of logical dependence, if these terms are used not in an abstruse sense, but as meaning imaginative consideration of the needs that call forth one mode of occupation, the devices and inventions that attach themselves, the way the invention reacts upon life and calls into play new powers, new modes of association, and leads to dealing with natural objects and forces hitherto unmastered. Orderly and cumulative narrative is, indeed, logic in its concrete form, the form which appeals to the child mind of this age.

3. This suggests the use which is made of the interest in the primitive and savage, which so many observers have noted as characteristic of this period of childhood. The aim is to avoid a mere excitation and indulgence of this interest, through dwelling in an unrelated way upon sensational or picturesque features of it, without regard to the motives lying behind them, the stimulus given to farther advance, or the ways in which men have got out of savagery into civilization. The effort is to lay hold of this interest in such a way as to use it as a projective—to bring out its defects as well as its dramatic incidents, to see how and why men worked their way out of it. The literary idealizations of such life—like Ab and Hiawatha—are used not as the basis and end of the work,

but as means of developing and vivifying the personal realization of some of its features. It should also be noted that the
use of material from primitive life does not mean that it is
supposed to have any pre-ordained or exclusive value in reference to this period of child life. It is simply one of many
possible modes of approach, selected chiefly because its
greater simplicity gives a means of analyzing *present* life as
indicated above.

4. The general principle mentioned [pp. 97–98], as to
the human setting of observation of natural things, may be
exemplified here with reference to geography. During the
previous year, there is continuous incidental attention to
natural features in connection with modes of life, bringing
up of different children's experiences of fields, woods, hills,
etc., observation of and comparison with the children's own
present surroundings. But in this year, there is an imaginative abstraction and arrangement of these natural features,
corresponding to the selection and sequence already spoken
of upon the historical side. With each phase of industry,
attention is concentrated upon its natural habitat—moun-
tainous woods for hunting, etc., and as one occupation succeeds to another, the children travel in imagination till they
find the locality especially suitable. Meantime in their clay
and sand maps each new environment is added to those previously brought up, until all the main features of physio-
graphic structure have been both introduced and placed in
their relationships to one another. Thus the child is left
with a picture of a typical section of the earth's surface, of
the way in which its various features, mountains, uplands,
river valley, and sea, connect with one another, and with the
activities of human life.

GENERAL INTRODUCTION TO GROUPS
V AND VI

In the general plan of the organization of the school three periods of work are noticed, corresponding to three phases of child growth (see pp. 337 and 338). The first is that in which the child is taken up with direct and outgoing activity, on the basis of the images and emotions that possess his mind. There is always physical, motor activity; and there is always a story, drama, image—a mental whole. But the two are not separate from each other. Acts are not (to the *child consciousness*, I mean) means for realizing ideas; they are just their spontaneous overflow and exhibition. The child's thoughts are not something *to be* realized; they are not projected in the future as ends; they are the living meaning and value that saturate whatever he does. Hence this is called the play period; the whole bent is toward acting out of images, thus giving them vividness and a place in life.

The work of the first four years of the school (from age four to eight) is based upon the working theory that the child's attitude is predominantly of this sort; and that it is premature to force upon him work whose essence, psychologically, is the separation of means and ends; the divorce of elements, steps, and acts from some idea for the sake of which they exist. Hence the relatively slight and incidental attention to reading, writing, and number during the sixth and seventh years, and the attempt to introduce geography and science in a synthetic, living, rather than analytic and morphological, way. (See pp. 97–98 and 224.) This is not because such things are "hard" and the child ought to be amused; it is not because the importance of forms and symbols in civilization and in individual development are not appreciated. It is simply because the child's psychical attitude at this time is less specialized than such work demands; be-

[First published in the *Elementary School Record,* no. 2 (1900): 49–52. Not previously reprinted.]

cause the latter introduces a separation of acts and ideas which tends to make the former conventional and mechanical, and the latter remote and incomprehensible.

But, of course, it is not supposed that conscious relating of means and ends is wholly absent in this period, or that there is no need of anticipating the later development. On the contrary, even with six-year-old children consciousness dawns of a certain sort of ends somewhat remote, and consequently the child is interested in regulating his acts so as to reach the end. In watching a group of six-year-old children playing "hide and hoop," I noticed the following: About half of the children played the game; i.e., they planned their movements to get to the goal first. The other half were carried away with what they were immediately doing; if the one who was "it" got to running away from the goal, he kept on running, in spite of the fact that others were making for the goal. Their present activity was so immensely satisfying that it was impossible to check and guide it by some result to be reached, even such a simple one as touching the goal first.

But the fact that some did thus direct their acts shows a change of attitude; it suggests that this change comes more easily, and hence earlier, in activities where the result is tangible and practical than where it is intellectual and abstract. It arises, for example, far more naturally in making a box, which the child is interested in putting to some use, or in cooking a cereal to be eaten at lunch, than in learning to read or calculate for the sake of some distant use. The active and constructive work of the children of ages six and seven (Groups III and IV) therefore includes activities which combine an immediate appeal to the child as outlet of his energy, with leading up, in an orderly way, to a result ahead. It thus forms habits of working for ends and of controlling present occupation so as, by a sequence of steps, to accomplish something beyond. These habits may be gradually transferred to ends more consciously conceived and more remote.

The eighth year seems to be markedly one of such transition; with the average nine-year-old there is evident dislike of attempting results to which the means at command are

felt to be inadequate. The child, for example, objects to the
kind of drawings formerly made with delight, because he sees
them as results, and hence as crude and even absurd, instead
of just feeling them as parts of his own present life. In the
tenth year there is often a conscious demand for "something
hard," something which will test and call out power, efficiency in selection and adaptation of means to ends. (See
p. 9 of *Elementary School Record* no. 1.)

Hence this is the period, in increasing measure, of acquisition of skill, of "technique"—something, of course,
which applies to geography as well as drawing, to cooking
as well as music, to history as well as reading. Its psychological reality is the mental presentation of an end to be
reached, making it necessary to select—to analyze—the required means (the elements, forms, symbols), and then to
follow regular order, method, "rules," in using the means to
get the result.

But in recognizing that this is the period of technique,
of getting facility, skill, in particular directions, we must
keep in mind certain fundamental principles. First, as already
intimated, the growth is gradual. It comes in reading before
in writing; in both before in numbers (this does not mean,
of course, that the child may not with great interest have
used numbers, as distinct from analyzing them and learning
the rules for their use), and in all of these subjects before
in science. It may well be questioned whether one of the
reasons for the comparatively small success of science in
elementary education up to this time is not to be found in
premature emphasis upon the strictly intellectual phases of
it. Our experience proves that children of eight and nine are
interested in experimental work in science; but it is not because they first conceive certain problems and ideas, and
then regard the experiment as a way of solving the problem
or testing the theory. On the contrary, such an interest hardly
shows itself before the age of thirteen or fourteen. They take
hold of the experimentation as they do of constructive work,
or cooking; it is the active performance of a series of steps
and seeing "what happens" at each step that occupy their
minds. And the technical interest in history and literature
comes even later; in such things the interest in the imagined

and felt totality, the story-form (see p. 97), lasts and resists objective analysis longest.

Secondly, the interest in technique, in acquiring skill, demands, in order not to lead to arrested development, a sufficient background of actual experience. Even if children of six and seven were psychologically ready for analysis, for attention to form and symbols and rules, very few of them have had the range of vital experience which would make it profitable for them to devote themselves very exclusively to the former at the expense of the latter. Hence, once more, attention must then be directed to positive subject-matter that enlarges and deepens their world of imagination and thought, rather than to analyzing an experience they have not yet got, or learning rules for doing things that make no personal appeal to them.

And, in the third place, the *introduction* to technique must come *in connection with ends that arise within the children's own experience, that are present to them as desired ends, and hence as motives to effort.* The too frequent assumption is that it is enough for the teacher to see the end; and that because, as matter of fact, a child is going to need a certain power, this is a sufficient basis upon which to engage him in its acquisition. But the prime psychological necessity is that the child see and feel the end as *his own end*, the need as his own need, and thus have a motive from within, an inherent and impelling motive, for making the analysis and mastering the "rules," *i.e.*, methods of procedure. This is possible only as the formal work is kept in connection with active, with constructive, and expressive work, which, presenting difficulties, suggests the need of acquiring an effective method of coping with them. This is the form which "correlation" takes at this period.

On account of these three principles, while the aim of the instructor is in this period to bring the child to the possession of certain powers, or skills, (1) there is no abrupt transition; (2) the child is still kept mainly occupied with positive subject-matter and with direct, expressive, and constructive activities in order to supply occasions for originating felt problems or difficulties, and motives for solving them; and (3) the technical exercises are selected from such

material. Moreover, in order that the circuit may be complete (4) additional concrete material or occupation is supplied upon or in which the child may use his newly acquired
power and thus realize its value.

THE PLACE OF MANUAL TRAINING
IN THE ELEMENTARY COURSE OF STUDY

As a matter of convenience, the studies of the elementary curriculum may be placed under three heads; this arrangement is also, I think, of some philosophic value. We have, first, the studies which are not so much studies as active pursuits or occupations—modes of activity which appeal to the child for their own sake, and yet lend themselves to educative ends. Secondly, there is the subject-matter which gives us the background of social life. I include here both geography and history; history as the record of what has made present forms of associated life what they are; geography as the statement of the physical conditions and theatre of man's social activities. At more advanced stages of education it may be desirable to specialize these subjects in such a way that they lose this direct relationship to social life. But in elementary education, of which I am speaking, I conceive that they are valuable just in the degree in which they are treated as furnishing social background. Thirdly, we have the studies which give the pupil command of the forms and methods of intellectual communication and inquiry. Such studies as reading, grammar, and the more technical modes of arithmetic are the instrumentalities which the race has worked out as best adapted to further its distinctively intellectual interests. The child's need of command of these, so that, using them freely for himself, he can appropriate the intellectual products of civilization, is so obvious that they constitute the bulk of the traditional curriculum.

Looking along the line of these three groups, we see a movement away from direct personal and social interest to its indirect and remote forms. The first group presents to the

[First published in *Manual Training Magazine* 2 (1901): 193–99. Reprinted in *Education Today*, ed. Joseph Ratner (New York: G. P. Putnam's Sons, 1940), pp. 53–61.]

child the same sort of activities that occupy him directly in his daily life; and re-presents to him modes of social occupation with which he is thoroughly familiar in his everyday surroundings. The second group is still social, but gives us the background rather than the direct reality of associated life. The third is social, but rather in its ultimate motives and effects—in maintaining the intellectual continuity of civilization—than in itself or in any of its more immediate suggestions and associations.

Manual training, constructive work (or whatever name we may care to employ), clearly belongs in the first group and makes up a very large part of it. Physical activity, the use of the bodily organs, is necessarily a phase of whatever directly occupies and absorbs the child. Plays and games obviously come here. So also do a variety of school resources that we might not at first sight put under this head: such as outdoor excursions, much of the more active observation and experimental work in nature study, etc. In this experimental work it is not so much the objective facts, much less the scientific laws, that concern the child, as it is the direct manipulation of materials, and the application of simple forms of energy to produce interesting results. Much of the meaning of art work with little children would also be lost, if we eliminated this aspect of the direct output of physical energy in realizing ideas. School gardens belong here, too. But it is of the manual training, the work with cardboard, wood, bent iron, the cooking, sewing, weaving, etc., that we have more directly to do. They so obviously involve modes of physical activity that the name used to designate them, "manual training," has been selected on this basis alone. No one any longer doubts the thorough training of hand and eye, and (what is of greater importance) of the hand and eye coordination, which is gained through these agencies. Recent psychology has made it unnecessary any longer to argue the fact that this training of hand and eye is also directly and indirectly a training of attention, constructive and reproductive imagination, and power of judgment. The manual-training movement has been greatly facilitated by its happy coincidence with the growing importance attached in psychological theory to the motor element. The old emphasis upon the strictly intellectual elements, sensations and ideas, has given way to the recognition that a motor factor is so closely bound up with the entire mental development that the latter cannot be intelligently discussed apart from the former.

I do not propose to repeat these arguments, but rather to assume them as both established in themselves and reasonably familiar to the reader, and go on to inquire whether there is not also something peculiarly appropriate, upon the *social* side, in demanding a considerable part in elementary education for this group of activities.

The idea of formal discipline, of the value of isolated and independent training of the so-called faculties of observation, memory, and reasoning, has invaded both physical culture and manual training. Here also we have been led to believe that there is a positive inherent value in the formal training of hand and eye quite apart from the actual content of such training—apart from its social relations and suggestions. Now, we ought to go deeper than this in our conception of the educational position of the constructive activities. We ought to see where and how they not only give formal training of hand and eye, but lay hold of the entire physical and mental organism; give play to fundamental aptitudes and instincts, and meet fundamental organic necessities. It is not enough to recognize that they develop hand and eye, and that this development reacts favorably into physical and mental development. We should see what social needs they spring out of, and what social values, what intellectual and emotional nutriment, they bring to the child which cannot be conveyed as well in any other way. And to carry the matter to this point, to recognize the substantial value of the educative material of which they are vehicles, is to connect them with social life; it is to conceive them from the standpoint of the social meaning they realize in child life.[1]

The culture-epoch theory in education, and the recapitulation theory in biology, have made us familiar with the notion that the development of life in the individual corresponds to the development of life in the race—that the

1. See my *School and Society*, pp. 21–36 [*Middle Works of John Dewey*, 1:6–15].

child achieves, in short years and months, that for which life upon the earth has required the slow ages. In spite of absurd pedagogical conclusions that have been drawn from this doctrine (through overlooking the fact that education is meant to accelerate and enrich this recapitulation instead of retarding and prolonging it), no one, I suppose, would deny to it a certain and important element of truth.

This element of truth, rightly apprehended, has, to my mind, a significant bearing upon the question of the place of manual training in education. The point is that the child, with his untried powers, his paucity of experience, is in much the same attitude toward the world and toward life as was early man. That the child should recapitulate the exact external conditions, performances, and blunders of primitive man is a ludicrous proposition. That he should assume a similar *attitude* is almost inevitable. The former conception leads to the notion that, since the race had to advance out of the errors of an animistic interpretation of nature to the truth as made known in science, the child must be kept in the mist of a sentimental and myth-enwrapped nature study before he can deal in any direct and truthful way with things and forces about him. The second conception means that it is the business of education to get hold of the essential underlying attitude which the child has in common with primitive man, in order to give it such play and expression as to avoid the errors and wanderings of his forefathers, and to come to the ends and realities toward which, after all, primitive man was struggling.

However, even admitting that this is the proper educational interpretation of the doctrine of recapitulation, what has it got to do with the place of manual training? Just this: both primitive man and the child are decidedly motor in their activity. Both are interested in objects and materials, not from a contemplative or theoretical standpoint, but from the standpoint of what can be done with them, and what can be got out of them. It needs no argument to show that primitive man must have mainly occupied himself with the direct problems of life—questions of getting food, fuel, shelter, protection. His concerns were the utensils, tools, instrumentalities that secured him a constantly improving life.

His interest in nature was based upon its direct and indispensable relation to his own needs and activities. His
nature-myths, his conception of natural forces as hostile and
favorable, his interpretation of the events of his daily life,
grew out of this industrial basis. His modes of associated
life, family relations, political control, etc., were intimately
dependent upon his industrial occupations.

Now, if there is anything at all in the doctrine of recapitulation, it indicates the probability, first, that we shall
find the child a reservoir of motor energy, urgent for discharge upon his environment; and, second, that this will be
likely to take forms akin to that of the social occupations
through which humanity has maintained and developed
itself.[2]

In one important respect, however, there is a fundamental difference between the child and primitive man.
Necessity, the pressure of getting a living, was upon the
savage. The child is, or should be, protected against economic
stress and strain. The expression of energy takes in his case
a form of play—play which is not amusement, but the intrinsic exhibition of inherent powers so as to exercise and
develop them. Accordingly, while the value of the motor activities of the savage was found chiefly in the external result
—in the game that was killed or the fish that was caught—
and only incidentally in a gain of skill and insight, with the
child the exact reverse is the case. With him the external
result is only a sign, a token; it is just a proof and exhibition
to himself of his own capacities. In it he comes to consciousness of his own impulses. He learns to know them
through seeing what they can effect. But the primary interest
and the ultimate value remain in precisely the culture of
the powers of action which is obtained in and through their
being put to effective use.

If there be any measure of truth in these conceptions,
then the forms of occupation, constructive work, manual
training (whatever name be given them), which are em-

2. In an article upon "The Culture-Epoch Theory," reprinted in the
   Second Herbart *Yearbook* [*Early Works of John Dewey*, 5:247–
   53], I have criticized the Herbart theory of making literature the
   basis of the curriculum from this standpoint.

ployed in the school, must be assigned a central position. They, more than any other one study, more than reading or geography, story-telling or myth, evoke and direct what is most fundamental and vital in the child; that in which he is the heir of all the ages, and through which he recapitulates the progress of the race. It was certainly a gain for educational theory and practice when appeal to personal and immediate sense-perception displaced reliance upon symbols and abstract ideas. But, after all, to have sensations, to receive impressions through sight or hearing, is not the ultimate thing. To do, to perform, to execute, to make, to control and direct activity—it is for the sake of such things that perceptions and impressions exist. Indeed, to see and to hear is more than to have impressions; to see and to hear is to do, to do in cooperation with head, arm, hand, and leg. It must remain part of the imperishable renown of Froebel that he first of all educational reformers seized upon the primordial significance of this phase of child nature, and insisted upon modes of education which should give it outlet. What his exercises did for the kindergarten, that, and more, constructive and occupation work of various sorts must do for the elementary school.

Hence manual training can never take its proper place in the elementary curriculum as long as its chief aim is measured either by the actual result produced or by the gain in technical skill that comes to the producer. These have their place, but this place is not large enough to cover the territory to be rightfully assigned. The first consideration must be to give play to the deep-lying motor instincts and demands of the child; to enable him to become conscious of his powers through the variety of uses to which he can put them; and thus to become aware of their social values. To give play, to give expression to his motor instincts, and to do this in such a way that the child shall be brought to know the larger aims and processes of living, is the problem. The saw, hammer, and plane, the wood and clay, the needle and cloth, and the processes by which these are manipulated, are not ends in themselves; they are rather agencies through which the child may be initiated into the typical problems which require human effort, into the laws of human production and

achievement, and into the methods by which man gains control of nature, and makes good in life his ideals. Out of this
larger human significance must grow gradually the interest
in the technical problems and processes of manual training.
When the interest becomes of the purely technical sort,
then of necessity manual training no longer occupies a central position; it belongs upon the level where all other forms
of special technique are found.

When manual training is so interpreted, there is a
necessary correlation between it and history and science. Just
as man came originally to know nature in its variety of forms
and forces through the active dealings which he had with
it, through his attempts to modify it to meet his needs, so the
child who in orderly fashion directs his motor powers to recapitulate social industries comes to know typical materials
and the typical causal forces upon which the outward facts
depend. In reassuming the motor attitude of the race, he recapitulates also the motives which induced the race to study
nature and find out its laws. He takes the position from which
the facts and truths of science are most easily accessible, and
from which they have the most vital significance. Correlation
of manual training with science is likely to be a rather external and artificial matter where the manual training itself
is conducted for technical ends—for ends which lie within
itself. But when it is treated as a means of organizing the
powers of the child in social directions, its scope is necessarily broadened to take in salient facts of geography, physics,
chemistry, botany, mathematics, etc.

Thus we return to the notion of the three groups of
studies with which I set out. If I have made myself clear in
what I have said, it is evident that manual training, properly
conceived, is an inevitable and indispensable introduction to
the studies of the second group, to history and geography, as
the background of social endeavor. It projects, it ramifies,
into these inevitably. It only remains for the teacher to be
alert to these connections and to take advantage of them. It
is the conception of formal discipline or a merely specific
benefit to be derived from these studies which limits them
to any narrower position. The restriction is due, not to their
own nature, but to the failure to take a large view of them

—failure to see them in their proper perspective. The connection with the third group of studies, those which have to do with the symbols and forms of distinctive intellectual advance, is equally important, even if more indirect. In number work it cannot even be said to be more indirect. Measurement, the application of number to limit form and arrange matters of shape and size, is a necessity. The child not only gets expertness in recognizing and handling certain number facts and relations, but, what is even more important, he gets a "number sense": he gets to be aware of the use and meaning of number; it becomes a reality to him, so that there is a vital motive in his own experience for pursuing it farther. Doubtless an ingenious and wideawake teacher will find natural connections also with the matter of reading and writing, but there is no need of forcing matters in this direction. Upon the whole, the connection here is indirect. But we may be sure that the training of the general intelligence which the child gets, his sense of reality, will arouse an interest in these matters. He will feel their necessity, even if he does not always have immediate motive for using them supplied by the constructive work. These tools of learning have been so integrally associated with productive work in the whole progress of humanity that the momentum which is secured from the pursuit of the latter will surely reflect itself, with increased effect, in devotion to the other.

If the term "primary" in the phrase "primary education" denotes anything more than merely a time element, if it means quality, if it means what is fundamental and basic, then the constructive arts and manual occupations have a claim to be considered distinguishing and characteristic features of primary education.

Review

THE WORLD AND THE INDIVIDUAL

Gifford Lectures, First Series: The Four Historical Conceptions of Being by Josiah Royce, Ph.D., Professor of the History of Philosophy in Harvard University. New York: Macmillan Co., 1900.

If the book before us lacked other noteworthy characteristics, it would be remarkable for the simplicity and force with which it grasps a single conception and follows it through its various forms, using it as an instrument of both criticism and construction. Natural religion, the topic *ex officio* of a Gifford lecture, is interpreted from the standpoint of the "nature of things" or ontology. The aim is so to define Being as to arrive at some conception of what is meant by the reality of God, and of the world and the human individual in relation to God. The originality of which I have spoken does not consist in this fact, nor yet in just taking the epistemological road towards Being. These things, as Professor Royce recognizes, are familiar enough. It is the special way in which the nature of the cognitive idea and its relation to Being are handled, the attempt to centre the whole discussion about the nature of the idea as such, that give the book force and freshness, and that challenge the reader to raise the problems anew for himself, to reëxamine his own conceptions, and modify his own method, even if at the end he, like the present writer, finds himself forced to dissent.

We are to start with the world as idea and not as fact. If we start from the world as fact, we are "sunk deep in an ocean of mysteries"; for it is a "defiant mystery." It bewilders, angers, and baffles us in its contrast of order and chaos, its combination of goodness and cruelty. Because this world of fact is persistently baffling, we turn to the world of idea to

[First published in *Philosophical Review* 9 (1900): 311–24. Not previously reprinted.]

get the key to unlock it. We find that the defect of the world of fact "is due at bottom simply to the fault of our human type of consciousness" (p. 18). So we must devote ourselves to a criticism of the latter. By this criticism we may purify it; we may raise it to a higher level and thus win insight into reality. This mode of approach at once compels the definition of an idea, and at least a preliminary conception of its relation to reality.

In defining idea, Mr. Royce starts from the familiar conception of recent psychology which views the ideational life from the standpoint of organism and environment, and thus connects it with the motor or behavior side of experience. An idea of a thing "always involves a consciousness of how you propose to act towards the thing of which you have an idea." Mr. Stout's remark that an idea is a plan of action, or way of constructing an object, is quoted with approval. The idea thus represents a sort of will or active meaning. It is an intention. Or, in the more technical definition, it is "any state of consciousness, whether simple or complex, which, when present, is then and there viewed as at least the partial expression or embodiment of a single conscious purpose" (p. 22). For example, in singing a melody we are conscious that this act partially fulfills and embodies a purpose; as such it constitutes a musical idea. The purpose, so far as embodied, constitutes the internal meaning of the idea.

But finite ideas always appear to have a meaning not exhausted in what is present as internal meaning, or fulfillment of purpose. They at least seem to refer beyond themselves, to objects. This secondary and problematic aspect we may call their apparent *external* meaning. The melody, for example, may be regarded not simply as the fulfillment of the musical purpose, but as meaning, attempting to copy or corresponding to, a certain theme of Beethoven. Indeed, in all our cognitive experience this external meaning *appears* to be fundamental. In knowing, "our ideas seem destined to perform a task which is externally set for them by the real world" (p. 28). Common sense would say that this reference of ideas to facts wholly apart from themselves, and the necessity of correspondence to these external facts in order to secure truth for ideas, is the important thing; and that the mere inner meaning, uncontrolled by such reference, is either just fancy or else a positive source of error. Yet there are reasons for doubting whether the contrast is as ultimate as it seems. In a certain sense the idea must have the primacy. Unless the idea has a meaning, a purpose of its own in relation to the object, unless it assigns its own special task of correspondence, there can be no question of the supposedly external object which is to serve as standard or model; there will be no telling what fact is to be used as basis for judging successful correspondence. The truth, for example, of the meaning that I put into my idea of a cow (so we may paraphrase Professor Royce), cannot be told by sheer reference to *any* object—to object as such; we must first find what object the idea itself means; what is the task of reference and correspondence that it sets for itself—what itself *means* or *intends*. Admitting, then, that we must go to an object, it is to an object selected and determined by the idea itself.

It is this conception that gives unity and characteristic originality to Professor Royce's discussion. It leads him in the end to declare that the whole external meaning, the reference to objects, must be interpreted in terms of the inner purpose of the idea itself. It leads to the interpretation of the apparent external meaning—the dependence upon external things— as in truth only an instrument of the adequate expression and development of a meaning partially fulfilled in the idea itself. It leads, that is, to the proposition that the whole distinction between inner and outer meaning, between the significance that an idea has as an idea, and that which it has as dependent upon an external object, is due to the difference between a partial and a complete embodiment of a purpose. The defect of our "present human form of momentary consciousness, lies in the fact that we just now do not know precisely what we mean" (p. 39). Our ideas, in other words, express our purposes only vaguely, abstractly, without determination—or, as it is afterwards put—they are mere universals. Hence our discontent with our ideas; hence our search for an "Other," for the object which, though appearing to be external to the idea, in reality is just the supplementation necessary to give complete fulfillment to the purpose only partially presented in the idea. This completeness of determination of meaning is the individual. Complete will, complete meaning, complete individuality (p. 40), are thus the "limits" of the development of all ideas. Here we get, in outline, the answer to the question, What is reality? "To be, means simply to express, to embody the complete internal meaning of a certain absolute system of ideas—a system moreover which is genuinely implied in the true internal meaning or purpose of every finite idea, however fragmentary" (p. 36; see also p. 341).

Thus far the discrepancy of external meaning from internal has been treated as problematic only, as due to the abstract reflection of the critic, (*e.g.*, p. 33). In discussing the root ideas that differentiate the various systems of ontology, Professor Royce appears however to indicate that, *for the finite consciousness as finite*, the discrepancy is inherent and necessary. "Experience comes to us, in part, as brute fact . . . merely immediate experience . . . apart from definition, articulation, and in general from any insight into its relationships." But experience "in addition to its mere presence possesses Meaning" (pp. 55–56). On this side, we have ideas. These two aspects are at war with each other. The brute, immediate facts are obstacles obdurate to our ideas. There is "endless finite conflict of mere experience and mere idea." So far as the ideas attempt to comprehend, to master the data in terms of themselves, there is thought. This is the collection of ideas contrasted with fact and yet trying to possess fact. So far as successful, we get an immediate experience luminous with meaning.

Four fundamental ontological conceptions arise as typically different modes of interpreting the relative significance of these two factors, fact and idea, immediacy and thought. The first, technically speaking, is realism; it emphasizes the external independence of the object, and defines reality from this point of view. Mysticism dwells upon that which is actually present in experience, the immediate, and hence defines reality as that in which all otherness is lost in immediacy, and all diversity is at an end. According to the third view, that of critical rationalism, the real is the object which gives truth or validity to our ideas: neither the idea nor the independent object is real, but an object of possible experience which would verify our idea (p. 61). The criticism of realism shows the necessity of defining Being as in essential relation to ideas; that of mysticism, the necessity of conceiving it as fulfilling, and not merely cancelling, the meaning of our fragmentary, finite experiences; while that of the "Possibility of Experience" theory shows the necessity of conceiving validity and truth to be actually and individually experienced, not merely universally and abstractly possible. The development of these three necessities of interpreting Being, leads inevitably to the fourth, Professor Royce's own conception: viz., that Being is the eternal, exhaustive, determinate, and individual presentation in immediate experiences of the really possible meanings of all ideas—a *totum simul* in a living experience of immediate appreciation of all valid significances, the absolute consciousness. And since, in its individuality, it fulfills the real purpose and strength of all finite consciousnesses, it preserves and validates within itself finite wills and individualities.

Limits of space prevent an adequate exposition of Mr. Royce's statement and criticism of realism and mysticism. Mr. Royce's position, however, is so coherent, so sequential, that if I have been at all successful in reporting it above, even a brief summary will not be wholly meaningless. Strictly consistent or extreme realism asserts the entire independence of the object as regards ideas; it is totally unaffected by them; it is "whether or no" they are. Hence the theory has really no way of defining Being except as that which is thus independent of ideas—*any* nature or content may be ascribed, and historically has been ascribed to it, provided only it remains wholly other than ideas. But, clearly, if its sole definition is to be independent of ideas, ideas cannot refer to it, cannot have connection, relation or community as regards it; certainly cannot correspond with it. Hence it is, for us, a realm of nothing at all; moreover, since by the realistic hypothesis this Being was to furnish the standard for truth and falsity of ideas, there is no longer any possibility of discriminating true from false. All ideas equally exist, are "existent entities" on the same footing—the "Forgotten

Thesis" of realism (p. 134). Realism thus contradicts itself in the most thoroughgoing way.[1]

Mysticism realizes that the discrepancy of idea and fact, immediacy and object, is the source of all struggle, failure, and disquietude. It sees the utter impossibility of ending this conflict in terms of the mere "other," the independent Being of realism, since it sees not only the contradictory character of such a Being, but also that its apparent or illusory presence is the source of all our woe, intellectual and moral. Hence it seeks Being in the escape from, or destruction of such external being, in the selfhood of sheer immediate distinctionless feeling. Hence the self-contradiction of mysticism; since it can define Being only as the goal of our struggle, only as a "contrast-effect," and if the struggle, the finite ideas, are absolutely illusory, Being itself remains absolutely without content. It is a "zero which is contrasted with nothing . . . and thus remains a genuine and absolute nothing" (p. 181).[2]

In the statement and criticism of the "Possibility of Experience" theory we enter, in effect, upon the exposition of Mr. Royce's own position, for he accepts it as true "as far as it goes," but holds that in order to retain the amount of truth which it possesses, it must be further developed. The transformation resulting from the required development gives his own conception of Being.

Even common sense is quite familiar with objects which obviously have Being only in relation to our ideas: it makes

1. It is only fair to say that in this condensation I have omitted reference to the nominally most characteristic feature of Professor Royce's discussion, namely, the consideration of Being as many or one. But, if I understand his argument, the above gives its *real* force; indeed, to be frank, the other phase of his argument seems to me to be either tautology, an elaborate reiteration of the fact that realism has no definition for its real except mere and complete independence of ideas, or else to be fallacious.

2. Personally I have found the discussion of mysticism one of the most interesting and enlightening portions of the book. But doubts arise as to the logical conclusiveness of the criticism. Can it be said that mysticism defines Being in terms of *total* contrast with our "finite" experience? Does it not rather define it exclusively in terms of *one phase* of our present experience—namely, the immediate phase—and insist, *not* upon the illusoriness of the whole "finite" experience, but upon that of objects "other than" this immediacy, and consequently upon the need of withdrawal from or negation of these externalities?

no difficulty, however, in ascribing objective reality to them. In this case objective reality clearly means *truth, validity*. Instances of such beings are the constitution of a state, social status, the commercial realm of credits and debts. Again, mathematical truths, the value of π, the fact that a function continuous within certain intervals need have no differential coefficients within those intervals; and, again, the moral order. In considering cases such as the reality of mathematical truths we come upon a most instructive characteristic. In one sense we seem here to be dealing merely with ideas or meanings, arbitrary constructions of our own definitions, having no necessity except to remain consistent with the intentions we ourselves embody in the definitions. But none the less it is a problem with the mathematician whether within his realm certain new (mathematical) objects may be found; he is liable to error in his assertions about such objects—as is illustrated in the case of the differential coefficient just alluded to, and, in general, he has to experiment, to produce, to wait and observe results, much as does the chemist or astronomer. Moreover, mathematical laws and results, originally quite independent of one another, finally often come together and reveal, in a fertile way, further quite new and unexpected truths—thus again simulating what happens in our knowledge of the physical world.

Philosophically it was Kant who first brought to consciousness the significance of reality as equivalent to validity, and generalized this conception as giving the clue to all Being—save, of course, to the things-in-themselves. He insisted that when we deal with objects other than our present ideas, we mean not objects independent of any knowledge, but *possible objects of experience*. Accordingly, the worth of ideas, the correspondence which they must possess, is decided, not by reference to Being independent of ideas, but by the determinate possibility of objects of experience which would make the ideas valid, true—such questions as arise with reference to the liquid or solid condition of the interior of the earth, the state of parts of the moon beyond direct observation, etc. The whole problem of Being is then one of the validity of ideas, not of the existence or nature of objects just other than ideas.

Mr. Royce, as already intimated, attributes worth to this conception "as far as it goes" (p. 251). He holds, however, that validity as such, or *mere* validity, is not valid; an idea must be immediately fulfilled to be completely or determinately true; it must be actually experienced, in order to be really *"possible."* The problem develops as follows: Validity, after all, is an ambiguous term (pp. 261 and 268). On one side, there is always some actual, present experience. Even in mathematics, one does not rely upon *mere* reasoning; one insists upon ability empirically to realize, in inner constructions, in observable symbols, diagrams, etc., the actual course of a certain development; and this, *a fortiori*, is true in what we would term physical truths. But, on the other hand, "the range of valid possible experience is viewed by me as infinitely more extended than my actual human experience" (p. 259). The mathematician goes straight on to assertions about an infinity of objects not actually present, but regarded as valid. Even empirically there are infinite valid possibilities about the commercial world which one does not immediately realize, which, indeed, one deliberately chooses not to realize, such as bankruptcy, bad investments.[3]

And so in the case of knowing a ship, unless it has for you, even as a merely valid object in the content of possible experience, more Being than you have ever directly verified, you would call it a figment of the imagination (p. 258). The second meaning of validity is, thus, that the realm of nature, of social life, of mathematical truth, has a character *not* tested, not exhaustively presented. To sum up: on one side is validity living, present in individual experience; on the other side, merely universal, formal, a mere general law. The first sense has the advantage of being given in experience, but the disadvantage of being only the "creature of the instant," a limited, fragmentary case. The second sense has the advantage of being eternal, infinite, exhaustive; but it is

3. It is not irreverent to say that in such cases we prefer the solid gains for ourselves, and prefer to leave the experiences of bankruptcy, etc., to God. Since they are "valid possibilities," the very point of Mr. Royce's argument is that they shall not remain *mere* possibilities, but be fulfilled. To deny their fulfillment in God would be to cut the nerve of the argument by which we pass from the third to the fourth conception.

merely and only possible, not actual. What is the solution of the ambiguity? Clearly, a conception of Being is indicated in which the meaning of validity shall lose this ambiguity, in which the relative advantages of these one-sided conceptions shall be combined in a harmonious, exhaustive whole.

Since for reasons that will appear later, I cannot, without taking too much space, give an exposition apart from criticism of the method by which Mr. Royce moves on from "Possibility of Experience" to an "individual life, present as a whole, . . . ; at once a system of facts, and the fulfilment of whatever purpose any finite idea, in so far as it is true to its own meaning, fragmentarily embodies . . . ; a life, which is the completed will, as well as the completed experience, corresponding to the will and experience of any one finite idea" (p. 341); I shall, at present, assume this step to be taken, and note the further characteristics of such Being.

In the first place, it solves for us the whole problem of the relation of inner and outer meaning. On one side, the object can have no essential character which is not predetermined by the purpose or meaning of the idea itself. The idea must *mean* the object; and it must also mean, must decide, the *kind* of correspondence that is required between itself and its object; for correspondence varies with the purpose in question, and if at times it demands copying or resemblance, at other times it does not; and even when it does, this is only because the idea itself set out to be just that kind of a copying idea. But since, on the other side, knowing requires effort, and since error is possible, the internal meaning *cannot* precisely predetermine the object, and external meaning is also necessary. The solution is in recognizing that our ideas are finite, fragmentary fulfillments of purpose. As *fulfillments* they predetermine their own objects; but, in so far as the idea is itself vague, abstract, indeterminate, it does not fully understand its own purpose, and to acquire completeness of meaning, individuality of purpose or will, has to hunt for its "other." But this is now seen to be no mere external "other"; it is just that which is required to make an idea truly valid, that is, adequate, determinate (pp. 300–311, 320–35). Thus, real Being is just that being in which idea, inner meaning, and object, external meaning, no longer stand apart, but idea is an exhaustive individual, and object is meaningful.

In the second place, such Being is Unity. Any valid idea must be a consciously experienced fact. Therefore, even if we assume that finite forms of consciousness are sundered, this, as true, valid idea, implies that they are all present in a single consciousness which realizes them all, and the fact of their mutual exclusiveness. "What is, is present to the insight of a single Self-conscious Knower" (p. 400). This abstract logical statement is reinforced by considerations of the material and psychological unity of experience—the unity of the world as known, and of its empirical knower.

In the third place, this unity is not subversive of the multiplicity of finite consciousnesses. Every idea or meaning is a purpose; as such it is a will, or act of will; for, so far as rational, it already embodies, however fragmentarily, a purpose. The complete or perfect reality can only be an exhaustive, an individualized, realization of these same meanings or wills. Every idea means or wills its own specific unique realization; and this is its individuality—its experience in such form that there can be no substitute for it.[4] Nothing can take its place. How then can the Absolute, which is precisely the complete realization of all purposes only partially fulfilled in us, do other than conserve and present all such wills, or individuals? The meaning of every life is unique, and uniquely maintained in the Absolute. This is just what ethical common sense means by *activity*. You alone mean just this purpose: that is activity. You are yourself, that unique individual, in your meaning, your purpose: that is freedom (pp. 468, 469). Such, then, is in outline the final conception of Being.

I have said that to save time it would be found expedient to combine exposition and criticism as regards the exact steps by which Mr. Royce, through his criticism of "the possible-experience" theory, passes on to his own. I now return to that point. So far as I can make out, the ambiguity which

4. Lack of space compels me to omit the interesting discussion of individuality, even in an object, as dependent upon purpose or will.

Mr. Royce attributes to the conception of validity, the contrast between actual, partial experience, and infinite, but merely possible experience, is not inherent in the theory criticized, but results from the fact that Mr. Royce himself gives two different, and quite inconsistent statements of it. If this ambiguity of his own be eliminated, his own theory may conceivably, of course, still be true, but so far as dependent upon the method by which it is arrived at, it falls to the ground.

What are these two differing statements? On the one hand, it is asserted that the theory is committed to "mere possibilities," "empirically valid general truths." It "consciously attempts to define the Real as explicitly and only the Universal" (pp. 240 and 241). Its realities are "merely more or less valid and permanent ideas" (p. 243). In defining possibilities of experience, it "tells you only of mere abstract universals" (p. 269). If we identify, as we must, the inner meaning with the universal, and the empirically experienced objects with the external meaning, then we can say that this theory regards "the antithesis of internal and of external as finally valid" (p. 288). It "leaves Reality too much a bare abstract universal" (p. 290). "All that is thus defined about the object is its mere *what*" (p. 357).

But upon other occasions we have it clearly enough stated that the validity of an idea is dependent upon an experience in which that idea shall be empirically verified—in other words, that an idea, *qua* mere idea, cannot be valid. A valid idea, and a possible experience are not synonymous; but the possibility of sense-experience is the test by which the validity of an idea is determined. And, moreover, this possibility is so far from being a *mere* possibility that it must be *necessarily* connected with what is actually experienced, it must, indeed, be necessary to the true, integral meaning of the present experience. The whole point of the argument of Kant is that you cannot draw a line and say this is merely actual, and that merely possible. If the idea of the liquidity of the earth is valid, it is because there is somewhat, which is directly present to us as real, which demands this idea as a part of its *own* meaning. It is only a construction of the present; *and the present apart from such construction* is, in turn, meaningless. That such is the case is brought out in Mr. Royce's quotation from Kant (p. 237) when the test of the validity of an idea is its connection with "our *perceptions according to the principle of the empirical synthesis of phenomena*" (italics mine). And, again, when Professor Royce says (p. 245) that the only basis for the assertion of an unexperienced Being is that an experience of facts sends us beyond themselves, and to further possible experience for their own interpretation. Again, it is a matter of recognizing that our "*present experience is interwoven* with the whole context of the realm of valid or of possible experience" (p. 248, italics mine. See also bottom of p. 242 and top of p. 243;—on pp. 254–56, it is shown that even mathematical ideas to be valid require immediate presentation).

There can be no question which of these two views comes nearer to representing the true spirit of Kant. Indeed, one rubs one's eyes when one finds the "attempt to define the Real as explicitly and only the Universal" associated with the name of Kant. That this view is the rationalism against which the Kant of *critical* rationalism asserted that thought in itself is empty, and can give only consistency, never validity, is of course obvious. Professor Royce confounds in his exposition three notions which Kant carefully distinguishes—and then uses this confusion not only to condemn the theory in question, but to furnish the terms of his own solution. These three notions are: (1) "The real" (in its phenomenal sense, of course, which alone is considered by Mr. Royce). This is immediate sense determined by thought, by mediate conceptions:—so far is Kant, from defining the real as merely universal, merely possible. (2) "The valid or true idea." Here, of course, his entire point is that the true idea is not a mere idea, any more than it is the real. It differs from the real in not being directly experienced; it differs from mere thought in that we have reason for assuming that there is a *possible* experience in which it would be directly presented in sense. (3) And thus there is "possible experience"—that which tests the validity of an idea. It is neither, *qua* possible, the same as the real, nor is it the same as the valid idea. It is not definable in terms of ideas as such, because of its necessary connection with the content of immediate experience. (On p. 247 it is correctly stated: "Experience furnishes the ground for truth.") Mr. Royce, however, assumes that these three notions are synonymous.[5] Except in so far as he does this, he has no basis for contrasting validity as immediate but fragmentary, with validity as universal, ideal but infinite;[6] and no basis for his own positive conception of the really valid idea as itself a living experience. So far as he does this, it is not surprising that he concludes that "all validity, as an incomplete universal conception needs another to give it final meaning" (p. 341).

I am forced to conclude, then, that Mr. Royce's own theory, so far as developed as affording the needed completion of the "validity" theory, rests upon an elaborate misinterpretation. Barely stated in this way the criticism is merely destructive. But what is enlightening is that precisely this oscillation is required *in order to give Mr. Royce's own conception its meaning.* From one point of view, our starting

5. Thus on p. 248 "experience as a whole" is identified with the "realm of truth," and both have a "valid constitution." The realms of "valid" and of "possible" experience are identified. On p. 259 we are told of "valid possible experience." In the first paragraph of p. 236 we deal with "objects of Possible Experience" (3) above; in the next paragraph with "experience as having a necessary constitution" (1) above; in the first paragraph of p. 239, it is a world of "valid empirical truth" (2) above. On p. 241, "substances," "causes," are instanced as cases of Kant's "empirical objects" (1), and these again are "empirically valid general truths"!

6. There is no space to make the point good here, but I would ask the reader to go carefully over the discussion of the "Universal and Particular judgments" (pp. 275–90) and see if there is not exactly the same ambiguity in the treatment of these ideas. Sometimes the universal appears as the abstract, the possibility, the ideal construction, as reasoning which while not real, *i.e.,* presented in experience, is valuable as an instrument for reducing indeterminateness by eliminating possibilities (*e.g.,* pp. 277–79); while at other times it appears as our actual present immediate experience of ideas, so far as this is finite, incomplete, and, therefore, *itself* indeterminate (*e.g.,* pp. 292, 295, and whenever the universal is identified with the "inner meaning" which is really experienced, but which as "finite," "fragmentary" needs an "other"). And, of course, the particular goes through similar transformations. At one time the particular judgments are what *"positively assert Being* in the object viewed as external"; hence, of course, they come in to give concreteness to the mere abstract universal, or ideal construction. But so far as the "universal" is our present but incomplete, inner meaning, the particulars appear as the ideal possibilities which, *if realized, would* give exhaustiveness or infinitude to our limited present meaning.

point is no idea, nor universal: it is actual, immediate experience. But this has to be contrasted with universals, possibilities, in order to be condemned as finite and fragmentary, in order to suggest the contrast of an infinite or exhaustive. Now the other side comes into play; if these possibilities are merely universals, merely possibilities, while the conception of them would convict our present experience of a certain limitation, it would give no basis for the reality of an *infinite experience*. So the scene shifts. It is now our experience, which as such, is *only* universal, only abstract, only indeterminate; and, hence, what it is contrasted with (previously only possibilities, abstractions) becomes the actual, immediate, individual experience.

Professor Royce's argument is in this predicament. Unless he can find something good to say of ideas, and of our experience, there is no ground for defining the Absolute in terms of ideas, or as experience. Hence, at times he insists that, even with us, the truly valid idea is that which is presented in our immediate experience. This point of view comes out in its essential meaning on page 422, when he says that it is "the wholeness and not the mere fragmentariness, the presence and not the mere absence of unity in our consciousness . . . which guides us towards a positive view of how the unity of Being is . . . attained." It finds expression again on page 424, when we are told that as to the "general form of the absolute unity, our guide is inevitably the type of empirical unity present in our own passing consciousness." When this necessary homogeneity or community is in mind (required in order intelligibly to describe the Absolute as experience or consciousness at all), validity means present actual experience. *It must mean this for us, or it cannot mean it for the Absolute.* So we have the emphasis on the genuinely Kantian interpretation of reality. But, on the other hand, pretty radical discredit must be cast on our ideas, on our experience; for otherwise there is no ground for making the radical distinction between ourselves as fragmentary, finite, etc., and the infinite or "completed" consciousness; otherwise we should end as well as begin with Kantianism, with experience as an organized system. Hence the necessity of conceiving our experiences, our ideas, which previously were

defined as immediate realities or *presented* purposes, as mere
meanings, indeterminate universals at large, and therefore
requiring the infinite experience to fulfill them. The dialectic
is this: (1) Our experiences are meanings, purposes fulfilled. Then, since reality cannot be conceived apart from
experience, *the* reality—absolute reality—is meaning fulfilled.
(2) But our purposes are only partially, inadequately, merely
universally or indeterminately, fulfilled. But since absolute
reality is meaning fulfilled in experience, it must be exhaustively, eternally fulfilled. The Absolute experiences all
at once, adequately and completely, that which we try to experience in pieces, in series and in distorted fashion. The
gist of my criticism is that the argument depends upon
taking propositions (1) and (2) alternately. They cannot be
taken together without destroying each other. Insist upon
(1) alone, and you get the system of experience as the Absolute; insist upon (2) alone, and you cannot get anywhere.
Mr. Royce, I say it in no flippant spirit, blows hot and cold
upon our "finite" experience. When he wishes to establish
the experienced, the significant character of his Absolute,
it is good enough. But when he wishes to give an all-embracing, single, exhaustive, *totum simul* character to his Absolute,
our finite consciousness appears in a condition which logically would justify no conclusion, and which, practically,
would not amount to enough even to suggest the problem of
its own nature—mere vague universals, indeterminate possibilities and the like!

     To put the matter somewhat more positively: If our
experience justifies us in entertaining the idea of the Infinite,
the Perfect, as valid, then we are not mere fragments or parts
in that Infinite; it is in and through us, and in such an
organic and pervasive way that the contrast between us and
it, as the "finite" over against the "infinite," the fragmentary
over against the complete, the serial over against the *totum
simul* is contradicted. If such be the case, we do not need a
definition of the Absolute which makes it the realization of
everything we intend but cannot effect; everything we mean,
but cannot express. What we need is a reconsideration of the
facts of struggle, disappointment, change, consciousness of
limitation, which will show *them*, as they actually are ex-

perienced *by us* (not by something called Absolute) to be significant, worthy, and helpful. On the contrary, if we are fragmentary and finite in such a way that our meanings and realizations are not presented in and to us, but only to and in the Absolute, what boots either the Absolute, or the struggle! Let us eat, drink and be merry—let us glean the satisfactions of our passing life, for as to serious meanings, only the Absolute knows what they mean; as to serious efforts, only the Absolute experiences their realization—and since he is Absolute, we cannot rob him of that in any case, nor will he grudge us such pleasures as we can snatch as we hurry along. Omar Khayyám knew such philosophy long ago.

Professor Royce has shown his capacity to be sceptical. He has declared that only through doubting does the truth appear. But the category of the "finite," the "fragmentary," the "flying moment," he seems never to have questioned. It is the one positive, fixed datum. Upon it he builds his whole conception of real or absolute Being—and yet to build upon it at all, he has to combine with it qualities such as meaning, purpose, fulfillment, which contradict this rigid finitude and require its reinterpretation.

I need hardly say in closing that it is quite possible to disagree pretty fundamentally with an author's conclusions, because one is not convinced as to his method, and yet recognize the scope and power of his work, and admire, to the point of envy, his skill in managing the course of his ideas and in presenting them to the reader. The book before us, together with its author's *Conception of God*, can be compared only with Mr. Bradley's *Appearance and Reality* in recent metaphysical thought. I should regret, even more than I do, the limitations which have confined me to the bare skeleton of Mr. Royce's argument, were it not that its many admirable traits are so obvious that they cannot fail to secure recognition from any competent reader. Meantime the serious effort critically to face Mr. Royce's method is the tribute—the highest of all tributes, it seems to me—which the importance of his work exacts.

The Educational Situation

Prefatory Word

In the following paper I have attempted to set forth the educational situation as it manifests itself in the three typical parts of our educational system. In so doing, I have revised papers originally prepared for three different bodies, namely, the Superintendents' section of the National Educational Association; the Conference of Secondary Schools affiliated with the University of Chicago; and the Harvard Teachers Association. If the following paper in the reading leaves with the reader the impression of a miscellaneous collection, not of an organic unity, it will hardly be worth while for me here to iterate that it is an attempt to apply a single social philosophy, a single educational philosophy, to a single problem manifested in forms that are only outwardly diverse. I may, however, be allowed to say that in each case I have tried to interpret the particular member of the school organism dealt with in its twofold relation: to the past which has determined its conditions and forms; and to the present which determines its aims and results—its ideals and its success or failure in realizing them. The school more than any one other social institution stands between the past and the future; it is the living present as reflection of the past and as prophecy of the future. To this is due the intensity of intellectual and moral interest attaching to all that concerns the school—if only our eyes are open to see.

1. AS CONCERNS THE ELEMENTARY SCHOOL

Horace Mann and the disciples of Pestalozzi did their peculiar missionary work so completely as intellectually to crowd the conservative to the wall. For half a century after their time the ethical emotion, the bulk of exhortation, the current formulæ and catchwords, the distinctive principles of theory have been found on the side of progress, of what is known as reform. The supremacy of self-activity, the symmetrical development of all the powers, the priority of character to information, the necessity of putting the real before the symbol, the concrete before the abstract, the necessity of following the order of nature and not the order of human convention; all these ideas, at the outset so revolutionary, have filtered into the pedagogic consciousness and become the commonplace of pedagogic writing and of the gatherings where teachers meet for inspiration and admonition.

It is, however, sufficiently obvious that while the reformer took possession of the field of theory and enthusiasm and preaching, the conservative, so far as concerns the course of study was holding his own pretty obstinately in the region of practice. He could afford to neglect all these sayings; nay, he could afford to take a part in a glib reiteration of the shibboleths because as matter of fact his own work remained so largely untouched. He retained actual control of school conditions; it was he who brought about the final and actual contact between the theories and the child. And by the time ideals and theories had been translated over into their working equivalents in the curriculum, the difference between them and what he as a conservative really wished and practiced became often the simple difference of tweedle

[First published as "The Situation as Regards the Course of Study," in *School Journal* 62 (1901): 421–23, 445–46, 454, 469–71. Also published in *Educational Review* 22 (1901): 26–49 and in *Proceedings and Addresses* of the National Educational Association, 1901, pp. 332–48.]

dum from tweedle dee. So the "great big battle" was fought with mutual satisfaction, each side having an almost complete victory in its own field. Where the reformer made his headway was not in the region of studies, but rather in that of methods and of atmosphere of school work.

In the last twenty or twenty-five years, however, more serious attempts have been made to carry the theory into effective execution in subject-matter as well as in method. The unconscious insincerity in continually turning the theory over and over in terms of itself, the unconscious self-deceit in using it simply to cast an idealized and emotional halo over a mechanical school routine with which it was fundamentally at odds, became somewhat painfully apparent; consequently the effort to change the concrete school materials and school subject-matter so as to give the professed ends and aims a *pou sto* within the school walls and in relation to the children.

Drawing, music, nature study with the field excursion and the school garden, manual training, the continuation of the constructive exercises of the kindergarten, the story and the tale, the biography, the dramatic episode and anniversary of heroic history found their way into the schoolrooms. We, they proclaim, are the working counterparts of the commands to follow nature; to secure the complete development of the child; to present the real before the symbolic, etc. Interest was transferred from the region of pedagogic principles and ideals as such, to the child as affected by these principles and ideals. The formulæ of pedagogics were reduced in importance and the present experience of the child was magnified. The gospel of the emancipation of the child succeeded the gospel of the emancipation of the educational theorist. This gospel was published abroad and verily its day seemed at hand. It was apparently only a question of pushing a few more old fogies out of the way, and waiting for others to pass out of existence in the natural course of events, and the long-wished-for educational reformation would be accomplished.

Needless to say the affair was not quite so simple. The conservative was still there. He was there not only as a teacher in the schoolroom, but he was there in the board of education; he was there because he was still in the heart and mind of the parent; because he still possessed and controlled the intellectual and moral standards and expectations of the community. We began to learn that an educational reform is but one phase of a general social modification.

Moreover certain evils began to show themselves. Studies were multiplied almost indefinitely, often overtaxing the physical and mental strength of both teacher and child, leading to a congestion of the curriculum, to a distraction and dissipation of aim and effort on the part of instructor and pupil. Too often an excess of emotional excitement and strain abruptly replaced the former apathy and dull routine of the school. There were complaints in every community of loss of efficiency in the older studies, and of a letting down of the seriousness of mental training. It is not necessary to consider how well founded these objections have been. The fact that they are so commonly made, the fact that these newer studies are often regarded simply as fads and frills, is sufficient evidence of the main point, viz., of the external and mechanical position occupied by these studies in the curriculum. Numbers of cities throughout the country point the moral. When the winds blew and the rains fell—in the shape of a financial stringency in the community and the business conduct of the school—the new educational edifice too often fell. It may not have been built entirely upon the sand, but at all events it was not founded upon a rock. The taxpayer spoke, and somehow the studies which represented the symmetrical development of the child and the necessity of giving him the concrete before the abstract went into eclipse.

It is, of course, agreeable for those who believe in progress, in reform, in new ideals, to attribute these reactions to a hard and stiff-necked generation who willfully refuse to recognize the highest goods when they see them. It is agreeable to regard such as barbarians who are interested simply in turning back the wheels of progress. The simple fact, however, is that education is the one thing in which the American people believe without reserve, and to which they are without reserve committed. Indeed I sometimes think that the necessity of education is the only settled article in the shifting and confused social and moral creed of America.

If then the American public fails in critical cases to stand by the educational newcomers, it is because these latter have not yet become organic parts of the educational whole—otherwise they could not be cut out. They are not really in the unity of educational movement—otherwise they could not be arrested. They are still insertions and additions.

Consider the wave by which a new study is introduced into the curriculum. Someone feels that the school system of his (or quite frequently nowadays her) town is falling behind the times. There are rumors of great progress in education making elsewhere. Something new and important has been introduced; education is being revolutionized by it; the school superintendent, or members of the board of education, become somewhat uneasy; the matter is taken up by individuals and clubs; pressure is brought to bear on the managers of the school system; letters are written to the newspapers; the editor himself is appealed to to use his great power to advance the cause of progress; editorials appear; finally the school board ordains that on and after a certain date the particular new branch—be it nature study, industrial drawing, cooking, manual training, or whatever—shall be taught in the public schools. The victory is won and everybody—unless it be some already over-burdened and distracted teacher—congratulates everybody else that such advanced steps are taken.

The next year, or possibly the next month, there comes an outcry that children do not write or spell or figure as well as they used to; that they cannot do the necessary work in the upper grades or in the high school because of lack of ready command of the necessary tools of study. We are told that they are not prepared for business because their spelling is so poor, their work in addition and multiplication so slow and inaccurate, their handwriting so fearfully and wonderfully made. Some zealous soul on the school board takes up *this* matter; the newspapers are again heard from; investigations are set on foot, and the edict goes forth that there must be more drill in the fundamentals of writing, spelling, and number.

Moreover, in the last year or two there are many signs that the older and traditional studies do not propose to be ig-

nored. For a long time, as already intimated, the conservative
was upon the whole quite content to surrender the intellectual
and emotional territory, the sphere of theory and of warmly-
toned ideals, to the reformer. He was content because he
after all remained in possession of the field of action. But
now there are symptoms of another attitude; the conservative
is, so to speak, coming to intellectual and moral consciousness himself. He is asserting that in his conservatism, he
stands for more than the mere customs and traditions of an
outworn past. He asserts that he stands for honesty of work,
for stability, for thoroughness, for singleness of aim and concentration of agencies, for a reasonable simplicity. He is
actively probing the innovator. He is asking questions regarding the guarantees of personal and intellectual discipline, of
power of control, of ability to work. He is asking whether
there is not danger of both teacher and child getting lost amid
the portentous multiplication of studies. He is asking about
the leisure requisite to intellectual and mental digestion, and
subsequent growth. He is asking whether there is not danger
to integrity of character in arousing so many interests and
impulses that no one of them is carried through to an effective result. These are not matters of mere school procedure
or formal arrangement of studies, but matters fundamental
to intellectual and moral achievement. Moreover some recent
magazine articles seem to indicate that some few, at least, of
the reformers are themselves beginning to draw back; they
are apparently wondering if this new-created child of theirs
be not a Frankenstein, which is to turn and rend its creator.
They seem to be saying: "Possibly we are in danger of going
too fast and too far; what and where are the limits of this
thing we are entered upon?"

My sketch, however inadequate, is yet, I hope, true to
the logic if not to the details of history. What emerges from
this running account? What does it all mean? Does it not
signify that we have a situation in process of forming rather
than a definitive situation? The history reflects both our lack
of intellectual organization and also the increasing recognition of the factors which must enter into any such organization. From this point of view, the renewed self-assertion, from
the standpoint of theory, of the adherents of the traditional

curriculum is a matter of congratulation. It shows that we are emerging from a period of practical struggle to that of intellectual interpretation and adjustment. As yet, however, we have no conscious educational standard by which to test and place each aspiring claimant. We have hundreds of reasons for and against this or that study, but no reason. Having no sense of the unity of experience, and of the definitive relation of each branch of study to that unity, we have no criterion by which to judge and decide. We yield to popular pressure and clamor; first on the side of the instinct for progress, and then on the side of the habit of inertia. As a result every movement, whether for nature study or spelling, for picture study or arithmetic, for manual training or more legible handwriting, is treated as an isolated and independent thing. It is this separation, this lack of vital unity, which leads to the confusion and contention which are so marked features of the educational situation. Lacking a philosophy of unity, we have no basis upon which to make connections, and our whole treatment becomes piecemeal, empirical, and at the mercy of external circumstances.

The problem of the course of study is thus in effect a part of the larger problem so pressing in all departments of the organization of life. Everywhere we have outgrown old methods and standards; everywhere we are crowded by new resources, new instrumentalities; we are bewildered by the multitude of new opportunities that present themselves. Our difficulties of today come not from paucity or poverty, but from the multiplication of means clear beyond our present powers of use and administration. We have got away from the inherited and customary; we have not come into complete possession and command of the present. Unification, organization, harmony, is the demand of every aspect of life —politics, business, science. That education shares in the confusion of transition, and in the demand for reorganization, is a source of encouragement and not of despair. It proves how integrally the school is bound up with the entire movement of modern life.

The situation thus ceases to be a conflict between what is called the old education and the new. There is no longer any old education save here and there in some belated geographic area. There is no new education in definite and supreme existence. What we have is certain vital tendencies. These tendencies ought to work together; each stands for a phase of reality and contributes a factor of efficiency. But because of lack of organization, because of the lack of unified insight upon which organization depends, these tendencies are diverse and tangential. Too often we have their mechanical combination and irrational compromise. More prophetic, because more vital, is the confusion which arises from their conflict. We have been putting new wine into old bottles, and that which was prophesied has come to pass.

To recognize that the situation is not the wholesale antagonism of so-called old education to the so-called new, but a question of the cooperative adjustment of necessary factors in a common situation, is to surrender our partisanship. It is to cease our recriminations and our self-conceits, and search for a more comprehensive end than is represented by either factor apart from the other. It is impossible to anticipate the exact and final outcome of this search. Only time, and the light that comes with time, can reveal the answer. The first step, however, is to study the existing situation as students, not as partisans, and having located the vital factors in it, consider what it is that makes them at the present juncture antagonistic competitors instead of friendly cooperators.

The question is just this: Why do the newer studies, drawing, music, nature study, manual training; and the older studies, the three R's, practically conflict with instead of reinforcing one another? Why is it that the practical problem is so often simply one of outward annexation or mechanical compromise? Why is it that the adjustment of the conflict is left to the mere push and pull of contending factors, to the pressure of local circumstances and of temporary reactions?

An answer to this question is, I believe, the indispensable preliminary to any future understanding. Put roughly, we have two groups of studies: one represents the symbols of the intellectual life, which are the tools of civilization itself; the other group stands for the direct and present expression of power on the part of one undergoing education, and for the present and direct enrichment of his life-experience. For reasons historically adequate, the former group represents the traditional education; the latter, the efforts of the innovator. Intrinsically speaking, in the abstract, there is no reason to assume any fundamental or even any minor antagonism between these two groups. Such an assumption would mean that the requirements of civilization are fundamentally at war with the conditions of individual development; that the agencies by which society maintains itself are at radical odds with the forms by which individual experience is deepened and expanded. Unless we are ready to concede such a fundamental contradiction in the make-up of life, we must hold that the present contention is the result of conditions which are local and transitory.

I offer the following proposition as giving the key to the conflict:

The studies of the symbolic and formal sort represented the aims and material of education for a sufficiently long time to call into existence a machinery of administration and of instruction thoroughly adapted to themselves. This machinery constituted the actual working scheme of administration and instruction. These conditions persist long after the studies to which they are well adapted have lost their theoretical supremacy. The conflict, the confusion, the compromise, is not intrinsically between the older group of studies and the newer, but between the external conditions in which the former were realized, and the aims and standards represented by the newer.

It is easy to fall into the habit of regarding the mechanics of school organization and administration as something comparatively external and indifferent to educational purposes and ideals. We think of the grouping of children in classes, the arrangement of grades, the machinery by which the course of study is made out and laid down, the method by which it is carried into effect, the system of selecting teachers and of assigning them to their work, of paying and promoting them, as in a way matters of mere practical convenience and expediency. We forget that it is precisely such things as these that really control the whole system even on its distinctively educational side. No matter what is the accepted precept and theory, no matter what the legislation of the school board or the mandate of the school superintendent, the reality of education is found in the personal and face-to-face contact of teacher and child. The conditions that underlie and regulate this contact dominate the educational situation.

In this contact, and in it alone, can the reality of current education be got at. To get away from it is to be ignorant and to deceive ourselves. It is in this contact that the real course of study, whatever be laid down on paper, is actually found. Now the conditions that determine this personal contact of child with child, and of children with teacher are, upon the whole, the survival of the period when the domination of the three R's was practically unquestioned. Their effectiveness lies in their adaptation to realizing the ends and aims of that form of education. They do not lend themselves to realizing the purposes of the newer studies. Consequently we do not get the full benefit either of the old or of the new studies. They work at cross-purposes. The excellence which the conditions would possess if they were directed solely at securing progress in reading, writing, and arithmetic, and allied topics, is lost because of the introduction of material irrelevant and distracting *from the standpoint of the conditions*. The new studies do not have an opportunity to show what they can do because they are hampered by machinery constructed for turning out another kind of goods; they are not provided with their own distinctive set of agencies. Granted this contradiction, the only wonder is that the chaos is not greater than it actually is; the only wonder is that we are securing such positive results as actually come about.

Let us study this contradiction somewhat more intimately, taking up one by one some of its constituent elements. On the side of the machinery of school work I mention first the number of children in a room. This runs in the graded schools of our country anywhere from thirty-five to sixty. This can hardly be said to be an ideal condition even from the standpoint of uniform progress in reading, writing, and arithmetic, and the symbols of geography and history; but it certainly is indefinitely better adapted to securing these results than that of the symmetrical and complete development of all the powers, physical, mental, moral, æsthetic, of each individual child out of the entire fifty. From the standpoint of the latter aim, the discrepancy is so great that the situation is either ridiculous or tragic. Under such circumstances how do we have the face to continue to speak at all of the complete development of the individual as the supreme end of educational effort? Excepting here and there with the genius who seems to rise above all conditions, the school environment and machinery almost compel the more mechanical features of school work to lord it over the more vital aims.

We get the same result when we consider not the number of children in a given grade, but the arrangement of grades. The distribution into separate years, each with its own distinctive and definite amount of ground to be covered, the assignment of one and only one teacher to a grade, the confinement of the same teacher to the same grade year by year, save as she is "promoted" to a higher grade, introduce an isolation which is fatal, I will not say to good work, but to the effective domination of the ideal of continuous development of character and personal powers. The unity and wholeness of the child's development can be realized only in a corresponding unity and continuity of school conditions. Anything that breaks the latter up into fractions, into isolated parts, must have the same influence upon the educative growth of the child.[1]

It may, however, be admitted that these conditions, while highly important as regards the aims of education, have little or nothing to do with the course of study—with the subject-matter of instruction. But a little reflection will show that the material of study is profoundly affected. The conditions which compel the children to be dealt with *en masse*, which compel them to be led in flocks, if not in hordes, make it necessary to give the stress of attention to those studies in which some sort of definite result can be most successfully attained, without much appeal to individual initiative, judgment or inquiry. Almost of necessity, attention to the newer studies whose value is dependent upon personal

1. This thought is developed in *Isolation in the School*, by Ella Flagg Young, especially pp. 33–40; 92–98.

appropriation, assimilation and expression is incidental and superficial. The results with the latter are naturally often so unsatisfactory that they are held responsible for the evil consequences; we fail to trace the matter back to the conditions which control the result reached. Upon the whole it is testimony to the vitality of these studies that in such a situation the results are not worse than they actually are.

Unless the teacher has opportunity and occasion to study the educative process as a whole, not as divided into eight or twelve or sixteen parts, it is impossible to see how he can deal effectively with the problem of the complete development of the child. The restriction of outlook to one limited year of the child's growth will inevitably tend in one of two directions: either the teacher's work becomes mechanical, because practically limited to covering the work assigned for the year, irrespective of its nutritive value in the child's growth; or else local and transitory phases of the child's development are seized upon—phases which too often go by the name of the interests of the child—and these are exaggerated out of all due bounds. Since the newer studies give most help in making this excessive and sensational appeal, these studies are held responsible for the evils that subsequently show themselves. As a matter of fact, the cause of the difficulty lies in the isolation and restriction of the work of the teacher which practically forbids his considering the significance of art, music, and nature study in the light of continuity and completeness of growth.

This unity and completeness must, however, be cared for somehow. Since not provided for on the basis of the teacher's knowledge of the whole process of which his own work is one organic member, it is taken care of through external provision of a consecutive course of study, external supervision, and the mechanics of examination and promotion. Connection must somehow be made between the various fractional parts—the successive grades. The supervisor, the principal, is the recourse. Acting, however, not through the medium of the consciousness of the class-room teacher, but through the medium of prescription of mode of action, the inevitable tendency is to arrest attention upon those parts of the subject-matter which lend themselves to external assignment and conjunction. Even music, drawing, and manual training are profoundly influenced by this fact. Their own vital aims and spirit are compromised, or even surrendered, to the necessities for laying out a course of study in such a manner that one year's work may fit externally into that of the next. Thus they part with much of their own distinctive and characteristic value, and become, to a considerable extent, simple additions to the number of routine studies carried by children and teacher. They serve no new purpose of their own, but add to the burden of the old. It is no wonder that when the burden gets too great there is demand that they be lopped off as excrescences upon the educational system.

The matter of promotion from grade to grade has a precisely similar effect upon the course of study. It is, from the standpoint of the child, just what the isolation and external combination already alluded to are from the side of the teacher. The things of the spirit do not lend themselves easily to that kind of external inspection which goes by the name of examination. They do not lend themselves easily to exact quantitative measurement. Technical proficiency, acquisition of skill and information, present much less difficulty. So again emphasis is thrown upon those traditional subjects of the school curriculum which permit most readily a mechanical treatment—upon the three R's and upon the facts of external classification in history and science, matters of formal technique in music, drawing, and manual training. Continuity, order, must be somewhat maintained—if not the order and method of the spirit, then at least that of external conditions. Nothing is gained by throwing everything into chaos. In this sense the conservative is thoroughly right when he insists upon the maintenance of the established traditions of the school as regards the tests of the pupil's ability and preparation for promotion. He fails, however, to recognize the other alternative: that the looseness and confusion, the vagueness in accomplishment and in test of accomplishment of which he complains, may be due not to the new studies themselves, but to the unfit conditions under which they operate.

I have already alluded to the fact that at present the

teacher is hardly enabled to get a glimpse of the educative process as a whole, and accordingly is reduced to adding together the various external bits into which that unity is broken. We get exactly the same result when we consider the way in which the course of study is determined. The fact that this is fixed by board of education, superintendent, or supervisor, by a power outside the teacher in the class room who alone can make that course of study a living reality, is a fact too obvious to be concealed. It is, however, comparatively easy to conceal from ourselves the tremendous import of this fact. As long as the teacher, who is after all the only real educator in the school system, has no definite and authoritative position in shaping the course of study, that is likely to remain an external thing to be externally applied to the child.[2]

A school board or a superintendent can lay out a course of study down to the point of stating exactly the number of pages of text-books to be covered in each year, each term and month of the year. It may prescribe the exact integers and fraction of integers with which the child shall make scholastic acquaintance during any period of his instruction; it may directly or indirectly define the exact shapes to be reproduced in drawing, or mention the exact recipes to be followed in cooking. Doubtless the experience of the individual teacher who makes the connections between these things and the life of the child will receive incidental attention in laying out these courses. But so long as the teacher has no definite voice, the attention will be only incidental; and, as a further consequence, the average teacher will give only incidental study to the problems involved. If his work is the task of carrying out the instructions imposed upon him, then his time and thought must be absorbed in the matter of execution. There is no motive for interest of a thoroughly vital and alert sort, in questions of the intrinsic value of the subject-matter and its adaptation to the needs of child growth. He may be called upon by official requirements, or the pressure of circumstance, to be a student of pedagogical books and journals; but conditions relieve him of the neces-

2. See, again, *Isolation in the School*, by Ella Flagg Young, pp. 31–32 and 106–9.

sity of being a student of the most fundamental educational problems in their most urgent reality.

The teacher needs to study the mechanics of successfully carrying into effect the prescribed matter of instruction; he does not have to study that matter itself, or its educative bearing. Needless to say, the effect of this upon the actual course of study is to emphasize the thought and time given to those subjects, and phases of subjects, where there is most promise of success in doing the exact things prescribed. The three R's are again magnified, while the technical and routine aspects of the newer studies tend to crowd out those elements that give them their deeper significance in intellectual and moral life. Since, however, the school must have relief from monotony, must have "interest," must have diversification and recreation, these studies become too easily tools for introducing the excitement and amusement supposed to be necessary. The judicious observer who sees below the surface, but not to the foundation, again discounts these studies. Meanwhile the actual efficiency of the three R's is hampered and lessened by the superaddition of the new ways of employing time, whether they be routine or exciting in character.

It may easily be said that the class-room teacher at present is not sufficiently educated to be entrusted with any part in shaping a course of study. I waive the fundamental question—the question of democracy—whether the needed education can be secured without giving more responsibility even to the comparatively uneducated. The objection suggests another fundamental condition in our present school procedure—the question of the status of the teacher as regards selection and appointment.

The real course of study must come to the child from the teacher. What gets to the child is dependent upon what is in the mind and consciousness of the teacher, and upon the way it is in his mind. It is through the teacher that the value even of what is contained in the text-book is brought home to the child; just in the degree in which the teacher's understanding of the material of the lessons is vital, adequate, and comprehensive, will that material come to the child in the same form; in the degree in which the teacher's understanding is mechanical, superficial, and restricted, the child's appreciation will be correspondingly limited and perverted. If this be true, it is obviously futile to plan large expansions of the studies of the curriculum apart from the education of the teacher. I am far from denying the capacity on the part of truth above and beyond the comprehension of the teacher to filter through to the mind of an aspiring child; but upon the whole it is certain beyond controversy that the success of the teacher in teaching, and of the pupil in learning, will depend upon the intellectual equipment of the teacher.

To put literature into a course of study quite irrespective of the teacher's personal appreciation of literary values—to say nothing of accurate discrimination as to the facts—is to go at the matter from the wrong end. To enact that at a given date all the grades of a certain city shall have nature study is to invite confusion and distraction. It would be comic (if it were not tragic) to suppose that all that is required to make music and drawing a part of the course of study is to have the school board legislate that a certain amount of the time of the pupil, covering a certain prescribed ground, shall be given to work with pencil and paper and to musical exercises. There is no magic by which these things can pass over from the printed page of the school manual to the child's consciousness. If the teacher has no standard of value in relation to them, no intimate personal response of feeling to them, no conception of the methods of art which alone bring the child to a corresponding intellectual and emotional attitude, these studies will remain what precisely they so often are—passing recreations, modes of showing off, or exercises in technique.

The special teacher has arisen because of the recognition of the inadequate preparation of the average teacher to get the best results with these newer subjects. Special teaching, however, shifts rather than solves the problem. As already indicated, the question is a twofold one. It is a question not only of *what* is known, but of *how* it is known. The special instructor in nature study or art may have a better command of the what—of the actual material to be taught—but be deficient in the consciousness of the relations borne by that particular subject to other forms of experience in the child, and, therefore, to his own personal growth. When this is the case we exchange King Log for King Stork. We exchange an ignorant and superficial teaching for a vigorous but one-sided, because over-specialized, mode of instruction. The special teacher in manual training or what not, having no philosophy of education—having, that is, no view of the whole of which his own subject is a part—isolates that study and works it out wholly in terms of itself. His beginning and his end, as well as the intermediate materials and methods, fall within manual training. This may give technical facility, but it is not (save incidentally) education.

This is not an attack upon special or departmental teaching. On the contrary, I have just pointed out that this mode of teaching has arisen absolutely in response to the demands of the situation. Since our present teachers are so largely an outcome of the older education, the so-called all-around teacher is for the most part a myth. Moreover it is a mistake to suppose that we can secure the all-around teacher merely by instructing him in a larger number of branches. In the first place, human capacity is limited. The person whose interests and powers are all-around is not as a rule teaching in grade schools. He is at the head of the great scientific, industrial, and political enterprises of civilization. But granted that the average teacher could master ten distinct studies as well as five, it still remains true that without intellectual organization, without definite insight into the relation of these studies to one another and to the whole of life, without ability to present them to the child from the standpoint of such insight, we simply add an over-burdened and confused teacher to the over-burdened and confused child. In a word, to make the teaching in the newer studies thoroughly effective, whether by specialists or by the all-around teacher, there must, in addition to knowledge of the particular branch, be sanity, steadiness, and system in the mental attitude of the instructor. It is folly to suppose that we can carry on the education of the child apart from the education of the teacher.

If I were to touch upon certain other matters fundamentally connected with the problem of securing the teachers who make the nominal course of study a reality, I should be started upon an almost endless road. However, we must not pass on without at least noticing that the question is one of political as well as of intellectual organization. An adequate view of the whole situation would take into account the general social condition upon which depends the actual supplying of teachers to the schoolroom. The education of the candidate, of the would-be teacher, might be precisely that outlined above, and yet it would remain, to a large extent, inoperative, if the appointment of school-teachers was at the mercy of personal intrigue, political bargaining, and the effort of some individual or class to get power in the community through manipulation of patronage. It is sentimental to suppose that any large and decisive reform in the course of study can take place as long as such agencies influence what actually comes in a living way to the life of the child.

Nor in a more comprehensive view could we be entirely silent upon the need of commercial as well as political reform. Publishing companies affect not only the text-books and apparatus, the garb with which the curriculum clothes itself, but also and that directly the course of study itself. New studies are introduced because some publishing firm, by a happy coincidence, has exactly the books which are needed to make that study successful. Old studies which should be entirely displaced (if there be any logic in the introduction of the new one) are retained because there is a vested interest behind them. Happy is the large school system which is free from the congestion and distraction arising from just such causes as these. And yet there are those who discuss the relative merits of what they are pleased to call old and new education as if it were purely an abstract and intellectual matter.

But we cannot enter upon these larger phases. It is enough if we recognize the typical signs indicating the impossibility of separating either the theoretical discussion of the course of study, or the problem of its practical efficiency, from intellectual and social conditions which at first sight are far removed; it is enough if we recognize that the question of the course of study is a question in the organization of knowledge, in the organization of life, in the organization of society. And for more immediate purposes it is enough to recognize that certain conditions imbedded in the present scheme of school administration affect so profoundly results reached by the newer studies, by manual training, art and nature study, that it is absurd to discuss the value or lack of value of the latter, without taking these conditions into account. I recur to my original proposition: that these studies are not having their own career, are not exhibiting their own powers, but are hampered and compromised by a school machinery originated and developed with reference to quite different ends and aims. The real conflict is not between a certain group of studies, the three R's, those having to do with the symbols and tools of intellectual life and other studies representing the personal development of the child, but between our professed ends and the means we are using to realize these ends.

The popular assumption, however, is to the contrary. It is still the common belief (and not merely in popular thought but among those who profess to speak with authority) that the two groups of studies are definitely opposed to each other in their aims and methods, in the mental attitude demanded from the child, in the kind of work called for from the instructor. It is assumed that we have a conflict between one group of studies dealing only with the forms and symbols of knowledge, studies to be mastered by mechanical drill, and between those that appeal to the vital concerns of child life and afford present satisfaction. This assumed opposition has been so clearly stated in a recent educational document that I may be pardoned quoting at length:

In regard to education we may divide the faculties into two classes—the doing faculties and the thinking faculties. By the doing faculties I mean those mechanical habits which are essential to the acquisition of knowledge, and are pure arts, such as the art of reading; that of performing arithmetical operations with rapidity and correctness; that of expressing thoughts in legible characters, and in words of grammatical arrangement. These arts can only be acquired by laborious drilling on the part of the teacher, and labor on the part of the pupil. They require little instruction, but repetition until they are performed with ease and almost pleasure. To neglect to impart these habits is to do a great injury to the child; nothing should be substituted for them, though instruction in other branches which require more thought and less art may be mingled as recreations with them.

I have never seen so condensed and comprehensive a statement of the incompatibility of aims and method for both teacher and pupil as is given here. On one side we have "doing faculties," by which is meant powers of pure external efficiency. These find their expression in what are termed "arts," which is interpreted to mean purely mechanical habits —sheer routine facility. These are acquired by continued drill on the part of the teacher, and continued laborious repetition on the part of the child. Thought is not required in the process, nor is the result "instruction"—that is, a real building up of the mind; the outcome is simply command of powers, of value not in themselves, but as tools of further knowledge, as "essential to the acquisition of knowledge." The scheme of contrasting studies is not so well developed. It is made clear, however, that they appeal to thought, not to mechanical habits, and that they proceed by instruction not by drill. It is further implied that their exercise is attended not so much with labor as with pleasure on the part of the child—which may be interpreted to mean that they have a present value in the life of the child, and are not mere instrumentalities of remoter acquisition. The situation as regards school work is contained in the proposition that the mechanical facilities based upon sheer drill and laborious repetition must make up the bulk of the elementary education, while the studies which involve thought, the furnishing of the mind itself, and result in a direct expansion of life, "may be mingled as recreations." They may be permitted, in other words, in the schoolroom as an occasional relief from the laborious drill of the more important studies.

Here is the dividing wall. The wall has been somewhat undermined; breaches have been worn in it; it has, as it were, been bodily pushed along until the studies of thought, of instruction, and of present satisfaction occupy a greater bulk of school time and work. But the wall is still there. The mechanical habits that are essential to the acquisition of knowledge, the art of reading, of performing arithmetical operations, and of expressing thought legibly and grammatically, are still the serious business of the schoolroom. Nature study, manual training, music and art are incidents introduced because of the "interests" they provide, because they appeal to ability to think, arouse general intelligence, and add to the fund of information. A house divided against itself cannot stand. If the results of our present system are not altogether and always satisfactory, shall we engage in crimination and recrimination—setting the old studies against the new and the new against the old—or shall we hold responsible the organization, or lack of organization, intellectual and administrative in the school system itself? If the old bottles will not hold the new wine, it is conceivable that we should blame neither the bottles nor the wine, but conditions which have brought the two into mechanical and external connection.

If my remarks in dwelling upon the split and contradiction in the present situation appear to be unnecessarily gloomy, it should be remembered that this view is optimism itself as compared with the theory which holds that the two groups of studies are radically opposed to each other in their ends, results and methods. Such a theory holds that there is a fundamental contradiction between the present and the future needs of the child, between what his life requires as immediate nutritive material and what it needs as preparation for the future. It assumes a fundamental conflict between that which nourishes the spirit of the child and that which affords the instrumentalities of intellectual acquisition. It proclaims a fundamental opposition to exist in the mental activity between the methods of acquisition of skill, and the methods of development. The practical consequences are as disastrous as the logical split is complete. If the opposition be an intrinsic one, then the present conflict and confusion in the schoolroom are permanent and not transitory. We shall be forever oscillating between extremes: now lending ourselves with enthusiasm to the introduction of art and music and manual training because they give vitality to the school work and relief to the child; now querulously complaining of the evil results reached and insisting with all positiveness upon the return of good old days when reading, writing, spelling, and arithmetic were adequately taught. Since by the theory there is no possibility of an organic connection, of cooperative relation, between the two types of study, the relative position of each in the curriculum must be decided from arbitrary and external grounds; by the wish and zeal of some strong man, or by the pressure of temporary popular sentiment. At the best we get only a compromise; at the worst we get a maximum of routine with a halo of sentiment thrown about it, or a great wish-wash of superficiality covering up the residuum of grind.

As compared with such a view, the conception that the conflict is not inherent in the studies themselves, but arises from maladjustment of school conditions, from survival of a mode of educational administration calculated for different ends from those now confronting us, is encouragement itself. The problem becomes first an intellectual and then a practical one. Intellectually what is needed is a philosophy of organization: a view of the organic unity of the educative process and educative material, and of the place occupied in this whole by each of its own parts. We need to know just what reading and writing and number do for the present life of the child and how they do it. We need to know what the method of mind is which underlies subject-matter in cooking, shop-work and nature study, so that they may become effective for discipline, and not mere sources of present satisfaction and mere agencies of relief—so that they too may become as definitely modes of effective preparation for the needs of society as ever reading, writing, and arithmetic have been.

With our minds possessed by a sane and coherent view of the whole situation, we may attempt such a gradual yet positive modification of existing procedure as will enable us to turn theory into practice. Let us not be too precipitate, however, in demanding light upon just what to do next. We should remember that there are times when the most practical thing is to face the *intellectual* problem, and to get a clear and comprehensive survey of the theoretical factors involved. The existing situation, with all its vagueness and all its confusion, will nevertheless indicate plenty of points of leverage, plenty of intelligent ways of straightening things out, to one who approaches it with any clear conviction of the ends he wishes to reach, and of the obstacles in the way. An enlightenment of vision is the prerequisite of efficiency in conduct. The conservative may devote himself to the place of reading and writing and arithmetic in the curriculum so that they shall vitally connect with the present needs of the child's life, and afford the satisfaction that always comes with the fulfillment, the expression, of present power. The reformer may attack the problem not at large and all over the entire field, but at the most promising point whether it be art or manual training or nature study, and concentrate all his efforts upon educating alike the community, the teacher, and the child, into the knowledge of fundamental values for individual mind and for community life embodied in that study. Both conservative and reformer can devote themselves to the problem of the better education of the teacher and of doing away with the hindrances to placing the right teacher in the schoolroom; and to the hindrances to continued growth after he is placed there. The American people believe in education above all else, and when the educators have come to some agreement as to what education is, the community will not be slow in placing at their disposal the equipment and resources necessary to make their ideal a reality.

In closing let me say that I have intentionally emphasized the obstacles to further progress rather than congratulated ourselves upon the progress already made. The anomaly and confusion have, after all, been of some use. In some respects the blind conflict of the last two generations of educational history has been a better way of changing the conditions than would have been some wholesale and *a priori* rearrangement. The forms of genuine growth always come slowly. The struggle of the newer studies to get a foothold in the curriculum, with all the attendant confusion, is an experiment carried out on a large scale; an experiment in natural selection, of the survival of the fit in educational forms.

Yet there must come a time when blind experimentation is to give way to something more directed. The struggle should bring out the factors in the problem so that we can go more intelligently to work in its solution. The period of blind striving, of empirical adjustment, trying now this and now that, making this or that combination because it is feasible for the time being, of advancing here and retreating there, of giving headway now to the instinct of progress and now to the habit of inertia, should find an outcome in some illumination of vision, in some clearer revelation of the realities of the situation. It is uneconomical to prolong the period of conflict between incompatible tendencies. It makes for intellectual hypocrisy to suppose that we are doing what we are not doing. It weakens the nerve of judgment and the fibre of action to submit to conditions which prevent the realization of aims to which we profess ourselves to be devoted.

My topic is the elementary educational situation. In a somewhat more limited and precise view than I have previously taken of the situation, I believe we are now nearing the close of the time of tentative, blind, empirical experimentation; that we are close to the opportunity of planning our work on the basis of a coherent philosophy of experience and a philosophy of the relation of school studies to that experience; that we can accordingly take up steadily and wisely the effort of changing school conditions so as to make real the aims that command the assent of our intelligence and the support of our moral enthusiasm.

2. AS CONCERNS SECONDARY EDUCATION

I should feel hesitant indeed to come before a body of teachers, engaged in the practical work of teaching, and appear to instruct them regarding the solution of the difficult problems which face them. My task is a more grateful one. It is mine simply to formulate and arrange the difficulties which the current state of discussion shows teachers already to have felt. Those concerned with secondary-school work have realized that their energies must be peculiarly concentrated at certain points; they have found that some problems are so urgent that they must be met and wrestled with. I have tried in the accompanying syllabus to gather together these practical problems and to arrange them in such form as to show their connections with one another; and by this classification to indicate what seemed to me the roots of the difficulty.

  I. *Problems relating to the articulation of the secondary school in the educational system.*
    1. Adjustment to the grades.
        a) Dropping out of pupils: extent and causes.
        b) Different sorts of preparation of teachers; methods of rectifying, etc.
        c) Abrupt change of ideals and methods of teaching and discipline.
        d) Introduction of traditional high-school studies into the upper grades; the science course, etc.
    2. Adjustment to college.
        a) Modes of entering college; examination, certification, etc.
        b) Varieties of entrance requirements.
        c) Different problems of public and private high schools.
        d) Coaching for specific results *vs.* training and method.

[Chapter 2 first published as "Current Problems in Secondary Education," in *School Review* 10 (1902): 13–28. Not reprinted elsewhere.]

II. *Problems relating to the adjustment of preparation for college to preparation for other pursuits in life.*
  1. Is it true that the same education gives the best preparation for both?
  2. If so, which shall be taken as the standard for measuring the character of the other?
  3. If not so, by what principles and along what lines shall the work be differentiated?
  4. If not so, shall specialized or definite preparation be made for other future callings as well as for the college student?

III. *The adjustment of work to the individual.*
  1. The nature and limits of the elective principle as applied to particular subjects, and to courses and groups of subjects.
  2. Acquaintance with the history, environment, and capacity of individuals with reference to assisting in the selection of vocation.
  3. Does the period of adolescence present such peculiarities as to call for marked modifications of present secondary work?

IV. *Problems arising from social phases of secondary-school work.*
  1. The educational utilization of social organizations: debating, musical, dramatic clubs; athletics.
  2. School discipline and government in their social aspects.
  3. Relations to the community: the school as a social centre.

V. *Preceding problems as affecting the curriculum: conflict of studies and groups of studies.*
  1. The older problem: adjustment of the respective claims of ancient and modern languages, of language and science, of history and social science, civics, economics, etc., of English literature and composition.
  2. The newer problem:
     a) The place of manual training and technological work.
     b) The place of fine art.
     c) Commercial studies.

In what I have to say this morning, I shall make no attempt to go over these points one by one. I shall rather try to set clearly and briefly before you the reasons which have led me to adopt the classification presented. This will take me into a discussion of the historic and social facts which lie back of the problems, and in the light of which alone I believe these problems can be attacked and solved. If it seems unnecessarily remote to approach school problems through a presentation of what may appear to be simply a form of social philosophy, there is yet practical encouragement in recognizing that exactly the same forces which have thrust these questions into the forefront of school practice are also operative to solve them. For problems do not arise arbitrarily. They come from causes, and from causes which are imbedded in the very structure of the school system—yes, even beyond that, in the structure of society itself. It is for this reason that mere changes in the mechanics of the school system, whether in administration or in the externals of subject-matter, turn out mere temporary devices. Sometimes, when one has made a delicate or elaborate arrangement which seems to him exactly calculated to obviate the difficulties of the situation, one is tempted to accuse his generation as stiff-necked when the scheme does not take—when it does not spread; when, in the language of the biologist, it is not selected. The explanation, however, is not in the hard-heartedness or intellectual blindness of others, but in the fact that any adjustment which really and permanently succeeds within the school walls must reach out and be an adjustment of forces in the social environment.

A slight amount of social philosophy and social insight reveals two principles continuously at work in all human institutions: one is toward specialization and consequent isolation, the other toward connection and interaction. In the life of the nation we see first a movement toward separation, toward marking off our own life as a people as definitely as possible to avoid its submergence, to secure for it an individuality of its own. Commercially we pursue a policy of protection; in international relations one of having to do as little as possible with other nationalities. That tendency exhausts itself and the pendulum swings in another direction. Reciprocity, the broadening of our business life through increased contacts and wider exchange, becomes the commercial watchword. Expansion, taking our place in the sisterhood of nations, making ourselves recognized as a world-power, becomes the formula for international politics. Science shows the same rhythm in its development. A period of specialization—of relative isolation—secures to each set of natural phenomena a chance to develop on its own account, without being lost in, or obscured by generalities or a mass of details. But the time comes when the limit of movement in this direction is reached, and it is necessary to devote ourselves to tracing the threads of connection which unite the different specialized branches into a coherent and consecutive whole. At present the most active sciences seem to be spelled with a hyphen; it is astro-physics, stereo-chemistry, psycho-physics, and so on.

This is not a movement of blind action and reaction. One tendency is the necessary completion of the other. A certain degree of isolation of detachment is required to secure the unhindered and mature development of any group of forces. It is necessary in order to master them in their practical workings. We have to divide to conquer. But when the proper degree of individualization is reached, we need to bring one thing to bear upon another in order to realize upon the benefits which may be derived from the period of isolation. The sole object of the separation is to serve as a means to the end of more effective interaction.

Now as to the bearings of this abstract piece of philosophy upon our school problems. The school system is a historic evolution. It has a tradition and a movement of its own. Its roots run back into the past and may be traced through the strata of the successive centuries. It has an independence, a dignity of its own comparable to that of any other institution. In this twenty-five-hundred-year-old development it has, of necessity, taken on its individuality at the expense of a certain isolation. Only through this isolation has it been disentangled from absorption in other institutions: the family, government, the church, and so on. This detachment has been a necessity in order that it might become a true division of labor and thus perform most efficiently the service required of it.

But there are disadvantages as well as advantages. Attention has come to be concentrated upon the affairs of the school system as if they concerned simply the system itself, and had only a very indirect reference to other social institutions. The school-teacher often resents reference to outside contacts and considerations as if they were indeed outside—

simply interferences. There can be no doubt that in the last two centuries much more thought and energy have been devoted to shaping the school system into an effective mechanism within itself than to securing its due interaction with family life, the church, commerce, or political institutions.

But, having secured this fairly adequate and efficient machine, the question which is coming more and more to the front is: What shall we do with it? How shall we secure from it the services, the fruits, which alone justify the expense of money, time, and thought in building up the machine?

It is at this point that particular conflicts and problems begin to show themselves. The contemporary demands—the demands that are made in the attempt to secure the proper interaction of the school—are one thing; the demands that arise out of the working of the school system considered as an independent historical institution are another. Every teacher has to work at detailed problems which arise out of this conflict, whether he is aware of its existence or not, and he is harassed by friction that arises in the conflict of these two great social forces. Men divide along these lines. We find one group instinctively rather than consciously ranging themselves about the maintenance of the existing school system, and holding that reforms are to be made along the line of improvement in its present workings. Others are clamorous for more radical changes—the changes that will better adapt the school to contemporary social needs. Needless to say, each represents a necessary and essential factor in the situation, because each stands for the working of a force which cannot be eliminated.

Let me now try to show how, out of this profound social conflict and necessity of social adjustment, the particular problems arise which I have arranged under five heads in the accompanying syllabus. Our first concern is with the articulation of the high school into the entire educational system. The high school looks towards the grades on one side and toward the college on the other. What are the historic influences which have shaped this intermediate position, and placed peculiar difficulties and responsibilities upon the secondary school? Briefly put, it is that the elementary school

and the college represent distinctly different forces and
traditions on the historic side. The elementary school is an
outgrowth of the democratic movement in its ethical aspects.
Prior to the latter half of the eighteenth century the elementary school was hardly more than a wooden device for
instructing little children of the lower classes in some of the
utilities of their future callings—the mere rudiments of reading, writing, and number. The democratic upheaval took
shape not merely in a demand for political equality, but in a
more profound aspiration towards an equality of intellectual
and moral opportunity and development. The significance of
such an educational writer as Rousseau is not measured by
any particular improvement he suggested, or by any particular extravagances he indulged himself in. His is a voice
struggling to express the necessity of a thoroughgoing revolution of elementary education to make it a factor in the intellectual and moral development of all—not a mere device for
teaching the use of certain practical tools to those sections of
society before whose development a stone wall was placed.
What Rousseau as a writer was to the emotions of the France
of his day, Horace Mann as a doer was to the practical situation of the United States in his time. He stood, and stood most
effectively, for letting the democratic spirit, in all of its
ethical significance, into the common elementary schools,
and for such a complete reorganization of these schools
as would make them the most serviceable possible instruments of human development.

In spite of all the influences which are continually
operative to limit the scope and range of elementary education, in spite of the influences which would bring back a
reversion to the type of the limited utilitarian school of the
seventeenth century, that part of the school system which
stands underneath the high school represents this broad
democratic movement. To a certain extent, and in many of
its phases, the high school is an outgrowth of exactly the
same impulse. It has the same history and stands for the
same ideals; but only in part. It has also been profoundly
shaped by influences having another origin. It represents also
the tradition of the learned class. It maintains the tradition
of higher culture as a distinct possession of a certain class of
society. It embodies the aristocratic ideal. If we cast our eyes

back over history, we do not find its full meaning summed up in the democratic movement of which I have just spoken. We find the culture of the ancient world coming down to us by a distinct channel. We find the wisdom and enlightenment of the past conserved and handed on by a distinct class located almost entirely in the colleges, and in the higher academies which are to all intents and purposes the outgrowth of the colleges. We find that our high school has been quite as persistently molded and directed through the agencies which have been concerned with keeping alive and passing on the treasure of learning, as through the democratic influences which have surged up from below. The existing high school, in a word, is a product of the meeting of these two forces, and upon it more than upon any other part of the school system is placed the responsibility of making an adjustment.

I do not mention the tradition of learning kept up in the universities of the Middle Ages and the higher schools of the Renaissance, and refer to it as aristocratic for the sake of disparaging it. Eternal vigilance is the price of liberty, and eternal care and nurture are the price of maintaining the precious conquest of the past—of preventing a relapse into Philistinism, that combination of superficial enlightenment and dogmatic crudity. If it were not for the work of an aristocracy in the past, there would be but little worth conferring upon the democracy of today.

There are not in reality two problems of articulation for the high school—one as regards the grades and the other as regards the college. There is at bottom but one problem— that of adjusting the demand for an adequate training of the masses of mankind to the conservation and use of that higher learning which is the primary and essential concern of a smaller number—of a minority. Of course, elementary school and college alike are affected by the same problem. Part of the work of the grades today is precisely the enrichment of its traditional meagre and materialistic curriculum with some-thing of that spirit and wealth of intelligence that are the product of the higher schools. And one of the problems of the college is precisely to make its store of learning more avail-able to the masses, make it count for more in the everyday life.

But the high school is the connecting link, and it must

bear the brunt. Unless I am a false prophet, we shall soon see the same thoughtful attention which for the past fifteen years has characterized discussion of the relation of high school and college, speedily transferring itself over to the problem of a more organic and vital relation between the high school and the grades. The solution of this problem is important in order that the democratic movement may not be abortively arrested—in order that it may have its full sweep. But it is equally important for the sake of the college and in the interests of higher learning. The arbitrary hiatus which exists at present reacts as unfavorably in one direction as in the other.

First, it limits the constituency of the college; it lessens the actual numbers of those who are awakened to the opportunities before them, and directed towards the college doors. Secondly, it restricts the sphere of those who sympathetically and vicariously feel the influence of the college, and are thus led to feel that what concerns the welfare of the college is of direct concern to them. The attitude of the mass of the people today towards the college is one of curiosity displaying itself from afar rather than of immediate interest. Indeed, it sometimes would seem that only athletic exhibitions form a direct line of connection between the college and the average community life. In the third place it tends to erect dams which prevent the stream of teachers flowing from the college walls from seeking or finding congenial service in the grades, and thereby tends automatically to perpetuate whatever narrowness of horizon or paucity of resource is characteristic of the elementary school. Fourth, it operates to isolate the college in its working relations to life, and thereby to hinder it from rendering its normal service to society.

I pass on now to the second main line of problems— those having to do with preparation for college on one side, and for life on the other. Ultimately this is not a different problem, but simply another outgrowth of the same question. A few years ago a happy formula was current: the proposition that the best preparation for college was also the best preparation for life. The formula was such a happy one that if formulæ ever really disposed of any practical difficulty, there would be no longer any problem to discuss. But I seem to observe that this proposition is not heard so frequently as formerly; and, indeed, that since it was uttered things seem to be taking their own course much as before.

The inefficiency of the formula lies in its ambiguity. It throws no light on the fundamental problem of Which is Which? Is it preparation for college which sets the standard for preparation for life, or is it preparation for life which affords the proper criterion of adequate preparation for college? Is the high-school course to be planned primarily with reference to meeting the needs of those who go to college, on the assumption that this will also serve best the needs of those who go into other callings in life? Or, shall the high school devote its energies to preparing all its members for life in more comprehensive sense, and permit the college to select its entrance requirements on the basis of work thus done?

I shall not attempt to solve this problem, and for a very good reason. I believe that there are forces inherent in the situation itself which are working out an inevitable solution. Every step in the more rational development of both high school and college, without any reference to their relationships to each other, brings the two more closely together. I am optimistic enough to believe that we are much nearer a solution of this vexed question than we generally dare believe. Quite independent of any question of entrance requirements, or of high-school preparation, the college is undergoing a very marked development, and even transformation, on its own account. I refer to such developments within the college course as the introduction not only of the Ph.B. and B.S. courses side by side with the older classical courses, but also to the forward movement in the direction of a specific group of commercial and social studies; and to the tendency of all universities of broad scope to maintain technological schools. I refer also to the tendency to adapt the college work more and more to preparation for specific vocations in life. Practically all the larger colleges of the country now have a definite arrangement by which at least one year of the undergraduate course counts equally in the professional course of law, medicine, or divinity as the case may be. Now, when these two movements have reached their fruition, and the high school has worked out on its own account the broadening of its own curriculum, I believe we shall find that the high school and the college have arrived at a common point. The college course will be so broad and varied that it will be entirely feasible to take any judicious group of studies from any well-organized and well-managed high school, and accept them as preparation for college. It has been the narrowness of the traditional college curriculum on one side, and the inadequacy of the content of high-school work on the other, which have caused a large part of our mutual embarrassments.

I must run rapidly over the problems referred to under my third and fourth main heads—those having to do with adjustment to individual needs, and to the social uses of the school. I take it that these illustrate just the same general principle we have been already discussing. The school has a tradition not only regarding its position in the educational system as a whole, and not only as regards its proper curriculum, but also as regards the methods and ideals of discipline and administration in relation to its students.

There can be no doubt that many of these traditions are out of alignment with the general trend of events outside the school walls—that in some cases the discrepancy is so great that the high-school tradition cuts abruptly across this outside stream. One of these influences is found in the tendency equally marked in the family, church, and state, to relax the bonds of purely external authority, to give more play to individual powers, to require of the individual more personal initiative, and to exact of him a more personal accountability. There may be difference of opinion as to the degree in which the school should yield to this tendency, or should strive to counteract it, or should endeavor to utilize and direct it. There can be no difference of opinion, however, as to the necessity of a more persistent and adequate study of the individual as regards his history, environment, predominant tastes and capacities, and special needs—and please note that I say needs as well as tastes. I do not think there can be any difference of opinion as to the necessity of a more careful study of the effect of particular school studies upon the normal growth of the individual, and of the means by which they shall be made a more effective means of connection between the present powers of the individual and his future career. Just the limits of this principle, and its bearings upon such problems as the introduction of electives, I shall not take up. We have no time for a detailed discussion of these disputed points. As I have just indicated, however, I do not see how there can be dispute as to the fact that the individual has assumed such a position as to require more positive consideration and attention as an individual, and a correspondingly different mode of treatment. I cannot leave the topic, however, without stating that here also I believe the ultimate solution will be found, not along the line of mechanical devices as to election or non-election, but rather through the more continued and serious study of the individual in both his psychological make-up and his social relations.

I have reserved the group of problems bearing upon the formation of a curriculum until the last. From the practical side, however, we probably find here the problems which confront the average teacher most urgently and persistently. This, I take it, is because all the other influences impinge at this point. The problem of just what time is to be given respectively to mathematics, and classics, and modern languages, and history, and English, and the sciences—physical, biological—is one the high-school teacher has always with him. To adjust the respective claims of the different studies and get a result which is at once harmonious and workable, is a task which almost defies human capacity. The problem, however, is not a separate problem. It is so pressing just because it is at this point that all the other forces meet. The adjustment of studies, and courses of study, is the ground upon which the practical solution and working adjustment of all other problems must be sought and found. It is as an effect of other deep-lying and far-reaching historic and social causes that the conflict of studies is to be treated.

There is one matter constantly accompanying any practical problem which at first sight is extremely discouraging. Before we get our older problems worked out to any degree of satisfaction, new and greater problems are upon us, threatening to overwhelm us. Such is the present educational situation. It would seem as if the question of adjusting the conflicts already referred to, which have so taxed the time and energy of high-school teachers for the past generation, were quite enough. But no; before we have arrived at anything approaching consensus of opinion, the larger city schools at least find the conflict raging in a new spot—still other studies and lines of study are demanding recognition. We have the uprearing of the commercial high school; of the manual-training high school.

At first the difficulty of the problem was avoided or evaded, because distinct and separate high schools were erected to meet these purposes. The current now seems to be in the other direction. A generation ago it was practically necessary to isolate the manual-training course of study in order that it might receive due attention, and be worked out under fairly favorable influences. Fifteen years ago the same was essentially true of the commercial courses. Now, however, there are many signs of the times indicating that the situation is ripe for interaction—the problem is now the introduction of manual-training and commercial courses as integral and organic parts of a city high school. Demands are also made for the introduction of more work in the line of fine art, drawing, music, and the application of design to industry; and for the introduction of a larger number of specifically sociological studies—this independent of those studies which naturally form a part of the so-called commercial course.

At first sight, as just intimated, the introduction of these new difficulties before we are half way through our old ones, is exceedingly distressing. But more than once the longest way around has proved the shortest way home. When new problems emerge, it must mean, after all, that certain essential conditions of the old problem had been ignored, and consequently that any solution reached simply in terms of the recognized factors would have been partial and temporary. I am inclined to think that in the present case the introduction of these new problems will ultimately prove enlightening rather than confusing. They serve to generalize the older problems, and to make their factors stand out in clearer relief.

In the future it is going to be less and less a matter of worrying over the respective merits of the ancient and modern languages; or of the inherent values of scientific *vs.* humanistic study, and more a question of discovering and observing certain broader lines of cleavage, which affect equally the disposition and power of the individual, and the social callings for which education ought to prepare the individual. It will be, in my judgment, less and less a question of piecing together certain studies in a more or less mechanical way in order to make out a so-called course of study running through a certain number of years; and more and more a question of grouping studies together according to their natural mutual affinities and reinforcements for the securing of certain well-marked ends.

For this reason I welcome the introduction into the arena of discussion, of the question of providing courses in commerce and sociology, in the fine and applied arts, and in technological training. I think henceforth certain fundamental issues will stand out more clearly and have to be met upon a wider basis and dealt with on a wider scale. As I see the matter, this change will require the concentration of attention upon these two points: first, what groups of studies will most serviceably recognize the typical divisions of labor, the typical callings in society, callings which are absolutely indispensable to the spiritual as well as to the material ends of society; and, secondly, not to do detriment to the real culture of the individual, or, if this seems too negative a statement, to secure for him the full use and control of his own powers. From this point of view, I think that certain of the problems just referred to, as, for instance, the conflict of language and science, will be put in a new perspective, will be capable of approach from a different angle; and that because of this new approach many of the knotty problems which have embarrassed us in the past will disappear.

Permit me to repeat in a somewhat more explicit way the benefits which I expect to flow from the expansion of the regular high school in making room for commercial, manual, and æsthetic studies. In the first place, it will provide for the recognition and the representation of all the typical occupations that are found in society. Thus it will make the working relationship between the secondary school and life a free and all-around one. It will complete the circuit—it will round out the present series of segmental arcs into a whole. Now this fact will put all the school studies in a new light. They can be looked at in the place they normally occupy in the whole circle of human activities. As long as social values and aims are only partially represented in the school, it is not possible to employ the standard of social value in a complete way. A continual angle of refraction and distortion is introduced in viewing existing studies, through the fact that they are looked at from an artificial standpoint. Even those studies which are popularly regarded as preparing distinctively for life rather than for college cannot get their full meaning, cannot be judged correctly, until the life for which they are said to be a preparation receives a fuller and more balanced representation in the school. While, on the other hand, the more scholastic studies, if I may use the expression, cannot relate themselves properly so long as the branches which give them their ultimate *raison d'être* and sphere of application in the whole of life are non-existent in the curriculum.

For a certain type of mind algebra and geometry are their own justification. They appeal to such students for the intellectual satisfaction they supply, and as preparation for the play of the intellect in further studies. But to another type of mind these studies are relatively dead and meaningless until surrounded with a context of obvious bearings— such as furnished in manual-training studies. The latter, however, are rendered unduly utilitarian and narrow when isolated. Just as in life the technological pursuits reach out and affect society on all sides: so in the school corresponding studies need to be imbedded in a broad and deep matrix.

In the second place, as previously suggested, the explanation of the high school simplifies instead of complicates the college preparatory problem. This is because the college is going through an analogous evolution in the introduction of similar lines of work. It is expanding in technological and commercial directions. To be sure, the branch of fine and applied arts is still practically omitted; it is left to the tender mercies of over-specialized and more or less mercenary institutions—schools where these things are taught more or less as trades, and for the sake of making money. But the same influences which have already rescued medical and commercial education from similar conditions, and have brought to bear upon them the wider outlook and more expert method of the university, will in time make themselves also felt as regards the teaching of art.

Thirdly, the wider high school relieves many of the difficulties in the adequate treatment of the individual as an individual. It brings the individual into a wider sphere of contacts, and thus makes it possible to test him and his capacity more thoroughly. It makes it possible to get at and remedy his weak points by balancing more evenly the influences that play upon him. In my judgment many of the problems now dealt with under the general head of election *vs.* prescription can be got at more correctly and handled more efficiently from the standpoint of the elastic *vs.* the rigid curriculum—and elasticity can be had only where there is breadth. The need is not so much an appeal to the untried and more or less capricious choice of the individual as for a region of opportunities large enough and balanced enough to meet the individual on his every side, and provide for him that which is necessary to arouse and direct.

Finally, the objection usually urged to the broader high school is, when rightly considered, the strongest argument for its existence. I mean the objection that the introduction of manual training and commercial studies is a cowardly surrender on the part of liberal culture of the training of the man as a man, to utilitarian demands for specialized adaptation to narrow callings. There is nothing in any one study or any one calling which makes it in and of itself low or meanly practical. It is all a question of its isolation or of its setting. It is not the mere syntactical structure or etymological content of the Latin language which has made it for centuries such an unrivaled educational instrument. There are dialects of semi-barbarous tribes which in intricacy of sentential structure and delicacy of relationship, are quite equal to Latin in this respect. It is the context of the Latin language, the wealth of association and suggestion belonging to it from its position in the history of human civilization that freight it with such meaning.

Now the callings that are represented by manual training and commercial studies are absolutely indispensable to
human life. They afford the most permanent and persistent
occupations of the great majority of human kind. They
present man with his most perplexing problems; they stimulate him to the most strenuous putting forth of effort. To
indict a whole nation were a grateful task compared with
labelling such occupations as low or narrow—lacking in all
that makes for training and culture. The professed and professional representative of "culture" may well hesitate to
cast the first stone. It may be that it is nothing in these
pursuits themselves which gives them utilitarian and materialistic quality, but rather the exclusive selfishness with
which he has endeavored to hold on to and monopolize the
fruits of the spirit.

And so with the corresponding studies in the high
school. Isolated, they may be chargeable with the defects of
which they are accused. But they are convicted in this respect
only because they have first been condemned to isolation.
As representatives of serious and permanent interests of
humanity, they possess an intrinsic dignity which it is the
business of the educator to take account of. To ignore them,
to deny them a rightful position in the educational circle, is
to maintain within society that very cleft between so-called
material and spiritual interests which it is the business of
education to strive to overcome. These studies root themselves in science; they have their trunk in human history,
and they flower in the worthiest and fairest forms of human
service.

It is for these various reasons that I believe the introduction of the new problem of adjustment of studies will help
instead of hinder the settlement of the older controversies.
We have been trying for a long time to fix a curriculum upon
a basis of certain vague and general educational ideals: information, utility, discipline, culture. I believe that much of
our ill success has been due to the lack of any well-defined
and controllable meaning attaching to these terms. The discussion remains necessarily in the region of mere opinion
when the measuring rods are subject to change with the
standpoint and wishes of the individual. Take any body of

persons, however intelligent and however conscientious, and ask them to value and arrange studies from the standpoint of culture, discipline, and utility, and they will of necessity arrive at very different results, depending upon their own temperament and more or less accidental experience—and this none the less because of their intelligence and conscientiousness.

With the rounding out of the high school to meet all the needs of life, the standard changes. It ceases to be these vague abstractions. We get, relatively speaking, a scientific problem—that is a problem with definite data and definite methods of attack. We are no longer concerned with the abstract appraisal of studies by the measuring rod of culture or discipline. Our problem is rather to study the typical necessities of social life, and the actual nature of the individual in his specific needs and capacities. Our task is on one hand to select and adjust the studies with reference to the nature of the individual thus discovered; and on the other hand to order and group them so that they shall most definitely and systematically represent the chief lines of social endeavor and social achievement.

Difficult as these problems may be in practice, they are yet inherently capable of solution. It is a definite problem, a scientific problem, to discover what the nature of the individual is and what his best growth calls for. It is a definite problem, a scientific problem, to discover the typical vocations of society, and to find out what groupings of studies will be the most likely instruments to subserve these vocations. To dissipate the clouds of opinion, to restrict the influence of abstract and conceited argument; to stimulate the spirit of inquiry into actual fact, to further the control of the conduct of the school by the truths thus scientifically discovered—these are the benefits which we may anticipate with the advent of this problem of the wider high school.

3. AS CONCERNS THE COLLEGE

The elementary school is, by the necessity of the case, in closest contact with the wants of the people at large. It is the public-school, the common-school, system. It aims at universality in its range, at including all children. It has a universal basis, coming home to every citizen as a taxpayer. The higher institutions of learning are less under the control of immediate public opinion, with the ebb and flow of popular sentiment. They are set apart, as it were, under the control of specially selected leaders. They are dominated by a more continuous system of educational principle and policy. Their roots are in the past; they are the conservators of the wisdom, insight, and resources of bygone ages. While they may be part of the state system, yet they touch the average citizen in a much less direct way than does the elementary school. The secondary school is intermediate: it is between the upper and the nether millstone. On one side, it is subject to pressure from current public opinion; on the other, to the pressure of university tradition. While the public high school is more sensitive in the former direction, and the private academy more sensitive in the latter, neither one can be free from both influences.

The elementary school has both the advantages and the disadvantages of its more direct contact with public opinion. It is thereby more likely to respond promptly to what the people currently want. But, on the other hand, it is rendered liable to the fluctuations and confusions of the public's expression of its own needs. The higher institution has the advantages and the disadvantages of its greater remoteness, its greater isolation. The advantage is in the possibility of

[First published as "Are the Schools Doing What the People Want Them to Do?" *Educational Review* 21 (1901): 459–74. Reprinted as "The People and the Schools," *Education Today*, ed. Joseph Ratner (New York: G. P. Putnam's Sons, 1940), pp. 36–52.]

more definite leadership by those consistently trained in continuous educational standards and methods—freedom from
the meaningless and arbitrary flux and reflux of public sentiment. The disadvantages are summed up in the unfavorable
connotation of "academic," the suggestion of living in the
past rather than the present, in the cloister rather than the
world, in a region of abstraction rather than of practice.

The lower schools are more variable, and probably vary
too easily and frequently as the various winds of public
sentiment blow upon them. They are freighted with too little
ballast. The traditional elementary-school curriculum was
so largely a formal thing, there was so little of substantial
content in it, that it could not offer much resistance to external pressure. There was also less ballast in the matter of
its teaching force, since the standard of requirement in
scholarship and training was so much lower than that of the
higher schools. But this in no respect detracts from their
being the public, the common, schools—that with which the
interests of the people are most closely and universally bound
up. It only emphasizes, after all, the necessity of their
being responsive to the needs of the people, and not to traditions or conventions from whatever source they arise.

The higher institutions are freighted with a definite
body of tradition. Their curriculum represents the enduring
experience and thought of the centuries. They are the connecting links binding us of today with the culture of Greece
and Rome and mediæval Europe. They are under the
guidance of men who have been subjected to uniform training, who have been steeped in almost identical ideals, and
with whom teaching is a profession and not an accident. In
their method of administration they are much more removed
from public opinion and sentiment than are the elementary
schools.

Does this mean, however, that the college is relieved of
the necessity of meeting public needs, of acting with reference to social considerations; or rather, that its problem, its
function with reference to this need, is a peculiar and distinctive one? Our answer is unhesitatingly the latter. If the
college derives more from the past, it is only that it may put
more effectually the resources of the past at the disposition

of the present. If it is more remote from immediate pressure of public demands, this should be regarded as imposing a duty, not as conferring an otiose privilege. It emphasizes the responsibility of steadying and clarifying the public consciousness, of rendering it less spasmodic, less vacillating, less confused; of imparting to it consistency and organization. The college has undertaken to maintain the continuity of culture. But culture should not be a protected industry, living at the expense of the freedom and completeness of present social communication and interaction. The sole reason for maintaining the continuity of culture is to make that culture operative in the conditions of modern life, of daily life, of political and industrial life, if you will.

It is comparatively easy to divorce these two functions. At one end of the scale we can erect the culture college; the college which, upon the whole, in its curriculum and methods ignores the demands of the present and insists upon the well-rounded and symmetrical education of the past—an education which is well-rounded simply because the insistent demands of the present are kept from breaking into it. At the other end of the scale is the distinctively professional technological school, which prepares specifically and definitely for the occupations of the present day; and which certainly is responding in consistent and obvious ways to current social needs and demands.

But, speaking for the higher institutions of learning as a whole, it is clear that both of these types of institutions solve the problem by unduly simplifying it. This is not to say that each has not its own place. It is only to say that that place is not the place of our higher institutions of learning taken in their entirety. Their problem is to join together what is here sundered, the culture factor (by which is meant acquaintance with the best that has been thought and said and done in the past) and the practical factor—or, more truly speaking, the social factor, the factor of adaptation to the present need.

But what, you may ask, is the working equivalent of this proposition? What effect would the attempt to carry it out have upon the existing college curriculum and method? How does it bear, for example, upon the mooted question of the relation of the languages or the humanities to the sciences? What bearing does it have upon the mooted question of the required *versus* the elective curriculum? What bearing does it have upon the question of the method of instruction? Shall it be dogmatic and disciplinary, so as to secure to the student the advantage of a stable point of view and a coherent body of material, or shall it be stimulating and liberating, aiming at ability to inquire, judge and act for one's self?

The problem of the multiplication of studies, of the consequent congestion of the curriculum, and the conflict of various studies for a recognized place in the curriculum; the fact that one cannot get in without crowding something else out; the effort to arrange a compromise in various courses of study by throwing the entire burden of election upon the student so that he shall make out his own course of study—this problem is only a reflex of the lack of unity in the social activities themselves, and of the necessity of reaching more harmony, more system in our scheme of life. This multiplication of study is not primarily a product of the schools. The last hundred years has created a new world, has revealed a new universe, material and social. The educational problem is not a result of anything within our own conscious wish or intention, but of the conditions in the contemporary world.

Take, for illustration, the problem of the introduction and place of the sciences. I suppose all of us sometimes hear arguments whose implication is that a certain body of self-willed men invented the sciences, and are now, because of narrowness of culture, bent upon forcing them into prominence in the college curriculum. But it needs only to make this implication explicit to realize what a travesty it is. These sciences are the outcome of all that makes our modern life what it is. They are expressions of the agencies upon which the carrying on of our civilization is completely dependent. They did not grow out of professional, but of human, needs. They find their serious application in the schools only because they are everywhere having their serious application in life. There is no pressing industrial question that has not arisen in some new discovery regarding the forces of nature, and whose ultimate solution does not depend upon some further insight into the truths of nature—upon some scientific advance. The revolution which is going on in industry because of the advance of natural science, in turn affects all professions and occupations. It touches municipal government as well as personal hygiene; it affects the calling of the clergy as significantly as, even if more indirectly than, that of the lawyer. An intellectual and social development of such scope cannot possibly take place and not throw our educational curriculum into a state of distraction and uncertainty.

When we are asked, "Why not leave alone all the new subjects not yet well organized in themselves, and not well elaborated as material for education; why not confine ourselves to the studies which have been taught so long as to be organized for purposes of instruction?"—when these questions are put to us, we come upon a logical self-contradiction and a practical impossibility.

The logical contradiction is found in the fact that the new studies are not so isolated from the old studies as to be lopped off in this arbitrary way. In spite of confusion and conflict, the movement of the human mind is a unity. The development of the new sciences is not a mere addition of so much bulk of information to what went before. It represents a profound modification and reconstruction of all attained knowledge—a change in quality and standpoint. The existing conflict between the sciences and the humanities in the contemporary college curriculum would not be terminated by eliminating the sciences. Precisely the same conflict would at once reflect itself within what is left over, the languages. The scientific method has invaded this region and claims it for its own. The lines would soon be drawn between those who represent the distinctively "scientific" aspects of language—phonology, philology, the strict historical development, the analytic determination of style, etc.—and those upholding the banner of pure literary appreciation. The point comes out more plainly by inquiring what we are to do with the modern social and historical sciences. No fact in controversy is more recurrent (or more amusing) than that while the contestants are struggling in the dark, the centre of the battle somehow manages to remove itself to another point; and when the smoke clears away there is not only a new battlefield, but an entirely new point at issue. While the struggle between the classicists and the scientists has been going on, a new body of studies has been gradually making its way, and is now reaching the point of conscious insistence upon its own claims. History, sociology, political science, and political economy may certainly claim to stand for the humanities. Quite as much as any linguistic phenomena, they represent fundamental values of human life. Yet they are the offspring of the scientific method. Apart from underlying biological conceptions, apart from the scientific conception of evolution, apart from that more intangible atmosphere which we call the scientific spirit, they would neither exist nor be making their way into the curriculum. The body of knowledge is indeed one; it is a spiritual organism. To attempt to chop off a member here and amputate an organ there is the veriest impossibility. The problem is not one of elimination, but of organization; of simplification not through denial and rejection, but through harmony.

The simple necessities of modern life would, however, force the college to face the problem of studies in its entire scope even if the philosophy of the sciences did not compel it. With the perspective of years, it will become clearer and clearer that the distinguishing characteristic of the nineteenth century is the development of applied science. The earlier years inherited the application to mechanics of the various uses of steam in the revolutionizing of industry. Succeeding years and decades widened the application to practically all forms of chemical and physical energy. The latter decades saw the development of the biological sciences to the point of application. We do not realize as yet the extent of the revolution which the profession of medicine is undergoing because of the ability to make application of chemistry, physiology, and bacteriology. But it is not merely medicine and public hygiene that are affected. Simple and fundamental industrial processes—agriculture, dairying, etc.—are being invaded more and more by applied science. The bacteriologist comes home to us, not only in the treatment of disease, but in the making of our butter, and cheese, and beer. The hour could be easily spent in simply mentioning the multiple and

important points of contact between science and the affairs
of daily life. The beginning of a new century surely sees us
upon the verge of an analogous translation of political and
moral science into terms of application.

Now it is absurd to the point of fatuity to say, under
such circumstances, we will restrict our curriculum to a certain group of studies; we will not introduce others because
they have not been part of the classic curriculum of the past,
and consequently are not yet well organized for educational
purposes. The problem which the college has to face is not
one which has grown up within the college walls, nor which is
confined there. The ferment which is happily going on in the
college is because the leaven of all modern life is at work.
There seems a certain lack of perspective, a certain lack of
sanity and balance in those arguments regarding the college
curriculum that assume that subjects are already in a settled
condition; that there are ready-made standards by which to
measure their various claims; and that it only remains to
pick out just so much of this and so much of that and put an
end to all the confusion and conflict which is troubling us.
Until the various branches of human learning have attained
something like philosophic organization, until the various
modes of their application to life have been so definitely and
completely worked out as to bring even the common affairs of
life under direction, confusion and conflict are bound to continue. When we have an adequate industrial and political
organization it will be quite time to assume that there is
some offhand and short-cut solution to the problem of educational organization. In the meantime it is somewhat ridiculous to argue as if there were somewhere a definite set of
specific educational recipes which the managers of the collegiate institutions might fall back upon, and then serve out
just such and such an intellectual diet to those eager for the
intellectual feast.

I have been speaking, thus far, of the problem as it
presents itself on the side of the curriculum—on the side of
the multiplication and conflict of studies. When we turn to
the matter of aims and methods, the moral end and the
fundamental intellectual attitude involved, we do not find
the state of things much changed. We talk, to be sure, about

character, and information, and discipline, and culture as setting our aims and controlling our methods. We ignore the fact that every generation must redefine these terms for itself, if they are to retain vitality. We speak as if each of these terms had a perfectly definite and well-recognized meaning attaching to it; we appear to believe that some sort of mathematical ratio is possible—that by taking such a per cent of culture, such a per cent of training, such a per cent of useful information, we may get a well-rounded education. Or, to take the problem in its more burning form, we imagine that we have just such and such a ratio between the authoritative determination of material for the student and his own personal choice—assuming that there is a certain ratio between external discipline and the play of individuality in the determination of character. All our universities are face to face, moreover, with the problem of the adjustment of what is ordinarily regarded as the strictly disciplinary and culture element in the curriculum to the professional element—the preparation for law, medicine, theology, or whatever. The common expedient, the device which works well on the practical side, is to allow the last year of the college course to count on both sides—for the degree which stands for general culture and discipline and also for the degree that stands for specific professional training. Turn from the matter of practical expediency and success to that of the philosophy of education, and what does this compromise mean? In terms of fundamental values, what is the relation between general culture and professional ability?

When we go below the surface, most of us, I think, would admit that we are in very great doubt as to what these terms really mean in themselves, to say nothing of their definite relationship to each other. What do we mean by character as a supreme end, or even incidental end, of college education? The topic lends itself gracefully to purposes of orations in which no cross-examination is permitted; but suppose one of us had to answer, honestly and definitely, what he took to be the exact connection between each of the studies of the college course, and each daily lesson in each study, and the attainment of a right character—what would the answer be? Indeed, just exactly what is the character at which we are aiming, or ought to aim, under modern conditions? Character involves not only right intentions, but a certain degree of efficiency. Now efficiency, as biologists have made us well aware, is a problem of adaptation, of adjustment to the control of conditions. Are the conditions of modern life so clear and so settled that we know exactly what organs, what moral habits and methods, are necessary in order to get the maximum of efficiency? Do we know how to adjust our teaching to securing this maximum?

Great as are the difficulties in reaching an adequate definition of what we mean by character and its relation to education, the problem is slight compared with what meets us when we ask about the significance of the terms discipline and culture.

What is discipline? I find the same persons who, in one connection, emphasize the necessity of conducting education so as to give training, are often also the persons who, in another connection, object to a certain kind of work on the very ground that it gives too much and too specific training. He who upholds the banner of discipline in classics or mathematics, when it comes to the training of a man for the profession of a teacher or investigator, will often be found to condemn a school of commerce, or technology, or even of medicine, in the university on the ground that it is too professional in character—that it smacks of the utilitarian and commercial. The kind of discipline which enables a man to pursue one vocation is lauded; the kind of training that fits him for another is condemned. Why this invidious distinction? The only clue to an answer that I have ever been able to get is the assumption of some mysterious difference between a general training and a special training—as if the training that the man got in the study of Latin and Greek were somehow distinctively the training appropriate to man as man, while the training which he gets in the application of, say, mathematics and physics to engineering, or of history, geography, and political economy to commerce, only touches some narrow segment or fraction of the man. Whence the justification of any such assumption? Is not the whole man required in the calling of an engineer or a captain of industry? If the whole man does not at present find opportunity and outlet for himself in these callings, is it not one of the main duties of the university to bring about precisely this result? The assumption that a training is good in general just in the degree in which it is good for nothing in particular is one for which it would be difficult to find any adequate philosophic ground. Training, discipline, must finally be measured in terms of application, of availability. To be trained is to be trained to something and for something.

This brings me to the question of culture. Doubtless, the current implication is that general culture and professional utility are quite independent of each other. The notion of absolute antagonism is, doubtless, wearing away. Like the similar conception of a fixed and obvious gulf between the elect and the unregenerated, it cannot stand the pressure of the free communication and interaction of modern life. It is no longer possible to hug complacently the ideal that the academic teacher is perforce devoted to high spiritual ideals, while the doctor, lawyer, and man of business are engaged in the mercenary pursuit of vulgar utilities. But we have hardly reconstructed our theory of the whole matter. Our conception of culture is still tainted with inheritance from the period of the aristocratic seclusion of a leisure class—leisure meaning relief from participation in the work of a workaday world. Culture, to use the happy phrase of one of my colleagues, has been prized largely as a means of "invidious distinction." If I were to venture into what might appear to you the metaphysical field, I think I could also show that the current idea of culture belongs to the pre-biological period—it is a survival of the time when mind was conceived as an independent entity living in an elegant isolation from its environment.

We come back here to the root of the whole matter. To very many the idea of culture covers adequately and completely that for which the college stands. Even to suggest that the college should do what the people want is to lay unholy hands on the sanctity of the college ideal. The people, the mob, the majority, want anything but culture—indeed they are capable of anything but culture. The college stands for the remnant. It is the fortress of the few who are capable of upholding high ideals against the utilitarian clamor of the many. To ask that the colleges do what society wants done is to surrender or compromise the idea of culture by requiring the introduction of the professional factor—a preparation for specific callings in life.

All this, I say frankly and emphatically, I regard as a survival from a dualistic past—from a society which was dualistic politically, drawing fixed lines between classes, and dualistic intellectually, with its rigid separation between the things of matter and of mind—between the affairs of the world and of the spirit. Social democracy means an abandonment of this dualism. It means a common heritage, a common work, and a common destiny. It is flat hostility to the ethics of modern life to suppose that there are two different aims of life located on different planes; that the few who are educated are to live on a plane of exclusive and isolated culture, while the many toil below on the level of practical endeavor directed at material commodity. The problem of our modern life is precisely to do away with all the barriers that keep up this division. If the university cannot accommodate itself to this movement, so much the worse for it. Nay, more; it is doomed to helpless failure unless it does more than accommodate itself; unless it becomes one of the chief agencies for bridging the gap, and bringing about an effective interaction of all callings in society.

This may seem pretty abstract, rather remote, in its actual bearing upon college affairs, but there is a definite body of fact which gives this general statement concreteness.

I have already referred to the fact that we are living in a period of applied science. What this means for present purposes is that the professions, the practical occupations of men, are becoming less and less empirical routines, or technical facilities acquired through unintelligent apprenticeship. They are more and more infused with reason; more and more illuminated by the spirit of inquiry and reason. They are dependent upon science, in a word. To decline to recognize this intimate connection of professions in modern life with the discipline and culture that come from the pursuit of truth for its own sake, is to be at least one century behind the times. I do not say that the engineer, the doctor, or lawyer, or even the clergyman, or the average man of commerce, has as yet awakened to the full necessity of this interdependence of theory and practice, to the full significance of the extent to which his activities are already dependent upon knowledge of the truth and the right attitude toward truth. I do not say that the professional classes are as yet fully aware of the dignity and elevation that thus come to their practical callings in life. But this very absence of clear and complete conscious-ness only makes the duty of the university the clearer. It is so to order its affairs that the availability of truth for life, and the dependence of the professional occupations upon science —upon insight into an ordered body of fact, and mastery of methods—shall become patent to all men.

Society needs the junction of that expert knowledge and skilled discipline which the college alone can supply, and the services of the professions, the businesses of life. All the forces and tendencies of college instruction and administra-tion are tending irresistibly, even if blindly, in this direction. To say that the reality of the present university is professional training would perhaps give little other than material for misunderstanding. It would seem to mean that what most would regard as the important and essential feature of the university was a mere preliminary or incident, and that the reality is located in the schools of medicine, law, engineering, etc. This is not what is meant. I do mean, however, that the business of the university is coming to be more and more the supplying of that specific knowledge and that specific train-ing which shall fit the individual for his calling in life. Just how the tendency shall work itself out on the formal and ex-ternal side is a matter of comparatively little moment. The fact is sure that the intellectual and moral lines which divide the university courses in science and letters from those of professional schools are gradually getting obscure and are bound finally to fade away.

What is termed general training and general culture is the function of the secondary school. A recent writer has stated that the college is threatened with attack from two sources: the high school on one side, the professional school on the other. This exactly states the situation to my mind— excepting that I should not regard these instrumentalities as foes, but rather as the twofold differentiation of function which the old-time amorphous college is assuming.

Formally, the first two years of college work probably belong to the secondary period. This is not the place or time to go into the question of what is meant by general training and its relation to secondary-school work. It certainly means, however, that the pupil shall be touched, shall be stimulated, on all sides; that he shall be given a survey, at least, of the universe in its manifold phases. Through this survey, through this elaboration, coming to know both himself and the universe, he may get his orientation—his placing of himself in the larger world. With proper economy of instruction, and harmonious organization instead of blind confusion in the curriculum, this result should certainly be attained by the time the average student is eighteen or twenty.

Having found himself, a student would then be prepared to enter upon that special training which is needed to equip him for the particular calling in life which he finds adapted to his own powers. This, by whatever name called, is professional training. The extent to which our larger universities have already moved in this direction is concealed, first, by the fact that they still retain considerable secondary work in the earlier years of their course; and secondly, by the fact that training for the calling of teaching, or of special research, is marked off in the public mind from training for the calling of doctor, lawyer, or engineer. In reality, the kind of training which students receive to make them professors or directors of laboratories is, of course, as professional as is that of the school of technology or medicine.

There is still, however, a great deal of reconstructive work to be done. There is still a good deal of so-called higher college or university work which is thoroughly anomalous in character. It is neither one thing nor the other. It does not give that kind of education which awakens the student to a sense of his own powers and their relation to the world of action, nor does it afford specific training for any particular walk in life. It is neither genuinely secondary nor yet manifestly collegiate in character. It is aimed in the air with the pious hope that something will come of it somewhere and somehow. Those who insist on the maintenance of the traditional college free from supposed encroachments of the high school on one side and the professional school on the other, are definitely contending, to my mind, for the perpetuation of this amorphous and artificial thing. Historically, the college, like the mediæval university, was a great vocational institution. Its original business was to prepare primarily for the ministry, and incidentally for other learned professions. That function gradually departed from it, and it took on more and more the form of an institution for general culture. Now the high school is appropriating this function, and in its legitimate extension is bound to absorb more and more of it. To give just more general culture at large, after the specific period for it has ceased; to prepare in a loose and vague way for future life—this is the anomaly to be corrected by restoring to the college its position as a vocational institution.

The movement is steady and, I believe, inevitable in one direction. There is to be a demarcation of the college into secondary work on one side, and into training for vocations on the other. The secondary period will be that of individual training and culture, awakening the mind to true self-consciousness—to a knowledge of self in its needs and capacities in relation to life about it, thus restoring to it freshness and vitality. The collegiate institution will then be an affair for specific training; for securing control of those specialized systems of knowledge and methods of research which fit the individual for the pursuit of his own calling in life.

All of us have callings, occupations—only the luxuriously idle and the submerged idle, only the leisure class of fashion and of pauperism violate this law. When higher education ceases to ignore the universality and significance, ethical as well as material, of this fact of occupations, when it recognizes it frankly and fully, and adapts its curriculum and methods to it, the college will be coherent in itself and in relation to the social whole. It is movement in the direction of the union of truth and use that defines the problems and aims of the existing collegiate situation.

Miscellany

THE UNIVERSITY ELEMENTARY SCHOOL

To the President of the University.

SIR: I submit herewith my report on the University Elementary School in connection with the Department of Pedagogy for the year 1898–99.

The School remained at 5412 Ellis Avenue. The average enrollment for the year was 95 pupils; the children being between the ages of 4 and 12 inclusive. The total expenses for the year were $12,870.26. The tuition receipts for the same period were $4,916, being an increase of $2,200 over the previous year. The University gave seven free scholarship tuitions, aggregating $840 in return for service in the school. The remainder of the sum needed was made up by personal gifts. The larger donations were as follows: The Castle family (for kindergarten) $1,500; Mrs. W. R. Linn $1,200; Mrs. C. R. Crane $1,000; Mr. and Mrs. A. C. Bartlett $750; Mr. Edward B. Butler $200; Mrs. William Kent $100; about $350 were realized from a series of three lectures given by the head of the department upon the work of the school. These lectures have since been reprinted in book form under the title, *School and Society.*

The chief item of expense was for salaries, being $9,160. It has proved more and more necessary each year to concentrate the expense upon this item in order to secure the service of specialists, competent not only to give good instruction, but also to develop subject-matter in a scientific way. Thirteen teachers, however, were on the pay roll for the year, being an average of almost exactly $700 per person. The comparative smallness of the sum is due in part to the fact that four of the teachers were not giving full time to the school. It is, however, even more due to the fact that

[First published in *The President's Report: July, 1898–July, 1899* (Chicago: University of Chicago Press, 1900), pp. 198–99. Not previously reprinted.]

many of the teachers are sacrificing more lucrative positions because of the great interest in this type of work. It would be manifestly unfair to count indefinitely upon this devotion, and consequently the problem of a general increase in the rate of salary paid is bound to arise in the early future.

Educationally the chief work of the year has been the formulation of the results of the three previous years' work in a course of study. The main points taken into consideration in the formation of this program are: 1) the different types of children's activities and interests in successive years, in order to select subject-matter and methods with the greatest probability of calling the whole child into activity at each stage; 2) a sequence in the subject-matter so that each year shall lead up naturally to the problems and material presented in the next, while the work of the following year utilizes that of the preceding in such a way as to give a review without literal repetition; 3) to provide for a gradual distinction of the subject-matter into its more specialized phases—history from science, biological science from physical science, etc.; 4) to provide demand and opportunity for the continuous introduction of symbols in reading, writing, and number, and the necessity for an increased use of books as auxiliaries. While the program as to one year in history, and some minor points in the sequence of the science work, is under reconsideration, upon the whole the outline adopted is found to work excellently, and it is believed that the period of experimentation in this direction is practically at an end.

The other chief educational problem engaging attention during the year was the formation of closer connections between the art work, the textile work, the shop work as three forms of expressive and constructive activity with the subject-matter in history and science. Valuable results have been reached in this direction, in particular the possibility of a practical and theoretical course in textiles which shall run parallel with the study of history, and give an introduction to fundamental historical ideas, has been demonstrated.

Time is affording an answer to questions often asked regarding the relation of work undertaken under unusual conditions to that of the public school. The objection is often raised that the conditions differ so much that results reached in the elementary school are not available for other school work. While the chief purpose is to demonstrate certain principles as fundamental in education, rather than to turn out methods and materials which can be slavishly copied elsewhere, experience indicates three lines of quite direct influence: I) the simple existence of the school following out new lines in a systematic way, serves insensibly but positively to modify the educational atmosphere and prepare public opinion for similar changes elsewhere. This influence is facilitated by the large number of visitors who throng the school on the days when it is open. Its results are specially manifest in the growing importance attached in all schools to constructive work. The textile work in making yarn, looms, doing weaving, etc., has already been introduced into a large number of the more progressive schools in the country. 2) The preparation of a large number of specialists who are imbued with the theory and practice of the school, and who are ready to undertake similar experimental work elsewhere. The demand is likely to exceed the supply here; but lack of funds is the only thing which stands in the way of a very large expansion. That eight or ten schools doing similar work, and located in different parts of the country, would exercise a tremendous influence, is a conservative statement. 3) The school is now arriving at a point where results of its work can be published in such form as to be more directly useful to teachers than heretofore. While it has required unusual conditions to work out this material for the first time, after it has been developed it is quite possible to employ it in more ordinary conditions. Here again the chief obstacle in the way of a large expansion of the school's influence is a financial and not a theoretical one.

The chief problems occupying the school in the immediate future will be the more systematic development of the modes of influence already spoken of; questions of organization and demonstration growing out of the increased size of the school; the larger number of special teachers whose various interests have to be harmonized; and the approach to the secondary-school period; the development of a more organic connection between the theoretical instruction in pedagogy in the University and the work of the school, including better provision for the pedagogical supervision of assistants, and a larger variety of more specific training courses.

The chief needs of the school remain as heretofore: 1) A building designed, constructed and equipped expressly for the use of the school. The educational principles and ideas involved cannot be exhibited or carried out as long as they are hampered by physical conditions which bear no direct relationship to the work done. 2) A permanent endowment. While we cannot too strongly express our gratitude to the generous friends who have guaranteed and extended the work each year in the past, yet the school must be on a precarious basis, and make undue demands upon the thought and anxiety of all concerned, until it has an assured annual income upon which it can count.

Respectfully submitted,
John Dewey, *Director*

WILLIAM JAMES'S *PRINCIPLES OF PSYCHOLOGY*

A remarkable union of wide learning, originality of treatment, and, above all, of never-failing suggestions. To me the best treatment of the whole matter of advanced psychology in existence. It does more to put psychology in scientific position, both as to the statement of established results and as stimulating to further problems and their treatment, than any other book of which I know.

[First published in *Talks to Teachers on Psychology and to Students on Some of Life's Ideals* by William James (New York: Henry Holt and Co., 1900), p. 303.]

Appendixes

THE UNIVERSITY ELEMENTARY SCHOOL:
HISTORY AND CHARACTER

The University Elementary School was opened in January 1896 with 16 pupils, aged from six to nine, Miss Clara I. Mitchell, formerly of the Cook County Normal School, being in charge. Soon afterwards Mr. F. W. Smedley, a graduate student of pedagogy, took direction of the manual training work. The school continued six months with numbers varying from 16 to 20. In October 1896 it was reopened at 5714 Kimbark Avenue with 32 children, aged from six to eleven, Miss Mitchell teaching literature and history, and Miss Camp, formerly of Pratt Institute, teaching science and the domestic arts. Mr. Smedley continued the manual training and three assistants gave part or all of their time to the school.

In January 1897, through the generosity of parents and friends, the school removed to the old South Park Clubhouse, corner of Rosalie Court and 57th Street, where it finds ample accommodation, much better light and air, and a large hall for a gymnasium. In the Spring Quarter Miss Mitchell resigned, and her place was taken by Mr. E. C. Moore, a graduate of Columbia College and Miss Churchill, a graduate of Smith College. At the same time Miss Andrews, also a graduate of Smith College, was secured as assistant in science. Because of the increased number of teachers new pupils were received, so that at present there is an enrollment of 46.

Studies and Methods

As another circular gives the relation of the work undertaken to the University and to educational interests in gen-

[First published in *University* (of Chicago) *Record* 2 (1897): 72–75. Reprinted in part in Katherine Camp Mayhew and Anna Camp Edwards, *The Dewey School* (New York: D. Appleton-Century, 1936), pp. 26, 27–30, 31, 32, 34, 36.]

eral, the present statement is confined to considering it from the point of view of the children in the school.

1. *Manual Training.*—Physical culture, conducted under the supervision of Miss Anderson of the Women's Gymnasium of the University, is a regular feature. In addition all the children (boys and girls being treated alike) have cooking, sewing and carpentry, besides incidental work with paper and pasteboard. From one hour to two hours per week are given to sewing, cooking and carpentry respectively. In the cooking each group of children prepares its own luncheon once a week, being responsible also for the setting of the table, reception of guests and the serving of the meal. This is found to afford a positive motive for the cooking as well as to give it a social value. In the carpentry shop no rigid series of exercises is followed. The aim is to adapt the tools and materials to the muscular and mental power of the child. The things made are, in the first place, the articles needed in the school work. For example, recently, wands, dumb-bell racks and wand-racks, have been made for the gymnasium; simple balances, with lead weights, test tube racks, and simple experimental apparatus, etc., for the laboratory. When articles are not needed in the school, the children are encouraged to plan and work out articles to take home. The favorite objects selected by the children are toy chairs, tables, etc. In sewing the same plan is followed, the children making aprons and sleeves for cooking; bean bags for gymnasium games, etc.

Great importance is attached to manual training for the following reasons:

1. The use of the hand, and other motor organs in connection with the eye, is the great instrument through which children most easily and naturally gain experience, and come in contact with familiar materials and processes of ordinary life. It affords unrivalled means for securing and holding attention. It is full of opportunities for cultivating the social spirit through the opportunities it affords for division of labor, and mutual cooperation, to say nothing of supplying the child with motives for working in ways positively useful to the community of which he is a member.

2. It is the best possible instrument for cultivating habits of industry and continuity in work, and of securing

personal deftness and dexterity, at the plastic period. When conducted in a free instead of mechanical spirit, it develops more than any other one instrumentality ingenuity in planning and power in execution. The constant testimony is that nothing compares with it as a means of arousing the child to a positive sense of his own power, and encouraging him in expression and construction.

3. It also affords constant opportunities for related work in other directions. Cooking, for example, is a natural avenue of approach to simple but fundamental chemical facts and principles, and to a study of the plants which furnish articles of food. A study of materials and processes involved is carried on in connection with the sewing. This includes a study of the history of invention, of geography (localities of production and manufacturing, with lines of distribution), and of the growth and cultivation of plants like cotton and linen. Recourse to measurement is had in these subjects. The carpentry work in particular constantly calls for calculation and gives the child a command of numerical processes in a related way, thus cultivating a genuine number sense.

II. *History and Literature.*—History is introduced at a very early period, and is conducted on the principle that it is a means of affording the child insight into social life. It is treated therefore, not as a record of something which is past and gone, but as a way of realizing what enters into the make-up of society, and of how society has grown to be what it is. The work thus far has been along two main lines. One a study of the typical epochs of human progress, beginning with the crudest form (when men lived in trees and natural caves) up to the introduction of iron; the other a study of Greek life, particularly in the Homeric period, in order to afford insight into a simple, natural life which expresses itself in a rich, artistic civilization. After this year the beginning will be made with a study of social occupation of the present time, taking up, particularly, the differentiation of country and city life and their interaction and mutual dependence. Attempt is made at every point to relate the present and the past; therefore, the so-called Culture Epoch Theory is not literally followed.

In the historical study, since it is treated as a mode of

insight into social life, great emphasis is laid upon the typical relations of humanity to nature, as summed up in the development of food, shelter, habitation, clothing and industrial occupations. This affords insight into the fundamental processes and instruments which have controlled the development of civilization. This method also affords natural and frequent opportunities for adjusting the work in history to that in manual training on the one side, and to science on the other.

As regards the study of literature, perhaps the most striking departure from methods pursued in other progressive schools is that literature is regarded as a social expression, and, therefore, is approached through the medium of history, instead of studying history through literature. It is believed that this method puts the subject in its proper perspective, and avoids the danger of distracting and overstimulating the child with stories which, to him (however it may be to the adult) are simply stories. In developing the work upon Greek life, for example, it was found that practically all the books for children are composed from the strictly literary side, many of them in addition making the myth fundamental instead of an incident to the intellectual and social development of the Greek people.

III. *Science.*—Both nature study (that is the study, through observation, of obvious natural phenomena) and experimental work, are introduced from the beginning. Children of six as well as those of ten, work in the laboratory, and with equal profit, both as regards the development of their intelligence, and the acquisition of skill and dexterity in manipulation. On this side indeed it is found that the laboratory work and manual training reinforce each other. With children of the age of the present pupils, the attempt is not to give them analytic knowledge of objects, or minute formulations of scientific principles. The object is to arouse the child's spirit of curiosity and investigation, to awaken him to a consciousness of the world in which he lives, to train the powers of observation, to instill a practical sense of methods of inquiry, and gradually to form in the mind images of the typical moving forces and processes involved in all natural change. The results thus far show that children respond eagerly and definitely to this mode of approach.

The school is fortunate in its connection with the University as regards the conduct of science work. Teachers and graduate students in the University have evinced much sympathy in making suggestions, helping the school to find material, and giving occasional talks to the children. The work in botany has been planned and carried out under the direction of Dr. Coulter, Head Professor of Botany. It is hoped that similar relations of cooperation will be gradually established with other departments. This, and the fact that the work is carried out by persons who are themselves specialists, insures that the children receive material which is worth while instead of being trivial; and get it in related and consecutive, instead of scrappy, form.

These subjects, the subjects which have a positive content and intrinsic value of their own, and which call forth the inquiring and constructive attitude on the part of the pupil, are the core of the school work. The school is conducted on the principle that formal studies, as reading, writing, spelling, and number, the technical aspects of geography and history should be developed out of, and in subordination to, content, or a positive body of facts. They are regarded as instruments and methods that the child must master, but which must be mastered as methods of doing something else (and therefore in relation to some positive end) and not as isolated things in themselves.

As frequent inquiries are made regarding the teaching of reading, and the attitude of the school towards the use of books, the following statement may be in place:

Books and the ability to read are regarded strictly as tools. The child must learn to use these, just as he would any other tools. This implies that he shall have arrived at some conception of what they are for, and have some end in view or motive for using them, and that the actual learning to read shall grow out of this motive. Accordingly no special effort is made to teach children to read in the sixth year, or even in the seventh, unless the indications are that the child is awakening to his needs in that direction. The premature teaching of reading in the present school system involves undue strain on the eyes and the nervous system, takes away time from subjects which have a positive content, and devotes it to a purely formal study which the child can master with much less strain and in shorter time when he is ready for it. Moreover, after the child has learned to read, there is very little material to put before him which is worth while.

The aim is thus to familiarize the child with the use of language as a means of discovering something otherwise unknown, and of sharing with others what he has himself found out. Hence reading is taught in close connection with other subjects as science, and history, not as a subject by itself. As soon as the child has an idea what reading is for, and has a certain amount of technical facility, printed material is supplied him, not as a text-book, but as an additional tool in his equipment. The prevalent use of text-books has two evils. First, the child forms a habit of depending upon them, and comes almost instinctively to assume that the book is the chief, if not the only way of getting information. Then, the use of books as text throws the mind into a passive and absorbing attitude. The child is learning instead of inquiring.

The chief difficulty which has to be met in connection with reading is the lack of suitable reading matter. The school hopes to add a printing press to its equipment next year by means of which the children will, to some extent, work out their own lessons, while the teachers can also use it to select and present proper material. After this material has been duly worked out and tested it will be published for general use.

Outline of Scheme of Organization

So far as the administrative organization of the school is concerned, the controlling principle is that education comprises three periods: elementary, secondary, and higher or university. These periods are not arbitrary divisions, but each one has its own dominant end or interest which determines the methods employed.

The University School will include the first two of these periods. The elementary begins at the age of four and extends to that of thirteen, nine school years. The aims of this period are: 1) to bring the child to an active, inquiring interest in, and consciousness of the world of society and nature about him; 2) to bring him to a positive consciousness of his own capacities, and 3) to introduce him gradually to a command of the technical tools required in further work, viz., reading, writing, and number.

The distinguishing aim of this period is not, therefore, to give the child technical facilities, or possession of a certain amount of information. It is to build up in his consciousness an orderly sense of the world in which he lives, working out from that which has most intimately touched him before coming to school, viz., the family and neighborhood life, and gradually extending the range. Orderly experience of a rich, varied, but consecutive sort, is the aim which controls the selection of materials and occupations.

The nine years of the elementary period are broken into three subdivisions or grades, although these breaks are not made outwardly prominent.

The first grade includes children from four to seven. It begins with the social experience which the child has already had, and endeavors, on one side, to bring the child to a clearer and more definite consciousness of what is involved in this life, and on the other side to form in him habits of social service, and ability to control his own powers of hand and eye. In the last year of this period, the child is informally introduced to the use of written language and (through his own use of foot rules, scales, etc.) to the typical numerical processes.

The second grade is from seven to ten. Its main object is to secure to the child a command of methods and through the use of these methods, to enable him to formulate his experience more definitely and accurately. These methods involve ability to use tools and utensils in cooking, the carpenter shop, and the laboratory, and to pursue a continuous line of work until it accomplishes definite results. It involves, also, an increasing use of reading, writing and number, not as separate studies, but with reference to making reports, keeping records, outlining plans, and conducting work in other studies.

In the third grade (from ten to thirteen) the controlling object is that the child shall acquire ability to conceive and formulate for himself, problems, and to select and define the methods which are appropriate to them. In the second grade it is supposed that the child has got practical command of the methods and of their uses. He now is capable of reflecting upon them, and of formulating them in more intellectual terms. This implies a more technical and formal use of books, as aids in investigation of problems in history, literature, geography, and science.

During the latter period one modern language, Latin, elementary algebra, and constructive geometry will be introduced. That one or two years will thus be saved in time of preparation for college, is not thought to be over-sanguine; while those who do not go on to college will go into their life work, not only with an active and aroused consciousness of the world in which they live, but in possession of the fundamental intellectual methods necessary to understand and deal with it.

Work in the secondary period is not as yet provided. Its main object, however, is more formal differentiation of various groups of study so that the individual pupil shall secure a well-balanced introduction into the whole region of human attainment, and also knowledge of the special direction in which his own interests and abilities lie, so as to prepare him for specialization in advanced work or in actual life. The secondary period really extends to the end of the present sophomore year in college. But naturally the University School is concerned with it only during its first three years. This secondary epoch is the time for formulating in generalizations the chief principles which are fundamental to various lines of study, and for amassing the detailed stores of information which embody and illustrate the general principles. If the elementary period has been adequately lived through, so that the child has secured positive experience in all these directions, has had intellectual hunger kept alive and quickened, and has acquired working use of the main methods of investigation, there is no doubt that a very large amount of technical generalization and of special detail can easily be acquired in a comparatively short time.

General

As regards the spirit of the school, the chief object is to secure a free and informal community life in which each child will feel that he has a share, and his own work to do. This is made the chief motive towards what are ordinarily termed order and discipline. It is believed that the only genuine order and discipline are those which proceed from the child's own respect for the work which he has to do, and his consciousness of the rights of others who are, with himself, taking part in this work. As already suggested, the emphasis in the school upon various forms of practical and constructive activity, gives ample opportunity for appealing to the child's social sense, and to his regard for thorough and honest work.

Along with this emphasis upon the social spirit of the school as furnishing the controlling moral motive, goes attention to the individuals as such. For purposes of convenience the children are divided into small groups from eight to twelve in each, according to the kind of work and the age of the children, and it is expected that in this group work the teacher will give attention to the specific powers and deficiencies of each child, so that the individual capacities will be brought out, and individual limitations made good. Individual attention extends to the physical as well as the intellectual side. Each child receives a personal physical examination in the gymnasium, and all defects observed are reported to the parent in order that the child may have the special exercises needed to build him up. Each child also undergoes an examination in the Psychological Laboratory in the University, with reference to his sense-organs and motor powers. Almost 20 per cent of the children in the school have thus been reported to their parents as needing either special exercise, or attention to eyes, ears, or throat, from a competent medical specialist.

Another general feature of the school is the fact that it is endeavoring to combine the services of specialists in manual training, science and history with unity of aim and method. There is a tendency to go to one extreme or the other. When specialists are employed the result often is that each does his work independently of the other, and the unity of the child's life is thus sacrificed to the tastes and acquisitions of a number of specialists. But the effort to avoid this through having each teacher take charge of the entire range of subjects, has equally serious evils in another direction. It is not a question of the specialist, but of the expert. When manual training, art, science and literature are taught, it is impossible that one person should be competent in all directions. Even if it were desirable it is a physical and mental impossibility. Superficial work is bound to be done in some direction and the child, through not having a model of expert workmanship to follow, acquires careless, and imperfect methods of work. The school, accordingly, is endeavoring to put the various lines of work in charge of experts, and yet maintain unity through continued consultation and cooperation, and through controlling the different studies and occupations by reference to the same general principles. The undue separation which often follows teaching by specialists, is not inherent in the method, but is the result of lack of supervision, cooperation and control by a unified plan.

THE UNIVERSITY ELEMENTARY SCHOOL: GENERAL OUTLINE OF SCHEME OF WORK

Introduction

GENERAL STANDPOINT

The school as a whole is organized on the basis of using as many connections as possible between everyday life and experience and the more formal work of the school. It is assumed that the processes that educate, the material that instructs, and the mental workings through which knowledge and discipline arise are the same within that they are without the school walls. Consequently the introductory work is a simple continuation, so far as possible, of the forms of experience and modes of expression with which the child is already familiar. Differentiation is gradually introduced, and at all times points of contact with everyday experience are kept up. Growth in character, involving of necessity advance in knowledge and control of mental powers is the end.

The problem of the school is thus to secure that organization of equipment and facilities which will give the children typical and varied contacts with the materials of experience, so arranged as to further consecutive and orderly growth. What the school can supply which the informal life of the home and the neighborhood lack is arrangement of materials and modes of action; such an arrangement that the information which is of most value shall be gained while the trivial is eliminated; such that there shall be constant growth of insight into the principles which underlie experiences; and that there shall be increasing command of methods of work, —of inquiry, discussion, and reflection. The school building is treated not as a collection of rooms in which lessons are learned and recited, but as a well-equipped and organized

[First published in *University* (of Chicago) *Record* 3 (1898): 253–54. Reprinted in part in Katherine Camp Mayhew and Anna Camp Edwards, *The Dewey School* (New York: D. Appleton-Century, 1936), pp. 53–54.]

environment for carrying on certain modes of work, and thus securing certain experiences and the formation of certain habits. It consists of carpenter shop, laboratory, studio, gymnasium, library, kitchen, and dining-room; a miniature textile factory for weaving and sewing, etc. The recitation room is the meeting room—the visiting room—in which the children and teachers exchange experiences, questions, and ideas. It is the belief that most is learned while there is least conscious attention to the process of learning; that most discipline is secured when attention is given to ends intrinsically valuable.

CORRELATION

When the natural forms of experience are carried over in the schoolroom, it is found that the problem of "correlation" largely solves itself—it disappears. The bonds that tie various studies and truths together are the same that hold together the various occupations in which the child engages and the various surroundings with which he comes in contact outside the school. There is a common fund of experience out of which all grow and to which all contribute. When subjects are not isolated from actual connection with the child's own life, forced correlation of one subject with another is not called for. Whenever a need, a motive, is felt for any special line of facts in any particular direction—as in number work, reading, writing, etc.—there is no hesitation in giving special work in that particular line. The necessity which the child feels, and the possibility of using what is gained to enrich and further some other subject, furnish all the threads of connection that are required.

More particularly, the various forms of constructive work, in kitchen and shop afford natural modes of experience, and give rise to problems that can be pursued in more technical and formal fashion in other classes. At the same time, they afford abundant and continued opportunities for applying whatever skill, practical or intellectual, is elsewhere gained. They introduce the children to materials, to tools, to processes and modes of handling materials which connect naturally and inevitably with arithmetic and geometry, geography, mineralogy, physics, chemistry, etc.

Moreover, when interrelation is made on the basis of need and possibility of application, certain subjects naturally fall together; as, for instance, geography with history on one side and science on the other; number with constructive activities and with science; language, both in reading, spelling, and writing, with all other subjects. Finally, art in music, line, and color is an indispensable mode of expressing and communicating values anywhere realized in experience.

DIFFERENTIATION OF STUDIES

In the organization of the Elementary School three stages, or periods are recognized. These, however, pass into one another so gradually that the children are not made conscious of the gaps. The first extends from the age of four to eight or eight and a half years.[1] In this period the connection with the home and neighborhood life is, of course, especially intimate. The children are largely occupied with direct social and outgoing modes of action, with doing and telling. There is relatively little attempt made at intellectual formulation, conscious reflection, or command of technical methods. As, however, there is continual growth in the complexity of work and in the responsibilities which the children are capable of assuming, distinct problems gradually emerge in such a way that the mastery of special methods is necessary.

Hence in the second period (from eight to ten) emphasis is put upon securing ability to read, write, handle number, etc., not in themselves, but as necessary helps and adjuncts in relation to the more direct modes of experience. Also in the various forms of hand work and of science, more and more conscious attention is paid to the proper *ways* of doing things, methods of reaching results, as distinct from the simple doing itself. This is the special period for securing knowledge of the rules and technique of work.

In the third period, lasting until the thirteenth year, the skill thus acquired is utilized in application to definite

---

1. This year the school (through the generosity of the Castle family) has children of four and five years of age, for the first time; consequently the sub-primary work is not as yet sufficiently formulated to be included in this report.

problems of investigation and reflection, leading on to recognition of the significance and necessity of generalizations. When this latter point is reached the period of distinctly secondary education may be said to have begun. This third period is also that of the distinctive differentiation of the various lines of work, history and science, the various forms of science, etc., from one another. So far as the methods and tools employed in each have been mastered, so far the child is able to take up and pursue each by itself, making it, in some sense, really a study. If the first period has given the child a common and varied background, if the second has introduced him to control of reading, writing, numbering, manipulating materials, etc., as instruments of inquiry, he is now ready for a certain amount of specialization without danger of isolation or artificiality.

PLAY AND IMAGINATION
IN RELATION TO EARLY EDUCATION*

It is hardly necessary to say that play does not mean amusement, nor yet games alone; it is a form of the child's activity. Dr. John Fiske has pointed out the significance of prolonged infancy for education and social evolution. Prolonged infancy means the postponement of the period in which the person permits his activity with reference to the necessities of life—of getting a living—and consequently a continued period of exercise of powers having no conscious end or aim beyond the satisfaction and the value inhering in the exercise and development of the powers for their own sake. This natural, unforced expression is play, and consequently *all* the child's activity so far as not controlled by necessity of reaching external ends is play. Hence three points follow:

1. *Plays* may be taught, but not play—that is, it is of the essence of play to be a growth, or an expression of the child's own attitude, disposition, images, etc. Others may take advantage of these spontaneous expressions and give them direction; may direct them through models, suggestions, and other stimuli, but the child must make them really his own, and then act upon them *as his own*, or else he is simply going through certain external motions, into which possibly the adult may read an ideal or spiritual significance, but which are either sensational or mechanical to the child.

2. We must avoid the separation of play and work which the adult makes when thinking of children. To the child, his play is his activity, his life, his business. It is intensely serious. He is absorbed, engrossed in it. It is an occupation. Hence many things which to the adult are work, or even

* Paper presented at the School of Psychology in Chicago, April 1899, under the auspices of the Chicago Kindergarten College.
[This summary report first published in *Kindergarten Magazine* 11 (1899): 636–40. Abstract also published in *School Journal* 58 (1899): 589. Not previously reprinted.]

drudgery, may be play to the child; like sweeping, dusting, washing dishes, etc.; it all depends upon the spirit in which the child enters into them. If he does them for the joy of doing them, it is play; if merely for some external result or necessity, then it is work in the adult sense. But naturally play is work to the child, and work (which really interests him) play.

3. We must avoid letting things down to the lower level, because we think the child must play. Just because the child is so serious and intent in his play, we may introduce positive material of value, which shall lead the child on. Hence he should pass naturally, and by continuous gradations, from play in the ordinary sense to the more definite study; to setting up and reaching ends appropriate to older children. In an ordinary school we could not tell where the kindergarten left off and the primary room began.

Imagination is simply the inner, the mental side of play. Aside from the games, which are largely the overflow and exercise of physical energy, the value of every play is measured by the imagery which finds expression in it. It is a mistake to suppose that the imagination is concerned only with make-believe and unreality. The child's very make-believe is taking one fragment of reality to stand for some larger reality, as when the little girl plays with her doll, or her dishes, and the boy with his steamboat or railway train. Through this extension of present reality to stand for the unseen the child enlarges his capacity, his insight, and his range of interests and sympathies. The healthy "symbolism" of the child is simply that which takes *one real element* to signify and gradually build up the wider, deeper whole, not a complete thing to stand for some unreal idea.

Hence the imagination must be really constructive; must find outlet in some actual building up of what to the child is reality. The image must result in doing, and in a doing which carries the child beyond his imperfect image and helps correct it, and so on. Hence the error of stimulating and exciting the imagination and not exercising it constructively. To arouse imagination and leave the matter there is to appeal simply to the sensational and emotional side, and thus to weaken character and dissipate mental energy, hence the danger in too many stories.

The child again finds culture of imagery in all his constructive activities so far as these have the play form. The child puts a filling of social and human values, of imagery of himself doing social service and being enlarged thereby, into many things which to the adult are prosaic and utilitarian. For the most part it is the everyday, homely activities and surroundings of the household and out-of-door life which give the most healthy media of culturing imagination. All occupation, all school study (history, geography, etc.), is as much a means of developing the creative imagination as are symbolic games, use of gifts, telling of highly idealized stories and literature.

Discussion

Dr. Dewey suggested that there was a series of educational instruments differing from Froebel. These might be the occupations of primeval man and his home; that these should be reproduced and considered not only as useful, but also educative.

In continuing the discussion, Dr. [William Torrey] Harris referred as follows to the questions raised by previous speakers:

The kindergartner must get the idea of what symbolism means. Instead of play being the object and result, play is a means. It is not a terminus, but we start with it to get away from it. The child thinks differently from the human being. The child gets hold of a fragment only. Reality is a series of things in a chain of causality. The child makes rapid progress with symbolism up to his sixth year; but he does not understand dynamics. He finds the kindergarten a great thing after all, with its semispontaneous play. In 1872–73 Froebel found the value of play, and selected the wisest of those already existing. No one had written before his time of the educational value of DOING. Froebel is a classic on that subject. It is important to get into Froebel's spirit. Without the latter he could not have carried out all the theory we find in his "Pedagogics of the Kindergarten." The kindergarten does not attempt to teach play, but includes causal activities. The child takes a mere fragment and makes believe. The kindergarten tries to bring the causal idea in a game of ball; the ball is merely the blank form of the struggle to beat the other side. It symbolizes something for which real struggle is waged. The kindergarten is not to teach symbols, merely taking the fragment for the whole, but rather teaches how we may take the thing for the process.

Mrs. McLeash said:

Dr. Dewey seems to have been providing for city rather than country children. Children naturally turn to the world of nature, animal and vegetable. The development of the constructive imagination is good. We must face the problem of keeping the balance between the artistic and constructive. First should come sympathy with nature and the animal world, then later opportunity for constructive work. This gives later a freedom from the drudgery of farm life. Such sympathy with nature goes far to ward the development of religious life. Feeling about God and the soul comes largely from intercourse with the world of nature. I have had experiment with two boys, to show the relation between the vegetable and animal world. Next day one boy exclaimed quite spontaneously, "How wonderful God is!" He had carried the experiment back to its cause in God. Too much storytelling has sad mental results. There are many cases where good minds have been frittered away.

Dr. Dewey closed this interesting discussion as follows:

As to the question, How far the child should be taken from familiar things, I would say that the work in his kindergarten is entirely planned by the kindergartner. When taking up the miner, the children carried each stage backward from those they knew to those which were unfamiliar to their experience. Balls and blocks are certainly historical toys. I would not rule them out. I plead not for restriction, but enlargement of material, and this depends on the insight, intelligence, and experience of the teachers. I agree with Dr. Harris as to the fragmentary character of symbols. We need to give a broad platform for principles.

Froebel was the greatest experimenter and investigator, unless we except Pestalozzi. We want to go on into the realities of child nature. He disclaims being the inventor of new games and occupations for the child. Try to find out what children did and what appealed to them.

In reply to the criticism that domestic and household work makes children prosaic and destroys spontaneity, Dr. Dewey said that he did not find dish-washing unimaginative and prosaic, for he had done it.

I think children get a cultivation of imagination in dish-washing. It is the child who is the poet and artist, and puts this into his work if we give him freedom of action. The child's thoughts are indefinite, vague, and emotional. He should be kept in sympathetic identification with the mother of the household. Imagination must work its way out into poetic elements. In the doll, what ethical and social elements are there, the child finds and puts these into it.

In answer to Mrs. McLeash, I have seen some of the kindergarten children playing that the bur was a cocoon and they the caterpillars or moths. This shows the city children had had some relations with nature.

TEXTUAL APPARATUS
INDEX

TEXTUAL PRINCIPLES AND PROCEDURES

These volumes of *The Middle Works of John Dewey, 1899–1924* offer a definitive critical text of his published writings arranged in a generally chronological order.

A text may be called "definitive," or "established," (a) when an editor has exhaustively determined the authority, in whole and in part, of all preserved documents containing the work under examination; (b) when the text is then based on the most authoritative documents produced in the work's publishing history; and (c) when the complete textual data of all appropriate documents are recorded, together with a full account of all divergences from the edition chosen as copy-text (the basis for the edited text) so that the student may recover the meaningful (substantive) readings of any document used in the preparation of the edited text.

A text may be called "critical" when an editor does not content himself with faithfully reprinting any single document without modification but instead intervenes to correct the faults or aberrations of the copy-text on his own authority or to alter it by reference to the corrections and revisions of some authoritative edition later than the edition or manuscript chosen as copy-text.[1]

The first step in the establishment of a critical text is the determination of the exact forms of the texts in the early editions and of the facts about their relationship one to another. An important distinction must be made immediately between an "edition" and a "printing" or "impression." Technically, an edition comprises a particular typesetting,

---

1. Various terms used here to describe textual principles and operations are discussed at length in Fredson Bowers, "Established Texts and Definitive Editions," *Philological Quarterly* 41 (1962): 1–17; and in "Textual Criticism," *The Aims and Methods of Scholarship in Modern Languages and Literatures*, 2d ed., ed. James Thorpe (New York: The Modern Language Association of America, 1970), pp. 29–54.

without regard for the number of printings made at different times from this typesetting or its plates.[2]

Textual variation is most commonly found when for one reason or another a publisher decides to make a new typesetting, since changes are inevitable in the mechanical process of transmitting the words from the copy to the new form. Some of these changes may have authority if the writer himself took the opportunity presented by the new edition to correct or to revise his work; the remaining changes can have no authority since they emanate from the publisher's readers or the compositors and may run the gamut from normal house-styling to positive though inadvertent error.

To establish texts for the present edition, all true editions up to Dewey's death in 1952 have been collated, their substantive variants recorded, and a decision made whether in any part the new editions seem to contain authorial revision, or whether on the whole they represent no more variation than is normally to be anticipated in a series of unattended reprints. When new editions do give every evidence that they were revised by the author, an attempt is thereupon made to distinguish his corrections and revisions from the normal variation of publisher and printer that can have no authority.

Ordinarily, Dewey did not revise his work merely for stylistic felicity but instead to clarify, amplify, and sometimes even to alter his meaning. For this reason, the nature of the changes usually provides sufficient evidence to determine whether or not Dewey had himself revised a new edition.

On the other hand, alterations of various kinds can be made in the plates in preparation for running off more copies to form a new impression, or printing. Often these changes originate with the publisher, whose readers have seen misprints or other actual or fancied errors in the earlier printing and now take the opportunity to correct the plates. Although these corrections may prove to be so necessary or

2. In the present edition the use of the bibliographical terms "edition," "impression" (or "printing"), "issue," and "state" follows that recommended in Fredson Bowers, *Principles of Bibliographical Description* (Princeton: Princeton University Press, 1949; offset by Russell and Russell, New York, 1962), pp. 379–426.

desirable that an editor will wish to accept them, they can have no basic authority, of course, when they were not ordered by Dewey himself. Moreover, it may happen that in the course of resetting a line to conform to the publisher's requested correction the printer may inadvertently make a different error that was not caught by the casual proofreading often adopted for plate-changes. In addition, similar errors may be found when for purely mechanical reasons, such as damage to plates in storage between printings, or an attempt to refurbish excessive wear attacking a plate, the printer without the knowledge of the publisher or author may reset a page in whole or in part to make a new plate or extensively to modify an old one.

Corrections, as distinguished from revisions, made by a publisher's reader are almost impossible to separate from the corrections of an author unless they seem to bring variants into conformity with house-style, in which case their non-authoritative origin is manifest. On the other hand, meaningful revisions such as Dewey ordered made in the first three chapters of *The School and Society* are always recognizable owing to their particular nature or extent.

Not only every new edition but even every printing during an author's lifetime carries within itself the possibility for authorial correction or revision that an editor must take into account. Hence the first step in the establishment of the present text has been the collection of all known editions and impressions of each work, followed by the determination of their order and relationship from the examination of internal as well as external evidence. That is, publishers' markings may indicate the order of separate impressions, as found in the American Book Company's reprints of *Psychology*; but sometimes no external evidence is available, or else (like a failure to change the date on a title page) it is untrustworthy, and then internal evidence based on the wear and deterioration of the plates, combined with their repair, must be utilized to separate one otherwise indistinguishable impression from another and to determine its order in the printing history of the plates.

Such evidence has been gathered by the scrupulous examination of available copies of every known edition on the Hinman Collator, which has enabled discovery of the alterations made from time to time in the plates during their printing history, all of which have been recorded so that the evidence may be made available of the total body of facts from which the editors worked. This full stemma, then, of the total number of editions and impressions of any Dewey work, and their order, establishes the necessary physical base for proceeding to the investigation of the complete body of evidence about textual variation and its order of development, a matter that has a crucial bearing upon the determination of the authority of the variants in any given edition or impression.

Modern critics have come to a general agreement about the following propositions for the determination of authority in the process of editing a definitive edition that attempts to establish an author's text, in every respect. For overall authority, nothing can take the place of the manuscript that was used by the printer, because it stands in the closest relation to the author's intentions. In only one respect can the printed edition manufactured from this manuscript exceed the manuscript in authority, and that is in the specific alterations made in proof by the author, which give us his final revised intentions. It is the editor's task to isolate these important readings from other variants such as errors made by the compositor that were overlooked in the proofreading. The distinction between authorial revision in proof and compositorial sophistication of a text is not always easy to make, but informed critical and bibliographical investigation of the corpus of substantive variants between manuscript and printed text will ordinarily yield satisfactory results.

That is, when meaning is involved distinctions can be made. But when meaning is not involved, as in the hundreds and sometimes thousands of variations between manuscript and print in respect to spelling, punctuation, capitalization, and word-division, the inevitable assumption holds that the author has not engaged himself to vast sums of overcharges for proof-corrections, and that the ordinarily expected housestyling has taken place, sometimes initiated by a publisher's reader, but always concluded by the compositors.

A distinction develops, hence, between the words of a

text—the "substantives"—and the forms that these words take in respect to their spelling, punctuation, capitalization, or division, what are known as the "accidentals" of a text.[3] Editorial criticism may attempt to assess the authority of the substantives, but one must take it that, as against a printer's-copy manuscript, no printed edition can have full authority in respect to the accidentals.

On the other hand, some authors—and Dewey was often among these—are extremely careless in the typing of the accidentals in their manuscripts since they are relatively indifferent to anomalies and expect the printer to set all right for publication. Thus in some respects it is not uncommon to find that the printed edition's accidentals may be superior to those of the manuscript in matters of consistency and even of correctness. Yet every author whether consciously or unconsciously, and often whether consistently or inconsistently, does use the forms of the accidentals of his text as a method for conveying meaning. For example, Dewey frequently capitalized words he expected to be taken as concepts, thus distinguishing them in meaning from non-capitalized forms of the same words. That he was not consistent does not alter the fact that he used such a device, which an editor must respect.

It follows that the words of the printed first edition have in general a superior, although not a unique, authority over those of the manuscript form of the text in view of the ever-present possibility that substantive variants in the print can represent authorial revision in proof. On the other hand, the author's accidentals, insofar as they are viable in correctness or consistency, have a superior authority in manuscript from that in the printed form that has undergone the ministrations of copyreaders and compositors.

In these circumstances, a critical text—which is to say

---

3. The use of these terms, and the application to editorial principles of the divided authority between both parts of an author's text, was initiated by Sir Walter Greg in "The Rationale of Copy-Text," *Studies in Bibliography* 3 (1950–51): 19–36. For an extension and added demonstration, see Fredson Bowers, "Current Theories of Copy-Text," *Modern Philology* 68 (1950): 12–20; "Multiple Authority: New Concepts of Copy-Text," *The Library*, 5th ser., 27 (1972): 81–115; "Remarks on Eclectic Texts," *Proof* 4 (1974): 13–58.

an eclectic text—will endeavor to join both authorities by printing each of the two major elements in the text from the form that is uniquely superior in its closeness to the author's own habits or intentions, although either element may be altered as necessary by editorial intervention to restore true authority, or purity.

This editorial principle can be extended logically to the situation when an author's manuscript has not been preserved, or is not available for use. In this circumstance the first edition, which is the only edition set directly from the author's manuscript, must necessarily take the place of the manuscript as the prime authority. If the author has not intervened to alter matters in any subsequent impression or edition, this first edition remains the single authority for both parts of the text and must therefore become the copy-text or basis for the definitive edition, although subject to editorial correction. Later impressions or editions may unauthoritatively alter, and even correct the text, but unless the author has himself ordered such alterations the changes have no authority and may only suggest necessary or advisable corrections to an editor. Indeed, the usual history of a text in these circumstances is one of chronological degeneration into ever more corrupt readings.

On the other hand, when in a later impression or edition the author makes his own revisions and corrections, these represent his altered intentions which must be respected by the editor. Special circumstances may call for special treatment, however, and thus two specific exceptions to the rule will be discussed later. At present it is necessary to remark only that the general principles of editing a single text in critical form call for the editorial acceptance of an author's altered wishes. The earlier readings should be recorded, because they must be made available to the reader concerned to study their historical position in the development of the author's thought; but in the text itself they obviously must be superseded by the author's final intentions in cases when the editor proposes to print only a single combined text. The substantive readings of a revised impression or edition, then, have a general authority superior to those in a preceding form.

Early editors were inclined to take as copy-text the last edition of a work published in the author's lifetime, on the supposition that if he had corrected or revised it this edition would contain the maximum authority. This procedure is no longer current, for in relieving the editor of the necessity to demonstrate that any authorial revision had indeed taken place it usually resulted (in cases when no authoritative intervention had occurred) in an editorial reprint of the most corrupt edition of all. And even when somewhere in the publishing history authoritative revision had appeared, the naïve editorial acceptance of *all* substantive variants in the last edition as necessarily authorial produced an unscholarly mixture of true revisions side by side with the inevitable corruptions of a reprint.

No uncritical acceptance of *all* substantive readings in any edition, whether or not revised, therefore, meets modern standards of scholarly textual criticism. It is the duty of an editor to assess all the variants that have accumulated in a text during its history and to choose on critical and bibliographical evidence those that appear to be authorial while rejecting those that appear to be printers' corruptions.[4]

As suggested above, however, in cases when the manuscript is not available the accidentals of a first edition must necessarily be more authoritative, as a whole, than those of any later reprint. House-styled as in part these first-edition accidentals may be, the fact that they were set directly from the author's manuscript will often have influenced the compositors to adopt the manuscript forms; and in any event, they must necessarily represent a closer approximation of the manuscript accidentals than can any reprint, which is only one printed edition further house-styled and set from another printed edition. What changes in the accidentals may take place in a revised edition at the order of an author are often impossible to isolate, but they must necessarily be fewer than

4. As a case-history the first edition of Nathaniel Hawthorne's *House of the Seven Gables* may be cited. In this, scrupulous editorial investigation established that two-thirds of the substantive variants between the manuscript and first edition were unauthoritative in the print and were to be rejected. See the Centenary Edition of Hawthorne, vol. 2 (Columbus: Ohio State University Press, 1965), pp. xlvii–lviii.

the substantive alterations that were the chief reason for his intervention, especially with an author like Dewey.

On the modern textual principle of divided authority, therefore, the copy-text for this edition of Dewey remains stable as the earliest authority closest to the author, usually the first edition;[5] and hence the accidentals for Dewey's texts are established as those of the first editions printed from his manuscripts, when the manuscripts are not available. Whenever it is ascertained that no authorial revision or correction took place in any subsequent impression or edition, the first edition remains the final authority for the substantives as well. On the other hand, when substantive revisions are made in later impressions or editions, and when these are of a nature that permit their incorporation into a single critical text, those variants believed to be authorial are adopted in preference to readings of the first edition, and thus an eclectic text is established that combines the highest authority in respect to the substantives drawn from the revised forms of the text with the highest authority of the accidentals drawn from the edition closest to the manuscript source. In short, in this form of critical text the copy-text

5. Few early Dewey manuscripts were preserved. Those that have been studied or utilized suggest that the copy given to the printer might vary widely in legibility and in styling. According to his associates, Dewey usually composed on the typewriter with a margin-stop set at the left but seldom at the right, with the result that some words might be typed on the platen instead of on the paper. Customarily the machine was set for double- or triple-spacing; revisions and additions were then typed in so that the final page might look as if it had been single-spaced. Handwritten comments might also be added, as well as handwritten revisions of the typed material. There is no evidence to suggest that Dewey made extensive use of professional typing services during these years as he did from the thirties on, but friends, colleagues, and trusted students are known to have helped put materials in shape for the printer.

Dewey was characteristically indifferent about his spelling, although more consistent in handwritten than in typewritten material; punctuation could be sporadic or altogether lacking. One of Dewey's long-time editors in Henry Holt and Co. has stated ". . . I tried a number of times to 'improve' his style, but whenever I made a substantial change I found that I also had changed the sense and therefore had to reinstate the original. I did go over many passages with him and he improved them. He permitted us to use our house style, but I kept as close to the original as I could." Letter from Charles A. Madison, 25 June 1964, Dewey Center, Southern Illinois University, Carbondale, Illinois.

remains the first edition, but into the texture of its accidentals are inserted the revised readings that have been selectively ascertained to represent Dewey's altered intentions.

When special circumstances exist, exceptions may be made to this now classic formulation of the principles of copy-text and the treatment of revised editions. First, like some other authors Dewey occasionally revised a work so extensively that it is necessary to print both the original and its rewritten revision for the benefit of readers concerned to read each version in its proper historical setting. Matter and idea may be so complexly and thoroughly altered in a revision (as in *Moral Principles in Education*, or *Ethics*, or *How We Think*) as to make impracticable the reader's reconstruction of the earlier form from the conventional list of variants. The two-text principle is sometimes the only answer to otherwise insoluble textual problems. Second, revision may be less thorough than that requiring the printing of both texts, as above, and in all such cases the practical possibility is present, therefore, of contriving the usual eclectic or critical text that would incorporate the revisions in the texture of the original. Yet in special circumstances it may so happen that the revision—usually at a considerably later time—may so blot out the essential ideas or point of view of the original and its corpus of ideas as to create what are, in effect, two independent documents. True, the apparatus list of the rejected earlier readings would still enable a reader to reconstruct the original and its differing content. Nevertheless, the presentation among the early works of such a text based on the revised substantives would occasionally clash sharply with and distort the historical perspective of the development of Dewey's thought gained by the chronological presentation of his works in the present edition. It would be a distinct anomaly, for example, suddenly to come in 1902 upon a developed body of ideas in full flower (as in a revised critical text) that Dewey, in fact, was not fully to formulate until 1931. Whenever this marked ideological difference exists in a revision, the original early version is retained in the *Works* volumes in its proper historical position. However, since this second category differs from the first in that a collational apparatus can enable a reader to sift the differences between the two versions, a historical collation of the variant revised readings is incorporated in the apparatus for the early text. A reader of such an early text, therefore, can if he wishes simultaneously investigate the nature of the later revisions.

In the process of editing, the principle has been adopted that each separate work is to be treated as an independent unit in respect to its accidentals. That is, each unit has its own problems of copy-text, with inevitable variation in the nature of the printer's copy and the house-styling given it, ranging from that found in all sorts of journals to that required by different book-publishers. Thus although an attempt has been made to secure uniformity of editorial result within each unit, certain features may vary between independent works within the present edition. For example, if the spelling or some other important feature of the accidentals differs within a given work, an attempt is made to reduce the variation to uniformity according to Dewey's own style as ascertained from his manuscripts. This principle has been extended to other spellings (with occasional forays into capitalization practices) which though uniform within the unit of the copy-text are demonstrably at odds with Dewey's own habits as recovered from his manuscripts and typescripts within the period. Thus when American house-styling has obscured the known forms of Dewey's own spelling habits, emendations have been made for authenticity but always with a record so that the original can be recovered from the apparatus provided. Except for presumptive error, however, the copy-text punctuation is preferred, since in most circumstances no such certainty about the recovery of an author's exact punctuation can obtain as is possible for his characteristic spellings.

Except for the small amount of silent alteration listed below, every editorial change in the chosen copy-text has been recorded, with its immediate source, and the original copy-text reading has been provided, whether in the substantives or the accidentals. The complete account will be found in the lists of emendations.

In most texts that have a reprinting history a certain

number of variants will be positive errors or else unnecessary changes that are unauthoritative and have not been adopted by the present editors. All substantives of this kind have been recorded whether occurring in new impressions or in new editions.[6] However, when in a new edition the text is reset throughout, the number of accidentals changes would be too large to list. In addition, since all such accidentals variants that seem to be either authoritative or advisable changes will have been incorporated as emendations of the copy-text, no useful purpose would be served by listing the hundreds and hundreds of discarded publishers' or printers' unauthoritative normalizings of the text on which they had worked.

Since the number of rejected variants of the kind noted above that qualify for recording[7] is comparatively limited, no separate list has ordinarily been made and this group of variants has usually been incorporated with the appropriate emendations lists.

In the emendations lists an asterisk prefixed to the page-line number indicates that the emendation, or the refusal to emend, recorded in this item is discussed in the Textual Notes that precede that list.

In special cases separate lists within the textual material may substitute for part of the basic emendations list. For example, in the early articles as represented in Volume 1 of *The Early Works*, the importance of capitalization to indicate concept meanings as distinct from non-concepts called for a certain amount of editorial emendation to correct the required sense from the inconsistent copy-text usage. The importance for meaning of these key words that have been emended is best called to the attention of the student in a separate list, whereas they might be overlooked if buried among a mass of material of other import in the general list of emendations. As explained on pp. 355–56, a new form

6. Changes made in the plates that correct errors that would otherwise have been silently made in the copy-text by editorial intervention (see below) are recorded for the sake of completeness.
7. Such rejected readings from editions later than the copy-text are to be distinguished from copy-text readings rejected in favor of subsequent revision or correction. These are recorded as emendations, of course.

of list may appear which provides the substantive variants of
a later revision when the decision has been made to print
the original text in this volume and textual conditions make
it possible by such a list to inform the reader of the changes
made later. In several volumes, a list of full and correct quotations has also been provided as a supplement to the Checklist of Dewey's References, as described below.

A number of silent alterations have been made in the
copy-text. These concern chiefly the mechanical presentation of the text and have nothing whatever to do with meaning, else they would have been recorded.

The most general class of these silent alterations has
to do with Dewey's system of references whether within the
text, in footnotes, or in lists of authorities that he might
append. These references have been checked for accuracy,
and the details of capitalization, punctuation, and of bibliographical reference have been normalized for the reader's
convenience. When a reference is within the text, its form
may be condensed following Dewey's own pattern when the
expanded information required by the reader to check the
reference will be found in an appended list of authorities.
Except for the silent emendations mentioned and changes
which appear in the emendations lists, Dewey's footnotes are
kept in their original form and position, since their references are completed in the appended Checklist of Dewey's
References.

In most of Dewey's edited texts, quotations have been
retained just as he wrote them even though not always
strictly accurate, since that was the form on which he was
founding his ideas. The section entitled Correction of Quotations gives the correct quotation and will be helpful to the
reader in determining from the form of the quotation—
whether accurate or sketchy—whether Dewey had the source
open before him or was relying on his memory. However,
when special circumstances in a specific text require the correction of quotations within the text itself, as in the *Study of
Ethics*, special notice is given the reader.

All references in footnotes or within the text (and also
in the rejected readings of the copy-text) that relate to
points taken up within the work in question (whether by

backward or by forward reference) have had the appropriate pages of the present edition substituted for their original page numbers applying to the copy-text itself.

A second large class of silent alterations concerns itself with the articles that Dewey published in England, wherein the English printer had styled in his own manner the American spellings, punctuation system, and other forms of the accidentals or general presentation such as the formal or typographical features of the punctuation. For the convenience of American readers, and in some part as a means of automatically returning to certain undoubted features of the manuscripts that served as printer's copy, the elements in such copy-texts that were styled in the English manner have been silently Americanized when these run contrary to what can be established as Dewey's own usage. Thus words like "emphasise" have been altered silently to "emphasize," "colour" to "color"; and the position of punctuation in relation to quotation marks has been altered to American usage. However, the case differs for Dewey's works published in American organs that had adopted certain characteristics of English accidentals, for in such circumstances it is impossible to differentiate such anglicizations from other features of the house-styling that in the present edition are normalized to conform to Dewey's own habits, but with a record. Hence the reader of these texts may expect that the English publications will have been silently normalized—in these respects only—to American (and to Dewey's) usage, but that in all texts originating in the United States emendations for normalizing purposes will be recorded.

For the rest, the silent changes are mechanical and concern themselves with making regular some anomalous typographical conventions or use of fonts, expanding most abbreviations, and so on. Typical examples are the removal of periods and dashes after headings, the expansion of "&c." to "etc.," changing syntactical punctuation after roman or italic words (or in italic passages) to follow a logical system, supplying accent marks in foreign words, and normalizing German "ue" to "ü" whether in lower case or capitals. Roman numbers in chapter headings are silently altered to arabic, as are all references to them.

These remarks concern the general treatment of most texts in the present edition. When unusual features call for unusual treatment, special notice in the respective textual commentaries will be given of modifications or of additions. The intent of the editorial treatment both in large and in small matters, and in the recording of the textual information, has been to provide a clean reading text for the general user, with all the specialized material isolated for the convenience of the student who wishes to consult it.

The result has been to establish in the wording Dewey's final intentions in their most authoritative form divorced from verbal corruption whether in the copy-text or in subsequent printings or editions. To this crucial aim has been added the further attempt to present Dewey's final verbal intentions within a logically contrived system of accidentals that in their texture are as close as controlled editorial theory can establish to their most authoritative form according to the documentary evidence that has been preserved for each work.

Fredson Bowers

10 *January 1974*

TEXTUAL COMMENTARY

Dewey's writings during this three-year turn-of-the-century period[1] present a range of textual complexity. Nine items[2] were printed only one time before the present edition; *The School and Society* had two editions, the first with eleven impressions and the second with seventeen, between 1899 and 1953, the year after Dewey's death. The nine items in the former group offer no editorial problems. Specific problems and editorial decisions related to each of the remaining items are discussed in the sections that follow.

The School and Society

In April of 1899, Dewey gave a series of three lectures about the University of Chicago Elementary School to an

1. In addition to the published writings that make up this volume, twelve other items—reports of addresses and transcripts of class lecture notes—from the 1899–1901 period are described at the end of this commentary.

   One item earlier attributed jointly to Josiah Royce and Dewey, "History of Philosophy," in the *Dictionary of Philosophy and Psychology*, edited by James Mark Baldwin (New York: Macmillan Co., 1901) 1:480–82, has been omitted here because it was written by Royce and approved by Dewey only as Consulting Editor. In the "Editor's Preface" to the first volume, James Mark Baldwin explained the system of initials used to sign articles (p. xii): "Another case is the signature by two persons with a comma—not a hyphen—between them: (A.B.C., X.Y.Z.) This indicates that the article was written by A.B.C. and accepted without alteration by X.Y.Z., who thus adds the weight of his authority to it." The "History of Philosophy" entry is signed (J.R., J.D.).

   Two articles on the University Elementary School appear here as Appendixes 1 and 2. Although neither was signed by Dewey, they were probably written by him and first distributed as pamphlets to inform parents and patrons about the work of the school.

2. These were: the review of Josiah Royce's *The World and the Individual*, First Series; Principles of Mental Development as Illustrated in Early Infancy; *Mental Development*; the two *Ele-*

audience made up largely of parents and students of the
school, which had opened in January 1896. From these talks
"about $350 were realized," part of the school's income for
that year.[3] Soon after making the talks, Dewey left for a
spring teaching position at the University of California. From
Berkeley, he went to Hawaii, returning to Chicago in October
after an absence of six months. During that period, *The
School and Society* was prepared for publication as a book by
combining a stenographic report, probably typewritten, of
Dewey's April lectures with the typewritten report, presum-
ably also stenographic, of another address "Three Years of
the University Elementary School," which had been presented
the preceding February. A "Publisher's Note" to the first edition remarks of the lectures, "Dewey revised them in part
from a stenographic report, and unimportant changes and
the slight adaptations necessary for the press have been
made in his absence."[4] These changes and adaptations were
made, as Dewey later noted in his "Author's Note" to the
second impression, by his "friends Mr. and Mrs. George
Herbert Mead." The first impression, then, appeared in November 1899, with no supervision of the text by Dewey.[5]

Publication of the first printing of 1,000 copies of *The
School and Society* was made possible by a gift of $510—
the total cost of the impression and its setting—from Anita
McCormick (Mrs. Emmons) Blaine, to whom the book was
dedicated. Costs of the second impression of 1,500 copies
were met by the proceeds from the first printing.[6]

Even though two-thirds of the second impression had

---

mentary School Record articles on Group IV, and Groups V and
VI; "The Place of Manual Training in the Elementary Course of
Study"; the two articles on the University Elementary School;
and the statement on James's *Principles of Psychology.*

3. See Dewey's report to President William' Rainey Harper on the
University Elementary School, this volume.

4. *School and Society,* p. 3.

5. "From [the Meads] came that interest, unflagging attention to
detail, and artistic taste which, in my absence, remade colloquial
remarks until they were fit to print, and then saw the results
through the press." "Author's Note" (for February 1900 printing), p. 3.

6. Newman Miller (Director, University of Chicago Press) to John
Dewey, 27 March 1900, Presidents' Papers, 1899–1925, Special
Collections, The Joseph Regenstein Library, University of Chi-
cago, Chicago, Ill.

been sold by the end of March 1900, the Press postponed discussing the possibility of a third printing until late April. By that time, Dewey had been approached by the newly formed McClure, Phillips & Company about a new "edition" of the book. Dissatisfied with the financial arrangements with the University of Chicago Press,[7] as well as with what the Press director himself described as the Press's "leisurely pace,"[8] Dewey reached an agreement with McClure, Phillips some time in June. The third impression of 5,000 copies appeared at once, in July 1900, printed from plates made from the standing type of the Chicago second impression and bearing the imprints of both McClure, Phillips and the University of Chicago Press. In all, McClure, Phillips published three impressions of *The School and Society*—the third, fourth, and fifth[9]—before Dewey once again designated the University of Chicago Press as publisher.

No records survive from McClure, Phillips to indicate when and how Dewey's association with the firm was terminated; subsequently, his first formal contract with the University of Chicago Press for *School and Society* was dated July 1905.[10] Manufacturing cards show that the University of Chicago bound some 1,500 sheets of the book in November 1906; these were apparently left over from the McClure,

7. Dewey's own letters making explicit complaints about the financial arrangements have not been located. Letters from Newman Miller to Dewey (27 March 1900, 21 April 1900, 11 June 1900) and to President Harper (23 June 1900) do, however, reflect his complaints about the lack of royalties and about high printing costs. Presidents' Papers, 1899–1925.
8. Newman Miller to W. R. Harper, 23 June 1900, Presidents' Papers, 1899–1925.
9. The third and fourth printings, both by McClure, Phillips, had a British issue with P. S. King and Son, London, also listed on the title page.
10. Dewey's earlier arrangement with the University of Chicago Press was informal; the lack of a signed contract seems not to have occurred to either side until Dewey began considering moving the book to McClure, Phillips. Newman Miller charged Dewey with taking advantage of the fact that there was no "definite contract." Dewey responded that "there has never been anything said to me from the start to indicate that the book was on any other than an ordinary basis of business agreement, covering a limited time & terminable at the pleasure of either party. Also whatever neglect there has been in the matter of a signed contract does not rest with me." Dewey to "Press Department," 12 June 1900, University of Chicago Press Langley Office; Dewey to Harper, 28 June 1900, Presidents' Papers, 1899–1925.

Phillips fifth impression of February 1905. The University
of Chicago Press resumed publishing the book from the plates
with the sixth impression, in August 1907. In this sixth impression, the title page was partially reset to change the date
and to omit Dewey's University of Chicago academic title,
but, curiously, not to delete McClure, Phillips from the imprint. The verso of the title page was reset and carried the
notice "Composed and printed by the University of Chicago
Press." The seventh-impression title page was redesigned and
completely reset just before books were bound 29 December 1909; the manufacturing card bears instructions to "omit
McClure from imprint," which was done. However, the spine
of the seventh-printing binding continued to carry the name
of McClure, Phillips. Printing records at the University of
Chicago Press go back only to the 1905 contract date, covering thus the sixth through the eleventh (and last) impression of the first edition, closing with the August 1913 nota-
tion, "number produced so far 19,619." This number tallies
with the printed copyright-page listing in I^{11} of the total number of copies printed of I^{1-11}, 19,500.

After the first two printings had been made from standing type, the remaining nine were all printed from a single
set of plates.[11] Although Dewey's lack of intervention in the
first impression of this first edition gives its accidentals
mixed authority, it nevertheless remains the choice of copy-
text as closest to the presumed typescript of a stenographic
report that served as printer's-copy manuscript. The copyright deposit copy of the November 1899 first impression
serves as copy-text for the first four chapters of the present
edition.

Copies of each impression except the ninth,[12] which
could not be located, have been collated against the first

11. Newman Miller to Dewey, 19 May 1900, "If you care to have the
    plates made at your own expense, in which case, of course, you
    would have control of them, the price will be 54¢ per page." See
    also Miller's reference to the type in note 13. Presidents' Papers,
    1899–1925.
12. I^1 Library of Congress copyright deposit LB875, 46623; I^2 South-
    ern Illinois University 370.1D519s; I^3 Dewey Center (a); I^4 Uni-
    versity of Cincinnati 57771; I^5 Dewey Center (a); I^6 Dewey
    Center (a); I^7 Dewey Center (b); I^8 Dewey Center; I^{10} University
    of Chicago LB875.D418c.3; I^{11} Dewey Center (a).

printing copy-text. Changes were found to have occurred in only the second and third impressions; the text remained invariant from the fourth through the eleventh impressions.

Dewey made a number of substantive changes in *School and Society* to prepare for the second impression, probably marking up a copy of the first,[13] which he had not seen until his return from Hawaii, and adding at this time his "Author's Note." The seventy-five substantive changes which first appeared in the second printing have been incorporated into the present edition as representing Dewey's intentions. Twenty-three changes in accidentals were made for I^2, of which sixteen seem to have Dewey's authority, and have been adopted here as emendations. Of these sixteen, six resulted directly from substantive alterations at 12.39, 18.24, 31.10, 31.12, 39.8, and 49.9; four changed the sense of sentences at 38.20, 39.16, and 46.15 (2); four clarified meaning at 5.22, 5.30, 13.23, and 14.36; a missing period was supplied at 18.39; "oriental" was capitalized at 54.9. Seven changes in accidentals, including three dropped marks of punctuation[14] restored in I^3, were rejected.

In the third impression, which was the first by McClure, Phillips, twenty-four additional substantive changes were made in the standing type before plating, all of which have been incorporated into the critical text as clearly Dewey's intended revisions and corrections. Besides the three punctuation marks restored, four accidental changes made in I^3 have been accepted as authoritative at 18.28–29 (2), 37.16, and 64.3.[15]

13. Evidence for Dewey's close attention to preparing copy for I^2 appears in Newman Miller's letter to Dewey on 21 April 1900, in which he justifies the cost of printing I^2, "I would say that this includes the proof reading and the correction of accidents which may have occurred in transportation of the type after its use on the first edition, as well as the new matter which you put in the second edition. The item of alterations, of course, will be understood." Presidents' Papers, 1899–1925.

14. These were the comma after "activity" at 15.34, the line-end hyphen in "schoolrooms" at 22.23, and the period after "pictures" at 54.23. Dropping punctuation marks would be the kind of accidents that Miller referred to in the letter quoted above. After the book was plated, no such omissions occurred in I^{3-11}.

15. Six reviews of this first edition of *The School and Society* appeared between 1899 and 1901, unanimous in praising the book and its author: *Transactions of the Illinois Society for Child-*

G. J. Laing of the University of Chicago Press started discussions with Dewey about a new edition of *The School and Society* some time early in 1915.[16] In May, he described the proposed volume in a memo to Press Director Newman Miller:

This title has been unusually successful and it is believed that a new edition in which shall be incorporated certain features, would revive the book and insure a sale for another ten or fifteen years. It is proposed that the revision shall include in addition to the first three chapters of the present volume the following essays reprinted from the Elementary School Record:
Froebel's Educational Principles
Psychology of the Elementary Curriculum
Psychology of Occupation [sic]
Reflective Attention
The Aim of History in Elementary Education
The last chapter of the present edition is to be omitted. The revision is to be made by the author himself, and the essays will occupy 45 pages of the size of the page in The School and Society. The last chapter of the present edition, which is to be omitted, is 17 pages, so that the net increase in the size of the volume would be but 28 pages.

In a covering letter, Laing noted that "[Dewey] has already returned the corrected proof of the first three chapters, . . . [and] has suggested the addition of one more essay of about ten pages."[17]

    Study (4 [1899]: 100–101); *Dial* (29 [1900]: 97–98); *Educational Review* (20 [1900]: 303–6); *University* [of Chicago] *Record* (5 [1900]: 159–60); *Chautauquan* (30 [1900]: 589–92); *Review of Education* (7 [1901]: 31). The restrained *Dial* commented that "small as it is, it is not impossible that the book will come to hold some such prominence among the pedagogical books of the time as the school itself is now holding among the schools of the country." W. S. Sutton said, with somewhat less restraint, in the *Educational Review*, "[Dewey] fully sustains his reputation for grasping essential truths and setting them before his listener or reader without indulging in feeble platitudes or effusive exhortation." The *Transactions of the Illinois Society for Child-Study* summarized the general critical response with, "The book is a model of clear statement, and simply invaluable to everyone interested in the improvement of either society or the school."

16. Even though the second edition of *The School and Society* was published fourteen years after the period covered by the present volume, all the material included in it was first published in 1899 and 1900.

17. The suggested addition included the School Reports, Groups I and II, and Group III, also from the *Elementary School Record* (Chicago: University of Chicago Press, 1900).

A companion volume, to be entitled The Record of an Educational Experiment, was proposed in the same memorandum but never published. That book would also have reprinted material from the *Elementary School Record* along with Dewey's statement "Three Years of the University Elementary School," which, as noted by Laing, was to be dropped from the second edition of *The School and Society*. The full combined version of *The School and Society* edited for the present volume includes that final chapter from the first edition as an integral part of the book.

Laing's prediction in 1915 that revision of *The School and Society* would "insure a sale for another ten or fifteen years" was timid indeed. The last impression from the 1915 second edition plates was the seventeenth, made in May 1953. An interoffice memo soon afterward indicated that copies found were not good enough for offset and that the book should be reset before reprinting. The stereotype plates were destroyed in 1955, after having been used to print some 14,000 copies of the book.

The second edition of *The School and Society* was made up of the first three chapters of the first edition and five new chapters that had originally appeared as six sections of the *Elementary School Record* (Chicago: University of Chicago Press, 1900).[18] The present edition includes, additionally, the fourth chapter of the first edition.[19] As indicated earlier, copy-

---

18. Although the second edition of *The School and Society* was twice the size of the first and considerably revised, it was not widely noticed. Brief mentions appeared in the *Boston Transcript* (25 August 1915), *Booklist* (12 [1915]), and *Education* (36 [1915–16]: 123), and two journals gave it more extended treatment: *Elementary School Journal* (16 [1915]: 67–69) and *Journal of Education* (82 [1915]: 357). The three-page *Elementary School Journal* review commented, "In the present edition the author has seen fit to omit [the] fourth chapter. Those who are familiar with the earlier edition will feel that there is a distinct loss in omitting this discussion of the important experiment which Professor Dewey inaugurated" (p. 68), and combined a reflective note about the first edition with praise for the second, "Certainly Professor Dewey may rest assured of the very great influence of his book. It is given only to a few men to write educational classics. Since Spencer wrote his essays there has not been a more important contribution to educational reform than Dewey's *School and Society*" (p. 69).

19. Although the fourth chapter was purposely omitted in the second edition, both Dewey and the publisher overlooked the original reference to it in the "Publisher's Note," I1+, which contin-

text for the first four chapters is the first impression of the
first edition. For the five new chapters of the second edition,
copy-text is the only previous printing of the articles in the
Elementary School Record.

Machine collation of the seventeen impressions of the
second edition collated for the present edition[20] has revealed
that in the second edition's forty-eight-year history of printings from a single set of plates, only two variants appeared,
both in the second impression. One, the addition of a comma
after "and" at 76.36, was apparently an editorial change, rejected for the present edition. The other change was the correction of a typographical error (satisfing) at 82.26. Five
typographical errors that have been corrected in the present
edition appeared in all printings of the second edition: "or-
ganzies" at 11.26, "arthmetic" at 55.2, repetition of the first
"a" at 36.16, of the syllable "com" at the end of 44.18, and
of the first "the" at 47.24.

The first three chapters (which had appeared in the first
edition) of the first impression of the second edition were
sight collated against two copies of I^{11}, revealing that 145
changes in accidentals and 42 changes in substantives were
introduced between the eleventh impression of the first edition and the first impression of the second edition. Removal
of italics and of the ligatures on "ae" accounts for the bulk
of the variants in accidentals; the spelling of some words was
restyled (fullness to fulness, guarantee to guaranty); and
many hyphenated compounds were closed up (textbook,
sandpapering, sawmill, gristmill). Among the changes in accidentals, five restored readings of I^1 that had been unauthoritatively altered in I^{2-11} by deleting a comma (12.27) and
adding a comma after "utilities" at 14.22, and by deleting a

---

ued throughout all printings of the second edition to include the
explanation, "As [the lectures] imply more or less familiarity
with the work of the Elementary School, Mr. Dewey's supplementary statement of this has been added" (p. xi).

20. II^1 Library of Congress copyright deposit A410258c.1; II^2 Dewey
Center (a); II^3 Dewey Center (a); II^4 Dewey Center (a); II^5
University of Pennsylvania 495038; II^6 University of Vermont
102.259, 191D515s2; II^7 Lexington [Ky.] Public Library 54605;
II^8 Temple University 26494; II^9 New York State Library 388194;
II^{10} Dewey Center (a); II^{11} Dewey Center (a); II^{12} Ohio State
University 377762; II^{13} University of California, Berkeley
M515954; II^{14} Dewey Center (a); II^{15} Dewey Center (a); II^{16}
Dewey Center (a); II^{17} Dewey Center (a).

comma after "proportions" (29.6) and overlooking two typographical errors in I[3-11], "recitaton" at 33.12 and "placer" at
33.13.

The second-edition substantive revisions have been incorporated into the copy-text, following what was probably
Dewey's own editorial process in preparing printer's copy. Of
the changes in accidentals, thirty-seven have been accepted
here as more nearly representing Dewey's characteristic usage than the readings in the first edition, as, for example,
spelling of "criticize" and the capitalization of "middle ages."
Some accepted changes in accidentals accompanied changes
in substantives, but markedly fewer by comparison than between the first and second impressions of the first edition. By
far the largest group of accidental emendations made on
the basis of new readings in II[1] were punctuation changes
made to clarify meaning; they were thought in each case to
reflect Dewey's intentions in this carefully revised edition.

Changes and emendations made in Chapter 4 of the
present edition have already been discussed as part of the
first edition; as noted, this chapter did not appear in the second edition.

The last five chapters of the second edition of *The School
and Society* first appeared in print as articles in the *Elementary School Record*, the only printing of that material before
it was typeset for the book. Sight collation of the *Elementary
School Record* forms against II[1] shows the same pattern of
accidental variation as in the first three chapters—i.e., chiefly
for restyling and for clarification of meaning. Of the total
of ninety-two, forty in the second category appear as emendations in the present edition, and the remaining fifty-two
were found to be unauthoritative. Twenty-one substantive
variants appear in the new edition; all have been incorporated into the edited text. Twenty-four other changes have
been made here to eliminate references to the original printing—changing titles and adding chapter numbers, deleting
addresses to write for *Record* material, and internal mentions
of "this journal."

In 1956, *The School and Society* was reset and combined
in a University of Chicago Press Phoenix paperback with
Dewey's *The Child and the Curriculum*, printed from plano-
graph negatives. The third edition, now in its eleventh im-

pression, has produced well over 260,000 copies in its paper and cased volumes.

" 'Consciousness' and Experience" ["Psychology and Philosophic Method"]

In May 1899, Dewey addressed the Philosophical Union of the University of California at Berkeley; his address was first published in August of that year as "Psychology and Philosophic Method" in the *University* [of California] *Chronicle* (2 [1899]: 159–79). After this initial appearance, the article was reprinted one time from standing type by the University of California Press for the Philosophical Union in August 1899 as a twenty-three-page pamphlet. The only changes made for the separate reprint were formal and typographical, including changes in pagination and removing *"University Chronicle"* from the running heads. The first printing in the *University* [of California] *Chronicle* (U) thus serves as copy-text for the present edition.

Eleven years after first publication, "Psychology and Philosophic Method" was revised by Dewey for inclusion in *The Influence of Darwin on Philosophy and Other Essays in Contemporary Thought* (New York: Henry Holt and Co., 1910) with the new title " 'Consciousness' and Experience." The book was registered for copyright upon publication 23 April 1910 with the number A26141. All copies located of the book carry the notice "Published April, 1910" on the copyright page. A partial inventory record in the Holt Publishing Co. Papers at Princeton University indicates a second printing was made, probably in 1917; collation of three copies[21] of Dewey's article in *The Influence of Darwin* (D) reveals no variants in the text of the article.

Comparison of the accidentals in the copy-text first impression with the revised 1910 edition reveals that most changes introduced in D were either formal or of the kind naturally associated with a revision of substantives. A num-

---

21. Library of Congress, copyright deposit A261481; Dewey Center (a) and (b). Both the copyright deposit copy and the Dewey Center (a) copy have the date 1910 on the title page; no date appears on the title page of the Dewey Center (b) copy, which is undoubtedly from the second printing.

ber of these changes have been retained as desirable emendations for the present edition: at twenty-seven points, D makes the single quotation marks used in U into double and the spelling of "equilibrium" was corrected at 19.6. Other emendations of copy-text accidentals have been made because the changes appeared to be authoritative: hyphens were inserted in "a-going" (124.26) and "subject-matter" (125.20). Substantive revisions led to the addition of the comma at 126.6 and deletion of another after "individualized" at 129.1; an exclamation point was added at 117.31; italics were used at 121.32, and quotation marks were added at 126.27; and at five places punctuation changes were made to clarify meaning (113.17, 113.18–19, 114.4, 125.30, 128n.23).

Dewey characterized the changes he made in the article for its inclusion in D in 1910 as "slight verbal changes, mostly excisions."[22] He did in fact eliminate many parenthetical expressions more natural for U, an address, but at the same time he brought a number of terms into line with his 1910 thought: "reality" largely disappears, becoming "fact" or "material"; "sensationalist school of psychology" changes to "analytic school of psychology"; "the psychical as such" becomes "experience."

One class of substantive changes that appears in D is the regular, frequent (twelve instances) and consistent substitution of "that" for "which" in restrictive clauses. As Dewey's own practice in this matter varied, a number of these changes may well have been instituted by an editor at Holt. But it is now impossible to distinguish the possible editorial regularization from Dewey's intended revision because some of these changes occur within passages rewritten by Dewey. These changes have therefore been accepted for the present edition, along with the large number of substantive changes that were beyond doubt Dewey's.

"Psychology and Social Practice"

Dewey's presidential address to the American Psychological Association meeting in New Haven in December

22. *Influence of Darwin*, p. 242.

1899, entitled "Psychology and Social Practice," first appeared in print the following March in both the *Psychological Review* (7 [1900]: 105–24) and in *Science* (n.s. 11 [1900]: 321–33).

In November, before delivering the address, Dewey had written to James McKeen Cattell, co-editor of the *Psychological Review*, "I am sorry to be the one to make a break in the custom of printing the presidential addresses in January, but I find it is going to be impossible for me to get the manuscript to you in time."[23] Cattell, a close professional associate of Dewey's, was editor of the journal *Science* as well as co-editor of *Psychological Review*; Dewey's delay in sending the material meant that Cattell would have received it some time in January or February, whereupon he published it in both periodicals. Although Dewey mentioned "manuscript," he probably sent a typescript as was his more common practice by 1900, and Cattell's dual editorial function would have made it possible for him to use a single typescript as printer's copy for both typesettings of the article. The two journals were published in New York, permitting Cattell to provide copy for *Psychological Review* first and to use the same copy in turn for the *Science* typesetting.

The two appearances of the article were apparently simultaneous. *Science* was published weekly; the number with Dewey's article is dated 2 March 1900. *Psychological Review*, a bi-monthly, usually went to press late in the month preceding the month of publication, thus making it possible that the *Science* printing appeared some days earlier than the one in *Psychological Review*, even though the latter was the traditional vehicle for publishing A.P.A. presidential addresses and had announced Dewey's forthcoming article in its January issue. Regardless of the order of appearance, the circumstances surrounding publication give each printing equal textual authority.

Sight collation of the two printings reveals twelve substantive variants and twenty variants in accidentals, as well as two possible accidental variants in compounds broken at the end of a line. Study of the variants in accidentals makes

23. Dewey to Cattell, 27 November 1899, Manuscript Division, Library of Congress.

it possible to reconstruct the details of Dewey's lost type-script. Of the twenty-two instances of accidental variation, including the two possible variants, the *Psychological Review* (PR) was on the whole more faithful to Dewey's typical prac-tice, correctly rendering it in fifteen cases; *Science*, however, was judged more faithful to his intentions in the remaining seven cases. Each journal has been credited with the inter-nal unambiguous reading of the two line-end hyphenated words: "text-book" (135.10) in S and "re-viewing" (145.23–24) in PR. "Re-viewing" might not seem to be an ambigu-ously broken word except that PR printed it within the text in that form, as the sense of Dewey's sentence requires. S did not use a comma at 132.33, where PR unauthoritatively makes "identity" apposite with "reality", and also did not use a comma at 135.22, where PR separates the subject from the verb with a comma. S has a comma at 146.36, where PR separates the clauses of a complex sentence with a semi-colon. At 135.31, 138.1, and 138.3, S uses Dewey's charac-teristic punctuation: a dash rather than a colon, and two commas omitted by PR. PR correctly rendered Dewey's usual spelling of "criticize" (146.9) and his hyphenation of "whole-hearted" (134.12) and "steam-engine" (150.19). In all other cases of variation, PR punctuation reproduced Dewey's char-acteristic usage more faithfully, and has been used here as copy-text.

The shorter period of time available for proofreading caused by *Science's* receiving the typescript later may ac-count for the fact that in all twelve cases of substantive variation the S readings have been rejected as non-authorial corruptions. In six instances, omissions of a letter or word probably resulted from compositorial slips: the word "in" dropped at 143.13; "the" dropped at 147.25; "law" for "laws" at 147.33; "ideas" for "ideals" at 148.1 and 148.28; "cate-gorial" for "categorical" at 148.7. Addition of an "s" to "view" (131.18) may also have been a compositorial slip, but seems more likely to have been an editorial change in Dewey's some-what unusual but intentional expression "the absence of elaborated and coherent view."

Two remaining substantive anomalies occurring in S were probably also corrected editorially by PR; they are typi-

cal Dewey oversights of lack of agreement between subject
and verb: at 137.35 in the S reading "Life functions, active
operations, are the reality which confront him," "confront"
is corrected to "confronts" in PR; and at 144.22, the S reading "the more economical is the discovery and realization of
human aims" is similarly corrected to "are" by PR.

The text of "Psychology and Social Practice" in the present volume is eclectic in its accidentals, which have been
selectively chosen from those of the two authoritative first
printings of the article; the present text follows PR in each
case of substantive variation between the two printings only
because the S variants in substantives were positive errors.

Dewey and Ella Flagg Young signed a contract in November 1901 with the University of Chicago Press for a
series to be called Educational Situations, a series that actually turned out to be the Contributions to Education;[24] the
original intended series title was assigned to Dewey's small
book of that name which also appears in the present volume.
"Psychology and Social Practice" was Dewey's first "Contribution" to this series, and in 1901, the University of Chicago
Press reset and published the article as a separate pamphlet
(C). The C printing was typeset from a clipping of the PR
text; it follows that printing in each case of substantive variation between PR and S, and agrees, in instances of variations
in accidentals, with seventeen accidentals in PR and only
five in S.

After the first impression from plates in 1901, a second
impression was made from the plates in 1909; a third and
final impression, once more from the stored plates, in 1916.
Machine collation of two copies of the first impression[25]
against two copies of the second[26] and one copy of the third[27]

24. The decision to name the series University of Chicago Contributions to Education was apparently reached very soon after the
contract was signed, as *Psychology and Social Practice* appeared
in 1901 as No. 2 in the series. Publishing records and correspondence of the University of Chicago Press cited throughout
this commentary are, unless otherwise noted, from Press records
at the Langley Office and are quoted with permission of the Press.
25. Ohio State University BF57D54c.2 and The Johns Hopkins University, LB5C2, No. 1–6.
26. Dewey Center (a) and Dewey Center (b).
27. University of Chicago Press Collection of Record Copies, Special
Collections, The Joseph Regenstein Library, University of Chicago, Chicago, Ill.

reveals only the changing of digits in the title-page date and the addition of a notice of the new impression on the copyright page. Although University of Chicago Press records are not complete for this particular publication, stock and manufacturing cards show that a total of 2,885 copies were printed of the three impressions. When stock from the 1916 printing was nearly exhausted, the Press decided not to reprint, and declared the publication out of print in June 1934.

The extent of Dewey's intervention in preparing copy for the University of Chicago Press edition is not known, but the large number of places—seventeen of a word or phrase—in which italics were added point to his having worked through the article copy very carefully.

At the same time, the University of Chicago Press editors apparently changed Dewey's punctuation freely, adding some forty-seven commas and five hyphens, and taking out or changing thirty other marks. The twenty-six changes in accidentals accepted as authoritative from C for the present edition include those that reflect Dewey's typical spelling, as in "today" (131.8, 132.24, 139.4, 144.14), "subject-matter" (133.31), "sense-organs" (139.38); the use of double quotation marks (133.22–23, 142.35); and eleven punctuation changes made to clarify meaning.

The italics were almost certainly added by Dewey and cannot be considered "accidentals" because the emphasis they introduce is substantive. The only other substantive change adopted from C is the correction of agreement between subject and verb at 143.32.

"Some Stages of Logical Thought"

"Some Stages of Logical Thought" first appeared in *Philosophical Review* (9 [1900]: 465–89). That version serves as copy-text for the present edition.

In 1916, the University of Chicago Press undertook a new edition of Dewey's contributions to *Studies in Logical Theory* (Chicago: University of Chicago Press, 1903). In the course of preparing that new edition, several articles previously printed in various journals were added and the collection was entitled *Essays in Experimental Logic* (EE).

One of the articles printed in revised form under that title was "Some Stages of Logical Thought," pp. 183–219.

Dewey said in the "Prefatory Note" to *Essays in Experimental Logic* that the added essays were "in part reprinted and in part rewritten, with additions, from various contributions to philosophical periodicals."[28] Dewey probably made his revisions in an offprint or clipping of the *Philosophical Review* printing of "Some Stages of Logical Thought," which then served as printer's copy for the University of Chicago Press edition.

The University of Chicago Press made three printings from a single set of plates of *Essays in Experimental Logic*, in June 1916, May 1918, and October 1920. After sales of the book fell to fewer than seventy-five a year, the book was allowed to go out of print in December 1925. In 1940, the Press still had the plates in its vault and ran off a set of proofs for Peter Smith, of Gloucester, Massachusetts, who was considering reissuing the book. Correspondence between Smith and the Press indicates, however, that no further reprinting from those plates occurred.

Machine collation of copies[29] of the second and third impressions of Dewey's article in *Essays in Experimental Logic* against the copyright deposit copy reveals no variation among them.

Comparison of the *Philosophical Review* (PR) printing with the revised article in *Essays in Experimental Logic* shows that by far the largest number of accidental changes made for the new edition were in formal matters such as the transposition of punctuation marks—quotation marks inside semicolons, for example; the removal of ligatures on "ae"; the correction of typographical errors; and twenty instances of substitution of double quotation marks for single. A number of commas were added and other punctuation was changed to improve style and clarify meaning, as at 154.24 and 154.38 where two sentences were joined with a semicolon, and at 164.34 where a comma separating subject and

28. *Essays in Experimental Logic*, p. v.
29. First impression, Dewey Center; second impression, University of Minnesota, 1329092; third impression, University of Chicago Press Collection of Record Copies.

verb was deleted. These kinds of changes have been accepted as desirable emendations for the present edition, as
have changes in hyphenation of compounds that more nearly
reflect Dewey's characteristic usage, as for instance, "re-
establishing" (154.18) and "thought-process" (173.34).

As the Emendations List shows, Dewey's substantive alterations in EE that have been introduced as authoritative
emendations in the present edition were intended to polish
style and sharpen meaning, and, though numerous, actually
represent fewer alterations in words used for concepts than
in, for example, his revision of " 'Consciousness' and Experience." In EE, Dewey revised primarily to delete parenthetical
expressions and unnecessary words, and on the whole to refine and clarify.

The Educational Situation

CHAPTER I, "AS CONCERNS THE ELEMENTARY SCHOOL"

On 28 February 1901, Dewey addressed the Department
of Superintendence of the National Educational Association
in Chicago on "The Situation as Regards the Course of
Study." The address was first published in three numbers of
the weekly *School Journal*, 20 and 27 April, and 4 May 1901.
In June of the same year, Dewey's revised version of the article appeared in the *Educational Review*; in November, the
same revised form of the article was also published in the
1901 *Proceedings and Addresses* of the National Educational
Association. The straight chronological order of appearance
of these printings might suggest a direct linear transmission
of the texts, with the *Educational Review* (ER) printing
made from a clipping of *School Journal* (SJ) marked with
Dewey's substantive revisions, and the *Proceedings and Addresses* (PA) printing based in turn on a copy of the ER
printing. But the evidence indicates that ER and PA are not
in this kind of direct relationship.

Dewey's substantive revisions provide clues to establish
the order of transmission. To make his changes in the SJ
version of the address before it was to appear in ER, Dewey

probably marked up a clipping of the three SJ installments. The fact that ER was published so soon after the last SJ installment on 4 May, however, does leave open the possibility that he reworked a carbon copy of the original typescript to prepare copy for the June ER publication.

Sixty-eight of Dewey's substantive changes from SJ that appear in the ER printing are also in the PA version. The concurrence of these two printings in this many revisions indicates that the two did not derive independently from SJ, a radiation for which one would need to hypothesize beyond probability that Dewey revised two copies of SJ (or of its typescript) identically in a number of readings.

The agreement in substantive revision of ER and PA could be explained if Dewey had used the ER printing as copy for the typesetting of the "official" PA publication of the address. The time sequence, with ER published in June and PA in November, would have permitted him to do that. But such a possibility is ruled out by the appearance in PA of SJ readings that had been altered in ER.

Four such changes were errors in ER that might have been corrected by editors or compositors at PA, as, for example, "he" for "it" at 272.19 and 272.22, "value" for "values" at 274.11, "forbid" for "forbids" at 270.25. Ten other substantive changes that are not errors, however, appear in ER where PA retains the SJ readings. ER added "has been made" at 261.17 and dropped "etc." at 261.25; ER used various forms of the word "education" to substitute for all forms of "pedagogy" (260.15, 260.16, 261.26, 261.28, 272.37); used "taken" for "taking" at 263.25, "I" rather than "we" at 276.31, and "last" rather than "least" at 276.1. In all these cases, PA has the same reading as SJ, thus establishing that PA could not have been based directly on ER.

The hypothesis that best explains the transmission of these documents is that a typescript and carbon were made up from a copy of SJ that Dewey had revised for the purpose. The ER substantive variants that disagree both with SJ and with PA appear to be editorial in the ER office since none is characteristic of Dewey. Revising forms of "pedagogy" to forms of "education" would be an expected editorial alteration in a journal that had the word "educational" in its title;

Dewey himself carefully distinguished "pedagogy," that is, teaching, from "education," a broad process. Two other typical items were editorially "corrected": "etc." was eliminated in one place, and "has been made" was added to make a complete sentence of Dewey's more characteristic expression that appeared in SJ and PA.

Errors could have appeared and editorial changes could have been made in ER in exactly the same manner if a marked copy of SJ had been used as the basis for both ER and for a new typescript later used by PA. But the extensive agreement of ER and PA in changes of accidentals supports instead the hypothesis that the two are in collateral relationship, both having been typeset from a common document, probably a new typescript and its carbon prepared either from a revised copy of SJ or from the revised carbon of Dewey's original typescript.

ER and PA concur in 150 changes from the SJ accidentals, too large a number to attribute to chance or to independent editorial regularization by each journal. Most of the changes are demonstrably not Dewey's and would therefore not have characterized his marking up of a copy of SJ; both the number and the kind of these sophistications point to the use of a new document for the typesetting of both ER and PA. Of the accidental changes common to ER and PA, 65 are added commas, more than two-thirds of them uncharacteristic of Dewey's pointing. A number, for example, are used to set off introductory words such as "indeed," "moreover," "thus," and "now," contrary to Dewey's usual practice. The changing of a semicolon to a dash at 260.14, the deletion of commas at 264.8 and 267.27, the changing of commas to other marks after "viz." at 262.19 and after "foot" at 263.36, and the substitution of a semicolon for a colon at 266.37 were similarly not revisions Dewey would ordinarily make.

The numerous accidental changes not attributable to Dewey were probably made by the typist in preparing copy for both ER and PA and in its subsequent styling for publication. Those associated with substantive revisions and those made to clarify meaning can readily be identified as Dewey's corrections, very likely in the marked copy itself. And,

whether in revising or in correcting the typescript, Dewey
followed his usual pattern and added hyphens in "long-
wished-for" (261.36), "self-assertion" (264.39), "face-to-
face" (268.4) and "school-teachers" (276.8). Typically, too,
he would have supplied quotation marks and a question mark
for the rhetorical question at 264.29–31; used a semicolon
to join two short sentences at 266.38–39; changed a semicolon to a comma after "point", (262.19); changed semicolons to colons (270.14, 271.35); and used his characteristic spelling "willfully" (262.32) and "Someone" (263.8). But
only two-fifths of the 150 accidental changes that appear in
ER and PA can be so classified, and the remainder are the
kind of sophistication, regularization, and changes in spelling and hyphenation that typists frequently made in Dewey
material and which he never troubled to alter.

Where substantive variants occur between ER and PA,
the degree of faithfulness of each to the new typescript and
its carbon can be determined by comparison with SJ; agreement either of ER or PA with SJ can be assumed to reflect
the reading of the typescript prepared from SJ. Of seventeen
instances of variation, PA and SJ agree at thirteen points,
ER and SJ at only four. Each independently introduced further substantive changes: those appearing in only ER have
been described; PA in addition regularized "her" to "his" at
270.30, deleted "in" from "or in its" at 273.5, inserted "of"
at 278.12, and made "gathering" at 260.16 into "gatherings."
Those changes, along with capitalizing "king log" and "king
stork" at 275.1, seem to be last-minute revisions Dewey could
have made before sending the typescript to PA.

In 1902, Dewey further revised "The Situation as Regards the Course of Study" and entitled it "As Concerns the
Elementary School" for its printing as the first chapter of
The Educational Situation (ES) (Chicago: University of Chicago Press, 1902). Printer's copy for the new edition was a
copy of the PA version; ES followed PA in each of the seventeen cases of substantive variation between ER and PA. In
addition to numerous revisions of wording, clearly Dewey's,
ES introduced some changes in accidentals: italics were
added at 263.35, 268.23, and 280.32; the twelve occurrences
of "thru" and "thoro" were restyled to "through" and "thor-

ough"; and the use of commas in series was regularized. ES also introduced one substantive error, repeating "the" at 277.3, which has been corrected here.

The present critically edited text of the first chapter of *The Educational Situation* has used the SJ printing as copy-text, incorporating as emendations Dewey's own revisions in substantives, with few exceptions. Also following standard editorial procedure, the accidentals of SJ are accepted as Dewey's intentions except where evidence suggests that he rather than an editor was responsible for changing them in later versions of the text.

In one class of substantive changes apparently introduced by the new typescript for ER and PA, it is difficult to determine the authority of the readings. In SJ, all pronoun references to teachers were "she" and "her." In ER and PA, except for one instance in ER, these references were made masculine. Because Dewey's own usage often vacillated between "her" and "his," both occurring within the course of a single lecture,[30] it seems likely that use of the feminine was made consistent editorially in SJ. The intention to regularize such references as masculine in the revision—whether wholly or in part Dewey's—is clear, and the regularization has been accepted as an emendation of the copy-text.

The SJ copy-text, with Dewey's characteristically light punctuation, otherwise has been followed in accidentals; only punctuation changes that clarify meaning or are associated with substantive revisions, or that reflect Dewey's known preferences for spelling and hyphenation, have been incorporated as emendations from the agreement of ER and PA. Despite the fact that two-thirds of the accidental changes in the typescript underlying ER and PA were rejected, that typescript was the source of the largest number of accidental emendations adopted, with several additional adopted from PA in cases where it was deemed to have followed copy more faithfully than did ER. From ES, only the added italics, two spelling changes, and the restyling of "thru" and "thoro" have been accepted.

30. "Principles of Education," University of Chicago, Spring Quarter, 1902 (mimeographed), pp. 18, 29, 30, 55, 63, 96, 121.

CHAPTER 2, "AS CONCERNS THE SECONDARY SCHOOL"

Choice of copy-text for Chapter 2 poses few problems, inasmuch as the only printing of the article before its revision for inclusion in ES was as the article "Current Problems in Secondary Education," in *School Review* (10 [1902]: 13–28). *School Review* was, like *The Educational Situation*, published by the University of Chicago Press and had the same basic style of accidentals.[31] Substantive alterations and additions have been accepted from *The Educational Situation* as representing Dewey's intended revisions in the text.

CHAPTER 3, "AS CONCERNS THE COLLEGE"

Chapter 3, similarly, had only one printing before its revision for *The Educational Situation*, that in the *Educational Review* (22 [1901]: 459–74), with the title "Are the Schools Doing What the People Want Them to Do?" The *Educational Review* printing has served as copy-text, with substantive emendations introduced from the revised form as it appeared in the book.

The Educational Situation

The Educational Situation, No. 3 in the University of Chicago Contributions to Education, was published in September 1902 and reprinted four times from a single set of plates—July 1904, July 1906, September 1910, and March 1916—and was declared out of print in June 1924. The electroplates that had been in storage since 1902 were destroyed in November 1924.

Collation of copies of the second through the fifth printings against the Library of Congress copyright deposit copy[32]

31. Dewey was, in fact, "Editor-in-Chief" of the *School Review* in 1902, but his correspondence with Wilbur Jackman during the period of his editorship indicates that he functioned more as General Editor than as a copy-editor. Dewey Papers, Special Collections, Morris Library, Southern Illinois University at Carbondale.

32. I¹ Library of Congress copyright deposit copy 24726c.B; I² University of Michigan 141083; I³ University of California 695980; I⁴ New York State Library 388516; I⁵ University of Vermont 87.742.

shows the only changes during the book's printing history to be in the preliminary pages, ranging from resetting of dates to resetting the title page. The text continued without change through the five printings, and the plates, used only for the small printings of 500 to 1,000, remained in excellent condition with only slight evidence of wear.

CHECKLIST OF SUMMARIES AND CLASS LECTURE NOTES, 1899–1901

1899   "The Method of the Recitation." Partial report of a course of lectures given at the University of Chicago; privately printed for use at Oshkosh, Wisconsin. 52 pp.

Summaries and parts of syllabus for series of five lectures on "The Life of the Child," presented through University Extension at Honolulu High School, in *Pacific Commercial Advertiser.*

"Advantages of Extension System," 7 August 1899

"Early Childhood, Play, Imagination," 18 August 1899

"Later Childhood, Interest and Attention," 22 August 1899

"Adolescence and Emotions," 25 August 1899

"General Principles of Growth," 29 August 1899

Summaries of first two lectures in series of five on "Movements in Nineteenth Century Thought," presented through University Extension at Honolulu High School, in *Pacific Commercial Advertiser.*

"Influence of Rousseau on French Political History and Literature," 1 September 1899

"Goethe and Schiller and the Ethics of Culture and Art," 5 September 1899

"Theory of Logic." Stenographic report of class lecture notes, 1899–1900, University of Chicago. 302 pp. H. Heath Bawden Collection, St. Louis University.[33]

"Pedagogy I B 19, Philosophy of Education." Stenographic report of class lecture notes, 1898–1899, University of Chicago. Grinnell College Library, Duke University Li-

33. H. Heath Bawden said of his notes, "I took all the Dewey notes in long hand, or rather in my abbreviated shorthand. . . . The other stenographic courses were the result of the cooperation of the members of the classes in hiring a stenographer." Letter to Ralph W. Gregory, 8 January 1947. Private collection of Ralph W. Gregory. For a fuller description of the preparation of the sets of class lecture notes, see Jo Ann Boydston, "A Note on the Texts," *The Early Works of John Dewey* (Carbondale: Southern Illinois University Press, 1972) 5:cxxxi–cxxxii.

brary. Published, New York: Random House, 1966. Ed. Reginald D. Archambault.

1900   "Logic of Ethics." Stenographic report of class lecture notes, Autumn Quarter, 1900, University of Chicago. XXIX Lectures, 85 pp. H. Heath Bawden Collection, St. Louis University.

1901[34]   "The Evolution of Morality." Stenographic transcript of a course of lectures delivered at the University of Chicago. Lecture I, 2 October 1901. 111 pp. (incomplete). Library of Henry Waldgrave Stuart, Stanford University, Palo Alto, California.

"The Psychology of Ethics." Stenographic report by Mary L. Read, Course 35, Winter Quarter, 1901. Philosophy Department, University of Chicago. 125 pp. H. Heath Bawden Collection, St. Louis University.

"Social Ethics." Stenographic report by Mary L. Read, Course 44, Spring Quarter, 1901. Philosophy Department, University of Chicago. 129 pp. H. Heath Bawden Collection, St. Louis University.

Educational Lectures. Ten lectures delivered before the Brigham Young Academy Summer School [1901]. Reports made by Alice Young and edited by N. L. Nelson. Utah State Historical Society.

"The Historical Method in Ethics." Typescript from notes of an address before the Philosophical Club, 4 December 1901, University of Chicago. 5 pp. H. Heath Bawden Collection, St. Louis University. Another copy, Library of Henry Waldgrave Stuart, Stanford University Library, 6 pp.

---

34. Three papers Dewey is reported to have given during 1900 and 1901 are apparently not extant: "Psychology and Education," to the Pedagogical Club, 12 January 1900; "An Educational Retrospect and Prospect," at Richmond, Virginia, 3 May 1901; and "Education and Everyday Experience," at St. Thomas, Canada, 10 May 1901.

TEXTUAL NOTES

30.14   children. Examination] "The example shown was made by the twelve-year-old children" has been deleted because no such example appears in the text or illustrations; at the time of the original address, such an example was probably displayed and Dewey's reference to it would have appeared in the stenographic report.

38.6   that] The second edition change of "that" to "which" has been rejected in favor of the first edition reading.

78.26   complaint] Although Dewey may well have made a natural verbal slip in his oral presentation and used the plural noun, it has been corrected here to agree with the verb "is".

79.14   results] In listing the "following points" he wanted to make, Dewey's intention of making general statements in the present tense is apparent in the "is" of the point before and the "is" of the point after; the copy-text past tense verb has been made consistent.

85.40   than] The erroneous reading "then" has appeared in all previous printings of this material, undoubtedly a typographical mistake repeatedly overlooked.

92.10   work] The copy-text reading "work herewith reported on" has been emended to omit the original reference to other articles in the *Elementary School Record* that did not, in fact, appear in II¹⁺.

107.1   but is suddenly] The necessary verb has been supplied.

177.11–12   disconnected] The copy-text reading "only a jungle of discontented facts" is assumed to be a typographical error that might easily have been overlooked in proofreading.

180.39   three] Dewey probably intended to mention only two reflexes when he started the sentence, but since three separate reflexes (taking food, clutching, crying) are mentioned, the number has been changed to conform to his listing.

181.14   child is simply] The lack of a verb has been remedied by supplying the necessary "is".

184.28   so in] The three words eliminated here had been mistakenly repeated in this line in the copy-text, probably when the compositor's eye had picked up the same words occurring in the line immediately above.

199.29   distinguishes] By analogy with succeeding verbs in the
          same paragraph (gives, makes, interests), this verb too
          should be in the present tense, which has been substi-
          tuted here to correct (in a typewritten document) the
          use of "d" for "s", a fairly frequent typographical error.

201.19   experienced] The typist's erroneous use of "s" for the
          clearly intended "d" has been corrected.

261.28   ideals] The use of "principles and ideals" and in the
          same sentence the reference to "these principles and
          ideas" make it clear that "ideas" in all printings of the
          text was a compositorial slip overlooked in proof-
          reading.

277.4   conditions] The substantive "considerations" introduced
          by the ES text has been rejected in favor of the copy-
          text reading. Dewey signalled his intention with the
          word "conditions" at 276.40 above. The reference here
          is still to "conditions", not "considerations".

277.7–8   machinery] Addition of the unnecessary "of" in ES may
          have resulted from a misunderstanding of the sense of
          the sentence by a copy-editor. The substantive change
          has been rejected because it distorts the meaning.

300.29   disadvantages] It is unlikely that Dewey intended to
          write "the advantages and the disadvantage". The "s"
          probably omitted by the compositor has been supplied
          here.

LIST OF SYMBOLS

A. Abbreviations used to identify sources in the emendations list are:

C   University of Chicago Contributions to Education (*Psychology and Social Practice*)
D   *Influence of Darwin*
E   *Elementary School Record*
EE *Essays in Experimental Logic*
ER *Educational Review*
ES *The Educational Situation*
ET *Education Today*
Mt *Mental Development* (typewritten)
PA *Proceedings and Addresses* of the National Educational Association
S   *Science*
SR *School Review*
I^{1-11} *School and Society*, 1899
II^{1-17} *School and Society*, 1915
U   *University* [of California] *Chronicle*

B. Other designations

Page-line number at left is from present edition; all lines of print except running heads are counted.

The abbreviation *et seq.* following a page-line number means that all subsequent appearances of the reading in that section are identical with the one noted.

Reading before bracket is from present edition.

Square bracket signals end of reading from present edition, followed by the symbol identifying the first appearance of reading.

W means Works—the present edition—and is used for emendations made here for the first time.

The abbreviation [*om.*] means the reading before the bracket was omitted in the editions and impressions identified after the abbreviation; [*not present*] is used where appropriate to signal material not appearing in identified sources.

The abbreviation [*rom.*] means roman type and is used to signal the omission of italics.

Stet used with an edition or impression number indicates a substantive reading retained from an edition or impression subsequently revised; the rejected variant follows the semicolon.

The asterisk before an emendation page-line number indicates the reading is discussed in the Textual Notes.

The plus sign + means that the same reading appears in all collated printings and editions later than the one noted.

For emendations restricted to punctuation, the curved dash ~ means the same word(s) as before the bracket, and the inferior caret ᴧ indicates the absence of a punctuation mark.

EMENDATIONS LIST

All emendations in both substantives and accidentals introduced into the copy-texts are recorded in the list that follows, with the exception of certain regularizations described and listed at the end of this introductory explanation. The reading to the left of the square bracket is from the present edition. The bracket is followed by the abbreviation for the source of the emendation's first appearance and abbreviations for subsequent editions and printings collated that had the same reading. After the source abbreviations comes a semicolon, followed by the copy-text reading. Substantive variants in all texts collated are also recorded here; the list thus serves as a historical collation as well as a record of emendations.

Copy-texts for each item are identified at the beginning of the list of emendations in that item; for items that had a single previous printing, no abbreviation for the copy-text appears in the list itself. Copy-text abbreviations are used for both *The School and Society* and *The Educational Situation*, which had composite copy-texts, and for "Psychology and Social Practice," in which accidental emendations were selected from two authoritative sources.

A number of formal, or mechanical, changes have been made throughout:

1. Book and journal titles have been put in italic type; articles and sections of books have been put in quotation marks.

2. The form of documentation has been made consistent and complete: "op. cit." has been eliminated and "ibid." is used only when a title is repeated within a single entry; section and chapter numbers are arabic and volume numbers are roman; abbreviations have been regularized; book titles have been supplied and expanded where necessary.

3. Superior numbers have been assigned consecutively throughout an item to Dewey's footnotes; the asterisk is used only for editorial footnotes.

4. To conform to Dewey's usual pattern, the following have been regularized: "viz.", "*i.e.*", "*per se*", "*e.g.*", and "*cf.*"; commas have been supplied after "etc." at 211.34, 213.36, 215.32, and after "*i.e.*" at 210.9.

5. Single quotation marks have been changed to double when not inside quoted materials; opening or closing quotation marks have been supplied where necessary.

6. In references, volume numbers were supplied for periodicals and the listing of authors' names was regularized; titles (Dr., Sir, Prof.) were omitted; only the surname of the author was used except in cases where an initial was used to distinguish between authors with the same surname.

The following spellings have been editorially altered in this volume to the characteristic Dewey forms, given to the left of the bracket:

centre] center 7.14, 15.14, 23.23, 23.30, 23.32, 23.34, 24.32, 44.30, 48.35, 63.32, 95.7, 98.31, 157.40, 191.40, 217.39, 241.20, 284.26, 304.39; (-d) 24.35, 52.11–12, 201.20; (-s) 6.31, 7.28, 10.30, 13.1, 13.26, 15.8, 86.39, 181.6, 183.22, 191.37; (self-centred) 29.12, 218.12
clue] clew 308.29
cooperate] coöperate 105.9
cooperating] coöperating 3.16, 191.35
cooperation] coöperation 4.13, 8.3–4, 10.23, 11.12, 11.33, 104.26, 121.16, 175.24, 182.34, 235.15, 326.36, 329.10, 334.15, 334.19
cooperative] coöperative 12.3, 81.20, 82.2, 84.31
coordinate] coördinate 62.16, 176.36; (-d) 188.4, 188.27
coordination] coördination 176.12, 176.13, 178.29, 179.29, 180.1, 180.9, 180.31, 181.19, 182.6, 183.19–20, 183.33, 184.22–23, 185.24, 191.26, 191.29, 191.34 (2), 191.38 (2), 191.39–40, 231.33; (-s) 176.21, 179.20, 180.17, 180.20, 181.21–22, 182.31, 186.21, 190.21, 190.36; uncoordinated 181.26
criticized] criticised 130n.16, 234n.3, 251.4
entrusted] intrusted 58.20, 66.13
fibre] fiber 14.11 (2), 14.14, 14.22, 14.36, 26.28, 282.6; (-s) 14.16, 14.25, 14.27, 14.31, 15.6, 15.13, 15.20, 183.22
fulfill] fulfil 67.29, 220.34, 255.2; (-ment) 210.2, 242.27–28, 242.31, 244.1, 248n.5, 256.19; (-ments) 249.32, 249.33; (-s) 242.23, 245.18
instill] instil 328.37
labelled] labeled 70.6
labelling] labeling 298.8
meagre] meager 24.22; (-ness) 165.19

modelling] modeling 61.30, 65.15, 74.4, 99.20
program] programme 318.9, 318.23
reinforce] reënforce (-d) 250.11; (-ment) 183.29
through] thru 339.22, 339.25, 340.26
travelling] traveling 204.3

The following instances of word division and hyphenation have been editorially altered in this volume to the known Dewey forms, given to the left of the bracket:

all-around] all around 133.11, 296.1
all-embracing] all embracing 255.20–21
child-study] child study 84.13, 132.11, 186.27
clay-modelling] clay modeling 65.15
common sense (noun)] common-sense 165.16–17
cooperative] co-operative 266.14, 279.39
cross-reference] cross reference 185.9, 185.26–27, 195.18
dining room] dining-room 48.33, 50.15
dish-washing] dishwashing 343.3
door-knob] door knob 195.21, 195.25, 196.14
door-knobs] doorknobs 194.22, 194.28
elementary-school] elementary school 301.11
everyone] every one 204.23
faculty-psychology] faculty psychology 178.6
far-reaching] far reaching 216.20–21
full-fledged] full fledged 197.2
interactions] inter-actions 198.33–34
life controlling] life-controlling 215.31–32
make-believe] make believe 200.28, 201.10
make-up] makeup 215.5
          make up 327.26
ready-made] ready made 180.25
reinforcing] re-inforcing 65.30–31
secondary-school] secondary school 319.38
self-confidence] self confidence 212.33
self-consciousness] self consciousness 216.3–4, 216.25
self-depreciation] self depreciation 213.1
self-explanatory] self explanatory 199.30–-31
sense-element] sense element 71.6
sense-organs] sense organs 62.15, 93.31, 185.14, 333.29
sense-training] sense training 71.11
seventy-five] seventy five 180.29
shop-work] shop work 74.4
sign-posts] sign posts 168.25
starting-point] starting point 113.25
subject-matter] subject matter 317.26, 318.11
today] to-day 115.18, 130n.21
well-defined] well defined 205.15

well-managed] well managed 292.7
well-organized] well organized 292.7

The School and Society

Emendations of the copy-texts are listed here to the left of the bracket followed by the abbreviation for the source of the emendation; the copy-text reading follows the semicolon. To identify the different parts of the composite copy-text, source abbreviations appear after the copy-text reading. Copy-text for the first four chapters is I^1, the November 1899 impression. For chapters 5–9, copy-text is the first impression of the chapters as articles in E: *Elementary School Record* (Chicago: University of Chicago Press, 1900). Editions and impressions collated are discussed in the Textual Commentary. The symbol II is used to mean all impressions of the second edition.

Substantive variants in texts collated are also noted in this list, even though rejected as emendations.

3.2–3	The first . . . before] II; The three lectures presented in the following pages were delivered before I^{1-11}
3.5	year 1899] I^{2+}; present year I^1
3.11	Mr.] I^{2+}; Professor I^1
3.14–4.16	*Author's Note* . . . January 5, 1900.] I^{2+}; [*not present*] I^1
3.15	printing] II; edition I^{2-11}
3.19	friends$_\wedge$] II; ~, I^{2-11}
3.19	Mead$_\wedge$] II; ~, I^{2-11}
4.8	tact,] II; ~$_\wedge$ I^{2-11}
4.16	January 5, 1900.] I^2; January 5, 1900$_\wedge$ I^{3-11}
4.17–30	*Author's Note* . . . July, 1915] II; [*not present*] I^{1-11}
4.29–30	change. July 1915] W; change. J. D. New York City/ July, 1915 II
5.16	is put] I^{3+}; it puts I^{1-2}
5.17	disposal] I^{2+}; disposition I^1
5.22	given,] I^{2+}; ~$_\wedge$ I^1
5.28	social,] II; ~$_\wedge$ I^{1-11}
5.30	teachers;] I^{2+}; ~, I^1
6.4	are changes] I^{2+}; are the changes I^1
6.9	character;] II; ~, I^{1-11}
6.9–10	it will cease] II; and will cease I^{1-11}
6.12	appear] I^{2+}; be seen I^1

6.16   witness it gives] I^{2+}; signs it shows I^1
6.20   training—] II; ∼, I^{1-11}
6.20   relation] I^{2+}; meaning I^1
6.20–21 to changed social conditions appears] I^{2+}; appears under changed social conditions I^1
6.22   point as well] I^{2+}; point I^1
6.22   innovations] I^{2+}; innovations as well I^1
6.23   dwelling] I^{2+}; dilating I^1
6.35   falls] I^{2+}; belongs I^1
7.4   facilitated,] II; ∼$_\wedge$ I^{1-11}
7.8–9 in some other than a formal] II; in other than formal I^{1-11}
7.17   part made] II; part not only made I^{1-11}
7.17   house; the] II; house, but the I^{1-11}
7.18   usually] I^{3+}; generally I^{1-2}
7.18   familiar also] II; familiar I^{1-11}
7.22   was followed] I^{3+}; stood revealed I^{1-2}
7.23   fat$_\wedge$] II; ∼, I^{1-11}
7.26   was produced] II; was I^{1-11}
7.30   materials$_\wedge$] II; ∼, I^{1-11}
7.36   even to] I^{2+}; even up to I^1
7.38   in this kind of life:] II; in this: I^{2-11}; in all this I^1
7.39   and in the] I^{2+}; and the I^1
9.9   in] II; with I^{1-11}
9.30   receptive] I^{3+}; perceptive I^{1-2}
9.34   seamstresses] II; sempstresses I^{1-11}
9.36–37 underestimate the worth of] I^{2+}; underestimate I^1
9.40   child.] I^{2+}; child, not to society. I^1
10.3   methods of living and learning,] II; methods of life I^{2-11}; methods, I^1
10.3–4 studies. [◖] We must] I^{2+}; studies of life on its active and social sides. We must I^1
10.7   as ways] I^{2+}; as the ways I^1
10.7–8 these needs] I^{2+}; these I^1
10.32   kitchen] I^{3+}; workshop I^{1-2}
10.39   absorbing] II; absorption I^{1-11}
11.7   accumulating,] II; ∼$_\wedge$ I^{1-11}
11.8   prevailing] II; prevalent I^{1-11}
11.14   on,] II; ∼$_\wedge$ I^{1-11}
11.34   such an aim] II; this I^{1-11}
11.34–35 of one sort of order] II; order of one sort I^{2-11}; order of the first sort I^1
12.1   the occupation] II; occupation I^{1-11}
12.9   as they are related] I^{2+}; in their vital relation I^1
12.14   when] II; where I^{1-11}
12.16   dominates$_\wedge$] II; ∼, I^{1-11}
12.31   streams] II; sources I^{1-11}

12.39   utilities,] I^{2+}; $\sim_\wedge$ I^1
12.39   this openness] I^{2+};   and openness I^1
13.20   developed] I^{2+};   finally fixed I^1
13.23   terms,] I^{2+}; $\sim_\wedge$ I^1
13.26   seamstresses] II;   sempstresses I^1
13.32–33   strikes more oddly upon the average intelligent visitor
           than] I^{2+};   strikes the average intelligent visitor as
           stranger than I^1
14.1   trace and] I^{2+};   begin to I^1
14.2   used] I^{2+};   he is using I^1
14.14   is$_\wedge$ that] II; $\sim$, $\sim$ I^{1-11}
14.18–19   gin only] II;   only gin I^{1-11}
14.23   averaging, say, one-third] II;   being one-tenth I^{1-11}
14.24   while the latter run to three inches] II;   while that of
           the latter is an inch I^{1-11}
14.36   fibre;] W;   fiber; I^{2+}; $\sim_\wedge$ I^1
15.17   appear] II;   usually appear I^{1-11}
15.18   usually pass] II;   pass I^{1-11}
15.27–28   historic and social values] II;   historic values I^{1-11}
15.28   With] I^{2+};   It ceases with I^1
15.29   knowledge it ceases] I^{2+};   knowledge I^1
15.31   organ of understanding] II;   organ I^{1-11}
16.7   than in] I^{3+};   than at I^{1-2}
16.8   exist] I^{3+};   be found I^{1-2}
16.9   consciousness of the one] I^{3+};   him I^{1-2}
16.10   himself] I^{3+};   him I^{1-2}
16.21   enables] I^{2+};   shall enable I^1
16.22   is in it] I^{2+};   is I^1
16.25   or the] II;   or to the I^{1-11}
16.29   as to] I^{2+};   into I^1
16.40   learning is] II;   learning was I^{1-11}
18.23   training] I^{2+};   the training I^1
18.24   culture,] I^{2+}; $\sim_\wedge$ I^1
18.24   or] II;   as I^{1-11}
18.24   the training] II;   that I^{1-11}
18.28–29   "workers,"] I^{3+}; $_\wedge\sim$, $_\wedge$ I^{1-2}
18.30   cent$_\wedge$] II; $\sim$. I^{1-11}
18.31   cent$_\wedge$] II; $\sim$. I^{1-11}
18.39   realization.] I^{2+}; $\sim_\wedge$ I^1
19.10–11   appeal] I^{3+};   do appeal I^{1-2}
19.12   find] I^{3+};   find that I^{1-2}
19.12   to] I^{3+};   would I^{1-2}
19.13   prolonged, containing more of culture.] I^{3+};   prolonged.
           I^{1-2}
19.21   often appear] I^{2+};   appear often I^1
19.22   to be] I^{2+};   as I^1
19.23   improvement] I^{3+};   improvements I^{1-2}

19.24   evolution] I²⁺; this change I¹
19.34   into] I³⁺; in I¹⁻²
21.12   great] II; good I¹⁻¹¹
21.20   great] II; good I¹⁻¹¹
21.23   at which the children may work] I²⁺; for the children
          to work at I¹
21.29   desks] I²⁺; the desks I¹
21.34   because] II; for I¹⁻¹¹
22.4   materials] I³⁺; results I¹⁻²
23.38   the child] I²⁺; him continually I¹
25.5   hidden] I²⁺; latent I¹
25.14   If] II; if I¹⁻¹¹
25.17   culture,] II; ~∧ I¹⁻¹¹
25.25   the paths followed.] I²⁺; these lines. I¹
28.12   childhood—] II; ~; I¹⁻¹¹
28.14   allowed] I²⁺; left there I¹
28.15   he] I²⁺; it I¹
*30.14   children. Examination] W; children. The example
          shown was made by the twelve-year-old children. Ex-
          amination I¹⁺
30.21   side:] II; ~. I¹⁻¹¹
31.10   comes: What are we] I²⁺; comes of what we are I¹
31.11   interest—are we] I²⁺; interest, I¹
31.11–12 out? Or shall we get] I²⁺; out; or whether, again, we
          shall get I¹
31.12   better?] I²⁺; ~. I¹
32.6   opportunity thus given] I²⁺; opportunity given in
          this I¹
32.12   provided occasion] I²⁺; gave opportunity I¹
32.16   supplied a demand] I²⁺; gave opportunity I¹
32.20   vent∧] II; ~, I¹⁻¹¹
32.23   needed] I²⁺; sought I¹
32.23   arrived at] I²⁺; worked out I¹
33.4   infinitely] II; indefinitely I¹⁻¹¹
33.7   facts] I²⁺; the information I¹
33.7   fixed lessons] I²⁺; lessons I¹
34.16   natural motive for] I²⁺; only natural use of I¹
34.22   taken away] II; taken I¹⁻¹¹
34.22   purpose] II; basis I¹⁻¹¹
35.39   *pulled*] II; *pulls* I¹⁻¹¹
36.11   are] II; were I¹⁻¹¹
36.16   a tumbler] *stet* I¹⁻¹¹; a a tumbler II¹⁻¹⁷
36.34   for] I²⁺; that I¹
36.35   to] I²⁺; should I¹
36.38   How] II; how I¹⁻¹¹
37.7–8   to control] II; control I¹⁻¹¹
37.9   supply] I²⁺; give all I¹

37.10	same results] II; results I[1-11]
37.15	condition] I[3+]; fashion I[1-2]
37.16	thing$_\wedge$] I[3+]; ~, I[1-2]
37.22	children$_\wedge$] II; ~, I[1-11]
37.36	imaginative values$_\wedge$] II; imaginative values, I[3-11]; values, of imagination I[1-2]
38.1	child$_\wedge$] II; ~, I[1-11]
*38.6	that] *stet* I[1-11]; which II
38.6	all$_\wedge$] II; ~, I[1-11]
38.9	Shall] II; shall I[1-11]
38.20	ability$_\wedge$] I[2+]; ~, I[1]
38.28	shall] I[3+]; will I[1-2]
39.8	children. Now] I[2+]; children, while I[1]
39.9	in relation both] II; both in relation I[1-11]
39.12	promotion of] I[2+]; to promote I[1]
39.16	school,] I[2+]; ~$_\wedge$ I[1]
40.8	in subjects] II; subjects I[1-11]
40.12	Middle Ages] II; middle ages I[1-11]
40.14	Middle Ages] II; middle ages I[1-11]
40.16	Middle Ages] II; middle ages I[1-11]
40.27	drawn] I[2+]; (*a-b*) I[1]
42.18	Middle Ages] II; middle ages I[1-11]
42.40	more into] II; into more I[1-11]
43.28	interrelation] II; inter-relation I[1-11]
44.13	use;] II; ~, I[1-11]
44.14	culture;] II; ~, I[1-11]
44.14	discipline;] II; ~, I[1-11]
46.15	work,] I[2+]; ~$_\wedge$ I[1]
46.15	tack$_\wedge$] I[2+]; ~, I[1]
46.18	year$_\wedge$] II; ~, I[1-11]
46.19	River] W; river I[1+]
47.24	the head] *stet* I[1+]; the the head II
48.16	mere] I[2+]; these I[1]
49.7	conforming] I[3+]; observing I[1-2]
49.9	sides—the] I[2+]; sides, but the I[1]
49.9	symbolizing] I[2+]; symbolizes I[1]
50.38	a] I[2+]; the I[1]
51.9–10	formulates . . . our] II; formulates almost all of our I[1-11]
51.20	B] W; A I[1+]
53.13	organs—] II; ~, I[1-11]
54.9	Oriental] I[2+]; oriental I[1]
54.13	*Odyssey*] II; [*rom.*] I[1-11]
54.13	because] II; only because I[1-11]
54.36	be able to live] II; live I[1-11]
55.15	organize,] II; ~$_\wedge$ I[1-11]
55.26	all things] I[2+]; everything I[1]

55.35   in the latter] I^{3+};   some time in the I$^{1-2}$
55.40   Teachers$_\wedge$] II;   ~' I$^{1-11}$
56.6   in turn will] I^{2+};   will in turn I^1
56.8   criticized] II;   criticised I$^{1-11}$
57.1–66.36 [Chapter 4]] I$^{1-11}$;   [*om.*] II
57.8   Street] W;   street I$^{1-11}$
57.9   Avenue] W;   avenue I$^{1-11}$
57.10   Court] W;   court I$^{1-11}$
57.12   Court] W;   court I$^{1-11}$
57.14   Avenue] W;   avenue I$^{1-11}$
58.2   school. Next] I$^{2-11}$;   school. The increase in number of
            pupils this year is 50 per cent. Next I^1
58.6   to the school] I$^{2-11}$;   in the school I^1
58.8–9   students . . . school.] I$^{2-11}$;   students. I^1
58.26   should] I$^{2-11}$;   would I^1
58.33   its administration] I$^{2-11}$;   the administration I^1
59.34   cent$_\wedge$] W;   ~. I$^{1-11}$
60.30   power;] I$^{2-11}$;   ~, I^1
60.32   the symbols.] I$^{2-11}$;   it. I^1
60.39   a few words] I$^{2-11}$;   little time I^1
61.7   upon] I$^{3-11}$;   on I$^{1-2}$
61.38   his acquisitions] I$^{2-11}$;   what he gets I^1
63n.2   *Record.*] W;   *Record.* Address The University of Chi-
            cago Press for particulars. I$^{3-11}$;   has been published,
            and may be obtained from The University Press. I$^{1-2}$
64.2–3   grasped. [¶ In] I$^{3-11}$;   grasped. In I$^{1-2}$
65.5   to] I$^{3-11}$;   they I$^{1-2}$
67.1   5] W;   iv II;   [*not present*] E
67.1–3   The Psychology of Elementary Education [¶] Naturally,
            most] II;   The Psychology of the Elementary Curricu-
            lum. [¶] As the current number closes the present series
            of monographs relating to the work of the Elementary
            School, a statement of the principles underlying its
            work may be in place. The present month happens also
            to end the fifth year of the school's existence, if further
            justification for the statement be required. [¶] Natu-
            rally, most E
67.10   the time] II;   time E
67.16   university] II;   University E
67.16   university] II;   University E
67.20   university] II;   University E
67.24–25   university] II;   University E
67.25   elementary school. Such a school] II;   elementary
            school. [¶] But since this phase is likely to be the last
            to show itself to the ordinary observer, since it is the
            most difficult to understand, there is ground for setting
            forth this university aspect of the work done in the ele-

mentary school of the University of Chicago. But most generally, the school E

68.7	child‿life] II; ~-~ E
68.7	themselves‿] II; ~, E
69.18	individual,] II; ~‿ E
69.22	and the] II; that the E
69.30	ways] II; way E
69.31	lives‿ acts‿] II; ~, ~, E
70.5	child‿mind] II; ~-~ E
70.21	character‿] II; ~, E
71.4	information‿] II; ~, E
71.28	but the size] II; but size E
72.13	Mr. W. S. Jackman] II; Mr. Jackman E
73.4	statement simply] II; statement (with more detailed illustrations, furnished in the various numbers of this RECORD) simply E
73.29	subject-matter] II; ~‿~ E
73.33	miniature] II; miniature E
74.13	formulate it.] II; formulate it.[1] . . . [1]This period has been dealt with at greater length in preceding issues. See the ELEMENTARY SCHOOL RECORD, pp. 12–15; 21–23; 143–151. E
74.22	broken up.] II; broken up (see RECORD 49–52). E
74.40	colonization)‿] II; ~), E
75.17	method involves] II; method (see RECORD, pp. 204–9) involves E
75.26	have] II; had E
75.26	met‿] II; ~, E
77.15	cent‿] II; ~. E
77.36	second-hand] II; second-handed E
*78.26	complaint] W; complaints E, II
78.32	constructive‿] II; ~, E
*79.14	results] W; resulted E, II
81.1	6] W; v II; [not present] E
81.2–3	the Elementary . . . is] II; the School is E
81.21	interdependence;] II; ~, E
81.32	use;] II; ~, E
81.33	foundation‿stones] W; ~-~ E, II
82.9	school] W; School E, II
82.17	It is necessary only] II; These are so clearly set forth in the accompanying article by Miss Scates that it is only necessary E
83.7	*Mother‿Play*] W; ~-~ E, II
83.10–11	criticize] II; criticise E
83.35	*Mother‿Play*] W; ~-~ E, II
84.36–85.1	models. [◖] Accordingly] II; models. Accordingly E
*85.36	than] W; then E, II
86.12	children] II; the children E

86.39   school] W;   School E, II
86.39   much] II;   largely E
88.13   that,] II;   ~∧ E
88.24   the year] II;   year E
88.34   habits;] II;   ~: E
89.17   standards.] II;   standards.¹ . . . ¹It is a pleasure to ac-
           knowledge our great indebtedness to Miss Bryan and
           her able staff, of the Free Kindergarten Association, for
           numberless suggestions regarding both materials and
           objects for constructive work. Our obligations are also
           due to Miss La Victoire, who, coming to the kinder-
           garten the previous year from successful primary work,
           was highly effective in affiliating the kindergarten to
           the spirit of the best modern primary work. E
90.27   what] II;   of what E
90.36   such] II;   both the E
90.37   the work of] II;   that of Group III, E
91.2   dependent;] II;   dependent (see RECORD, No. 1, p.
           12);   E
92.1   7] W;   VI II;   [not present] E
92.1–2   THE PSYCHOLOGY OF OCCUPATIONS [⊄] By occupation] II;
           Psychology of Occupations. [⊄] In the first number of
           the ELEMENTARY SCHOOL RECORD there was given some
           account of the mental attitude of little children as ex-
           pressed in the familiar terms of play and imagination.
           In the second number was a description of the change
           of attitude that takes place when the child becomes
           conscious of the distinction between means and ends,
           and of the necessity of adjusting the former to the
           latter. In this issue I shall speak of the psychology
           which controls the educational use of occupations—
           these remarks finding their immediate application in
           the accompanying paper by Miss Harmer upon the
           school textile work. [⊄] By occupation E
92.2   work∧"] II;   ~," E
*92.10   work.] W;   work herewith reported upon. E, II
95.32   one)] W;   one herewith reported on) E, II
97.1   8] W;   VII II;   [not present] E
97.1–2   THE DEVELOPMENT OF ATTENTION [⊄] The subprimary]
           II;   School Reports. [⊄] Groups I and II. [⊄] The Sub-
           primary E
97.7–8   knowledge. [⊄] Little children] W;   knowledge. A de-
           tailed statement of the work will be published later.
           [⊄] Little children II;   knowledge. A detailed state-
           ment of the work will be published later. [⊄] Group III.
           [⊄] Average age of children, six years;   seventeen in
           group, divided into two subgroups. The group is under
           the charge of Miss Katherine Andrews, and the details

of work are planned and carried out by her. [◖] A. General Principles of Work, Educationally Considered. [◖] Little children E

97.19–20   operation—inspection] II;   operation. Inspection E
97.23   Material provided by existing] II;   The material selected as the basis of this year's study, existing E
97.23   occupations‸] II;   ~, E
97.23–24   calculated] II;   designed E
97.24   In previous] II;   The previous E
97.27   may take] II;   take E
98.29   thing—] II;   ~, E
98.29   cat—] II;   ~, E
98.37   possible;] II;   ~, E
98.37   which,] II;   ~‸ E
100.7   familiar‸] II;   ~; E
100.9   with,] II;   ~; E
100.16   pleaded] II;   plead E
100.31–32 and enlarging. [◖] With the] II;   and enlarging. [◖] While, doubtless, there are many other subjects which would meet these demands, it is found that the one in question, existing social occupations, affords a sufficient answer to be worth following out. [◖] Reflective Attention. [◖] With the E
100.34–35 previous paragraphs we have been concerned with] II;   first number I spoke of E
101.9–10   in *Middle* . . . 102–3)] W;   in the second number) E, II
101.30–31 proper. [◖] In history work] II;   proper. [◖] It is illustrated in the reports upon Groups IX and X in this number—especially the latter. In history work E
101.38   is,] II;   ~; E
102.2   science] II;   science reported upon E
102.6   the practice.] II;   the practice. In Latin there is the change from hearing and reading stories, speaking and writing answers upon certain points, to problems of inflection and syntax—bringing to light the theoretical significance of matters already practically dealt with. E
102.7   process] II;   psychical process E
102.27   merely] II;   barely E
102.32–33 a bribe] II;   bribe E
102.33   interesting";] II;   ~;" E
102.34–35 non-promotion] II;   ~‸~ E
103.32   and power.] II;   and power. [◖] Here I have spoken only of the fundamental nature of reflective attention —as depending upon interest in a conscious problem. In a later number I shall speak of the methods employed in the school to secure this interest. E
104.1   9.] W;   VIII II;   [*not present*] E

104.32   motors—] II; ~, E
*107.1   but is suddenly] W; but suddenly E, II
107.15   hand,] W; ~? E, II
107.18   form?] W; ~. E, II
108.2   and does] II; and it does E
108.21–22   education. [¶] In this general scheme] II; educa-
            tion. [¶] The principle stated, together with the appli-
            cations indicated to industrial history, to biography and
            story, and to chronological sequence, will explain, in a
            general way, the program of historical study outlined
            in Miss Bacon's article. In this general scheme E
108.30   effects] II; effect E
109.27   child$_\wedge$] II; ~; E

" 'Consciousness' and Experience" ["Psychology and Philosophic Method"]

Copy-text is the first printing "Psychology and Philosophic Method" in the *University* [of California] *Chronicle* 2
(1899): 159–79. Emendations not made editorially have
been adopted from the revised edition, " 'Consciousness' and
Experience" in D: *The Influence of Darwin on Philosophy
and Other Essays in Contemporary Thought* (New York:
Henry Holt and Co., 1910), pp. 242–70.

113.1   "CONSCIOUSNESS" AND EXPERIENCE[1]] D; Psychology
            and Philosophic Method.*
113.4   that] D; which
113.12   arouse interest] D; interest
113.14–15   They are revealed] D; It is
113.15   life.] D; life that they are revealed.
113.17   individuality;] D; ~,
113.18–19   experience;] D; ~,
113.21   a different temper.] D; very different tempers.
113.26   In this conviction] D; It is in this conviction that
113n.1–5   1. Delivered . . . mostly excisions.] D; *Address
            before the Philosophical Union, May, 1899, by Professor
            John Dewey, Ph.D., Head Professor of Philosophy in
            the University of Chicago.
114.4   There is] D; Put briefly and as clearly as may be in
            advance of detailed argument, the point is this:
            There is
114.4   apparently$_\wedge$] D; ~,
114.10–11   *qua* consciousness;] D; *qua* consciousness, just as
            consciousness;

114.12	fact that] D; reality which
114.13	purposes,] D; purposes at least,
114.14	this conception be true, there] D; this be true, I hardly need point out that the question concealed in my title, is already answered in the negative. There
114.19	is out] D; is obviously out
114.23	self-sufficient,] D; self-sufficient unto itself,
114.24	inquiries] D; the inquiries
114.25	only preliminary.] D; preliminary and instrumental only.
114.26	"Consciousness" is but a symbol,] D; We have here but a symbol having its translation in social activity;
114.27	natural and social operations.] D; its social operation.
114.28	letter,] D; letter exactly,
114.29	a] D; an understood
114.30	signified. If this view be correct,] D; signified, the social spirit. In this case,
114.35	This] D; It is clear that this
114.36	attack] D; attack *in toto*
114.36	venture] D; have ventured
114.37	appear] D; may appear
115.1	issues.] D; issues of reality.
115.3	"as such"] D; '~'
115.4	an isolation of each such as] D; such isolation of each as
115.5	statement] D; such statement
115.6	order such as] D; order as
115.7	or as] D; or
115.7	give] D; give us
115.9	each state] D; each
115.13	objective] D; ultimate
115.19	general] D; this general
115.21	of] D; with
115.22	Others] D; With others it is
115.25	philosopher.] D; philosopher proper.
116.4	happily] D; so happily
116.11	against] D; to do battle against
116.12–13	at a certain point,] D; in the first place,
116.13	"consciousness as such."] D; '~.'
116.14	limitation is final.] D; professed limitation follows.
116.15	"consciousness" or "state of consciousness"] D; '~' or '~'
116.23	It] D; To come to the point, it
116.24	significant] D; objective
116.25	things] D; Reality
116.26	existence] D; Reality
116.27	handling] D; handling, for treatment

116.30   nor are they] D;   they are not
116.31   a] D;   that
116.33   such.] D;   such—or, to go a step beyond, with shaded
          colors as such.
116.35   twilight] D;   twilighted
116.37   phenomena] D;   the phenomena
116.38   So the preoccupation] D;   So, to return to our problem,
          the preconception
116.40   material,] D;   Reality
117.3   To him, however,] D;   But he
117.4   psychology, the state] D;   psychology must interpret
          this preoccupation in quite another sense. To him the
          state
117.10   existence before] D;   existence 'as such'—to employ the
          favorite term once more—before
117.11   existence. What] D;   existence. In asking a certain
          question, he operates to secure the media of answering
          it, and this medium is 'consciousness' as the psycholo-
          gist treats it. What
117.16   an inclusive] D;   the inclusive
117.16   course] D;   whole
117.19   The] D;   An illustration may save argument and con-
          dense reasons. The
117.23–24 yet he . . . existences] D;   yet it is not as exist-
          ences he deals with them
117.25   critic] D;   omnipresent critic
117.31   space!] D;   ~.
117.36–37 The difference is in his] D;   It is just in the
117.37   His] D;   The
118.2   problem.] D;   problem and interest.
118.10   fallacy":] D;   ~:"
118.13   The psychologist begins] D;   The simple fact is that
          the psychologist always begins
118.14   functions as] D;   as
118.16   to control] D;   controlling
118.17   to afford] D;   affording
118.18   Acts such as] D;   It is such acts as
118.18   loving give] D;   loving, that give
118.20   To understand] D;   It is to understand
118.21   analysis] D;   that the analysis
118.24   may be translated] D;   are translated
118.24   acts.] D;   such experienced realities.
118.25   much as] D;   much so as
118.29   "objects."] D;   ∧~.∧
118.29   But there is] D;   But the comparison suggests its own
          extension. There is
118.29   that] D;   which

118.31   the structure] D;   these structures
118n.5   that, moreover,] D;   moreover, that
118n.11   Reflection] D;   Continued reflection
119.3–4   to concentrate] D;   in concentrating
119.4   function] D;   functions
119.5   gives him] D;   gives
119.6   that] D;   which
119.7   that] D;   which
119.7   that] D;   which
119.9   Reference to function] D;   It is reference to function
            which
119.10   trivialities] D;   trivalities
119.12   desert] D;   surface of desert
119.12–13   translation. States] D;   translation. Even a puzzle
            assumes some point, some possible interpretation, in
            the seeming mass of blind and brute circumstance.
            Even so states
119.16–17   of acts, attitudes, found in experience.⁴] D;   of re-
            sults reached, the sorts of value that are brought into
            experience.†
119.18   "empirical sort,"] W;   "~ₐ" D;   '~ₐ'
119.21   a self-existent.] D;   self-existent somewhats.
119.21   always defined] D;   defined
119n.4   explaining] D;   arranging or explaining
119n.23   acts,] D;   just acts in experience,
119n.24   the point] D;   just the point
119n.24   "state of consciousness"] D;   '~'
119n.25   appliance.] D;   appliance of reflection.
120.1   extraneous] D;   confessedly extraneous
120.2   The] D;   Indeed the
120.3   aspect on this basis.⁵] D;   aspect.*
120.6   imagine] D;   even imagine
120.7   while] D;   it is as meaningless as
120.8   occurrenceₐ] D;   ~,
120.9   a natural] D;   natural
120.9   straightforward undertaking.] D;   straightforward.
120.11   themselves.] D;   themselves (not as forms which the
            process of experience assumes when examined with ref-
            erence to the genesis of its various modes.)
120.12   we again have] D;   here again we have
120.13   that] D;   which
120.14   habit, of neural action, or else] D;   habit, or else of
120.15   in the object.⁶] D;   in the content or object, thus ad-
            mitting in either case that it is neither the states which
            are associated (habits connect acts, not states; content
            belongs to the things associated, not to the states) nor
            are they the means by which the association is ef-
            fected.†

120.17–18   is the subject.] D;   the whole subject is.
120.20   scandal] D;   scandals
120.24   that] D;   which
120.28   between them.] D;   between them—forgetting that the origin and *raison d'être* of the state of consciousness was but to define and get hold of the act or operation as experienced.
120.29–30   this procedure explains away rather than explains,] D;   it is to explain away, rather than to explain,
120.31   certain] D;   these
120.31   themselves] D;   themselves also
120n.6–7   "states of consciousness"] D;   '~'
120n.7   "synthetic unity"] D;   '~'
120n.9   "states of consciousness"] D;   '~'
120n.10–11   "state of consciousness"] D;   '~'
120n.12–13   analysis.] D;   analysis. In this particular case 'states' and 'habits' are the correlative factors appearing when we analyze a series of experiences of a certain type.
121.2   "states,"] D;   '~,'
121.4   contents] D;   states
121.4   analytic] D;   sensationalist
121.8–9   these "spiritual faculties" are] D;   these are
121.9   reduced] D;   classified and reduced
121.9   one comprehensive] D;   comprehensive
121.12   a function] D;   some function
121.13–14   if the functions digestion and vision] D;   if digestion and vision as functions
121.14–15   from organic structures] D;   from the activity of each constituent organic structure
121.15   them] D;   these
121.16   them!⁷] D;   them!ₐ
121.21   "synthetic"] D;   '~'
121.22   Both] D;   The difficulty is that both
121.23   "reality"] D;   '~'
121.27   first has] D;   has first
121.32–33   the *course* of the acts that constitute experiencing.] D;   the course of experiencing as such as distinct from its special contents.
121.37   and] D;   and in
121n.1–3   7. The "functions". . . fearing.] D;   [*not present*]
122.2–3   "consciousness as such"—in] D;   'consciousness as such,' as material by itself—in
122.4   that] D;   which
122.8   "transcend"] D;   ₐ~ₐ
122.11   Just and only because experience] D;   It is just because the psychical as such
122.11–12   "states of consciousness"] D;   '~'

122.12   does] D;   that
122.13   have any meaning. The entire] D;   is raised. It is
          hardly too much to say that the entire
122.21   that] D;   which
122.21   logical] D;   the logical
122.23–25 make philosophic . . . scientific facts?] D;   make
          these special problems soluble only either by ignoring
          them entirely or else by arbitrarily wrenching them?
122.28   experience, as . . . we] D;   experience, do we
122.30   science?] D;   science, and not a piece of cloudy meta-
          physic?
122.32   We] D;   But we
122.32   to keep] D;   keep
122.32–33 facts involved] D;   realities
122.33–34 Experience to avoid this danger.] D;   Experience
          and not lose ourselves in its mere generality.
122.35   facts] D;   sorts of facts
123.1   led] D;   led on
123.3   in] D;   into
123.4   inevitableness to] D;   absolute inevitableness into
123.8–9   life itself; the structures] D;   the life itself; *they*
123.9   signature] D;   signatures
123.21–22 of science. The conception] D;   of science. It ex-
          hibits, to be sure, an accumulation of information, of
          knowledge of this and that; but the important matter
          is the change in attitude and method—in interest. The
          conception
123.24   isolated] D;   isolate
123.27   the problem.] D;   from the inside.
123.35   Not] D;   It is not
123.36–37 unverifiable] D;   unveriable
123.37–38 introduced; but] D;   introduced. It is
123.38–39 a process of actions in its adaptations] D;   the proc-
          ess in its various adaptations
123.39   circumstance. If we] D;   circumstance, and success is
          measured by our ability to place each special fact in the
          particular position it occupies. If we
124.2–3   marking] D;   making
124.3   equilibrium] D;   equilibrim
124.4   use] D;   import
124.5   sensations] D;   sensation
124.5   for] D;   with reference to
124.6   perception] D;   feeling, or perception
124.8   recognition] D;   consciousness
124.17   conditions.] D;   conditions. But to return; the question
          of perception passes insensibly into that of attention,
          into that of interest and will, and so carries with it in-
          evitably the whole problem of the part played by indi-

viduality in constituting the objective world of things and events.

124.19   make] D; cover
124.23   from detecting] D; from the detection of
124.23   act] D; fact
124.24   out] D; it out as
124.25   discovering] D; the discovery of
124.26   to keep] D; in keeping
124.26   a-going] D; agoing
124.26   course of action.] D; whole course of experience.
124.30–31 the natural history of the course of experience.] D; the course of experience itself whose history is to be written.
124.32–33 deals, it is said, with] D; deals with
124.35   that] D; that it is
124.36   analysis] D; analysis that
124.36   a survival] D; to survive
124.37   It indicates] D; It is
124.37   an assured] D; the assured
124.38   as the] D; as it is the sign of the
124.39–40 mathematicians] D; mathematics
125.6   that] D; which
125.10–11 no more and no less] D; no more
125.14   its beginning] D; the beginning
125.16   successive] D; the successive
125.16   appear,] D; appear in their simplicity and purity,
125.18   valuable] D; most valuable
125.20   way to sort out the results flowing] D; way, in the results reached, to sort out those flowing
125.20   subject-matter] D; ~∧~
125.21   itself from] D; itself, and
125.24   existence] D; reality
125.30   ones: it] D; ones. It
125.32   accordingly it] D; it accordingly
125.40   their] D; and their
126.1   while] D; and
126.2   afford to] D; afford through being the one event that is meet and fit to
126.2   their whole is their meaning. The] D; the whole. This
126.5   constitution] D; constitutions
126.6   philosophy,] D; ~∧
126.6   a brand of philosophic dualism:] D; just a brand of the dualism of the philosophy that conceives it:
126.7   are] D; are somehow
126.9   There are] D; Here we strike a deeper level. There are
126.10–11 flow of behavior, arrested for inspection, made] D; the arrested flow of experience, and made

126.11–12   reconstruct experience in its life-history. Yet in] D;
             reconstruct it in its life-history through studying the or-
             gans, the structures, by which it executes its habits and
             realizes its aims. Yet in
126.15   Experience, they say, is] D;   This experience is
126.16   tells] D;   tell
126.18   But, they say, reality] D;   But the reality
126.18   reality] D;   it
126.20   goal] D;   reality
126.27   "Reality"] D;   ∧~∧
126.28   outside] D;   quite outside
126.29   The Reality] D;   the Reality
126.35   Some] D;   It is some
126.35   lies] D;   that lies
126.39–40   objects] D;   realities
127.1   is] D;   is something
127.2   world.] D;   universe itself.
127.3   beyond] D;   outside of
127.6   directly] D;   obviously
127.9   of itself. Even in] D;   of itself. So it usually gives back
             through some round-about method or special organ a
             part of what it takes away from the every-day, straight-
             forward experience of man. But it is more pertinent
             upon this occasion to dwell upon the fact that even in
127.13   position] D;   position of which
127.13   time of] D;   time
127.14   practical and social.] D;   practically and socially has
             possession.
127.14   The] D;   This
127.16   the notion] D;   this notion
127.19   must] D;   may
127.23–24   control action] D;   penetrate to the truths of experi-
             ence
127.27   perception and purpose] D;   consciousness and pur-
             poses
127.28   external] D;   seemingly external
127.30   intrinsic] D;   self-contained
127.30   is inevitable. Under such] D;   is inevitable. The worth
             of experience is measured by no self-set standard; its
             ideal is no reflection of its own process; its success is
             through no assured method of its own. Under such
127.32–33   uncertainty. The necessity] D;   uncertainty. Individ-
             uality, the self-functioning and the self-culmination of
             experience, is lacking. The necessity
127.33   external control] D;   the external control
127.33   external redemption] D;   redemption
127.34   a low] D;   the low

127.37   its theology] D;   the theology
127.38–39   as that . . . cosmology.] D;   as that it should be
            simply a part of cosmology with the Greeks—an account
            of how the fixed world of reality is shared.
127.40   this, the assertion] D;   this, I hope it will not seem just
            braggadocio if the assertion
127.40–128.1 psychology,] D;   psychology as
128.1   knowledge] D;   the knowledge
128.2   experience,] D;   experience and thus with the general
            method of philosophy,
128.5–6   achievement . . . affair.] D;   achievement is the most
            complete and centred statement of reality open to us.
128.13   that] D;   which
128.16–17   Modern life involves] D;   It is
128.22   This] D;   In this
128n.16   things experienced] D;   the realities experienced
128n.16–17 in either mechanical or miraculous relations] D;   in
            mechanical relations
128n.17   It is] D;   From the standpoint of the discussion, it
            is
128n.18   already] D;   constantly
128n.20–21 existences in reference to concrete action.] D;   re-
            ality in concrete experiencing.
128n.23   considerations,] D;   ~∧
129.1   individualized∧] D;   ~,
129.1   finds] D;   it finds
129.3   aspect] D;   aspects
129.3   presents itself.] D;   presents itself. It is the theoretical
            counterpart of the will to exhibit in action the complete
            connectedness, the full organic quality, of every hu-
            man being.
129.5–6   involves for philosophy the] D;   involves a
129.8   truths and the] D;   particular set of truths, or the
129.9   values] D;   fixed set of values
129.11–12   with science. Philosophy . . . partial] D;   with sci-
            ence. I certainly would not sacrifice the depth and
            comprehensiveness of genuine philosophy to the partial
129.15   must] D;   in which it must
129.18   claims for itself] D;   claims
129.18   fact,] D;   fact for itself,
129.22   things] D;   reality
129.24   existences] D;   realities
129.25   Such] D;   For such
129.26   *might*] D;   [*rom.*]
129.27   experience] D;   actual experience
129n.1   may] D;   must
129n.4   things] D;   reality

129n.5   which they turn.] D; which it turns—and the value
          in which it culminates.
130n.1–22 [NOTE: I . . . philosophy.]] D; Must I say, need I
          say, in concluding, that I have not this evening at-
          tempted to argue, but only to propose? Would that I
          had such clearness that I might say, expose! My inten-
          tion is not to convince, but to utter a conviction. Such
          an evening's address as I could make, even to this
          audience, might have only the semblance of logically
          demonstrative discourse, and at best it should develop
          only the emotion of persuasion. But if I may show you
          an attitude which it is possible to take; if I can acquaint
          you, even at a distance, with a certain spirit in which
          it is possible to pursue psychology; if I can loosen
          somewhat of the rigidity which perhaps the bounds and
          metes of the philosophic disciplines have assumed;
          if I can suggest that all these technical divisions and
          definitions are at the mercy of our historical life, and
          must dissolve and re-form at its human touch, I shall
          have abundantly satisfied my most ardent desire. To
          this end, I bespeak the hospitality of your thoughts.

"Psychology and Social Practice"

Copy-text is the article in PR: *Psychological Review* 7
(1900): 105–24; accidental emendations have been made
on the authority of S: *Science*, n.s. 11 (1900): 321–33.
Emendations have also been adopted from the pamphlet C:
Psychology and Social Practice, University of Chicago Contributions to Education, no. 2 (Chicago: University of Chicago Press, 1901), 42 pp. C means the three impressions of
the pamphlet edition, which were found to be invariant.

131.8   today] C; to-day PR, S
131.18   view] PR, C; views S
131n.1   before] PR, C; of S
131n.2   New Haven, 1899.] PR, C; New Haven meeting, De-
            cember, 1899.] S
132.17–18   material,] C; ~∧ PR, S
132.20   *mechanism*] C; [*rom.*] PR, S
132.24   today] C; to-day PR, S
132.33   identity∧] S, C; ~, PR
132.33   reigns,] C; ~; PR, S

133.4	*specific*] C; [*rom.*] PR, S
133.7	*growth*] C; [*rom.*] PR, S
133.9	*forming*] C; [*rom.*] PR, S
133.17	*full growth*] C; [*rom.*] PR, S
133.17	*skills*] C; [*rom.*] PR, S
133.22–23	"little men and women."] C; '~.' PR, S
133.31	subject-matter] C; ~ₐ~ PR, S
134.12	whole-hearted] PR, C; ~ₐ~ S
134.17	namely] C; Namely PR, S
134.17	*conditions*] C; [*rom.*] PR, S
134.32	ends,] PR, C; ~ₐ S
135.1	*Alertness*] C; [*rom.*] PR, S
135.2	*docility*] C; [*rom.*] PR, S
135.10	text-book] S; ~ₐ~ PR, C
135.22	effectₐ] S, C; ~, PR
135.25	itselfₐ] PR, C; ~, S
135.31	theorist—] S; ~: PR, C
135.36	does,] C; ~ₐ PR, S
135.39	Münsterberg,] W; [*not present*] PR, S, C
136.28	sciences] W; science PR, S, C
136.29	suggest,] PR; ~ₐ S, C
137.5	*empiricism and quackery*] C; [*rom.*] PR, S
137.8	millsₐ] PR, C; ~, S
137.13–14	*consciousness*] C; [*rom.*] PR, S
137.35	confronts] PR, C; confront S
138.1	magic,] S; ~ₐ PR, C
138.3	empiricism,] S; ~ₐ PR, C
138.12	*as if*] C; [*rom.*] PR, S
139.4	today] C; to-day PR, S
139.28	naked;] PR, C; ~, S
139.38	sense-organs] C; ~ₐ~ PR, S
140.9	necessityₐ] PR, C; ~, S
140.10–11	*causal mechanism*] C; [*rom.*] PR, S
140.24	emphasis)ₐ] PR, C; ~), S
141.1	numberₐ are,] C; ~, ~ₐ PR, S
141.1	themselvesₐ] C; ~, PR, S
141.26	*partial*] C; [*rom.*] PR, S
141.34	view,] C; ~; PR, S
142.20	fatigue,] C; ~; PR, S
142.22	curvatures,] C; ~; PR, S
142.35	"yellow journal,"] C; '~,' PR, S
143.2	pathology,] C; ~ₐ PR, S
143.11	aims,] W; ~; PR, S, C
143.13	and in complexity] PR, C; and complexity S
143.14	person,] W; ~; PR, S, C
143.17	*psychical*] C; [*rom.*] PR, S
143.32	is] C; are PR, S

144.14   today] C;   to-day PR, S
144.20   obvious:] PR, C;   ~;   S
144.22   are] PR, C;   is S
144.23   spite of,] PR, C;   ~ₐ S
144.33   trained;] C;   ~, PR, S
145.5   psycho-physical] PR, C;   psychological S
145.23–24   re-viewing] PR, C;   re-|viewing S
146.9   criticize] PR;   criticise S, C
146.24   objectsₐ] PR;   ~, S, C
146.36   practice,] S;   ~;   PR, C
147.2   idea, at least,] C;   ~ₐ ~ₐ PR, S
147.4   politics,] PR, C;   ~ₐ S
147.25   of the abstraction] PR, C;   of abstraction S
147.28   object,] C;   ~;   PR, S
147.33   laws] PR, C;   law S
148.1   ideals] PR, C;   ideas S
148.7   categorical] PR, C;   categorial S
148.28   ideals] PR, C;   ideas S
149.11   or] C;   [rom.] PR, S
149.19   interrelations] S;   inter-relations PR, C
149.39   and of its application to life] C;   [rom.] PR, S
150.19   steam-engine] PR, C;   ~ₐ~ S

"Some Stages of Logical Thought"

Copy-text is the first impression in *Philosophical Review* 9 (1900): 465–89. Emendations have been adopted from the revised new edition in EE: *Essays in Experimental Logic* (Chicago: University of Chicago Press, 1916), pp. 183–219.

151.12–13   reasonable certainty] EE;   certainty
151.30   a] EE;   the
152.7   The result, of course,] EE;   Of course, the likely result
152.10–11   of efficiencyₐ] EE;   efficiency,
152.14   initial stage] EE;   first
152.15   hardly] EE;   barely
152.18   suppositionsₐ (of ideas),] EE;   ~, ₐ~ₐ,
152.27   beliefs] EE;   ideas
152.31   recognition] EE;   consciousness
152.32   ideas] EE;   the ideas
152.33   static meanings] EE;   these static ideas
152.34   originated] EE;   have originated
152.34   have been] EE;   been
152.36   "there,"] EE;   '~,'
152.36   they] EE;   so

152.38   fallen] EE;   extraneously fallen
153.3   general] EE;   the general
153.5   as] EE;   just as
153.21   present] EE;   present to the mind
153.21–22 something] EE; something in the psychology of the
          mind itself
153.22   names] EE;   terms
153.32   than] EE;   than is
153.35   Ideas, or meanings fixed] EE;   Meanings, or ideas as
          fixed
153.40   expressing] EE;   as expressing
154.5–8   of ideas. Or, coming . . . of understanding.] EE;   of
          ideas.
154.9   We find] EE;   Turning to social psychology, we find
154.10   rules which] EE;   and which
154.14   judicial utterance] EE;   their judicial statement or ut-
          terance
154.15   anyone] EE;   the one
154.18   re-establishing] EE;   reëstablishing
154.18–20 certainty. An individual . . . necessary.] EE;   cer-
          tainty.
154.20   the] EE;   a
154.21   that ideas are psychical] EE;   of ideas as *merely* psy-
          chical
154.22   significance] EE;   real significance
154.23   rule of judgment is] EE;   rule is, after all,
154.24   facts;] EE;   ∼,
154.24   as such it is] EE;   and as such is
154.30   as] EE;   with reference
154.30   in] EE;   used in
154.35   citizens] EE;   supporters
154.35   that an] EE;   that it was an
154.37   offended_∧] EE;   which had offended,
154.38   case;] EE;   ∼,
155.2   Inquiry takes effect,] EE;   It is expressed,
155.3   among] EE;   from among
155.13   manner] EE;   mode
155.18–19 which law is] EE;   the one which is
155.20   its] EE;   its entire
155.24   way in which] EE;   way
155.28   these] EE;   such
155.28   they] EE;   the latter
155.29–30 separated] EE;   quite separate
155.30   present] EE;   all
155.30   application] EE;   all application
155.31–32 any thinking] EE;   thinking
155.33   remains] EE;   still remains

155.34   is a] EE;   is
155.36   that is,] EE;   ~∧
156.6   instilling in advance] EE;   instilling
156.9   group] EE;   society
156.12   interesting] EE;   interesting from the side of social psy-
          chology
156.17   importance] EE;   importance which may be
156.19   immobilization] EE;   their immobilization
156.20   conserving] EE;   historic conserving
156.24   than such] EE;   than
156.31   alternative] EE;   only alternative
156.32   importation to ideas] EE;   ascription to the ideas
156.37   practice";] EE;   ~;"
156.40   "positing"] EE;   '~'
156.41   hardening   meanings] EE;   a   certain   hardening   of
          meaning
157.2   a] EE;   a necessary
157.6   "essence."] EE;   '~.'
157.11–13   using them. Hence . . . definition.] EE;   using them.
157.17–18   by which to decide] EE;   in deciding
157.18   that] EE;   a
157.18–19   of ideas which] EE;   of the ideas such as
157.19   fit,] EE;   fit into one another,
157.23   conditions] EE;   social and psychological conditions
157.27–28   "why" and "how."] EE;   '~' and '~.'
157.37   possessing] EE;   regarded as possessing
157.41   systematization] EE;   systemization
158.19   considerations] EE;   ideas
158.24   to meet] EE;   meet
158.29   beliefs] EE;   ideas
158.30   tearing] EE;   the tearing
158.33   carried] EE;   first carried
159.7   beliefs] EE;   ideas
159.14   "subjectivity."] EE;   ∧~.∧
159.16   expressions] EE;   products
159.23   opinion] EE;   personal opinion
159.30   different] EE;   quite different
159.30   to be merely] EE;   a merely
159.31   it is considered to be at least] EE;   at least it is con-
          sidered as
159.32   things.] EE;   things, taking us further and further
          away from reality into what is merely subjective.
159.33   of] EE;   of one's own
159.36   reflection, for it] EE;   reflection. It
159.37   proof that] EE;   proof either that
160.1   thought to measure] EE;   thought, as measuring
160.2   thinking] EE;   the thinking

160.2   we cannot] EE;   the point is that we cannot
160.3   "fact,"] EE;   '~';
160.3   adequate] EE;   simple
160.4   stimulus] EE;   very stimulus
160.4   arises] EE;   has arisen
160.4   "facts"] EE;   '~'
160.5   committed] EE;   embodied
160.7   "colligating"] EE;   '~'
160.7   insists] EE;   insists both
160.9   and also that] EE;   and that
160.11–12 order."¹ [❡] Reflection involves] EE;   order."¹ [no ❡]
           Subjective reflection involves
160.14   in] EE; into
160.14   two,] EE;   two and avoid their incompatibilities,
160.15   view,] EE;   view and
160.17   and the greater] EE;   the greater
160.17   resultant] EE;   consequent
160.19   the] EE;   this
160.19   "mere thinking."] EE;   '~.'
160.20   but] EE;   yet
160.23   is thus] EE;   thus
160.24   while] EE;   while still
160.29   than] EE;   than they are
160.32   say,] EE;   ~∧
160.33   absence] EE;   presence or absence
160.33   "mere thinking,"] EE;   '~,'
160.33   presence of conditions] EE;   conditions
160.34   its results;] EE;   the results of the latter,
161.4–5   specific meanings] EE;   ideas
161.9   not interested] EE;   interested not
161.10   and a] EE;   and consequent
161.13   mutual] EE;   necessary mutual
161.14–15 of the operation of a standard permanent meaning]
           EE;   of the presence of an arbiter
161.17   dissolution,] EE;   dissolution which were going on,
161.18   Idea] EE;   idea
161.19   may] EE;   may as a matter of fact
161.20   doubt,] EE;   mere doubt, by
161.21   so throwing an] EE;   thus throwing the
161.22   also involves] EE;   involves also
161.23   thus putting] EE;   and thus puts
161.24   This] EE;   It was this
161.25   and abiding intellectual object] EE;   idea
161.27   animated] EE;   that animated
161.29   Ideas] EE;   ideas
161.31   prove] EE;   justify
161.38   of clues,] EE;   supplying clues, and

161.38   object of interest] EE;   interest
162.10   confused] EE;   though confused
162.10   impose] EE;   yet impose
162.15   To insist upon this] EE;   However strong and finally
          unresisted may have been this tendency, to insist
          upon it
162.18   which otherwise is just manipulation] EE;   other than
          just futile manipulation
162.19   prejudices] EE;   prejudice
162.19   is] EE;   is certainly
162.21   opinionated,] EE;   opinionated and
162.22–23   as that contrasted] EE;   as contrasted
162.23   subject-matter] EE;   assured subject$_\wedge$matter
162.24   mere views] EE;   merely personal views
162.24   argumentations] EE;   argumentation
162.27   as] EE;   as it was
162.28   recognized] EE;   had recognized
162.30   was] EE;   then was
163.2   probative] EE;   proving
163.6   a summary] EE;   its summary
163.7–8   a conclusion.] EE;   the conclusion. Hence the possi-
          bility of forming a scheme for defining the exact mode
          of credibility attaching to any proposition.
163.9   there now is] EE;   we have now
163.10   marked] EE;   quite marked
163.24   remote,] EE;   ∼$_\wedge$
163.37   *practical*] EE;   [*rom.*]
164.10   afterward] EE;   soon
164.10   in] EE;   in the question of
164.12   *ubique*$_\wedge$ *omnibus*$_\wedge$] EE;   ∼, ∼,
164.21   was] EE;   is
164.24–28   as such. It was . . . the play of subjective] EE;   as
          such. Without such truths we are still in the bonds of
          uncertainty. We are still within the play of subjective
164.30   is] EE;   is still
164.31   reasoning] EE;   theory of reasoning
164.32   securing demonstration,] EE;   securing
164.34   followers$_\wedge$] EE;   ∼,
164.35   players] EE;   not philosophers, but players
164.37   assurance.] EE;   assurance in cases of doubt.
164.40   the bundles] EE;   their bundles
165.2   Scriptures] EE;   scriptures
165.7   scant] EE;   decidedly scant
165.13   need for] EE;   the need of
165.14   all important beliefs] EE;   customs were dissipated
          through their mutual clash, and hence ideas
165.16–17   power, for . . . natural tradition.] EE;   power.

165.19   supplemented] EE;   compensated for
165.20   the] EE;   and the
165.23   authoritative] EE;   the terms of authoritative
165.28   that they have] EE;   having
165.31–32   only contingent.] EE;   only contingent, unstable
            and divagating. The doubt attaching to them is in no
            sense a result of the thinking process; it does not arise
            organically within the latter, but is rather its external
            precondition.
165.34   by] EE;   because of
165.34   It stands] EE;   In itself it stands
166.1   degrees in] EE;   degrees of
166.3   active,] EE;   ~∧
166.3   itself∧] EE;   ~,
166.4   fixed] EE;   the fixed
166.5   which] EE;   that they
166.7   rests] EE;   hits
166.7   direction all] EE;   direction doubt is itself arrested. All
166.7–8   "matters of fact," all "empirical truths"] EE;   '~,' all
            '~'
166.14   objectified] EE;   fixed
166.15   arrested] EE;   objectified, and thereby arrested
166.17   less] EE;   less had
166.17   Uncertainty] EE;   Uucertainty
166.19   meaning] EE;   own meaning
166.20–21   interpretation to be given thought] EE;   interpreta-
            tion of thought possible
166.29   things] EE;   those
166.30   application] EE;   application, however,
166.31   unchanged] EE;   quite unchanged
166.34–35   anything already current may be] EE;   it may be
166.40–167.1 man specifically is] EE;   man is
167.2   There is no] EE;   It is not an
167.4   a question] EE;   just a question
167.5   some proposition] EE;   a proposition
167.10   things] EE;   things it is that
167.13   for] EE;   since
167.14   suggestiveness, by] EE;   suggestiveness of
167.14   lead to. The mind] EE;   lead to, and thus the mind
167.16   an actuary] EE;   the expert
167.21   regards,] EE;   ~∧
167.21   say,] EE;   ~∧
167.22   are] EE;   are thereby
167.35   unchanged∧] EE;   ~,
167.35–36   claim . . . principles.] EE;   claims to credence.
168.11   those] EE;   those which are
168.14   "pass"] EE;   '~'

168.18   things] EE;   facts,
168.21–22   "inference."] EE;   ∧~·∧
168.23   "goes . . . unknown."] EE;   '~.'
168.24   not at] EE;   not with
168.26   beliefs] EE;   ideas
168.26   but is a] EE;   but a
168.31   "proof."] EE;   '~.'
168.39   fixed] EE;   equally fixed
168.40   possible] EE;   possible and
169.2   out in advance] EE;   out
169.12   camera∧] EE;   ~,
169.16   to accomplish this,] EE;   to effect this the
169.16   "facts"] EE;   ∧~∧
169.18   intrusion] EE;   all intrusion
169.22   is] EE;   is also
169.31   not] EE;   rather than
169.32   Hence] EE;   Hence also
169.35   which may suggest] EE;   suggest
169.41–170.1 to consist] EE;   consist
170.11   *propria*] EE;   *propia*
170.15–16   that scientific power is generally] EE;   that gen-
            erally scientific power is
170.18   employed∧] EE;   ~,
170.23   Hence the notion] EE;   The notion
170.23   something] EE;   something of superior kind
170.24   events from on high;] EE;   events,
170.28   attitude.] EE;   attitude of thought.
170.29   forces] EE;   then forces
170.32   breeds their degeneration.] EE;   breeds degeneration.
170.32–33   When . . . facts] EE;   Their service is dependent
            upon the assumption of fixed universals as real es-
            sences; since their business is the ceremony of bringing
            these essences down into facts, the universal becomes
            the established order of the facts
170.33   themselves,] EE;   themselves, and then
170.39–40   irregular,] EE;   rectilinear
171.2   were] EE;   are
171.13   are not] EE;   cannot be
171.17   control] EE;   control of experience
171.21   is,] EE;   ~∧
171.27   which] EE;   for that
171.40   devising and using of suitable instrumentalities] EE;
            device and use of instrumentalities
172.1   we] EE;   we also
172.3   discovery] EE;   thought
172.9   give] EE;   gave
172.10   is] EE;   was
172.14   marks] EE;   makes

172.15   scientific] EE;   this scientific
172.20   which] EE;   that
172.21   has] EE;   it has
172.22   startlingly] EE;   startingly
172.28   framework] EE;   frame-work
172.29   "empirical"] EE;   '~'
172.31   "proved."] EE;   '~.'
173.1   reason,] EE;   ~;
173.9   gymnastic] EE;   subjective gymnastic
173.20   my discussion] EE;   discussion
173.24   deny] EE;   deny alike
173.24   all of the three] EE;   all three
173.25   voicing] EE;   voice
173.27   supplying both its] EE;   at once supplying its
173.33–34   material given ready-made] EE;   ready-made ma-
            terial given
173.34   thought-process] EE;   ~ʌ~
173.34–35   and externally limiting inquiry] EE;   and, therefore,
            that they externally limit inquiry
173.36   search] EE;   investigation or search
173.38   "in itself"] EE;   ʌ~ʌ
173.39   inquiry] EE;   doubt or inquiry
173.39   it is taken to be] EE;   it is
174.1   "finite,"] EE;   '~,'
174.3   "thought"] EE;   '~'
174.4   fixed.] EE;   fixed. It is *per accidens* an object of in-
            quiry, but not its organic content.
174.11   account] EE;   account or theory
174.14   etc.,] EE;   ~ʌ
174.14   *infinitum*] EE;   *indefinitum*

Principles of Mental Development as Illustrated in Early Infancy

Copy-text is *Transactions of the Illinois Society for Child-Study* 4 (1899): 65–83.

177.1   they have done the work] W; the work they have done
*177.11–12 disconnected] W; discontented
178.4   arms] W;   arm
178.35   locomotion.] W;   ~ʌ
179.12   makes] W;   make
179.18   environment.] W;   ~,
179.23   *Mental*] W;   Warner's *Mental*
179.25   namely,] W;   ~ʌ
*180.39   three] W;   two

181.6   develop_Λ] W;   ∼,
181.14   seeing,] W;   ∼_Λ
*181.14   child is simply] W;   child simply
181.33   which,] W;   ∼_Λ
*184.28   so in] W;   so that it is in
186.27   *Child-Study*] W;   Child_ΛStudy
187.3   dulled] W;   dull
189.5   sorts] W;   sort
191.27   affords] W;   afford
191.35   order.] W;   ∼_Λ
191.38   up,] W;   ∼_Λ

"Mental Development"

Copy-text is University of Chicago, Department of Philosophy and Pedagogy, © 1900, by John Dewey, mimeographed; a second copy, Henry Suzzallo Papers, University of Washington, Mt: typescript, which derives from the copy-text, is noted as the first appearance of emendations that would have been adopted editorially.

192.5   *Social and Ethical Interpretations in Mental Development.*] W;   "Mental Development—Social and Ethical Interpretations".
192.7   Chamberlain] Mt: Chamberlaic
192.21   Harris.] W;   [*not present*]
192.23   "Harris's *Psychologic Foundations of Education.*"] W; "Review of Psychologic Foundations of Ed."
192.26   *The First Yearbook of the Herbart Society*] W;   "The Herbartian Year Book"—No. I
192.28   "Herbartian System of Pedagogics,"] W;   "Herbartian Pedagogics"
192.30   Common Schools] W;   Schools
192.34   III] W;   V, IV
193.1   "The Relation of Play to Education."] W;   "Psychology of Play".
193.10   on] W;   of
193.18   on] W;   of
193.36   *Childhood*] W;   Child
193.41   of] W;   in
193.43–44   Children and Adolescents."] W;   Adolescents".
193.46   V] W;   II
193.48   XI] W;   II
196.17   is] Mt;   to
196.19   doing,] W;   ∼;
196.33   choo."] W;   ∼_Λ"

196.40   child had] W;   child has
197.10   response.] W;   ~∧
198.4   object,] W;   ~∧
198.7   all:∧] W;   ~: -
198.37   animals] Mt;   animal
198.37   play] Mt;   plays
198.40   play] W;   plays
199.16   nurseries] W;   nurser-
*199.29   distinguishes] W;   distinguished
200.2   school,] W;   ~∧
200.11   be] W;   by
*201.19   experienced] W;   experiences
202.34   incongruities,] W;   ~∧
203.13   196–97] W;   [not present]
203.16   whoa, whoa,] W;   ~, ~∧
203.21   lines,] W;   ~.
203.40   the same] Mt;   the the same
205.14   have seen,] Mt;   have see,m
206.12   complex] W;   conples
206.23   simply] Mt;   simple
207.29   becomes] W;   bacomes
207.37   purpose.] W;   ~∧
209.14   gap] Mt;   gap chasm
210.9–10   directed)] W;   ~—
211.20   are∧] W;   ~:
214.10   at] W;   as
214.36   Barnes's] W;   Barnes'
215.32   is] W;   are
216.25–26 manifestations] Mt;   manifestation
218.15   they] Mt;   there
218.21   principle,] W;   ~∧
218.40   plant,] Mt;   plantm∧
219.31   circulating∧] W;   ~,

Group IV, Historical Development of Inventions and Occupations

Copy-text is: *Elementary School Record*, no. 1 (1900), pp. 21–23.

222.9, 31 said *. . .* Pp. 97–100, this volume.] W;   said about
           Group III,
224.9   mentioned [pp. 97–98]] W;   mentioned, under Group
           III,
224.21   and as] W;   and (as will be seen from the follow-
           ing account) as

General Introduction to Groups V and VI

Copy-text is: *Elementary School Record*, no. 2 (1900), pp. 49–52.

225.5   growth (see . . . 338).] W;   growth (see pp. 2 and 3 of "Outline of Course of Study").
225.28   way (see pp. 97–98 and 224).] W;   ~. (See pp. 13 and 23 in *Elementary School Record* No. 1.)
226.11   hoop] W;   coop
228.1   (see p. 97),] W;   (see p. 12 of *Elementary School Record* No. 1),

"The Place of Manual Training in the Elementary Course of Study"

Copy-text is MT: *Manual Training Magazine* 2 (1901): 193–99.

232n.1   36 [*Middle* . . . 20].] W;   36.
234n.2–3 *Yearbook* [*Early* . . . 37],] W;   *Yearbook,*

Review of The World and the Individual, *First Series*

Copy-text is: *Philosophical Review* 9 (1900): 311–24.

244.34   realism;] W;   ~,
250.27   Absolute.] W;   ~∧
253n.7   in] W;   on
253n.11   truths"!] W;   ~!"
253n.14   275] W;   274
253n.22   indeterminate∧] W;   ~,

The Educational Situation

Copy-text for the "Prefatory Word," p. 258, is the first and only previous appearance of that material in ES: *The Educational Situation*, University of Chicago Contributions to Education, no. 3 (Chicago: University of Chicago Press, 1902); this work is noted throughout by the abbreviation ES without impression numbers, as no variation was found among the five impressions. Copy-text for the three chapters is: for Chapter 1, pp. 260–82, SJ: "The Situation as Regards the Course of Study," *School Journal* 62 (1901): 421–23, 445–46, 454, 469–71; for Chapter 2, pp. 283–99, SR: "Current Problems in Secondary Education," *School Review* 10 (1902): 13–28; and for Chapter 3, pp. 300–313, ER: "Are the Schools Doing What the People Want Them to Do?" *Educational Review* 21 (1901): 459–74.

Substantive variants are also noted from two other 1901 impressions of Chapter 1: ER, *Educational Review* 22 (1901): 26–49 and PA, *Proceedings and Addresses* of the National Educational Association, 1901, pp. 332–48. The list that follows is thus not only an emendations list but a historical collation as well.

The reprint of Chapter 3, entitled "The People and the Schools," in ET: *Education Today* (New York: G. P. Putnam's Sons, 1940), pp. 36–52, is also noted as the first appearance of emendations that would have been made editorially in the present edition.

258.6   Superintendents'] W; Superintendent's ES; [*not present*] PA, ER, SJ
260.1–2   I. AS CONCERNS THE ELEMENTARY SCHOOL] ES; The Situation as Regards the Course of Study PA; III The Situation as Regards the Course of Study[1] . . . [1]An address delivered before Department of Superintendence of the National Educational Association at Chicago, Ill., February 28, 1901. ER; The Situation as Regards the Course of Study.* . . . *All rights reserved by the author. SJ
260.7   catchwords] ER, PA, ES; catch words SJ
260.8   have] ES, PA, ER; having SJ
260.14   revolutionary,] ER, PA, ES; ~ₐ SJ
260.15   pedagogic] ES, PA, SJ; educational ER
260.16   pedagogic] ES, SJ; educational ER
260.16   gatherings] ES, PA; gathering SJ, ER
260.18   is] ES, PA, ER; is not SJ
260.18–19 the reformer took possession of the field] ES; the field SJ, ER, PA
260.20   preaching, the] ES; preaching was taken possession of by the reformer, the SJ, ER, PA
260.20   as concerns the] ES; as the SJ, ER, PA
260.21   study was] ES; study is concerned, was SJ, ER, PA
260.22–23 sayings;] ER, PA, ES; ~, SJ
260.28   ideals] ES; the ideals SJ, ER, PA
260.31   practicedₐ] ER, PA, ES; ~, SJ

260.31   of] ES;   between SJ, ER, PA
261.1   from] ES;   and SJ, ER, PA
261.5   of atmosphere] ES;   atmosphere SJ, ER, PA
261.8   execution in subject-matter] ES;   execution in the
            school-|room, in subject-matter PA;   execution in the
            schoolroom, in subject-matter ER;   execution in the
            school-room, regarding subject-matter SJ
261.8   in method] ES;   method SJ, ER, PA
261.16   *pou sto*] ES, PA, ER;   prestige SJ
261.16   walls and] ES, PA, ER;   walls SJ
261.17   children.] ES, PA, SJ;   children, has been made. ER
261.22   schoolrooms] ER, ES;   school-rooms SJ;   school-|rooms
            PA
261.25   symbolic, etc.] ES, PA, SJ;   symbolic. ER
261.26   pedagogic] ES, PA, SJ;   educational ER
*261.28   ideals] *stet* SJ, ER, PA;   ideas ES
261.28   pedagogics] ES, PA, SJ;   education ER
261.36   long-wished-for] ER, PA, ES;   ~∧~∧~ SJ
262.1   there∧ because] ER, PA, ES;   ~, ~ SJ
262.19   point,] ER, PA, ES;   ~; SJ
262.21 *et seq.* throughout] ES;   thruout SJ, ER, PA
262.32   willfully] ER, PA, ES;   wilfully SJ
263.8   Someone] ER, PA, ES;   Some one SJ
263.9–10   behind] ES, PA, ER;   somewhat behind SJ
263.25   taken] ER;   taking SJ, PA, ES
263.31   they are] ES;   they also are SJ, ER, PA
263.33   inaccurate,] ER, PA, ES;   ~; SJ
263.35   *this*] ES;   [*rom.*] SJ, ER, PA
264.11 *et seq.* thoroughness] ES;   thoroness SJ, ER, PA
264.16   getting] ES;   being SJ, ER, PA
264.16   amid] ES;   in SJ, ER, PA
264.17   portentous] ES, PA, ER;   pretensions and SJ
264.21 *et seq.* through] ES;   thru SJ, ER, PA
264.25   few,] ER, PA, ES;   ~∧ SJ
264.25   least,] ER, PA, ES;   ~∧ SJ
264.27   new-created] ER, PA, ES;   ~∧~ SJ
264.29   "Possibly] ER, PA, ES;   ∧possibly SJ
264.31   we are] ES;   we have SJ, ER, PA
264.31   upon?"] ER, PA, ES;   ~?∧ SJ
264.37   and also the increasing] ES;   and the developing SJ,
            ER, PA
264.39   self-assertion,] ER, PA, ES;   ~∧ SJ
264.40   theory,] ER, PA, ES;   ~∧ SJ
264.40   adherents] ES, PA, ER;   inherence SJ
265.2   a period] ES;   the period SJ, ER, PA
265.20–21   circumstances. [¶] The problem] ES, PA, ER;   cir-
            cumstances. [¶] The Root of the Problem. [¶] The prob-
            lem SJ

265.27   difficulties of] ES, PA, ER;   difficulties SJ
265.27   today] PA, ES;   to-day SJ, ER
266.1   definite] ES;   definitive SJ, ER, PA
266.9   prophetic,] ER, PA, ES;   ~∧ SJ
266.9   vital,] ER, PA, ES;   ~∧ SJ
266.13   to] ES;   by SJ, ER, PA
266.20   time, and] ER, PA, ES;   ~∧ ~ SJ
266.21–22   situation as] ES;   situation impartially, as SJ, ER, PA
266.24–25   friendly cooperators] W;   friendly co-operators ES;
            co-operative forces SJ, ER, PA
266.26   Why] ER, PA, ES;   why SJ
266.29   reinforcing∧] W;   re-enforcing∧ SJ;   re-enforcing, ER;
            reinforcing, PA, ES
266.38–39   itself; the] ER, PA, ES;   itself. The SJ
267.1   life-experience] ER, PA, ES;   ~∧~ SJ
267.2   adequate,] ER, PA, ES;   ~∧ SJ
267.3   latter,] ER, PA, ES;   ~∧ SJ
267.17   sort∧] ER, PA, ES;   ~, SJ
267.20 *et seq.* thoroughly] ES;   thoroly SJ, ER, PA
267.22   These conditions persist] ES;   The conditions thus con-
            stituted persist SJ, ER, PA
268.1   accepted] ES, PA, ER;   adopted SJ
268.4   face-to-face] ER, PA, ES;   ~∧~∧~ SJ
268.6   situation] ES, PA, ER;   system SJ
268.11–12   personal contact . . . are,] ES;   personal relation-
            ship are, SJ, ER, PA
268.17   do not] ES;   never SJ, ER, PA
268.18   old] ES, PA, ER;   older SJ
268.23   *from the standpoint of the conditions.*] ES;   [*rom.*] SJ,
            ER, PA
268.25   they are hampered] ES;   hampered SJ, ER, PA
268.27   agencies] ES;   instrumentalities SJ, ER, PA
269.1–2   æsthetic,] PA, ES;   esthetic, SJ;   æsthetic— ER
269.4   situation is] ES, PA, ER;   situation becomes SJ
269.9   compel] ES, PA, ER;   compels SJ
269.18   introduce] ES, PA, ER;   introduces SJ
269.26   child.[1]] ES, PA;   child.[2] ER;   child.∧ SJ
269.27   conditions,] ER, PA, ES;   ~∧ SJ
269.28   education,] ER, PA, ES;   ~∧ SJ
269.34   make] ES, PA, ER;   makes SJ
269.37   attention] ES, PA, ER;   it compels attention SJ
269n.1–2   1. This thought . . . 92–98.] ES;   [1]I am indebted to
            Mrs. Ella F. Young's thesis *Isolation in the School* for
            many suggestions. PA;   [2]I am indebted to Mrs. Ella F.
            Young's thesis, *Isolation in the school* (Chicago: 1900),
            for many suggestions. ER;   [*not present*] SJ
270.1   expression is] ES, PA, ER;   expression, to be SJ
270.2   often] ES, PA, ER;   then often SJ

270.10   he] ES, PA, ER;   the teacher SJ
270.13–14   directions:] ER, PA, ES;   ∼;   SJ
270.17   local] ES;   less local SJ, ER, PA
270.17   transitory] ES;   transitive SJ, ER, PA
270.25   forbids] ES, PA, SJ;   forbid ER
270.25   his] ES, PA, ER;   her SJ
270.29   provided] ES;   looked out SJ, ER, PA
270.30   his] ES, PA;   her SJ, ER
270.31–33   external provision . . . supervision,] ES;   external
            supervision∧ SJ, ER, PA
270.37   the consciousness] ES, PA, ER;   consciousness SJ
270.38–39   of prescription of mode of action,] ES;   of external
            prescription and advice, SJ, ER, PA
271.4   for] ES, PA, ER;   of SJ
271.10   own,] ER, PA, ES;   ∼∧ SJ
271.24   readily a] ES;   readily of a SJ, ER, PA
271.28   somewhat] ES;   somehow SJ, ER, PA
271.29   least that] ES;   least SJ, ER, PA
271.35   alternative:] ER, PA, ES;   ∼;   SJ
272.7   class∧room∧] ES;   classroom, ER;   class-room∧ SJ, PA
272.13   that] ES, PA, SJ;   it ER
272.15   child.²] W;   child.¹ ES;   child.∧ SJ, ER, PA
272.19   It] ES, PA, SJ;   He ER
272.22   it] ES, PA, SJ;   he ER
272.30   If his] ES, PA, ER;   Her SJ
272.31   him,] ES, PA, ER;   her;   SJ
272.32   then his] ES, PA, ER;   her SJ
272.32   must] ES, PA, ER;   will SJ
272.35   and its adaptation] ES, PA, ER;   or its organic adapta-
            tion SJ
272.35   needs] ES, PA, ER;   specific needs SJ
272.36   He] ES, PA, ER;   She SJ
272.37   pedagogical] ES, PA, SJ;   educational ER
272.38   him] ES, PA, ER;   her SJ
272n.1–2   2. See, again, . . . 106–9.] W;   ¹See, again, Num-
            ber 1 of this series, pp. 31–32 and 106–109. ES;   [not
            present] SJ, ER, PA
273.2   reality.] ES, PA, ER;   and real presentation. SJ
273.5   he] ES, PA, ER;   she SJ
273.5   or its] ES, PA;   or in its ER, SJ
273.6   say,] ER, PA, ES;   ∼∧ SJ
273.10   while] ES;   and SJ, ER, PA
273.13   life. Since] ER, PA, ES;   life. [⌐]Since SJ
273.15–16   for introducing the excitement] ES;   for the intro-
            duction of the supposedly necessary excitement SJ, ER,
            PA
273.16–17   supposed to be necessary.] ES;   of the child. SJ, ER,
            PA

273.22 easily be] ES, PA, ER; be easily SJ
273.34 his] ES, PA, ER; her SJ
273.36 child;] ER, PA, ES; ~– SJ
274.3 apart from] ES; beyond SJ, ER, PA
274.11 values] ES, PA, SJ; value ER
274.12 the facts] ES, PA, ER; facts SJ
274.14 study$_\wedge$] ER, PA, ES; ~, SJ
274.19 pupil,] ER, PA, ES; ~$_\wedge$ SJ
274.36 art$_\wedge$] ER, PA, ES; ~, SJ
275.1 King Log] PA, ES; king log SJ, ER
275.1 King Stork] PA, ES; king stork SJ, ER
275.2 teaching$_\wedge$] ER, PA, ES; ~, SJ
275.3 over-specialized,] ER, PA, ES; ~-~$_\wedge$ SJ
275.5 education–] PA, ES; ~, SJ; ~,– ER
275.6 part–] PA, ES; ~, SJ; ~,– ER
275.9 fall] ES, PA, ER; all fall SJ
275.18 him] ES, PA, ER; her SJ
275.20 all-around] PA, ES; ~$_\wedge$~ SJ; ~-round ER
276.1 least] ES, PA, SJ; last ER
276.4 condition] ES; conditions SJ, ER, PA
276.5 schoolroom] ER, PA, ES; school-room SJ
276.8 school-teachers] ER, PA, ES; ~$_\wedge$~ SJ
276.19 also$_\wedge$] ER, PA, ES; ~, SJ
276.19 that directly] ES; in direct fashion$_\wedge$ PA, ER; in direct fashion, SJ
276.20 publishing] W; pushing SJ, ER, PA, ES
276.24 one)$_\wedge$] ER, PA, ES; ~), SJ
276.31 But we] ES, PA, SJ; But I ER
277.3 the] *stet* SJ, ER, PA; the the ES
*277.4 conditions] *stet* PA, ER, SJ; considerations ES
*277.7–8 machinery] *stet* PA, ER, SJ; of machinery ES
277.17 authority)$_\wedge$] ER, PA, ES; ~), SJ
277.24 that] ES; which SJ, ER, PA
277.27 length:] ER, PA, ES; ~. SJ
277.28 $_\wedge$In] ER, PA, ES; "~ SJ
277.31 and are] ES, PA, ER; and SJ
277.32 reading;] ER, PA, ES; ~, SJ
277.40 *et seq.* though] PA, ES; tho SJ, ER
277.41 art$_\wedge$] ER, PA, ES; ~, SJ
277.42 them.$_\wedge$] ER, PA, ES; ~." SJ
278.4 faculties,"] ER, PA, ES; ~$_\wedge$" SJ
278.10 that is,] ER, PA, ES; ~$_\wedge$ SJ
278.12 of value] ES, PA; value SJ, ER
278.21 remoter acquisition.] ES; further advancement. SJ, ER, PA
278.28 schoolroom] ER, PA, ES; school room SJ
278.33 of present] ES, PA, ER; present SJ
278.38 schoolroom] ER, PA, ES; school room SJ

278.39   art$_\wedge$] ER, PA, ES;   ~, SJ
278.40   "interests"] ES; $_\wedge$interests$_\wedge$ PA, ER; $_\wedge$interest$_\wedge$ SJ
279.12   connection.] ES;   relation to each other. SJ, ER, PA
279.14   to be] ES;   to take an SJ, ER, PA
279.15   gloomy, it] ES;   gloomy view of the situation, it SJ, ER, PA
279.18   theory] ES, PA, ER;   theory I repeat, SJ
279.22   assumes] ES, PA, ER;   assumes also SJ
279.24–27 intellectual acquisition. . . . methods of development.] ES;   social progress. SJ, ER, PA
279.30   schoolroom] ER, PA;   school room SJ, ES
279.31   extremes:] ER, PA, ES;   ~;   SJ
279.36   upon] ES, PA, ER;   to SJ
279.38   an] ES, PA, ER;   any SJ
279.38   of] ES, PA, ER;   any SJ
280.3   we get] ES;   we can get SJ, ER, PA
280.5   superficiality] ES, PA, ER;   sentimentality SJ
280.6   the residuum] ES, PA, ER;   a minimum SJ
280.7   view] ES, PA, ER;   rule SJ
280.9–10   of a mode] ES, PA, ER;   of mode SJ
280.10   calculated for] ES;   that was adapted to SJ, ER, PA
280.11   those now confronting us,] ES;   those which now appeal to us, SJ, ER, PA
280.16   know just] ES, PA, ER;   know, that is to say just SJ
280.19   subject-matter] ER, PA, ES;   ~$_\wedge$~ SJ
280.20   shop-work$_\wedge$] ES;   shopwork, SJ;   shop work, ER;   shop-work, PA
280.24   society$_\wedge$] ER, PA, ES;   ~, SJ
280.24   as ever] ES;   as SJ, ER, PA
280.25   have been.] ES;   have ever been. PA, ER;   have ever been, nay, even more so. SJ
280.29   theory] ES, PA, ER;   it SJ
280.29   practice.] ES, PA, ER;   practical effect. SJ
280.32   intellectual] ES;   [rom.] SJ, ER, PA
280.34   situation,] ER, PA, ES;   ~$_\wedge$ SJ
280.34   vagueness] ES;   rigidity SJ, ER, PA
280.36   things] ES, PA, ER;   itself SJ
280.37   out,] ER, PA, ES;   ~$_\wedge$ SJ
280.39   of efficiency] ES, PA, ER;   to efficiency SJ
281.1–2   so that] ES, PA, ER;   in such a way that SJ
281.4   fulfillment] ER, PA;   fulfilment SJ, ES
281.9   into the knowledge of] ES, PA, ER;   in the SJ
281.9   values for] ES;   methods of PA, ER;   method of SJ
281.10   for] ES;   of SJ, ER, PA
281.10   embodied] ES, PA, ER;   which are embodied SJ
281.11   Both conservative and reformer] ES;   All SJ, ER, PA
281.11   themselves] ES, PA, ER;   themselves alike SJ
281.12   and of] ES, SJ;   and ER, PA

281.13   to placing] ES, PA, ER;   of placing SJ
281.14   schoolroom] ER, ES;   school-|room SJ, PA
281.14   and to] ES;   to PA, ER;   and SJ
281.14   hindrances to] ES;   hindrances of SJ, ER, PA
281.15   he] ES, PA, ER;   she SJ
281.19   a reality] ES, PA, ER;   reality SJ
281.22   ourselves] ES;   you SJ, ER, PA
281.27   rearrangement] ER, PA, ES;   re-arrangement SJ
281.31   of the survival] ES;   in the survival SJ, ER, PA
281.32   forms] ES, PA, ER;   species SJ
281.34   is to] ES, PA, ER;   should SJ
281.39   retreating] ES, PA, ER;   retarding SJ
282.2   vision,] ER, PA, ES;   ~;   SJ
282.3   the situation. . . . uneconomical] ES;   the situation.
          As this comes, the time grows ripe for scientific experi-
          mentation; that is, for a more organized philosophy of
          experience in education, and for a corresponding at-
          tempt to regulate conditions so as to make actual the
          aims recognized as desirable. It is uneconomical PA,
          ER;   the situation. As this comes the time grows ripe
          for scientific experimentation; that is for a more or-
          ganized philosophy of experience in education, and for
          a corresponding attempt to regulate conditions so as to
          make actual aims recognized as desirable. It is uneco-
          nomical SJ
282.9   elementary educational situation.] ES;   situation as
          regards the course of study. SJ, ER, PA
282.15   and a philosophy of] ES;   and of SJ, ER, PA
282.17   wisely] ES, PA, ER;   sanely SJ
282.18–19 of our intelligence and the support of our moral en-
          thusiasm.] ES;   of intelligence. SJ, ER, PA
283.1   2. AS CONCERNS SECONDARY EDUCATION] ES;   Current
          Problems in Secondary Education. SR
283.20   of teachers] ES;   for teachers SR
283.22   change] ES;   changes SR
284.21   secondary-school] ES;   ~ˌ~ SR
284.24   athletics.] W;   ~, SR, ES
284.25   aspects] ES;   aspect SR
284.26   school as a] ES;   school a SR
284.33   problem:] ES;   ~. SR
284.42   problems] ES;   problem SR
285.21   walls˄] W;   ~, SR, ES
285.35   exchange,] ES;   ~˄ SR
287.20   he is] stet SR;   is he ES
287.22–23 themselves] ES;   itself SR
287.26   that] stet SR;   which ES
287.28   each] ES;   each group SR
289.1   history,] ES;   ~˄ SR

289.13   a product] ES;   the product SR
289.33   affected] *stet* SR;   effected ES
291.23   other,] W;   ~∧ SR, ES
291.23   brings] W;   bring SR, ES
296.23   satisfaction] ES;   satisfactfon SR
298.21   it is] ES;   is SR
298.22   account] ES;   an account SR
298.34   ideals:] ES;   ~;   SR
299.13   the abstract] ES;   abstract SR
300.1–2   3. AS CONCERNS THE COLLEGE [◖] The elementary] W;
          III As Concerns the College [◖] The elementary ES;   III.
          ARE THE SCHOOLS DOING WHAT THE PEOPLE WANT
          THEM TO DO? The answer to the question, whether the
          schools are doing what the people want done, depends,
          as the other speakers have clearly brought out, upon
          the conception of what the people want. And there is a
          good deal of difficulty in finding this out; when we do
          find out, we see that they want very diverse things—
          things so divergent as to be contradictory. The school
          cannot really do what the people want until there is
          unity, an approach to system and organization, in the
          needs of the people. We are told that when the sewing
          machine was first invented and an attempt was made
          to introduce it, the agents had almost to break into peo-
          ple's houses in order to get it into use. If the people
          wanted the sewing machine, they did not know that
          they wanted it. There are many things in education of
          which a similar thing must be said. The people may
          need these things very badly, but they have not awak-
          ened to a lively consciousness of the fact.
              I happen recently to have heard two gentlemen
          speaking of educational matters, both of whom are in
          positions of responsibility, and both marked successes
          in their respective affairs. One of these men would or-
          dinarily be called a conservative. He gave as a reason
          for his conservatism that he had to conform to condi-
          tions, that it was impossible for a successful school to
          be far in advance of the conditions about it. In other
          words, he thought that what the people wanted was
          just about what they had been accustomed to getting.
          The other, of a more radical type in educational mat-
          ters, propounded as the utmost reach of his anticipa-
          tions of reform the desire that the schools should be-
          come a reflex of existing conditions. One thought that
          he was limited to education of rather a routine, cus-
          tomary type because that is what the conditions call
          for, and hence what the people want; the other's high-
          est flight of imagination regarding the reform of the

school is to have an education which shall be a reflex of existing conditions, and hence what is really wanted.

The two remarks are apparently contradictory. Yet each appeals to us as possessing a certain truth. How are we to explain this state of affairs? One was thinking of what people consciously want, of what people in specific instances bring to bear in way of pressure upon the school authorities. The other had in mind what he conceived to be the meeting of the *actual* wants or necessities of the case, quite apart from their conscious recognition on the part of the people. He was thinking of breaking into people's educational houses in order to provide them with the agencies, the instrumentalities, they really want, but of the need of which they have not become aware.

I see practically no other way of answering this question. If we ask whether the schools, upon the whole, are doing what the people want—yes, certainly, if we keep in mind the more conscious and definitely formulated wants of the people growing out of the experiences and customs and expectations of the past; no, to a very considerable degree, if we mean an effective response of school aims, methods, and materials to the underlying wants which arise in the movement of modern society.

My thesis, then, is a twofold one. The schools are not doing, and cannot do, what the people want until there is more unity, more definiteness, in the community's consciousness of its own needs; but it is the business of the school to forward this conception, to help the people to a clearer and more systematic idea of what the underlying needs of modern life are, and of how they are really to be supplied.

I take it that I am expected to speak to-day more particularly of the third story of the educational edifice— the college and its relations to the needs of the people. This requires some placing of the college in connection with the elementary and secondary forms of education in order to see how its points of contact with popular needs vary from those of the other two forms, and how its methods of meeting the popular needs must also be differentiated. [¶] The elementary ER

300.5	It has] ES; It also has ER
300.27	public's] ES; public ER
*300.29	disadvantages] W; disadvantage ER, ES
301.5	"academic,"] ES; the term academic, ER
301.16	lower] ES; less ER
301.16	that of] ES; that demanded in ER

301.18   with] ES;   in ER
301.26   today] ES;   to-day ER
301.35–36 acting . . . considerations;] ES;   doing what the
           people want done;   ER
302.4–5   public consciousness,] ES;   consciousness of the peo-
           ple, ER
302.12   operative] ES;   operative and determining ER
302.20   breaking into] ES;   impinging upon ER
302.23   and which] ES;   which ER
302.25   current social needs and demands.] ES;   the needs of
           the people. ER
302.36   present need.] ES;   present need of the people. ER
303.13–14 crowding something else out;] ES;   crowding out
           something else;   ER
303.15–16 burden of election upon the student] ES;   burden
           upon the student of election ER
303.19   system in our scheme of life.] ES;   system, in the di-
           rection of the people's needs. ER
303.23   is] ES;   is thus ER
303.27   is] ES;   seems to be ER
303.35   professional] ES;   scholastic ER
304.3   science,] ES;   ~∧ ER
304.6   significantly as,] ET;   significantly, ER, ES
304.6   indirectly than,] ET;   indirectly, as ER, ES
304.11   asked,] ET;   ~∧ ER, ES
304.11   the] ES;   these ER
304.19   to be] ES;   to be capable of being ER
304.25   in] ES;   in its ER
304.25   standpoint] ES;   method ER
304.32   language∧–] ES;   ~,– ER
304.34   etc.∧–] ES;   ~.,– ER
305.6   science,] ES;   ~∧ ER
305.7   may certainly claim] ES;   can hardly be denied ER
305.8   phenomena,] ES;   ~∧ ER
305.18   of simplification not] ES;   not of simplification ER
305.18 et seq. through] ES;   thru ER
305.21   studies in its] ES;   its ER
305.22   compel] ES;   itself compel ER
305.30   development] W;   development ES;   evolution ER
305.31   extent] ES;   rapidity ER
305.36   processes∧–] ES;   ~,– ER
305.36   etc.∧–] ES;   ~.,– ER
306.2   beginning of a new century] ES;   close of the century
           ER
306.3   translation of] ES;   translation on the part of ER
306.4   science] ES;   sciences ER
306.6   circumstances, we] ES;   circumstances, that we ER
306.7   studies; we] ES;   studies;   that we ER

306.16   subjects] ES;   the subjects ER
306.17   condition;] ES;   ~, ER
306.18   claims;] ES;   ~, ER
306.20   all the] ES;   all this ER
306.22   like philosophic] ES;   like a philosophic ER
306.24   bring] ES;   put ER
306.25   direction] ES;   scientific direction ER
307.2–4   our methods. We ignore . . . retain vitality. We speak]
          ES;   our methods. We speak ER
307.8   cent$_\wedge$] ET;   ~. ER, ES
307.8   cent$_\wedge$] ET;   ~. ER, ES
307.9   cent$_\wedge$] ET;   ~. ER, ES
307.11   imagine] ES;   may assume ER
307.13   assuming] ES;   thus assuming ER
307.30   these] ES;   all these ER
308.4   well] ES;   very well ER
308.10   as are] ES;   as ER
308.10   in] ES;   would be in ER
308.20   the banner of discipline] ES;   mental training ER
309.3–4   is good in general] ES;   is general ER
309.8   and for something] ES;   and for somewhat ER
309.15   the free communication and interaction] ES;   the in-
          teraction ER
309.23–26 workaday world. Culture, . . . "invidious distinc-
          tion." If I were] ES;   workaday world. If I were ER
310.1   what society wants done] ES;   what the people want
          ER
310.5   this,] ES;   ~$_\wedge$ ER
310.5   emphatically,] ES;   ~$_\wedge$ ER
310.7   dualistic politically] ES;   dualistic practically and po-
          litically ER
310.13   ethics] ES;   ethic ER
310.14   aims] ES;   ends ER
310.27   which gives] stet ER;   by which to give ES
310.27–28 concreteness.] ES;   sufficient concreteness. ER
311.1   or the] ES;   or much less the ER
311.3–4   to which] ES;   in which ER
311.11   occupations] ES;   occupation ER
311.12–13 mastery of methods] ES;   the possession of the right
          attitude of inquiry ER
311.14   Society . . . knowledge] ES;   I thus come back to the
          original question: is the college doing what the people
          want? No; for the people do not know what they want.
          They need illumination, and it is the business of the
          university to reveal them unto themselves. Yes; for
          what the people need is the union of that expert knowl-
          edge ER
311.15–16 and the services] ES;   with the direction ER

311.16   life. All] ES; life;   and all ER
311.20   other] ES;   less ER
311.25   This is] ES;   This, of course, is ER
311.31   lines which divide] ES;   lines, dividing ER
311.32–33   of professional schools∧] ES; of the professional
            schools, ER
311.33   getting obscure] ES; relaxing ER
311.34   fade away.] ES; fade away. And this is what the
            people want—it is the answer to their deepest needs.
            ER
311.35–36   is the] ES; is to be the ER
312.3   probably] ES;   may perhaps ER
312.4   period. This is not] ES; period. I am not speaking,
            however, of externals, but of the educational substance.
            This is not ER
312.12   of instruction] ES;   and instruction ER
312.15   eighteen or twenty.] ES;   twenty or twenty-one. ER
312.18–19   adapted to his own] ES;   adapted to the freest and
            most effective expression of his own ER
312.28   as is] ES;   as ER
312.32   thoroughly] ES;   thoroly ER
312.33–34   does not give] ES;   gives neither ER
312.37–313.38 walk in life. . . . existing collegiate situation.]
            ES;   walk in life. It is aimed in the air, with the pious
            hope that something will come of it in some direction or
            other.
                The movement, however, is steady, and I believe in-
            evitable, in one direction: the demarcation of second-
            ary work as the period of general training and culture,
            thus restoring to it freshness and vitality by making it
            what it should be, the renaissance of the individual
            mind, the period of self-consciousness in the true sense,
            of knowledge of self in relation to the larger meanings
            of life; and the reservation of the higher institution for
            specific training, for gaining control of the particular
            body of knowledge and methods of research and verifi-
            cation which fit the individual to apply truth to the
            guidance of his own special calling in life. All of us
            have callings, occupations—only the luxuriously idle
            and the submerged idle, only the leisure class of fash-
            ion and of pauperism, violate this law. When educa-
            tion ceases to ignore this fact, when it recognizes it
            frankly and fully, and adapts its curriculum and
            methods to it, the university will be coherent in
            itself and also doing what the people really want done.
            ER
313.4   artificial] W;   artifical ES;   [not present] ER

"The University Elementary School: History and Character; Studies and Methods"

Copy-text has been the first printing in *University* [of Chicago] *Record* 2 (1897): 72–75. The partial reprinting in DS: *The Dewey School* by Katherine Camp Mayhew and Anna Camp Edwards (New York: D. Appleton-Century, 1936) is also cited as the first appearance of emendations that would have been made editorially.

325.11	Avenue] W; avenue
325.18	Street] W; street
325.30	the] W; The
326.5	of the] W; of The
327.4	is∧] DS; ∼,
328.3	habitation,] W; ∼∧
328.12	expression,] W; ∼;
329.3	the] W; The
329.5	the] W; The
329.6–7	to find material] W; to material
329.40	system∧] W; ∼,
332.39	detail∧] W; ∼,
333.12	gives] DS; give
333.21	powers∧] W; ∼,
333.30	the] DS; The
333.30	sense-organs] DS; sense∧organ
333.31	per cent∧] W; ∼.
333.33	ears] DS; ear

"The University Elementary School: General Outline of Scheme of Work"

Copy-text has been the first printing in *University* [of Chicago] *Record* 3 (1898): 253–54.

337.25	handle∧] W; ∼,

"Play and Imagination in Relation to Early Education"

Copy-text has been the only previous printing, *Kindergarten Magazine* 11 (1899): 636–40.

340.3	If] W; if
343.2	*prosaic*] W; mosaic

LINE-END HYPHENATION

I. Copy-text list.

The following are the editorially established forms of possible compounds which were hyphenated at the ends of lines in the copy-text.

8.15	grist-mill	175.12	pigeon-holes
22.23	schoolrooms	176.35	sub-headings
32.12	arrow-head	178.39	standpoint
46.11	schoolroom	233.23	underlying
64.36	stepladder	233.34	standpoint
65.6	hand-work	262.7	overtaxing
100.5	subject-matter	269.3	standpoint
102.34	counterirritants	274.34	twofold
103.17	ready-made	281.14	schoolroom
119 n.11	footnote	285.38	world-power
135.10	text-book	294.20	interaction
141.25	psycho-physical	309.28	pre-biological
142.31	psycho-physical	330.15	text-books
145.5	psycho-physical	340.25	steamboat
145.22	re-approximation	343.5	*dish-washing*
157.15	reappears		

II. Critical-text list.

In quotations from the present edition, no line-end hyphens are to be retained except the following:

6.10	over-ingenious	84.26	far-fetched
8.21	sense-organs	89.25	non-psychological
9.21	half-hearted	90.11	so-called
34.1	text-book	90.36	subject-matter
38.2	make-believe	97.12	story-form
47.38	mind-killing	98.36	pseudo-science
59.25	subject-matter	102.34	non-promotion
61.15	hand-work	103.31	self-directed
61.27	hand-work	122.38	rock-structures

123.1	world-forming	199.30	self-explanatory
123.24	stepping-stone	216.3	self-consciousness
124.8	thing-and-/quality	275.2	one-sided
125.24	pigeon-holes	285.11	subject-matter
130.8	soul-substance	285.15	stiff-necked
140.11	net-work	285.18	hard-heartedness
140.12	sensori-motor	286.8	psycho-physics
145.23	re-viewing	292.10	high-school
158.11	right-mindedness	318.31	subject-matter
181.15	cross-reference	340.22	make-believe
183.30	so-called	342.23	story-telling
185.26	cross-reference	343.5	*dish-washing*
195.9	door-knob		

CORRECTION OF QUOTATIONS

Dewey represented source material in varying ways, from memorial paraphrase to verbatim copy, sometimes citing his source fully, in others mentioning only authors' names, and in still others, omitting documentation altogether.

To prepare the critical text, all material inside quotation marks, except that obviously being emphasized or restated, has been searched out and the documentation has been verified and emended when necessary. Steps regularly used to emend documentation are described in Textual Principles and Procedures, but Dewey's variations from the original in his quotations have been considered important enough to warrant a special list.

All quotations have been retained within the texts as they were first published, except for corrections required by special circumstances and noted in the Emendations List. Substantive changes that restore original readings in cases of possible compositorial or typographical errors are similarly noted as "W" emendations. The variable form of quotation suggests that Dewey, like many scholars of the period, was unconcerned about precision in matters of form, but many of the changes in cited materials may have arisen in the printing process. For example, comparing Dewey's quotations with the originals reveals that some journals housestyled the quoted materials as well as Dewey's own.

Dewey's most frequent alteration in quoted material was changing or omitting punctuation. He also often failed to use ellipses or to separate quotations to show that material had been left out. No citation of the Dewey material or of the original appears here if the changes were only of this kind—omitted or changed punctuation, including ellipses. In the case of omitted ellipses, attention is called to short phrases; if, however, a line or more has been left out, no attention has been called to the omission.

Italics in source material have been treated as accidentals: when Dewey omitted those italics the omission is not noted, though Dewey's added italics are listed. If changed or omitted accidentals have substantive implications, as in the capitalization of some concept words, the quotation is noted. The form of listing the quotations, from Dewey as well as from his source, is designed to assist the reader in determining whether Dewey had the book open before him or was relying on his memory.

Notations in this section follow the formula: page-line numbers from the present text, followed by the text condensed to first and last words or such as make for sufficient clarity, then a square bracket followed by the symbol identifying the Dewey item. After a semicolon comes the necessary correction, whether of one word or a longer passage, as required. Finally in parentheses, the author's surname and shortened source-title from the Checklist of Dewey's References are followed by a comma and the page-line reference to the source.

Two quotations at 156.35–39 from Hegel and at 277.28–42 from "a recent educational document" have not been located. Extensive searching and comparison of sources suggest that Dewey probably translated the Hegel material directly from the German.

SS: The School and Society

5.24–25 is growing, one former is worth a thousand re-formers.] SS; that *grows*, one right *former* will accomplish more than a thousand *re*-formers. (Mann, *Life and Works*, vol. 2, 264.7–8)

70.35–36 middle department which we sometimes take to be final, failing to see, amid the] SS; middle stage. Sometimes we think it final, and sometimes we fail to see, amid the (James, *Will to Believe*, 124.1–3)

70.37 diversity of] SS; diversity in (James, *Will to Believe*, 124.3)

70.37 complications] SS; complication (James, *Will to Believe*, 124.4)

70.38–39 function—the function] SS; function, and that the one we have pointed out,—the function (James, *Will to Believe*, 124.5–6)

72.16   because starting] SS;   because, by starting (Jackman,
          "School Grade a Fiction," 462.5)
72.18   then] SS;   thus (Jackman, "School Grade a Fiction,"
          462.7)

L: "Some Stages of Logical Thought"

160.9   us] L;   the mind (Mill, *Logic*, 457.46)
163.17   a proposition] L;   it, or claim credence for it, (Mill,
           Logic, 122.16)
163.19–20 it is] L;   that it is (Mill, *Logic*, 122.10)

PM: "Principles of Mental Development as Illustrated in Early Infancy"

186.31   and he] PM;   and, with an absorbed expression, he
          (Hall, "First Five Hundred Days," 466.23–24)
187.1   it] PM;   this, (Preyer, *Senses and Will*, 87.25)
187.20   effort] PM;   efforts (Hall, "First Five Hundred Days,"
          399.1)
187.22   himself; this] PM;   himself—his strength was slightly
          reinforced—this (Hall, "First Five Hundred Days,"
          399.4)
187.25   his hands] PM;   hands (Hall, "First Five Hundred
          Days," 399.7)

M: "Mental Development"

204.32   that's not] M;   That not (Sully, *Studies of Childhood*,
          442.16)
204.33   that's E's] M;   Dat E.'s (Sully, *Studies of Childhood*,
          443.13)

WF: *Review of* The World and the Individual, *First Series*

242.14   thing] WF;   things (Royce, *World and Individual*, 1st
          Ser., 22.5)
242.15   an idea] WF;   ideas (Royce, *World and Individual*, 1st
          Ser., 22.6)

243.34 we] WF; you (Royce, *World and Individual*, 1st Ser., 39.13)

243.35 we] WF; you (Royce, *World and Individual*, 1st Ser., 39.14)

246.16 which] WF; that (Royce, *World and Individual*, 1st Ser., 181.29)

246.17 thus remains] WF; remains thus (Royce, *World and Individual*, 1st Ser., 181.30)

249.12 fragmentarily] WF; already fragmentarily (Royce, *World and Individual*, 1st Ser., 341.22–23)

249.12–13 embodies . . . ; a life, which is] WF; embodies. This life is (Royce, *World and Individual*, 1st Ser., 341.23)

252.4 principle] WF; principles (Royce, *World and Individual*, 1st Ser., 237.21)

252.10 with] WF; in (Royce, *World and Individual*, 1st Ser., 248.26)

253n.5 of] WF; of *Mögliche Erfahrung* (Royce, *World and Individual*, 1st Ser., 236.2–3)

253n.14 and] WF; and the (Royce, *World and Individual*, 1st Ser., 275.13–14)

253n.27 *positively assert Being*] WF; positively *assert* Being (Royce, *World and Individual*, 1st Ser., 282.26)

254.22 which guides] WF; which, from this point of view, guides (Royce, *World and Individual*, 1st Ser., 422.28)

CHECKLIST OF DEWEY'S REFERENCES

Titles and authors' names in Dewey references have been corrected and expanded to conform accurately and consistently to the original works; all corrections appear in the Emendations List.

This section gives full publication information for each work cited by Dewey. When Dewey gave page numbers for a work, the edition he used was identified exactly by locating the reference. Similarly, the books in Dewey's personal library have been used to verify his citations of a particular edition. For other references, the edition listed here is the one from among the various editions possibly available to him that was his most likely source by reason of place or date of publication, or on the evidence from correspondence and other materials, and its general accessibility during the period.

Bacon, Georgia F. "History." In *Elementary School Record*, edited by John Dewey and Laura L. Runyon, pp. 204–9. Chicago: University of Chicago Press, 1900.

Baldwin, James Mark. *Mental Development in the Child and the Race: Methods and Processes*. New York: Macmillan Co., 1895.

———. *Social and Ethical Interpretations in Mental Development: A Study in Social Psychology*. New York: Macmillan Co., 1897.

Barnes, Earl. *Studies on Children's Games*. Palo Alto, Calif.: Leland Stanford Junior University, 1896.

———. "A Study on Children's Drawings." *Pedagogical Seminary* 2 (1892): 455–63.

———, ed. *Studies in Education*. Stanford: Stanford University Press, 1896–97.

Bradley, Francis Herbert. *Appearance and Reality: A Metaphysical Essay*. London: Swan Sonnenschein and Co., 1893.

Burk, Frederic. "Growth of Children in Height and Weight." *American Journal of Psychology* 9 (1898): 253–326.

Burnham, William H. "The Study of Adolescence." *Pedagogical Seminary* 1 (1891): 174–95.

Chamberlain, Alexander Francis. *The Child: A Study in the Evolution of Man.* London: Walter Scott, 1900.

Cushman, Lillian S. "Principles of Education as Applied to Art." In *Elementary School Record,* edited by John Dewey and Laura L. Runyon, pp. 3–11. Chicago: University of Chicago Press, 1900.

Daniels, Arthur H. "The New Life: A Study of Regeneration." *American Journal of Psychology* 6 (1893): 61–106.

Defoe, Daniel. *Robinson Crusoe.* Edited by Edward R. Shaw. Standard Literature Series, no. 25. New York: University Publishing Co., 1897.

De Garmo, Charles. "The Herbartian System of Pedagogics." *Educational Review* 1 (1891): 33–45, 244–52, 453–62.

Dewey, John. *The School and Society.* 2d ed. Chicago: University of Chicago Press, 1915. [*The Middle Works of John Dewey, 1899–1924,* edited by Jo Ann Boydston, 1:2–109. Carbondale: Southern Illinois University Press, 1974.]

———. "General Introduction to Groups V and VI." In *Elementary School Record,* edited by John Dewey and Laura L. Runyon, pp. 49–52. Chicago: University of Chicago Press, 1900. [*Middle Works,* 1:225–29.]

———. "Harris's Psychologic Foundations of Education." *Educational Review* 16 (1898): 1–14. [*The Early Works of John Dewey, 1882–1898,* edited by Jo Ann Boydston, 5:372–85. Carbondale: Southern Illinois University Press, 1972.]

———. "Historical Development of Inventions and Occupations, General Principles." In *Elementary School Record,* edited by John Dewey and Laura L. Runyon, pp. 21–23. Chicago: University of Chicago Press, 1900. [*Middle Works,* 1:222–24.]

———. "Interpretation of the Culture-Epoch Theory." *Public-School Journal* 15 (1896): 233–36. [*Early Works,* 5:247–53.]

———. "The Psychology of Infant Language." *Psychological Review* 1 (1894): 63–66. [*Early Works,* 4:66–69.]

———. Review of *The World and the Individual,* First Series, by Josiah Royce. *Philosophical Review* 9 (1900): 311–24. [*Middle Works,* 1:241–56.]

Donaldson, Henry Herbert. *The Growth of the Brain: A Study of the Nervous System in Relation to Education.* London: Walter Scott, 1895.

Froebel, Friedrich Wilhelm August. *Friedrich Froebel's Pedagogics of the Kindergarten; or, His Ideas concerning the Play and Playthings of the Child.* Translated by Josephine Jarvis. New York: D. Appleton and Co., 1895.

———. *The Mottoes and Commentaries of Friedrich Froebel's Mother Play.* Translated by Susan E. Blow and Henrietta R. Eliot. International Education Series, edited by William Torrey Harris, vol. 31. New York: D. Appleton and Co., 1895.

Groos, Karl. *The Play of Animals*. Translated by Elizabeth L. Baldwin, with a Preface and Appendix by James Mark Baldwin. New York: D. Appleton and Co., 1898.

Hall, G. Stanley. "The Moral and Religious Training of Children and Adolescents." *Pedagogical Seminary* 1 (1891): 196–210.

Hall, Mrs. Winfield S. "The First Five Hundred Days of a Child's Life." *Child-Study Monthly* 2 (1897): 394–407, 458–73.

Harmer, Althea. "Textile Industries." In *Elementary School Record*, edited by John Dewey and Laura L. Runyon, pp. 71–81. Chicago: University of Chicago Press, 1900.

Harris, William Torrey. *Psychologic Foundations of Education: An Attempt to Show the Genesis of the Higher Faculties of the Mind*. International Education Series, edited by William Torrey Harris, vol. 37. New York: D. Appleton and Co., 1898.

Jackman, Wilbur S. "Constructive Work in the Common Schools." *Educational Review* 17 (1899): 105–23.

———. "The School Grade a Fiction." *Educational Review* 15 (1898): 456–73.

James, William. *Psychology*. American Science Series, Briefer Course. New York: Henry Holt and Co., 1893.

———. *The Will to Believe*. New York: Longmans, Green and Co., 1897.

Johnson, G. E. "Education by Plays and Games." *Pedagogical Seminary* 3 (1894): 97–133.

Kant, Immanuel. *Kritik der reinen Vernunft*. 2d ed. Riga: Johann Friedrich Hartknoch, 1787.

Lancaster, E. G. "The Psychology and Pedagogy of Adolescence." *Pedagogical Seminary* 5 (1897): 61–128.

Longfellow, Henry Wadsworth. *The Song of Hiawatha*. Standard Literature Series, no. 37. New York: University Publishing Co., 1898.

Lukens, Herman T. "Preliminary Report on the Learning of Language." *Pedagogical Seminary* 3 (1896): 424–60.

———. "A Study of Children's Drawings in the Early Years." *Pedagogical Seminary* 4 (1896): 79–110.

Mann, Horace. *Life and Works of Horace Mann*. Edited by Mary Mann. 2d ed., vol. 2. Boston: Lee and Shepard Publishers, 1891.

Mead, George Herbert. "The Relation of Play to Education." *University* [of Chicago] *Record* 1 (1896): 141–45.

Mill, John Stuart. *A System of Logic, Ratiocinative and Inductive: Being a Connected View of the Principles of Evidence and the Methods of Scientific Investigation*. 8th ed. New York: Harper and Bros., 1874.

Münsterberg, Hugo. *Psychology and Life*. Boston: Houghton Mifflin Co., 1899.

Oppenheim, Nathan. *The Development of the Child*. New York: Macmillan Co., 1898.

O'Shea, M. V. "Some Adolescent Reminiscences." *Journal of Pedagogy* 11 (1898): 299–316.

Preyer, William. *The Senses and the Will*. Translated by H. W. Brown. International Education Series, edited by William Torrey Harris, vol. 7. New York: D. Appleton and Co., 1888.

Rosenkranz, Johann Karl Friedrich. *The Philosophy of Education*. Translated by Anna C. Brackett. 2d ed., rev. International Education Series, edited by William Torrey Harris, vol. 1. New York: D. Appleton and Co., 1887.

Rowe, Stuart Henry. *The Physical Nature of the Child and How to Study It*. New York: Macmillan Co., 1899.

Royce, Josiah. *The Conception of God: A Philosophical Discussion concerning the Nature of the Divine Idea as a Demonstrable Reality*. Publications of the Philosophical Union of the University of California, vol. 1. New York: Macmillan Co., 1897.

———. *The World and the Individual*. First Series: The Four Historical Conceptions of Being. New York: Macmillan Co., 1900.

———. *The World and the Individual*. Second Series: Nature, Man, and the Moral Order. New York: Macmillan Co., 1901.

Salisbury, Albert. "A Child's Vocabulary." *Educational Review* 7 (1894): 289–90.

Scates, Georgia P. "The Subprimary (Kindergarten) Department." In *Elementary School Record*, edited by John Dewey and Laura L. Runyon, pp. 129–42. Chicago: University of Chicago Press, 1900.

Street, J. R. "A Study in Language Teaching." *Pedagogical Seminary* 4 (1897): 269–93.

Sully, James. *Studies of Childhood*. New York: D. Appleton and Co., 1896.

Tracy, Frederick. *The Psychology of Childhood*. Boston: D. C. Heath and Co., 1893.

———. "The Language of Childhood." *American Journal of Psychology* 6 (1893): 107–38.

"The University Elementary School." *The President's Report: July, 1898–July, 1899*, pp. 198–99. Chicago: University of Chicago Press, 1900. [*Middle Works*, 1:317–20.]

"The University Elementary School: General Outline of Scheme of Work." *University* [of Chicago] *Record* 3 (1898): 253–54. [*Middle Works*, 1:335–38.]

Van Liew, C. C. "The Educational Theory of the Culture Epochs: Viewed Historically and Critically." In *The First Yearbook of the Herbart Society*, edited by Charles A. McMurry, pp. 70–121. Bloomington, Ill.: Public-School Publishing Co., 1895.

Warner, Francis. *A Course of Lectures on the Growth and Means of Training the Mental Faculty*. New York: Macmillan Co., 1890.

——. *The Nervous System of the Child: Its Growth and Health in Education*. New York: Macmillan Co., 1900.

——. *The Study of Children and Their School Training*. New York: Macmillan Co., 1897.

Young, Ella Flagg. *Isolation in the School*. University of Chicago Contributions to Education, no. 1. Chicago: University of Chicago Press, 1901.

INDEX

Goethe, Johann Wolfgang von:
objective idealism of, xvii
Grades: arrangement of, 268;
secondary, problems of, 282
Grammar school: origin of, 42
Growth: stages of, in child,
related to education, 73–80;
mental, of child, 133–35

Hall, G. Stanley: culture-epoch
theory in educational thought
of, xvn; influence of German objective idealism on,
xviii; mentioned, xiii
Hall, Mrs. Winfield S.: on infant coordination, 186–87
Harris, William Torrey: influence of German objective
idealism on, xviii; on pathological use of psycho-physical mechanism, 142; men-
tioned, 341, 342
Harvard Teachers Association,
258
Hegel, Georg Wilhelm Friedrich: objective idealism of,
xvii; on Verstand, 156
Heidbreder, Edna: on Dewey's
reflex-arc concept, xiii
Herbart, Johann Friedrich: influence of German objective
idealism on, xviii
Hiawatha: related to social
study, 107; mentioned, 223
High school: intermediate position of, 287–300 passim
History: Dewey's emphasis on,
xxi; as taught in University
Elementary School, 62–63,
327, 333–34; American, 63;
Greek and Roman, 63; American, related to growth stage
of child, 74–75; use of, in
elementary education, 104–
9; periods of, related to
child's stages of development, 108–9; related to social life, 230

Home life: used as subject
matter in kindergarten, 87–
88
Household: as centre of industrial occupation, 7; ideal,
with child as centre, 23–24
How We Think: Dewey's theory of inquiry refined in,
xiv–xv; mentioned, ix–x
Human Nature and Conduct,
xii
Hume, David, 115

Idea: world as, 241–42; defined by Royce, 242–56
Idealistic philosophy: Dewey's
early work in, compared to
middle work in, x–xi
Ideas: fixed, in thinking process, 153–54; treatment of, in
primitive communities, 155;
fixed, in judicial procedure,
155–56; Platonic hierarchy
of, 161
Image: related to child play,
198, 225, 340–41
Imagery: need for variety of,
in child, 203–6
Imagination: cultivation of, in
child, 37–38; as developed
in play and games, 85–86;
development of child's, 99–
100, 201–2; defined in terms
of play, 340
Individual: Dewey on changing
of, xxi; psychology of, 113–
14
Inductive science: as stage of
thinking, 168
Industrial revolution: its effect
on society, 6–7
Infancy: prolonged, in humans,
180; eye coordination in,
181; importance of use
of thumb in, 182; development of distance judgment
in, 185; creeping stage in,
187–88; mental development